SPENSER STUDIES

XXII

SPENSER
STUDIES

A Renaissance
Poetry Annual
XXII

Volume XXII edited by

David Galbraith and *Theresa Krier*

SPENSER STUDIES GENERAL EDITORS

William A. Oram
Anne Lake Prescott
Thomas P. Roche, Jr.

AMS PRESS, INC.
NEW YORK

SPENSER STUDIES
A RENAISSANCE POETRY ANNUAL

edited by Anne Lake Prescott, William A. Oram, and Thomas P. Roche, Jr.

is published annually by AMS Press, Inc. as a forum for Spenser scholarship and criticism and related Renaissance subjects. Manuscripts must be double-spaced, including notes, which should be grouped at the end and should be prepared according to *The Chicago Manual of Style*. Authors of essay-length manuscripts should include an abstract of 100–150 words and provide a disk version of the article, preferably in a Windows-compatible format. One copy of each manuscript should be sent to Thomas P. Roche, Jr., 425 West Rio Salado Parkway, Unit 320, Tempe, AZ 85281; one copy to Anne Lake Prescott, Department of English, Barnard College, Columbia University, 3009 Broadway, New York, NY 10027–6598; and one copy to William A. Oram, Department of English, Smith College, Northampton, MA 01063.

Please send inquiries concerning subscriptions or the availability of earlier volumes to AMS Press, Inc., Brooklyn Navy Yard, 63 Flushing Ave.—Unit 221, Brooklyn, NY 11205-1005, USA.

ISSN 0195-9468
Vol. XXII ISBN-10: 0-404-19222-x
Vol. XXII ISBN-13: 978-0-404-19222-8

CONTENTS

Illustrations

Index

DAVID GALBRAITH AND THERESA KRIER

Spenser's Book of Living

*T*he papers in this volume emerge from the conference "Spenser's Civilizations" held in Toronto in May 2006. We heard many strong, innovative papers, and noted new interests and new takes on traditional critical topoi. There was a finely tuned focus on conditions of embodiment, the energies of bodily life, affect and sympathy, and less emphasis on the love poetry, eros, and gender politics than in earlier Spenser scholarship. By contrast, the elegiac poems, particularly *The Ruines of Time* and *Daphnaïda*, received a good deal of attention from conference participants for their intersections of rhetoric, affect, and memory. Spenser's Ireland proved a less central occupation than it had even five years ago, at the 2001 Spenser conference in Cambridge. There was a resurgence of interest in rhetorical studies, and in the relationship between rhetoric, memory, and temporality that Paul Alpers's work had opened up. There was also a shift in focus from specifically Reformation and biblical forms to ethics. Fueling the whole conference was an impetus to move from a vigilant or suspicious mode of reading to an intimate one. We hope that the essays in this volume demonstrate the vitality and promise of scholarship today; as we edited them we were cognizant of our gratitude to all the conference participants.

This volume moves from the political project of empire—in Paul Stevens's essay, derived from his plenary—to creatural life and process, and sheer vitality, in the concluding essays. In several pieces in this collection, Spenser's civilizations enter into complex transactions with the natural world, because both he and his twenty-first century readers understand civility as taking shape within natural processes. Linda Gregerson's powerful evocation of *oikos* as an ethically ambivalent engagement of humans with their earthly environment speaks to a critical turn from *space* as a central metaphor for understanding Spenser's worlds to an emerging emphasis on *place*, habitation and

Spenser Studies: A Renaissance Poetry Annual, Volume XXII, Copyright © 2007 by AMS Press, Inc. All rights reserved.

dwelling. Much recent Spenser criticism has of course emphasized politics as the central category that mediated the poem and the world. Now the political yields some of this privilege to other systems in which beings are embedded or experience their being alive. It seems fitting that Gryll adamantly dwells in many of these essays, garnering more attention than Acrasia does.

Three papers in this volume were presented in a session entitled "Animal Being." Each of these, by Elizabeth Jane Bellamy, Joseph Loewenstein, and Elizabeth Harvey, speaks to aspects of Spenser's ecology—of the ways that Spenser's human and fairy protagonists inevitably dwell in a common place not only with nymphs but also with gnats. In Spenser's poem, all of us living beings inhabit not the abstract space that Coleridge saw as characteristic of fairy land but places filled with other animate beings and, more broadly, with highly specific kinds of matter. At the conference's concluding roundtable, Katherine Eggert observed the ubiquitous theme of *dirt*—with papers attending to georgic, to animals, to current archeological work at Irish sites—but matter figured as well in a spacious attention to early printed editions of Spenser's work and to the history of the book.

The turn to ethics in post-modernist criticism noted by Elizabeth Jane Bellamy at the start of her essay has wide-ranging consequences for Spenser studies, and complicates older forms of thinking about politics and religion. Paul Stevens exemplifies this turn from religion to ethics when he juxtaposes his analysis of the relevance of Protestant ideas of grace to the imperial project with an account of his own military service in Ireland. Stevens's paper foregrounds the complexity of our transactions with others whose inhabitation of the same ground gives them claims that require recognition. Theological discourses are muted elsewhere, too: we were struck by the absence of the biblical concept of dominion from discussions of animals and the natural world, for instance.

The discipline of rhetoric shows new discursive links in these essays, as its multiple forms of locus, topos, and place are deployed to craft fine-grained accounts of literary friendships and imaginative transactions between Spenser and his contemporaries. Richard McCabe reads Spenser's patronal relations in the early stages of his career through the Ciceronian rhetoric of *amicitia*. His account illuminates in loving detail Spenser's relationship with Gabriel Harvey, his Pembroke College near-contemporary. Rebeca Helfer explores the ways that these relations, and particularly Spenser's association with Sidney, inform the lived process of memory in *The Ruines of Time*. Lindsay Reid and Andrew Wallace focus a conference-wide attention to the ethics of reading in the episode of Busirane's Ovidian tapestries.

Andrew Escobedo's discussion of agency, choice, and will in Milton and Spenser entails Renaissance magical theory, but also attention to rhetoric and its particular figures of animation: for him *prosopopoeia* as the trope of animation suggests close links between rhetorical and poetic techniques and creatural vitality. Historicism remains methodologically central to many of Spenser's best readers. Both focus and method have shifted, however, from foundational oppositions—between the aesthetic and the political or between suspicious and naïve modes of reading—to the historicizing of discourses in order to gain proximity to *le vécu* of earlier people. Judith Owens, for example, draws on early-modern discourses to ground her reading of Amavia's legacy to the infant Ruddymane and to articulate the elusive affect in the language of inheritance. This rangy attention to multiple discourses informs the papers of all three participants in the essays on animal being, by Bellamy, Harvey, and Loewenstein.

Place and boundary assume a heightened importance for accounts of Spenser's poem insofar as the contributors to this volume work freely across many fields, discourses, and disciplines. Gordon Teskey's reflections on thinking, moving, and the moment in the process of reading Spenser draw on the great Romantic aestheticians and twentieth-century continental philosophers alike. James Nohrnberg, in a tight mesh of close reading, historicist vigilance, and persistence with the erotic—brings the erotic dynamics of *The Faerie Queene* III into close association with *A Midsummer Night's Dream* by seeing both texts as imaginative refractions of spousal negotiations of Elizabeth and Mary Stuart, and as studies of the real–life stakes of reproductive politics. He thus demonstrates that all our present claims about topics and approaches that have receded must be taken as provisional and partial. Finally he reminds us that the sustained generativity of Spenser's work for generations of readers arises from a poetic force that abides our question, whatever that question is.

For C. S. Lewis at the end of *The Allegory of Love*, Britomart's victory over the enchanter Busirane offered a corrective to a modernity characterized by psychoanalysis and feminism—among other modern errors. The power of Lewis's reading, even as a provocation, is without doubt. As Gordon Teskey notes in his essay, Lewis's *Allegory* "did more than any other single text outside *The Faerie Queene* to draw three generations of Spenserians into the study of their poet." But the twenty-first century seems not to promise a return either to the "monogamic idealism" of romantic love or to anything we take as the critical naïveté of an earlier era. Twentieth-century approaches like psychoanalysis, feminism, and historicism have not disappeared

but are metamorphosing and expanding into a historical phenomenology of lived experience. Readers have always loved this life-
force in Spenser's worlds, referring it to his never-ending story, or
to his animism, or to his verdant woods, or to the process of reading
him, which is like living. But until recently, we have had little critical
vocabulary for elaborating these questions.

★   ★   ★

We were extraordinarily fortunate in the support and goodwill we
received from many people and institutions. On behalf of the conference organizers we would like to thank the three sponsoring organi-
zations: the International Spenser Society, the Department of English
of the University of Toronto, and Victoria College at the University
of Toronto. We are grateful for generous support from the Social
Sciences and Humanities Research Council of Canada and The Con-
naught Committee,

   The editors of this collection extend profuse thanks to their fellow
members of the conference organizing committee: Elizabeth Harvey,
Anne Lake Prescott, and Christopher Warley. All the participants
owe a debt of gratitude to Travis De Cook, our indefatigable local
coordinator, and to the University of Toronto graduate students who
assisted at the event: Heather Ladd, Philip Loosemore, and Lindsay
Reid. We're also grateful to the National Gallery of Canada and the
Thomas Fisher Rare Book Library. The conference was anchored
by four very strong plenary speakers, whose contributions we acknowledge gratefully: Linda Gregerson, Gail Kern Paster, Paul Stevens, and Gordon Teskey. We would also like to thank the editors
of *Spenser Studies*, William Oram, Anne Lake Prescott, and Thomas
Roche, for facilitating the appearance of this collection as a special
number of the journal. And each of the co-editors of this issue, David
and Terry, is beholden to the other for being so stalwart in good
times and bad.

David Galbraith, University of Toronto
Theresa Krier, Macalester College

PAUL STEVENS

Spenser and the End
of the British Empire

Over the last decade or so the term "empire" has acquired a
dramatic new currency. Like its cognate term "imperialism,"
the term Joseph Schumpeter's work did so much to illuminate
in the 1950s, empire is a catch-all phrase, usually taken to mean
some kind of aggressively expansive entity or polity whose
claims to authority are absolute. My principal aim in this essay
is to enlist Spenser's aid in coming to a fuller understanding of
what we might mean by empire. My argument falls into two
parts: first, I want to focus on the role Protestantism, specifically
its articulation of the argument of grace, played in stimulating
and shaping English or British imperial expansion; and second,
I want to consider what it might tell us about the larger significance of the term empire.

*I*N MARCH 1975, THE PROTESTANT ORANGE Order of Bel-
fast celebrated the opening of a new headquarters building on Dublin
Road in the central Sandy Row area of the city. The celebration
attracted some 25,000 members, bowler hats, marching bands, and
masses of prancing teenagers clad in denim or in the tartan-faced
uniforms of the Bay City Rollers rock band. In order to reach the
new building one contingent of Orangemen planned to march north
through the Catholic area along the Ormeau Road. My troop, 8
platoon of the First Royal Regiment of Wales, was tasked to cordon
off one of the Catholic side streets, Hatfield Street, in order to keep
Protestant marchers and Catholic residents apart. As the Orangemen
came up the main road, drums beating and red cross banners flying,

I ordered my guys to roll out the barbed wire and seal off our side street. The Catholic crowd now caught behind the wire became increasingly angry, and I tried to placate them: "Look, they'll only be 20 minutes," I said. "Come on, it's not that big a deal—I'm a Catholic just like you." What seemed to me a rhetorical master-stroke was greeted with derision—"No you're not. You're a fucking soldier." Far from upsetting me, I found this response surprisingly gratifying. What the man who said it meant and what I understood by the word "soldier" were radically different. What the man meant was that I was nothing more than a mercenary—someone who had sold out whatever sense of common decency he might have had to assist the Orangemen in their triumphalism, in their deliberate at-tempt to humiliate and break the spirit of their fellow citizens. He meant that I was complicit in what was to him a self-evident act of injustice. I never really understood this until long after, for I was shielded from it by the heat of the moment and the formidable power of my own cultural memory. His appellation or calling me into being as a "soldier" was gratifying because it confirmed me in the identity I most desired—it confirmed my sense-of-being within a specific *habitus* of reassuring permanence and enormous affective power. For in my mind we were not soldiers in any mercenary sense. That was impossible. We were members of a unique community, not merely the Army but the sons of working-class Welsh people, boys from Cardiff, Newport, Swansea, and the South Wales valleys whose fa-thers and grandfathers had served in the same regiment on the Somme and in the Western Desert. We played rugby, sang hymns and arias, and were completely confident in our good-natured decency. Most importantly, our badges and regimental regalia remembered the apotheosis of our humble origins as the physical arm of a great world empire only now fading into history—we were the imperial regiment who had defeated James II at the Boyne and the Zulus at Rorke's Drift. For all the protective power of our cultural memory, however, my Catholic interlocutor had the last laugh, for in the pride of who we were we wore our green-flashed black berets instead of steel helmets and when the stones began to fly we came to feel his pain.

Over the last decade or so the term "empire" has acquired a dra-matic new currency. Like its cognate term "imperialism," the term Joseph Schumpeter's work did so much to illuminate in the 1950s,[1] empire is a catch-all phrase, usually taken to mean some kind of aggressively expansive entity or polity whose claims to authority are absolute. My principal aim in this essay is to enlist Spenser's aid in coming to a fuller understanding of my experience on the Ormeau Road and what we might mean by empire. My argument falls into two parts: first, I want to focus on the role Protestantism played in stimulating and shaping English or British imperial expansion; and second, I want to consider what it might tell us about the larger significance of the term empire. Let me begin with David Armitage's impressive analysis of empire in his recent book, *The Ideological Origins of the British Empire* (2000).[2]

THE ORIGINS OF THE BRITISH EMPIRE

It is a measure of Armitage's ambition that he opens his book with a parody of Gibbon's *Decline and Fall* that is only slightly self-mocking. According to the logic of Armitage's somewhat arch allusions, the British Empire in the middle of the eighteenth century had reached a point of stability and definition comparable to that of the Roman Empire in the Age of the Antonines: "The frontiers of that extensive monarchy were guarded by a common religion and by the Royal Navy," he says; "[t]he gentle, but powerful influence of laws and manners had gradually cemented the union of the provinces. Their free, white inhabitants enjoyed and produced the advantages of wealth and luxury" (1). Armitage's purpose is not, however, to explain the decline and fall of this great, albeit imperfect, empire but to reveal its origins. More importantly, his purpose is to transume or out-do Gibbon by showing how origins as Gibbon might have understood them, origins as deep-rooted, underlying, or necessary causes, are a fiction. What is remarkable about Armitage's book is its unusually thoughtful emphasis on contingency. He does not doubt that the British Empire in the 1740s identified itself as "Protestant, commercial, maritime, and free" (8), but he sets out to demonstrate that this self-identification was a post-hoc rationalization of characteristics that had actually emerged in a random, bewilderingly complex, and often contradictory manner. There is nothing inevitable, necessary, or natural about Armitage's empire. Deeply influenced by Quentin Skinner's version of Nietzsche, he knows only too well that aetiology, the study of origins, can become "teleology in reverse" (5) and is determined to construct a genealogy of empire which avoids that danger. In one sense, his book is about how the first British Empire came to be what it was before its collapse during the American revolution. In another sense, it is a sustained polemic against the explanatory force of ideology as identity, that is, an argument against those master narratives which aim to show how a specific system of beliefs might interpellate or, as Gibbon would put

it, gently insinuate itself into the minds of men, derive vigor from
opposition, and finally erect an empire. Most immediately, it is this
polemic that I wish to contest—I wish to do so because in its empiri-
cism it limits ideology to political argument or "sectional interest"
and effectively constitutes a nominalist assault on any general theory
of empire.

Armitage's method is to proceed both synchronically and dia-
chronically, taking each of the British Empire's defining characteristics and analyzing it as it comes most powerfully into focus. In each
case, he is determined to show how the characteristic in question,
whether it be "empire" itself, Protestantism, or any of the other
characteristics he feels relevant, emerged dialogically, almost accidentally as "a contribution to political argument, not a normative, self-
conception" (172). For Armitage, these arguments are always textual,
dominated by a surprisingly limited number of key discourses, and
almost always unresolved. They usually "fail to square the circle," as
he likes to put it, because they fail to meet Skinner's legitimation
principle. Almost all the contenders for the role of "taproot," *arche*,
or origin of empire turn out to be vulnerable when subjected to the
acid test of Skinner's belief that "what it is possible to do in politics
is generally limited by what it is possible to legitimise."[3] Thus, the
legacy of Rome, the explanatory force of the term "empire" itself,
is extremely limited, for while the language and symbolism of empire
could provide early modern polities, especially composite monarchies
like Spain or multiple kingdoms like England-Scotland-Ireland "with
the resources for the legitimation of their independence" (34), they
could not produce arguments capable of legitimizing the suppression
of internal differences, especially those between the three kingdoms
of the British archipelago. Similarly, the ability of Protestantism to
explain the ideological origins of the empire are limited. Protestantism fails because although the imperatives of Scripture "encouraged
and legitimated migration and even evangelicisation," they could
not provide a lawful justification for either possession or sovereignty
(96). In Armitage's view, the breakthrough comes not with a theory
or even a political debate but with an event. It is the spectacular
growth of overseas trade in the decades after the Restoration that
provides the insight that allows British people to rationalize their
burgeoning empire. As the growth of trade is seen to encourage and
be encouraged by both individual liberty and overseas expansion, so
it becomes possible to theorize commerce and legitimize the idea
"that liberty and empire might be reconciled within [one] political
economy" (147). And so, he concludes, the "association of religious

and political liberty with freedom of trade became an enduring ideological foundation of the British Empire" (167).

The chief value of Armitage's learned and forcefully argued book is
as a corrective to overly thematic or what he calls "straight line" (24)
stories of empire. Armitage's favorite self-representation is that of an
iconoclast or Talus-like breaker of myths. The book's most immediate weakness is the iconoclast's over-dependence on the flail of the
legitimation principle. The principle itself assumes a rationalism in
politics that is hard to reconcile with either experience or early modern textual evidence. In this case, it consistently underestimates the
extraordinary ingenuity of politicians, merchants, and settlers in justifying their behavior. And in doing so it shifts attention away from
the crucial category of *motivation*. Once we return our focus to the
desires that drive legitimation, then ideology as identity looms as
large as ever. In the book's longest and most fiercely argued chapter,
after conceding that Protestantism should have provided "the solvent
of difference" in state and empire (61), Armitage concludes that there
were in fact "no identifiably or exclusively Protestant origins of British imperial ideology" (99). This is quite a stretch. Only a narrowly
held concentration on the letter of Protestant doctrine and the *apparent* limitedness of its specifically legal role in justifying colonial practice could allow such a conclusion. The spirit tells a different story.
It reveals the degree to which the Protestant emphasis on the argument of grace pervades English culture, insinuates itself into the minds
of men and women in all three of Britain's kingdoms and moves so
many of them to imagine a new kind of empire, an empire in which
the working of grace manifests itself in what Paul Kennedy calls
the "initiative, endurance, and will" of its mercantile class.[4] As the
examples of Catholic empires like those of Portugal, Spain, and
France make abundantly clear, early modern European expansion
cannot be explained in terms of Protestantism alone. That would be
absurd. But while no form of Christian belief was immune from the
expansive imperatives of the Gospels, in Protestantism, to the degree
that God's grace was perceived as a direct and unmediated gift to the
individual believer, those imperatives seem to have taken on a peculiar force in shaping England's imperial ideology.

In order to emphasize the relative poverty of that ideology, Armitage quotes D. A. Brading: "what is there in English literature to
compare to the letters of Hernan Cortes or the 'true history' of Bernal
Diaz?" (qtd. 63). The answer is easy. Consider Spenser or Shakespeare. Consider something as familiar as Shakespeare's universalizing
account of the opposition between the law and gospel in *The Merchant*

of Venice. There the argument of grace, the quality of mercy itself, is secularized in Antonio's risk-taking merchant adventuring and so made to idealize the very overseas trade that so ironically provides Armitage with the way out of the impasse his over-zealous genealogical argument creates.[5] As Antonio explains to Shylock, capital "venture" is a divine thing, a thing not in the adventurer's "power to bring to pass/But swayed and fashioned by the hand of heaven" (I.iii.88–90). And so, for so many of the Elizabethan nationalists who associated themselves with Leicester House, was empire itself. If the circulation of grace as it appears in Shakespeare served to idealize the radical expansion of overseas trade, so the descent of grace as it appears in Spenser served to idealize many things, but, most immediately, overseas military expansion in Ireland and America. My point is that the desires aroused by Scripture, especially as they were politicized, secularized, and increasingly aestheticized, proved a potent inducement to their subsequent legitimation.

THE ARGUMENT OF GRACE

The role of grace in stimulating the military origins of British imperial ideology might at first sight seem more than a little counterintuitive. But the Christian emphasis on grace is from the beginning rooted in an act of textual violence against its own cultural origins in the Hebrew scriptures. Central to the polemical purpose of the gospel is the desire to distinguish its "good news" from the Mosaic law. John's gospel puts it this way: "For the law was [indeed] given by Moses, but *grace and truth came by Jesus Christ*" (John 1:17–18, my emphasis).[6] The assertion that grace in its largest sense of surplus, forgiveness, going beyond the law, of a giving that produces more and more giving, is peculiar to the Christian scriptures is, of course, a misrepresentation, an act of appropriation or to use Harold Bloom's term "transumption." Yahweh's willingness to redeem Sodom and Gomorrah in the Hebrew scriptures, for instance, or his decision to speak directly to Job, to answer his complaints about the inequity of the law and still justify him, these are clearly acts of grace. But since Christian doctrine considers grace the unique result of Christ's redemptive sacrifice, it can only tolerate other accounts of grace as types or imperfect models of its own truth. Its *locus classicus* is the Sermon on the Mount in Matthew 5–7. There, Christ offers a detailed explanation of the relationship between the law and the gospel, that the new dispensation does not mean the abrogation of the law but its fulfillment. It means that not only are we to observe the law but to exceed it—we are to be perfect as our heavenly father is perfect, that is, we are to imitate the grace of his Son in giving, in turning the other cheek, going the extra mile, and most importantly in loving our enemies and praying for them, especially those who persecute us (Matt. 5:44). This articulation and the general significance of grace is constantly being reinterpreted and developed throughout the epistles, but in the Epistle to the Ephesians it takes a radical turn.

Paul, or whoever it actually was who composed the letter to the Ephesians,[7] wrote it from prison and clearly had great difficulty praying for those who were persecuting him. On the one hand, his account of grace is, as one would expect, expansive, boundless, and utterly inclusive. Grace in the epistle even goes beyond Christ's sermon and completely abolishes the Mosaic law, "*even* the law of commandments *contained* in ordinances" (Eph. 2:15). It does so in order to transcend the critical distinction between Jew and Gentile, and so create, the author says, "one new man" or one humanity in place of two (Eph. 2:15). On the other hand, however, the letter immediately proceeds to reinscribe difference, articulating an intensely combative determination to identify the other and contest the gathering power of its enemies. Even as it insists that "we wrestle" against spiritual not physical enemies, the distinction collapses as the letter focuses all too ambiguously on "rulers" and the "spiritual wickedness in high places" (Eph. 6:12). Similarly, even as the letter welcomes Gentiles into the new dispensation of grace, it reminds them of what they once were and proceeds to express anything but love for those who have refused grace: they are degenerate, says the letter—having their "understanding darkened, being alienated from God through the ignorance that is in them, because of the blindness of their heart," being "past feeling" and having "given themselves over unto lasciviousness, to work all uncleanness with greediness," they are clearly beyond the pale (Eph. 4:18–19). Over and again, the focus of the epistle is on the *reception* rather than the *donation* of grace. Such reception is only possible through faith, the letter insists, but faith in Ephesians is not so much a matter of belief as one of strength, muscularity, or will to power—"be strong in the Lord," the Ephesians are admonished, "be strong in the Lord and in the power of his might" (Eph. 6:10). Only by putting on the "whole armour of God," the "shield of faith," and the "sword of the Spirit" can the Ephesians hope to receive the grace that will finally enable them to stand against the Devil (Eph. 6:11–17). Grace, it is implied, is a surplus of explicitly military power coming to the rescue. Like Ezekiel's vision or Milton's chariot of paternal deity, grace has become a matter of shock and awe.

In much the same way that the spiritual tenor of the parable of the talents is co-opted by its economic vehicle, so here the same spiritual tenor is co-opted by its military vehicle, and it is entirely fitting that the Epistle to the Ephesians should be the principal biblical text with which Spenser opens his chivalric romance, *The Faerie Queene,* in his prefatory letter to Ralegh:

> In the end the Lady told him [the soon to be revealed St. George] that unlesse that armour which she brought, would serve him (that is the armour of a Christian man specified by Saint Paul v. Ephes.) that he would not succeed in that enterprise, which being forthwith put upon him with dewe furnitures thereunto, he seemed the goodliest man in al that company, and was well liked of the Lady.
>
> (*FQ* Letter of the Authors 17)[8]

My point here is that Spenser's often monstrous militarism is not simply a function of his colonial situation, but that there is a degree to which his colonial situation is itself an effect of Scripture's totalizing imaginations, especially as they are read and re-read in various early modern Protestant communities searching for political guidance. In order to develop this point we need to look more closely at Spenser.

GRACIOUS SPENSER I: POSSESSION AND SOVEREIGNTY

The argument of grace is as important as it is, because of the enormous *confidence* it afforded Protestants in their expansive enterprises. As it appears in a text like Ephesians, grace seems specifically designed to confront and overawe the degenerate, whether they be Roman authorities or Irish kerns. The most persuasive prevailing representation of Spenser is that of a profoundly conflicted, Mulcaster–educated humanist, whose poetics, to use Richard McCabe's telling phrase, "interrogate his politics."[9] From Ciaran Brady to McCabe's magisterial study, Spenser is taken to exemplify the tragedy of Renaissance humanism rendered monstrous by its being "imposed on a colony rather than inculcated in a people" (McCabe 6). There is much to this view, but its limitation, so it seems to me, is that it tends to turn

Spenser into Conrad's Kurtz; and, as Thomas Herron has suggested, it underestimates the extraordinary resilience of Protestantism in shaping identity and behavior[10]—most importantly, I would add, it underestimates the power of grace in reassuring Protestants of their election and so stimulating expansive action. Whatever despair Spenser might feel on contemplating the heart of his own darkness, there stands universal truth ready to reassure him about the efficacy of grace, just as she would Redcross Knight: "What meanest thou by this reprochfull strife?" she asks, "Is this the battell, which thou vauntst to fight." Do not "let vaine words bewitch thy manly hart,/ Ne diuelish thoughts dismay thy constant spright./In heavenly mercies hast thou no part?/Why should thou then despeire, *that chosen art*?" Remember "Where iustice growes, there growes eke greater grace" (*FQ* I.ix.52–53, my emphasis).[11] Therefore, rise up, she says, leave this place and take possession of Una's promised land. As John Bradley has pointed out, the motto over the entrance to the New English Lismore castle read—"God's providence is our inheritance."[12] Even now at the end of empire, the echoes of the argument of grace can still be heard among Ulster's Protestants, the Orangeman who lauded it over their Catholic neighbors on the Ormeau Road. A decade after the Hatfield Street riot, forced to confront the might of Gloriana Redux in the form of Mrs. Thatcher, the Reverend Ian Paisley invokes the parable of the mustard seed. In that parable, grace says if you have faith the size of a mustard seed, you can move mountains—"nothing will be impossible to you" (Matt. 17:20). So in his December 1985 sermon, "A Prime Text for a Prime Minister," Paisley says this—"God has a purpose for this province and this plant of Protestantism sown here in this north-eastern part of this island. The enemy has tried to root it out, but it still grows today, and I believe like a grain of mustard seed, its future is going to be mightier yet."[13] Armed with the Word, Paisley has none of Kurtz's self-doubt or sense of horror.

Nowhere is the confidence-sustaining power of grace more crucially deployed than in Spenser's *View of the Present State of Ireland*. The situation of the New English in April 1598 when the *View* was first registered was fast becoming as desperate as that of the Ephesians in Paul's epistle, and the emphasis in Spenser's text, just as it is in Paul's, is on receiving rather than giving grace. At the climax of the dialogue, Eudoxus and Irenius have arrived at an impasse. Rational discourse has done all that it can do, and the desire for moral balance that animates the law's governing concept of equity has been cruelly frustrated. It is vain, says Irenius, "to prescribe lawes where no man careth for keeping of them, nor feareth the daunger for breaking of them."[14]At this moment, Irenius could be speaking to Armitage: it is vain to talk of Skinner's legitimation principle when these people will not do what we require of them. Both Irenius and Eudoxus feel that the reformation of Ireland now needs "the strength of a mightier power" (92). That power reveals itself in Irenius's draconian plan to go beyond the law by resorting to the sword. As they begin to discuss it, it is clear that the argument of grace is in Spenser's mind because Eudoxus and Irenius act out the roles of Abraham and Yahweh from Genesis 18[15]—the same passage that Milton uses in *Paradise Lost,* Book III, to articulate the Son's amplification of the Father's intention that "Man should find grace" (III.145).[16] To do otherwise says the Son, quoting Genesis 18: "that be from thee far,/That far be from thee" (III.153–54). In Genesis 18 itself, Yahweh decides that the degenerate cities of Sodom and Gomorrah are to be cut off. Abraham objects but with a speech act indicating his faith in Yahweh's justice: "Wilt thou also destroy the righteous with wicked?" he enquires. "*That be far from thee* to do after this manner, to slay the righteous with the wicked" he affirms. "[A]nd that the righteous should be as the wicked, *that be far from thee*: Shall not the judge of all the earth do right?" (Gen. 18:23–25, my emphasis). Yahweh relents and offers to spare both cities if one righteous man be found in either of them. His grace is evident in his willingness to go beyond the needs of equity and spare the wicked on behalf of the righteous. In the event, no righteous are found and his grace is transformed into the mighty power that saves the angels from sodomy and destroys the cities. In Spenser's text, it is Eudoxus who objects and Irenius's response with its tell-tale emphasis on the phrase "far be it from me" assimilates Yahweh's gracious concession into the words of Abraham's challenge: "by the sword which I named," says Irenius, "I did not meane the cutting off [of] all that nation with the sword, which *farre bee it from mee*, that I should ever thinke so desperately, or wish so uncharitably" (93, my emphasis). In the event, all those who oppose the Yahweh-like power arrogated by Irenius to "the royall power of the Prince" (93) will be cut off, and mercy in the *View*, unlike in grace in *Paradise Lost*, collapses into justice. That is, in Spenser's text the grace of the Sermon on the Mount collapses into the "imperiall" justice of Artegal (*FQ* V.Proem.10) and the merciless, providential power of his squire, Talus. But grace does this, it needs to be emphasized, not simply through the distorting pressures of Spenser's colonial situation, but through the independent, mediating agency of Christian Scripture itself. As Linda Gregerson puts it, "the subject is formed in subjection

by the power of words,"[17] and the power of the Word is always
there with Protestant nationalists like Spenser constantly shaping and
directing understanding and action. This is not to say that the argument of grace functions like some vast monological machine, some
mindless "dominant ideology," but that under certain circumstances
and in particular textual communities it provides a repository of
rhetorical triggers and strategies of great authority for the legitimation
of expansion.

As Scripture moves Spenser, so it does innumerable other English
empire-builders throughout the seventeenth century. In his widely
publicized letter of 1614 to the governor of Virginia, for instance,
John Rolfe legitimizes his union with Pocahontas specifically by
attributing his love for her to the promptings of grace overturning
the Mosaic law's prohibition against marrying outside the nation.[18]
In his 1625 tract "Virginias Verger," Samuel Purchas appeals to the
gracious donation of dominion in Genesis 1:28 to claim possession
and sovereignty in Virginia.[19] In his 1655 *Declaration against Spain,*
Oliver Cromwell appeals to the universalizing argument of Acts 17:26
to claim possession and sovereignty in the Caribbean.[20] In fact, despite
Armitage's argument to the contrary, there is hardly a point when
English colonial possession and sovereignty in the late sixteenth and
early seventeenth centuries is not legitimized by an appeal to some
version of the Gospel's argument of grace. Most strikingly, it is the
argument of grace that animates James Harrington's theory of empire
in his *Oceana* of 1656, a theory that was to play such an important
role in the intellectual genesis of the United States constitution.[21]
J. G. A. Pocock makes the point this way: "Oceana is to be a commonwealth for expansion, but . . . there is no hint of ultimate doom,"
of impermanence or that at some point the empire will decline;
"Harrington seems to have discerned messianic or apocalyptic possibilities for his republic, which permitted him to turn from *virtu* to
grace in the completion of his vision."[22] Harrington's imperial republic is imagined as a function of grace at work in the world and its
specific political purpose is "patronage," that is, the propagation of
balanced popular sovereignty, civil liberty and liberty of conscience
across the globe (332).[23] Such patronage or imperial expansion is
understood as an imperative: "if the empire of a commonwealth be
patronage, to ask whether it be lawful for a commonwealth to aspire
unto the empire of the world is to ask whether it be lawful for her
to do her duty, or to put the world in a better condition than it was

before" (328). At the climax of this passage, Lord Archon, an ideal-ized representation of Cromwell, insists on England's imperial excep-tionalism—that the empire of Oceana is our first world, the garden of God, "the rose of Sharon, and the lily of the valley" (333).[24]

Critical as this point is, Spenser's representation of grace has an-other more important insight to offer. Not only does it stimulate the English to expansion, but even in its very virtue it insulates them against difference and cultural mutability, most significantly by en-abling belief to overwhelm irony.

GRACIOUS SPENSER II: IMMUTABILITY

One of the most sacred moments in *The Faerie Queene*, so John Milton and Henry Vaughan clearly felt, was the epiphany of grace on Mount Acidale in Book VI. For Milton, Mount Acidale provides one of the principal sources for his representation of paradise. In Spenser's poem as in *Paradise Lost*, it is the original *locus amoenus*, "a place, whose pleasaunce did appere / To passe all others," says Spenser; "For all that euer was by natures skill / Deuized to work delight, was gathered there" (*FQ* VI.x.5–6). As Milton's recreation of Acidale in Eden makes clear, discovering this hill-top meadow "bordered with a wood / Of matchless hight" (6) is like entering our first world. It is profoundly moving. More than anything else it is the home of innocence and boundless grace. For there, "airs, vernal airs," says Milton, "Breathing the smell of field and grove, attune / The trembling leaves, while Universal *Pan* / Knit with the *Graces* and the *Hours* in dance / Led on th'Eternal Spring" (*PL* IV: 264–68). For Vaughan in *Silex Scintillans,* Mount Acidale becomes the home of Christ's grace in the fullness of its regenerative agency.[25] The wind which is heard but not seen in the hill-top's "fair, fresh field" ("Re-generation" 27) recalls Christ's words to Nicodemus in John's Gos-pel. Grace in the form of the spirit of the Word, that is, Christ himself, cannot be summoned at will: it blows "where it listeth and thou hearest the sound thereof, but canst not tell whence it cometh, and whither it goeth: so is every one who is born of the Spirit" (John 3:8). So it is here on Spenser's Acidale. For as Colin, that is, the poet and creator of the graces himself, explains to Calidore, the graces cannot be summoned; once they have disappeared, "none can bring them in place, / But whom they of them selues list so to grace" (*FQ* VI.x.20). The Senecan graces invoked on Mount Acidale are being assimilated into Christian revelation and made to exemplify the surplus or circulation of grace as it is imagined in the Sermon on the Mount—giving, not demanding or summoning, produces plenitude. Spenser's graces dance in such a way as to exemplify boundless liberality—that "good should from us goe, then come in greater store" (*FQ* VI.x.24). Here classical civility and Christian grace become one. For people of my generation and for older scholars like Edgar Wind or Thomas Roche, this epiphany of grace even when located in a colonial landscape was not seen as a grand gesture of poetic isolation, a futile act of cultural hypocrisy, but a moment when we came to see Renaissance culture at its ideal.[26] "Colin's explanation of the vision of the dance," says Roche, "is the most self-conscious artistic act in Renaissance poetry." The poet in the persona of his character Colin, Roche continues, enters the poem to emphasize that grace is "the source of civilization" (1227). Grace as it manifests itself in civility, not least the civility of Spenser's own art, repairs the ruins of our first parents and transforms us into people who are truly human. These three graces, Euphrosyne, Aglaia, and Thalia, says Colin, "on men all gracious gifts bestow,/Which decke the body and adorne the mynde." Most importantly, they teach us how to negotiate difference—"They teach us, how to each degree and kynde/We should our selues demeane, to low, to hie;/To friends, to foes, which skill men call Ciuility" (*FQ* VI.x.23). After 30 years of postcolonial critique, however, it is difficult to accept this idealism without wanting some kind of qualification. It now requires an act of imagination to see *The Faerie Queene* in quite the uninflected way Wind or Roche did. Because it is now so hard to forget colonial Ireland's suffering, we may feel that on Mount Acidale we're looking into the heart of darkness, but Spenser and his older interpreters clearly did not—they are staring into the heart of light. This incongruity or discrepant awareness is central to my argument about empire.

The immediate effects of Spenser's vision are for us, his postcolonial readers, profoundly ironic. Calidore returns to his duty, and grace most immediately manifests itself in the urbanity with which he deceives the brigands, the scarcely disguised Irish runnagates who have kidnapped Pastorella. After "gently waking them" and allaying all their fears, he wreaks massive slaughter on them—"through dead carcasses he made his way" (*FQ* VI.xi.38, 47). Grace, so Spenser might argue, enables the less than competent Calidore to recover Pastorella and return the world to the moral balance or order civility promises. Grace, we might argue, does something quite different. It

insulates Spenser against the incongruity of his own violence. It protects him against the irony or relativism that civility in the form of
humanist education would teach. My point is that it's not so much
Spenser's poetics that interrogate his politics as we, his critics, and
that we do so in the way we do is a measure not of our superior
virtue, but of our historicism, not necessarily our "new historicism"
but of the degree to which Spenser's early modern world is perceived
as a discrete culture or foreign country. It is a measure of our historicism or cultural relativism that the lines that now haunt contemporary
Spenser studies are not those of Mount Acidale but those from the
View describing Munster's rebels as so many anatomies of death, their
terrible suffering dismissed in a line as a fate that "they themselves
had wrought" (102). But for Spenser, their suffering is as nothing
compared to the vision of grace on Acidale, where change is no
longer as "perillous" as Eudoxus and Irenius imagine (92) because it
is aestheticized in the circulating dance of the graces and so made to
signify the liberating permanence, immutability, the eternal stability
of the world Spenser's culture promises him. The wide-ruling, ever-
expanding argument of grace is as important as it is, especially when
it is recreated in the sublime poetry of *The Faerie Queene,* because it
enables Spenser to protect his way of being in the world against
difference and mutability. Nowhere is this more clear than in the
final cantos of the poem where the very real horror of change, death,
decay, and difference is *aestheticized* by grace from the outset. In the
very act of allegorizing mutability her threat is *anaesthetized*—as she
enters the presence of the Gods, her words "marked well her grace"
(*FQ* VII.vi.28) and her beauty, so Jove discovers, "could the greatest
wrath turn to grace" (31). Jove's empire is saved before the debate
has begun. For mutability personified is not real change but only
change reassuringly imagined as a function of Nature's benign order.
Clearly, Jove's empire and maybe all empires have something to do
with the longing for cultural permanence.

    At the end of the British Empire things seem different, but only
in this sense. It is not Protestant grace so much as its secularization
in the nation's cultural memory, its aestheticization in narratives and
cultural artifacts precisely like those of Spenser's poetry, that protects
so many British people against difference and the impermanence of
empire. In the late sixteenth-century, at the beginning of the empire,
cultural memory in the specific form of the nation's Protestant history
is clearly a site of intense contention;[27] by the mid-twentieth century,
however, at the end of the empire, cultural memory is dominated
by the nation's progressive history, the unfolding story of popular
liberties and parliamentary government. For so many British people

what Herbert Butterfield called the "Whig interpretation" of history had become a fiction felt as fact. In order to make this clear, let me turn to Spenser's most illustrious descendent, Winston Churchill.

THE END OF THE BRITISH EMPIRE

Despite Spenser's own best efforts to associate himself with the Spencers of Althorp in *Prothalamion* (130–31) and *Colin Clout's Come Home Againe* (536–39), there was in fact, as everyone knows, no immediate blood relationship between him and that "house of ancient fame," nor consequently with their relatives, the Churchills.[28] But Spenser and the greatest of the Churchills, Winston Spencer-Churchill, are related in more substantial ways than those of genealogy. Between them, they comprehend the British Empire. Not only do they mark out its beginning and end, but they allow us considerable insight into its longing for liberating permanence.

One of the most resonant images in the recent history of the West, especially as it's been cultivated, revived, and elaborated since September 2001, is that of Churchill refusing to appease the Nazis, staying the course, and leading Britain over the summer of 1940 in her lonely stand against Hitler's Germany. At that moment, so we are reminded, the West faced extinction and only Churchill's indomitable will saved us. While Churchill's courage and intelligence really are incontrovertible, his story has become a shaping fantasy of enormous power and he himself has become a growth industry not only in Britain but even more so in the United States.[29] The British statesman who was best known before the advent of Hitler for his refusal to appease the democratic aspirations of Mahatma Gandhi and before that the naval ambitions of U.S. President Calvin Coolidge has somewhat ironically become an American icon—an exemplar of the grit the United States needs to show if its unique way of being in the world is to prevail. The rise of Churchill, it might be argued, is a sure-fire indication of the degree to which America has come to think of itself as an empire.

   In his single most famous speech, the radio speech he delivered at the fall of France on June 18, 1940, Churchill talked of the end of the British Empire both in terms of its purpose and its final termination. While he imagined its purpose as the survival of what he called "Christian civilization," he projected its termination into a distant millenarian future. As he urged his fellow citizens to duty and resistance, he prophesied that "if the British Commonwealth and Empire should last a thousand years, men will still say, 'This was their finest hour.' "[30] In the event, it only lasted another seven years, effectively disappearing in the summer of 1947 with the abandonment of Palestine and more importantly with the independence of India.[31] But in Churchill's romantic wartime imagination, the essential meaning of the British millenium would be made manifest in this, its finest hour, an epiphany that would transcend time.[32] The speech, like much of Churchill's rhetoric, is carefully calibrated to enlist the prestige of Scripture without being explicitly religious, and in so doing it identifies itself with a genre of mystical English nationalism that flourished in the 1930s and 1940s and whose most authentic, genuinely religious expression was T. S. Eliot's *Four Quartets*. The complete version of Eliot's poem was published in 1944 just after the Normandy landings and within months of Olivier's *Henry V,* Powell and Pressburger's wonderful *Canterbury Tale,* and C. S. Lewis's Clark lectures on Sidney and Spenser. For Lewis, Spenser represents the "ordered exuberance" of English culture.[33] Eliot would have agreed for there in the *Four Quartets*, in that poem written in wartime London while Eliot listened to Churchill's speeches, England stands on Mount Acidale. At the beginning, in "Burnt Norton," we enter our first world and stare into the heart of light. At the end, in "Little Gidding," England stands at the still point of the turning world: "the communication/ Of the dead is tongued with fire beyond the language of the living," Eliot explains. The dead are alive because England is the specific location of an eternal present. "Here the intersection of the timeless moment/Is England and nowhere" (50–53).[34] If we were to look at Churchill's prophecy and Eliot's revelation through the skeptical eyes of a postcolonial critic or a contemporary anthropologist like Marshall Sahlins,[35] what we might see is the degree to which history has been reduced to a function of culture. That is, history has ceased to be a disinterested inquiry into the past, sensitive to discontinuity, inconstancy, and the frighteningly unpredictable lurches of contingency, but has become a function of a particular culture's determination to assimilate the past, aestheticize change, and maintain its identity. What Churchill's rhetoric and Eliot's poetry have in common is the representation of the past not simply as cultural memory, but as their own culture's *very selective* memory.

In Eliot's highly influential 1919 essay "Tradition and the Individual Talent," the process of selection itself suggests how the aesthetic might be deployed to persuade the culture to believe more fully in its quest for permanence.[36] In that essay, the past is represented not so much as a collection of fragments desperately shored against our ruin but as a resilient, ever-evolving structure of words, beliefs, and practices known as "tradition." There is nothing of Milton's violent, revolutionary contempt for tradition in Eliot's vision. It is not the peculiar amalgam of "unchewed notions and suppositions" that would sow up Milton's "womb of teeming truth,"[37] but an ideal order of great beauty only to be perceived by what Eliot calls the "historical sense." This historical sense is paradoxically, but predictably, intensely anti-historicist, that is, aggressively antipathetical to any sense of the past as a foreign country or genealogy of discrete cultures. The historical sense is the principle by whose possession writers select themselves as great or truly memorable. It "involves a perception not only of the pastness of the past," says Eliot, "but of its presence; the historical sense compels a man to write not merely with his own generation in his bones, but with the feeling that the whole of the literature of Europe from Homer and within it the whole of the literature of his own country has a simultaneous existence and composes a simultaneous order" (14). No poet, no artist, neither Spenser nor Milton, has his complete meaning outside this order. This, Eliot insists, is "a principle of aesthetic, not merely historical, criticism" (15). At this point, it becomes clear that what Eliot means by aesthetic criticism is something more than the simple apprehension or evaluation of beauty; it is the perception of one's culture as a complete synchronic order idealized in such a way that change as in the dance of the graces only perfects that order. Culture is Europe or Western culture, and it is imagined, to use Northrop Frye's term, as a "secular scripture" in which the new only reveals more fully the universal truths of the old. From an anthropologist's perspective, this constitutes a form of cultural solipsism of an extraordinarily high order, but most importantly, a form of solipsism whose political equivalent is empire.

In the same way that empire, from Jove's "high empire" in the Mutability Cantos to Hardt and Negri's new world order, from Harrington's *Oceana* to Robert Kagan and William Kristol's Project for the New American Century, seeks to arrest mutability and represent itself as the once and future *telos*, so does Eliot's aesthetic tradition. My point is that the end of empire imagined by Churchill and other imperial thinkers aspires to the same kind of absolute cultural synchronicity imagined by Eliot and before any of them by Spenser. Michael Hardt and Antonio Negri put the idea this way: "Empire exhausts historical time, suspends history, and summons past and future with its own ethical order. In other words, Empire presents its order as permanent, eternal, and [morally] necessary."[38] Change is not change but the endless reproduction of novel simulacra of this final synchronic order. The Churchill whom neoconservatives like Niall Ferguson love to quote never really gives up on the empire but imagines it reproducing itself in the form of a great Anglo-American empire called "the English-speaking peoples"[39] and the Bush administration lectures academics on the way that not only the past but the future and indeed change itself is now government property: "We are an empire now," an anonymous Bush official recently said, "and when we act, we create our own reality. And while you are studying that reality—judiciously, as you will—we'll act again, creating new realities which you can study too, and that's how things will sort out"[40] The critical problem is this—by focusing on the fantasy of their absolute synchronicity cultures at their most imperial erase the possibility of a plurality of ways of being in the world. The failure of early new historicism, certainly as it was articulated in classic essays like Greenblatt's wonderful "Invisible Bullets" (1981), was that it took the claims of empire or what it called the "dominant ideology" at face value and refused to see its totalizing power as a cultural fiction.[41] As the Iraq War has most recently demonstrated, empires to the degree that they indulge their tendency to solipsism routinely overestimate their power and underestimate their fragility. For all their claims to unchanging synchronicity, they are wracked with the fear of cultural mutability.

No one felt the fear of impermanence more powerfully than Spenser, but so at their darkest moments did Churchill and Eliot, and it seems significant that at these moments they both invoke not so much grace as the memory of Spenser as a metonym for cultural continuity. For Churchill, after the Second World War, as he tries to recreate the British Empire in the history of the English-speaking peoples, he looks back for reassurance to Elizabethan England and Spenser's vision of Gloriana, a moment, he says, focusing on *The Faerie Queene,* when the English people first "awoke to consciousness of their greatness" (II:133). In this, he joins nationalist historians like Arthur Bryant and A. L. Rowse in the hope of a new Elizabethan age. More pointedly, for Eliot, after the First World War, as he gathers fragments to shore against the ruin of his culture, he dwells on Spenser's *Prothalamion*. In *The Waste Land*, he sits down by the waters of the now polluted Thames and weeps, invoking the implicit resolve of Psalm 137—"By the rivers of Babylon there we sat down [and] wept when we remembered Zion . . . if I forget thee, O Jerusalem . . . ." The fear is that England is no longer England, but Babylon —"How shall we sing the Lord's song in a strange land?" The gracious answer is by remembering Zion in the specifically English form of Spenser's refrain: "Sweet Thames, run softly till I end my song" (*Waste Land* 183). The irony is that Eliot invokes the aesthetic resonances of Spenser's memory in almost exactly the same way that Spenser invokes the argument of grace. In *Prothalamion,* the poem Eliot remembers, the departed river nymphs return and sanctify the betrothal of the Somerset daughters with boundless grace, "endlesse Peace" and "blessed Plentie" (101–02). But most importantly, the betrothal erases the memory of decay and ushers in the prospect of imperial renewal. For out of Leicester House, the home of Spenser's former patron, Robert Dudley, Earl of Leicester, comes a new star, the patron of the betrothed, Robert Devereux, Earl of Essex, "Great Englands glory and Worlds wide wonder . . . Faire branch of Honor, flower of Cheualrie, / That fillest England with thy triumphes fame" (146–51). Because he comes like "Radiant *Hesper*" (164), it is difficult not to believe that it's morning again in England.

CONCLUSION

Let me conclude by returning to the imperial theorists with whom we began, Schumpeter and Armitage. For both these scholars, the defining characteristic of empire is spacial expansion. For Schumpeter, imperialism is "the objectless disposition on the part of a state to unlimited forcible expansion" and because expansion has no end but itself, empires tend "to transcend all bounds and limits to the point of exhaustion" (6). What I'm suggesting is that the argument of grace as it manifests itself in the work of a great poet like Spenser and as it is reproduced in the cultural memory of so many people at the end of the British Empire indicates something different. That the key to understanding empire is not spacial but temporal. That the driving force at the heart of empire is a culture's longing for its own permanence, what I've been calling its absolute synchronicity, and that it articulates this longing in imaginations of ending history or transcending time on Mount Acidale, Arlo Hill, or indeed the Ormeau Road.

NOTES

1. Joseph Schumpeter, *Imperialism [and] Social Classes: Two Essays* (1919; 1927), trans. Heinz Norden (New York: Meridian, 1972). Hereafter cited in the text.

2. David Armitage, *The Ideological Origins of the British Empire* (Cambridge: Cambridge University Press, 2000). Hereafter cited in the text.

3. Quentin Skinner, *Liberty before Liberalism* (Cambridge: Cambridge University Press, 1998), 105.

4. Paul Kennedy, *The Rise and Fall of British Naval Mastery* (Harmondsworth: Penguin, 1976), 24.

5. See Paul Stevens, "Heterogenizing Imagination: Globalization, *The Merchant of Venice*, and the Work of Literary Criticism," *New Literary History* 36:3 (2005): 425–37. Shakespeare is quoted from *The Merchant of Venice*, ed. Jay L. Halio (Oxford: Oxford University Press, 1994).

6. The Bible is quoted from the 1611 Authorized Version.

7. The letter was probably written by Ignatius, Bishop of Antioch, around 110–17 AD—see, for instance, *The Cambridge Companion to the Bible*, ed. Howard Clark Kee et al. (Cambridge: Cambridge University Press, 1997), 565–67.

8. *The Faerie Queene* is quoted from Edmund Spenser, *The Faerie Queene,* ed. Thomas P. Roche (1978; rpt. Harmondsworth: Penguin, 1987).

9. Richard A. McCabe, *Spenser's Monstrous Regiment: Elizabethan Ireland and the Poetics of Difference* (Oxford: Oxford University Press, 2002), 4. Hereafter cited in the text. See also Ciaran Brady, "Spenser's Irish Crisis: Humanism and Experience in the 1590s," *Past & Present* 111 (1986): 17–49, and Paul Stevens, "Spenser and Milton on Ireland: Civility, Exclusion, and the Politics of Wisdom," *ARIEL* 26:4 (1995): 151–67.

10. Thomas Herron, "Guyon's Angel," Paper, *Spenser's Civilizations*, International Spenser Society Conference, University of Toronto, May 2006.

11. Obviously, the doctrine of election was double-edged and could lead to despair—but it is extraordinary how little of the temptation to doubt one's own election enters public arguments for imperial or colonial expansion.

12. John Bradley, Response to "Archaeologies of Spenser," *Spenser's Civilizations*, International Spenser Society Conference, University of Toronto, May 2006.

13. Ian Paisley, "A Prime Text for a Prime Minister" (15 December 1985), quoted in Steve Bruce, *God Save Ulster: The Religion and Politics of Paisleyism* (Oxford: Clarendon, 1986), 269–70.

14. The *View* is quoted from Edmund Spenser, *A View of the State of Ireland* (1633), ed. Andrew Hadfield and Willy Maley (Oxford: Blackwell, 1997). Hereafter cited in the text.

15. See Stevens, "Spenser and Milton on Ireland."

16. Milton is quoted from *John Milton: Complete Poems and Prose*, ed. Merritt Y. Hughes (Indianapolis: Odyssey, 1957).

17. Linda Gregerson, *The Reformation of the Subject: Spenser, Milton, and the English Protestant Epic* (Cambridge: Cambridge University Press, 1995), 236.

18. John Rolfe, Letter to Sir Thomas Dale, in Ralph Hamor, *A True Discourse of the Present Estate of Virginia* (London, 1615).

19. Samuel Purchas, "Virginias Verger" (1625), in *Hakluytus Posthumus, or Purchas his Pilgrimes*, 20 vols. (1906; rpt. New York: AMS, 1965).

20. Oliver Cromwell, *A Declaration of His Highness, by the Advice of His Council . . . against Spain* (1655), in *The Works of John Milton*, ed. Frank Allen Patterson et al., 18 vols. (New York: Columbia University Press, 1931–38), XIII: 509–63.

21. The classic account is H. F. Russell-Smith, *Harrington and His Oceana: A Study of a 17th-Century Utopia and Its Influence in America* (Cambridge: Cambridge University Press, 1914). See also J. G. A. Pocock, ed., *The Political Works of James Harrington* (Cambridge: Cambridge University Press, 1977), esp.128–52; James Holstun, *A Rational Millenium: Puritan Utopias of Seventeenth-Century England and America* (Oxford: Oxford University Press, 1987), and David Norbrook, *Writing the English Republic: Poetry, Rhetoric and Politics, 1627–1660* (Cambridge: Cambridge University Press, 1999), esp. 357–78.

22. Pocock, *Harrington*, 19.

23. *Oceana* is quoted from Pocock's edition. I am indebted to Philip Loosemore for drawing my attention to this passage.

24. While Armitage (137–39) shows no interest in the religious quality of Harrington's republican vision, Norbrook (357–78), somewhat more surprisingly, shows little or no interest in the overtly imperial quality of what he calls English republicanism's "most important text" (357).

25. Vaughan is quoted from *The Works of Henry Vaughan*, ed. L. C. Martin, 2nd ed. (Oxford: Clarendon, 1957).

26. See, for instance, Edgar Wind, *Pagan Mysteries in the Renaissance*, rev. ed. (New York: Norton, 1958).

27. Building on the work of scholars like Richard Helgerson, especially in *Forms of Nationhood: The Elizabethan Writing of England* (Chicago: University of Chicago Press, 1992), there is now a wealth of imaginative scholarship on Spenser and the construction of English national history: see, for example, David Galbraith, *Architectonics of Imitation in Spenser, Daniel, and Drayton* (Toronto: University of Toronto Press, 2000); Andrew Escobedo, *Nationalism and Historical Loss in Renaissance England* (Ithaca: Cornell University Press, 2004); Philip Schwyzer, *Literature, Nationalism, and Memory in Early Modern England and Wales* (Cambridge: Cambridge University Press, 2004); and Bart Van Es, *Spenser's Forms of History* (Oxford: Oxford University Press, 2002).

28. See, for instance, Richard Rambuss, "Spenser's Life and Career," in *The Cambridge Companion to Spenser Studies*, ed. Andrew Hadfield (Cambridge: Cambridge University Press, 2001), 14–16. Spenser's shorter poems are quoted from *The Yale Edition of the Shorter Poems of Edmund Spenser*, ed. William Oram et al. (New Haven: Yale University Press, 1989).

29. For a perceptive overview of this phenomenon, see Geoffrey Wheatcroft, "A Man so Various: The Misappropriated Winston Churchill," *Harper's Magazine* (May 2006), 86–94.

30. Quoted from Roy Jenkins, *Churchill* (London: Macmillan, 2001), 621.

31. As Willy Maley reminds me, in strict Harringtonian terms the empire lingers on in the sovereign state of the United Kingdom of Great Britain and Northern Ireland: both Marpesia and the northern part of Panopea are still subject to Oceana.

32. On Churchill's romanticism, see Paul Stevens, "Churchill's Military Romanticism," *Queen's Quarterly* 113:1 (2006): 70–85.

33. C. S. Lewis, *English Literature in the Sixteenth Century, excluding Drama* (Oxford: Clarendon, 1954), 393.

34. Eliot's poetry is quoted from T. S. Eliot, *The Complete Poems and Plays, 1909–1950* (New York: Harcourt, Brace, 1971).

35. See Marshall Sahlins, *Apologies to Thucidydes: Understanding History as Culture and Vice Versa* (Chicago: University of Chicago Press, 2004).

36. T. S. Eliot, "Tradition and the Individual Talent" (1919), *Selected Essays* (1932; rpt. London: Faber, 1969), 13–22. Hereafter cited in the text.

37. John Milton, *The Doctrine and Discipline of Divorce* (1643), in Hughes, 697.

38. Michael Hardt and Antonio Negri, *Empire* (Cambridge: Harvard University Press, 2000), 11.

39. Winston S. Churchill, *A History of the English-Speaking Peoples,* 4 vols. (1956; rpt. New York: Dodd, Mead & Co., 1966). Hereafter cited in the text. See Niall Ferguson, *Empire: The Rise and Demise of the British World Order and the Lessons for Global Power* (New York: Basic, 2002) and David Reynolds, *In Command of History: Churchill Fighting and Writing the Second World War* (London: Penguin, 2004).

40. Anonymous Bush administration official quoted in the Toronto *Globe and Mail* (February 4, 2006), A26.

41. Stephen Greenblatt, "Invisible Bullets: Renaissance Authority and its Subversion," *Glyph* 8 (1981): 40–61. See especially Jonathan Dollimore's critique in *Political Shakespeare: New Essays in Cultural Materialism,* ed. Jonathan Dollimore and Alan Sinfield (Manchester: University of Manchester Press, 1985), 11–13.

JUDITH OWENS

Memory Works in *The Faerie Queene*

Ruddymane's episode in *The Faerie Queene* reveals that Spenser is deeply interested in the process by which the affective dynamics of family life could be transferred to the moral and spiritual life of a nation. But he is acutely aware that such transference is difficult and costly to effect, partly because the work of memory in joining strong affect to virtuous intent in the service of the commonwealth remains fractured, and fracturing. This essay focuses these matters through the lenses provided by wills and wardships, a context we are invited to adduce when Guyon becomes the *de facto* executor of Amavia's nuncupative will and establishes the terms of wardship for Ruddymane. Wills and wardship cast into high relief the contradictions informing memory's role in the creation of heroic agency in the service of the commonwealth

I

*B*OOK II OF *THE FAERIE QUEENE* INTRODUCES its extensive concern with memory in the first stanza of the Proem:

Right well I wote most mighty Soveraine,
  That all this famous antique history,
  Of some th'aboundance of an ydle braine
  Will judged be, and painted forgery,
  Rather then matter of just memory,
  Sith none, that breatheth living aire, does know,
  Where is that happy land of Faery,
  Which I so much do vaunt, yet no where show,
But vouch antiquities, which no body can know.[1]

Spenser Studies: A Renaissance Poetry Annual, Volume XXII, Copyright © 2007 by AMS Press, Inc. All rights reserved.

The phrase "matter of just memory" initially seems unprepossessing, subordinated grammatically and seeming merely to mean *not* "th'aboundance of an ydle braine" and "painted forgery." Closer consideration of the phrase nets a finer set of discriminations—and correspondences— between "memory" and the (imaginative) products of "idle" brains, however, correspondences that will prepare us to understand memory to be a faculty that is both creative and essential to heroic agency.[2]

When the several available meanings of "just" are brought into play, with "just" in the adverbial sense of "simply" or "merely" being the least likely, because probably not yet available, the apparently sharp distinction between, on the one hand, "aboundance of an ydle brain" and "painted forgery" and, on the other, "matter of just memory" proves to be something of a red herring. Leaving aside for the moment the matter of "forgery," we can observe that to understand "just" in its senses of "impartial," "righteous," "equitable," "lawful," or "honourable in one's social relations" is to grant to memory capacities and functions that are every bit as creative as, and even more active than, those ascribed to the idly abundant faculty of imagination or fancy.[3] We are, moreover, primed to make precisely this concession by Mary Carruthers's wide-ranging study of medieval "crafts" of memory.[4]

We find ample evidence in Book II that, for Spenser, memory does not simply store knowledge, it makes knowledge. In the critically much-visited chamber of Eumnestes in Alma's Castle, for instance, we learn that Memory, despite his advanced age, remains remarkably active: laying up and making records, and "tossing and turning" those records without end (ix.57–58). He is so active, in fact, that Guyon and Arthur "wonder" at his "endless exercise." With his endless tossing and turning, Eumnestes, who is initially distinguished from Phantastes along a range of indices, in fact rivals him in restlessness; although Phantastes is described as restless, he does nothing more than sit amidst the flittings and fleetings that keep his chamber buzzing with activity. More compellingly, Memory's ceaseless activity is not idle, in the sense of purposeless or without consequence. This is evidenced by the allegorical logic that directs relevant histories into the hands of Arthur and Guyon respectively: Memory, (pseudo-)historical here rather than personal and individual, produces narrative trajectories with which these two heroes must align themselves, an alignment that shapes their courses of action and so helps to fashion the commonwealth.[5]

When memory is considered to be a creative faculty rather than merely a storehouse or an inert recorder, then the "matter" of memory does not need to be tied exclusively to sense impressions or indeed to any aspect of material reality—a premise that both permits the claim that the "antique history of Faery land" *is* a "matter of just memory" rather than the "aboundance of an ydle brain," and aligns the workings of memory with those of imagination, a faculty that in Spenser's anatomy is seldom fettered to material reality. Faery land is intelligible reality, not coterminous with, although it can inform—indeed should provide the meaning, or pattern, for—an objectively verifiable reality. By the same token, faery land both represents the past *and* looks to the future. As the analogies in the proem, which are drawn from contemporary new-world discoveries and projected out-of-this-world lunar discoveries, as these analogies indicate, Spenser's just memory is a faculty or condition that should aim to secure the future of an England verging on expansionisms of several kinds (territorial in Ireland, religious on the continent, economic in the Americas).[6] Such a forward-looking and fundamentally socio—and geo-political function is assigned to "just memory," not only by these farfetched analogies, but also by the meanings of "just" canvassed above: all of them suppose a profoundly social milieu in which actions and decisions both affect others and establish conditions for future action. With this context in mind, we can return to the proem's opposing of "painted forgery" to "matter of just memory" to surmise that "forgery" here refers primarily to the forging of the metals out of which are fashioned the shields and spears of knights. Spenser is predicting that the skeptics he addresses in the proem will suppose the heroic exploits recorded in his antique history to be "painted" rather than real, a supposition he is at pains to dispel throughout *The Faerie Queene*.

Construed in these interrelated ways, as forward-looking, as socio—and geo-political in its functioning and effects, as integral to the project of English nationhood, memory is a faculty that proves crucial to heroic agency. Like the rest of *The Faerie Queene*, Book II has extensive investments in fashioning not only a gentle person but also a civil commonwealth—it has, that is, both "Ethice" and "Politice" aims, to use terms from the *Letter to Ralegh* (715). Given Book II's pronounced interest in memory, a primary question with respect to this book becomes how does or how can memory create the conditions for heroic agency. The connections between heroic agency and memory, as well as forgetting, and the relations of these to history have been examined from various stimulating perspectives recently, by such critics as Chris Ivic, Alan Stewart, Garrett Sullivan, Grant Williams, and others.[7]

I would like to contribute to this developing critical discussion by thinking more closely about the complexities that attend memory's role in the creation of heroic agency, especially in a nation that is not only expanding in the ways identified above, but that is still in transition, from Catholicism to Protestantism, neo-feudalism to centralism, other-worldliness to this-wordliness. To do so, I will focus in detail on the Ruddymane episode of Book II, because this episode draws its energies from these transitional cultural moments, and because it underlines the integral, but potentially fractured, work of memory in such founding enterprises. Ruddymane's story demonstrates that if memory is to create the conditions for heroic agency, it needs to be personal and public, familial and national, and, above all, strongly affective in order to work for the commonwealth. Ruddymane's story *also* predicts that such alignments can be damaging, costly, and difficult to forge.

I will focus less on Ruddymane's eponymously bloody hands than on the largely unremarked facts that Guyon becomes the *de facto* executor of Amavia's nuncupative will—a responsibility enjoined upon him by his overhearing of her last testament—and that Guyon establishes terms of wardship for Ruddymane when he entrusts the orphaned babe to the care of Medina. Wills and wardships in early modern England furnish an exceptionally useful lens for focusing these matters because the practices, assumptions, and provisions of these legal mechanisms grow from and in turn affect *both* family and larger communal imperatives. Both wills and wardships serve to memorialize families—by preserving through redistribution the property belonging to, and at least partly defining, a family, as well as by perpetuating a family's values through the provisions frequently made for the education of surviving minor heirs. To the extent that both wills and wardships affect individuals and institutions beyond the immediate family—the poor recipients of bequests, for instance, or the local church in which a monument will be erected, or the guardian who buys and perhaps in turn sells a wardship—these contracts also underwrite the commonwealth. This is especially true with respect to wardship, a regulatory mechanism which was developed to serve the military needs of king and country in feudal England. More pertinently still, for the concerns of this essay, both wills and wardship reflect the strains that accompany the socio-cultural transitions identified above, thereby casting into relief the contradictions informing memory's role in the creation of heroic agency in the service of commonwealth.

II

To begin my analysis, as Guyon does his intercession in Ruddymane's life, with wills, I would observe that the vocabulary of, and desire for, remembrance run like a leitmotif through many wills of the period—intimating that testators were animated by more than the desire to dispose of goods and property. Even post-Reformation testators wanted to be remembered, if not through prayers and masses like their pre-Reformation counterparts, then through the specific items bequeathed to friends and family members, through remembrance rings to be purchased with precisely allotted portions, through monuments to be erected in their names, through carefully designated grave-sites. And even in the more secularly-oriented wills of post-Reformation England, the desire to be remembered retains a distinctly spiritual dimension. The standard organization of topics in wills—from commending the body to the grave and the soul to Christ; to bequeathing alms for the poor; to allotting portions to distant relatives and servants; to, finally, providing for closer family members—this arrangement arcs from eschatological (and so spiritual) concerns through charitable (and so spiritual) concerns to secular, pragmatic matters, in a way that establishes the controlling context as a spiritual one (or at least one that is far from exclusively material). We can thus surmise that, when there are surviving children, the allotting of portions carries expectations of returns, of what Ralph Houlbrooke calls "spiritual caretaking" on the part of the children: children are to remember parents, both by fashioning themselves according to parental wishes and values, and by not discrediting the parents.[8] Here, remembrance shades into memorializing. It is not just that testators, usually fathers, want to be held in memory; they want their survivors to be living memorials to them, to the family itself. With surprising frequency, a testator will set conditions that must be met if an heir is to inherit, conditions pertaining to a son's treatment of his mother, for instance, or conditions aiming more generally at a son's conduct.[9] We can add to this the point that wills, as formulaic as they are, nevertheless carry a strong affective charge, privileging us with brief glimpses into lives sustained—or strained—by family and community ties.

The imaginative literature of the period encourages us to understand that such memorializing might weigh heavily upon a descendent, as well as to consider how such memorializing might or might not foster heroic agency. "Remember me," intones Hamlet's ghostly father on the midnight platform at Elsinore.[10] "To thy mother dead attest," beseeches Amavia to Ruddymane in the minutes before her death (II.i.37.6). I have coupled these two literary moments, not only because both of them suggest—the former very famously—just how weighty the burden of memorializing parents can be, but also because both moments register this burden while inaugurating revenge stories in a highly charged emotional atmosphere. However, while the ghost king conscripts his son into an already largely formulated plot, one in which to memorialize, by avenging, the father is also (supposedly) to cleanse the body politic, Amavia conscripts her son into a plan intended to address personal and familial, but not national, grievances. This particular difference between these two highly charged memorial moments reveals that Spenser is deeply interested in the process by which the imperatives of family moralities *might* be aligned with those of the commonwealth, particularly the means by which the affective dynamics of family life could be transferred to the moral and spiritual life of a nation. He is also acutely aware, we shall find, of the difficulty of doing so.

Amavia's situation is one that aligns virtue, personal and familial imperatives, and strong feeling. Her recounting of her plight, of the whole sordid tale of her husband's abandonment to Acrasia and of her own efforts to rescue him, shows her to be admirably, almost heroically, determined, resourceful, and courageous—as well as certain of her moral bearings: she is able to "recure" Mortdant to "a better will" through her "wise handling and faire governaunce" before Acrasia's parting curse takes effect (II.i.54.6–7). Her plight is also a powerfully moving one. We cannot miss her anguish at saying farewell to Ruddymane, a leavetaking that is rendered all the more poignant by our sense that Amavia, longing to be removed from this world's woes and to be shut from this world's "long lent loathed light," has already distanced herself from the son who has yet to make his way in the world (II.i.36.7). Guyon, who has been repeatedly referred to as a warrior and who, in the episode just prior to this one, had learned the value of tempering unthinking emotional response, is "constraine[d]" by his hearing of Amavia's lament "to stoupe, and show his inward pain" (II.i.42.8–9).

Although Amavia introduces the idea of revenge early in her lament-cum-testament, however, citing the apparent failure of the heavens to wreak vengeance on her behalf, she stops well short (as befits a loving mother) of assigning to Ruddymane the role of revenger or of assigning to him any role in defeating Acrasia—who figures the threat to commonwealth posed by intemperate sensuality as well as the even more considerable hazard of believing that the world is not fallen and therefore not in need of heroic action. Amavia's hard-earned perspective on Acrasia, coupled with her understandable motherly reluctance to engage her son's life in any organized campaign against Acrasia, leads her to adopt the position that every knight must fend for himself. Her own quest had been motivated by desire to free her husband from Acrasia's trap, not to bind Acrasia; and she counsels Guyon simply to "shonne" Acrasia's land (II.i.51.7), a course of action that would defeat the logic of Guyon's quest and leave her current thrall, Verdant, (with all that his name promises for renewal of the commonwealth) disarmed and suspended from militant actions of the kind Spenser believed were necessary to English, Protestant, expansionist and reformist designs.

A closer reading of Amavia's last will and testament suggests that, for Spenser, the difficulty of forging heroic agency of the kind needed in Protestant England, or in (unreclaimed) Ireland, stems partly from belief in Purgatory. Abolished officially in 1561, Purgatory retained a strong hold over the metaphysical and eschatological beliefs of many. What the transactions attending Amavia's will indicate is that, for Spenser, trust in Purgatory endures as cultural remnant that both inhibits necessary heroic action *and* paradoxically proves necessary to it. For Amavia, Ruddymane, with his bloodied hands, is to serve not as avenger but as witness to her innocence, more specifically, to the fact that her suicide was not a "criminall" act. "Live thou," says Amavia,

> and to thy mother dead attest
> That cleare she dide from blemish criminall:
> Thy litle hands embrewed in bleeding brest
> Loe! I for pledges leave. So give me leave to rest.
>
> (II.i.37.6–9)

As I remarked above, wills of the period frequently tax heirs with spiritual caretaking. Amavia's bequest certainly assigns to Ruddymane spiritual custodianship of the first order: in begging leave to rest, Amavia is trusting that Ruddymane's memorializing of her innocence will be sufficient to keep her ghost from restless walking—a fate frequently predicted for suicides.

The repetition of "leave" in the lines "Thy litle hands embrewed in bleeding brest/Loe! I for pledges leave. So give me leave to rest" places Ruddymane in an untenable position, however. This rhetorical device—antanaclasis—whose effect is magnified by the caesura in the line, seems to establish equivalence between Amavia's bequest to Ruddymane and her request of him ("I will leave you this portion; you, in turn must do this for me"). In fact, the antanaclasis masks a great imbalance: the hoped-for spiritual benefit to Amavia outweighs the gains to Ruddymane, indeed, exacts a cost to him—because in purgatory-free Reformation theology Ruddymane can never discharge the debt. Amavia's portion to Ruddymane is thus no portion at all, but, were he to know it, a burden. Clare Gittings and others have suggested that in the shift from pre- to post-Reformation theology, there remained in will-making strong vestigial traces of old patterns of belief, such as death-bed charitable bequests, made in what Gittings calls a "last-minute bid for salvation."[11] Amavia's petition for "leave to rest" appears similarly vestigial, in its wish for lasting intercession on her behalf and its implicit assumption of Purgatory, in its demand, that is, for a kind of individualized memorializing no longer possible in the Protestant England of Spenser's day.

This is not to say that Amavia's legacy to Ruddymane could not also include the memory of her determined and virtuous actions in finding and re-curing Mordant. That surely seems to be part of *her* intention in saying "to thy mother dead attest/That cleare she dide from blemish criminall." And the Palmer, rightly and reasonably, construes the babe's bloodstained hands as a monument to the innocence of his mother and to the reputation of all chaste women (II.ii.10). But Guyon is the executor, and in that capacity he takes advantage of the considerable leeway afforded executors at this time in history (especially with respect to funeral preparations) to refigure Ruddymane's portion in order to shift the focus of Amavia's will from the next world to this, from strictly familial and personal welfare to the moral health of the commonwealth—overriding the familial legacy of virtue in the process, as we shall see, while compounding the emotional charge and adding a revenge clause. This calculation of Ruddymane's portion harnesses for personal memory—Guyon's and, subsequently, Ruddymane's—the pathos of the circumstances.

In the immediate aftermath of Amavia's death, Guyon remains vague regarding its moral and eschatological implications: he draws pat, generalized, and so not precisely pertinent lessons, from the spectacle—all to do with the frailty of mortals, none to do with what had been virtuous and good in Amavia or in Mortdant; he fudges a little on the whole matter of the suicide; he neglects to distinguish between Amavia and Mortdant as victims of Acrasia. What he is absolutely clear about is the pathos. With the Palmer's help, Guyon performs a burial service that begins in seemliness but then exceeds the bounds of due observance, in order to heighten the emotion:

"Sir *Guyon* more affection to increace,/Bynempt a sacred vow, which none should aye releace" (II.i.60.8–9). Guyon's heightening of the affective charge accomplishes two things in the interests of heroic agency. To begin, it binds Guyon more closely to the course of revenge against Acrasia: in ways not entirely dictated by reason, in ways that exploit the powerful connection of the living with the dead that belief in Purgatory assumes, in ways that make *instrumentally memorable* the "pitifull spectacle" of Amavia's plight.

Throughout the deliberations over Amavia's burial, Guyon remains slightly at odds with the Palmer, who aims to check Guyon's inclination to moralize and to judge (II.i.57) with the gentle admonition "Reserve her cause to eternall doome" (II.i.58.9). Guyon's ready assent to this advice —"after death the tryall is to come," he acknowledges—does not quite suppress his urge to moralize, however:

Palmer, quoth he, death is an equal doome
    To good and bad, the commen In of rest;
    But after death the tryall is to come,
    When best shall bee to them, that lived best:
    But both alike, when death hath both supprest,
    Religious reverence doth buriall teene,
    Which who so wants, wants so much of his rest:
    For all so greet shame after death I weene,
As selfe to dyen bad, unburied bad to beene.

                                                            (II.i.59)

Guyon, seemingly, cannot temporarily suspend moral judgment as does the Palmer, but must keep in view the moral categories of "good" and "bad" even if he refrains from saying outright that Amavia falls into the latter category. By the end of his vow, he assigns guilt to Acrasia, but only equivocally, since he does not name her, referring instead vaguely to "guiltie blood," an evasive locution that does not exclude Amavia (II.i.61.8). His keeping in view these categories generates strong feeling in Guyon, an access of emotion registered formally in the repetitions, caesurae, alliteration, and assonance of lines 7 to 9 in stanza 59. And it is this strong feeling that enables him to act: to benefit the dead—in this case, to give rest to Amavia—and to undertake revenge on her behalf.

While we might not blanch at Guyon's willed assumption of the role of avenger—he represents a classical virtue, after all, and frequently acts in ways not consonant with Christianity—we must be struck by just how powerfully incantatory are the rites and language of Guyon's "sacred vow" of revenge. (We might recall in this context that "sacred" can also mean "accursed," its primary meaning in the initial description of Acrasia's Bower of Bliss [II.xii.37.8].) In performing his "sacred vow," Guyon not only "meddles" together the *matter* of Amavia, Mortdant, and the earth, but mingles his own blood, hair, and fate, as well as Ruddymane's (an assumption permitted by the possessive pronoun "their"), so thoroughly with their matter as to suggest that Guyon must fuse with the dead to create energy for his heroic quest:

> The dead knights sword out of his sheath he drew,
>   With which he cutt a lock of all their heare,
>   Which medling with their blood and earth, he threw
>   Into the grave, and gan devoutly sweare;
>   Such and such evil God on *Guyon* reare,
>   And worse and worse young Orphane be thy payne,
>   If I or thou dew vengeance doe forbeare,
>   Till guiltie blood her guerdon doe obtaine:
> So shedding many teares, they closd the earth agayne.

(II.i.61)

In thus compounding the affective interest of the tableau in front of him and yoking that emotional power to moral purposes, Guyon makes it memorable and, accordingly, as we shall see in a moment, instrumental in his heroic quest.[12]

Guyon's heightening—perhaps "deepening" is more precise—of emotion also conscripts Ruddymane, as Amavia's will did not, into that course of action. Following the improvised obsequies and in the face of the baby's happy obliviousness to his circumstances, Guyon takes the "litle babe up in his armes," literally and figuratively—extending immediate protection to the infant, but also foretelling his eventual assumption of arms in the knightly sense. Still in his capacity of executor, Guyon recalculates Ruddymane's portion:

> The litle babe up in his armes he hent;
> Who with sweet pleasaunce and bold blandishment
> Gan smyle on them, that rather ought to weepe,
> As careless of his woe, or innocent
> Of that was doen, that ruth emperced deepe
> In that knights heart, and wordes with bitter teares did steepe.

Ah lucklesse babe, borne under cruell starre,
    And in dead parents balefull ashes bred,
    Full little weenest thou, what sorrowes are
    Left thee for porcion of thy livelyhed.

(II.ii.1.4–9; 2.1–4)

Guyon increases markedly the burden of sorrows to be borne by Ruddymane. Where Amavia sought to lighten that burden in her farewell blessing to Ruddymane—"Long maist thou live, and better thrive withall" (II.i.37.4)—Guyon apportions only sorrows untold. It is not quite the case that Ruddymane was "in dead parents balefull ashes bred," however. I suggested above that Amavia's stipulated portion to Ruddymane amounts to no portion at all because the benefits, could they accrue, would accrue only to her. But, while Guyon's assigning "sorrows" as Ruddymane's portion does disburse *something,* this execution of Amavia's estate disregards vital aspects of his parents' legacy to him—especially Amavia's determined exercising of virtue on behalf of her wayward husband. Guyon's unwillingness to draw on that in determining Ruddymane's portion is gauged nicely by his remaining oblivious to the promise buried in his own imagery of ashes, the promise of spiritual resurrection, figured for many Renaissance writers and mythographers by the Phoenix. Moreover, as it is subsequently retold by Guyon to those gathered at Medina's castle, the tale of Amavia, Mortdant, and Ruddymane testifies to wretchedness and woe, and is received by the listeners as "a dolefull tale" of "sad ruth," "unhappie bale," and "mortall payne," an "ensample" of the "ill" effects of "pleasures poyson" (II.ii.44,45).

I suggested above that, as one consequence of Guyon's heightening of the pathos of Amavia's plight, Guyon is furnished with a memorable occasion whose recollection can spur him on his way. Having sojourned with Medina, Guyon grows "mindfull of his vow yplight"—the vow taken so dramatically over the graves of Amavia and Mortdant—and "address[es]" himself to the course of revenge against Acrasia (II.iii.1.5–7). Notably, he turns to this quest *as if for the first time.* This version of the inception of Guyon's quest contradicts significantly other versions. In the *Letter to Ralegh* appended to the 1590 *Faerie Queene,* the Palmer comes to Glorianna's court to request help against Acrasia, accompanied by the bloody-handed babe, and Guyon is assigned the task. The frequent inconsistencies between the *Letter* and the poem are well documented. But this particular discrepancy seems deliberate, a claim that can be pressed because the Medina canto itself offers a version that, like the *Letter*'s, places the

start of Guyon's quest at Glorianna's castle (II.ii.43). The implication
of the dramatized, as opposed to the versions related to us, is that
virtue alone is insufficient to this enterprise; to be effective in this
quest, to exercise heroic agency, Guyon—already grounded in virtuous intent—must be moved, as he is by Amavia and Ruddymane, to
"ruth and pity."

III

Strong affect must be joined to virtuous intent in the service of the
commonwealth. It is just this alignment that the terms of wardship
established by Guyon for Ruddymane aim to produce. When Guyon
entrusts the orphaned Ruddymane to the care of Medina, he "con-
jures" her to raise the boy, not just to manhood, but to heroic agency:

> Then taking *Congé* of that virgin pure,
>   The bloody-handed babe unto her truth
>   Did earnestly committ, and her conjure,
>   In vertuous lore to traine his tender youth,
>   And all that gentle noriture ensueth:
>   And that so soone as ryper yeares he raught,
>   He might for memory of that dayes ruth,
>   Be called *Ruddymane*, and thereby taught,
> T'avenge his Parents death on them, that had it wrought.
>
> (II.iii.2)

Guyon's terms stipulate that two instructional regimens must be followed in conscripting Ruddymane into the quest to subdue the threat
to commonwealth represented by Acrasia: the first program relying
on "gentle noriture," the second on the triggering of a highly charged
personal, particular, and painful memory; the first designed to inform
the tender boy with "vertuous lore," the second to stimulate the
adult Ruddymane to seek revenge; the first providing Ruddymane
with a moral compass, the second paying out his portion to him in
the form of "ruth."

Guyon's parting injunctions to Medina represent these programs
as dovetailing smoothly—an assurance reflected rhetorically and most
immediately, in lines 5 and 6 of the stanza just quoted, by the repeated
"And," the anaphora, that links the second phase of instruction to

the first. Guyon's interest in melding these two programs and in creating the "memorie of that days ruth" is to forge for Ruddymane heroic agency in the service of the commonwealth, to align moral and emotional bearings, virtue and feeling, as they could not be aligned by Amavia's will. In this regard, we should observe that Guyon's proposed pedagogy—grounding in virtue followed by incentive to revenge—reproduces the narrative and epistemological logic, described above, of his own inculcation into the quest to quell Acrasia, a fact confirming that Spenser is profoundly interested in the means by which the affective charge of family dynamics can be harnessed to strengthen the moral and spiritual life of a nation.

Spenser is also, I am contending, keenly aware (as Guyon is not) of the difficulties and costs of doing so. His verse here attests to this difficulty. The syntactical breach, faulty parallelism, that is almost, but not quite, smoothed over by Guyon's repeated "And," suggests that we should *not* share Guyon's seeming assurance that vertuous lore and revenge can be readily aligned—either ethically or epistemologically. What Spenser understands, and what the Ruddymane episode demonstrates, is that the jointure of affect, ethos, and action envisioned in Guyon's pedagogy, and aimed at in his terms of wardship, is hard to secure when institutions, some of them long-standing, prove no longer adequate to the demands of a changed—and changing—society, and when the workings of memory collide, as they do in the instructional program devised by Guyon.

To turn first to wardship. In Elizabethan England, wardship no longer served readily, or at all, the functions for which it was originally designed.[13] Guyon's adjurations to Medina stress that her primary responsibility as the boy's guardian is his education. But to judge from contemporary commentators, petitions, letters, court cases, or from, say, Orlando's treatment at the hands of his older brother in Shakespeare's *As You Like It,* guardians frequently shirked this duty. In his *De Republica Anglorum* (a work Spenser almost certainly knew, likely through Gabriel Harvey), Thomas Smith observes with dismay that wardships in England are sought after only because of the profit they bring. More pertinently, he rehearses the common conviction that wardship, as practiced in the England of his day, "will be the decay of the nobilitie and libertie of England" because the "buyer" of a ward, who is frequently unrelated by blood and so unmotivated by "natural care," will "not suffer his warde to take any great paines . . . in study."[14] Indeed, wardships "provide the occasion . . . why many gentlemen be so evil brought up touching virtue and learning" (129). Guyon's directives to Medina seem intended to allay precisely such anxieties; he "conjure[s]" her "In vertuous lore to traine his tender youth,/And all that gentle noriture ensueth (II.iii.2.3–5). As the vocabulary here attests, Guyon intends that under Medina's tutelage Ruddymane *will* receive an education befitting a gentleman, an education designed specifically to train him up in virtue.

We will return in a moment to the matter of "vertuous lore," to what it might entail and to the kind of memory work required in the learning of it, but first I would like to follow the line of inquiry suggested by the summative phrase "all that gentle noriture ensueth," which points to something other than instruction in virtue, something quite apart from humanist education. Once again, Smith furnishes a useful perspective. When he repeats the belief, cited above, that deficiencies in providing for the education of wards will inevitably lead to ruination, Smith has in mind not only the material and social "decay" of noble families, through the wasting of properties and revenues (one meaning implied by his phrasing), but also the "decay" of nobility as an aspect of character. More tellingly still, in declaring that the "libertie of England" is also threatened, Smith implies that nothing less than the very security of the commonwealth is at stake. When he touches briefly on the question of wardship in an earlier section of *De Republica Anglorum*, the context makes it even more clear that Smith considers wardship (despite the corrupted practices of his day) to be instrumental to the maintenance of the commonwealth. In a chapter entitled, "Of the Monarch King or Queene of England," Smith lists wardship as one of the "absolute" powers of the monarch, along with the power to wage war or determine peace, to control coinage, to waive laws in the interests of equity, to assign offices, and to authorize writs and executions—all powers to do with the governance of the state (85–87). In the course of answering the argument that wardship should be wrested from crown control because it has become corrupted, Smith introduces a telling analogy, one suggesting just how thoroughly he understands wardship to be (or, to have been at one time) conducive to the *heroic* agency necessary for the maintaining of the commonwealth. The royal prerogative of wardship, he observes, "being once graunted by act of Parliament (although some inconvenience hath beene though to have growen therof, and sith that time it hath beene thought verie unreasonable) yet once annexed to the crowne who canne take the clubbe out of *Hercules* hand" (87). Hercules is far from a simple figure for Renaissance mythographers and writers, but the reference to the club indicates that Smith is thinking of Hercules specifically as an exemplar of heroic action—an ascription that underlines Smith's understanding of wardship as a social mechanism designed to fashion military heroes to serve the commonwealth.

Smith's look back at the feudal origins of the institution, when the education of a ward was so far from being neglected that it followed a carefully prescribed two-stage course, both emphasizes these intended ends of wardship and points unwittingly to the socio-cultural shift that in his day complicates the accomplishment of these ends. "As for the education," Smith observes, "our common wealth was at the first *militaire*, and almost in all things the scope and designe thereof is *militaire*." Accordingly, it was likely "that noble men, good knights, and great captains would bring up their wards in their own feats and vertues" before marrying them "into like race and stocke where they may finde . . . friends, who can better look to the education or better skill of the bringing up of a gentleman" (130). Smith's recollection of past practices thus suggests that at one time the fitting education of a ward (ideally) involved training in several arenas: chivalric arms; learning; social graces. Additionally, Smith seemingly conflates, under the auspices of the first guardian, training in arms and instruction in moral philosophy; there is nothing in Smith's phrase—"noble men, good knights, and great captains . . . bring up their wards in their own feats and vertues"—to distinguish military from moral education, and nothing to apportion proper spheres of influence among noblemen, knights, and captains.

Smith cannot conceive of "learning"—training in virtue—as entirely a chivalric prerogative, however: when he turns to the second stage of the ward's training, he remarks that "friends" (who are not "noble men, knights, or captains") can "better look to the *education*" or "bringing up of a gentleman," with "education" here undoubtedly meaning university education rather than instruction in gentlemanly airs and conduct. Classical scholar, professor of civil law, ambassador, secretary to a king and a queen, Smith had advanced to positions of influence on the strength of his humanist training—a circumstance that no doubt inflects his analysis of the extent to which chivalric ideals could ever have been adequate to secure the commonwealth. Nominated by Muriel Bradbrook as the "most notable Elizabethan example of a pure scholar turned successful politician," Smith himself is evidence that a significant shift has occurred in sixteenth-century England, away from promotion and governance through feudal privilege toward advancement through talent, skill, and learning.[15]

With the context provided by Smith in mind, we can return to the terms of wardship established for Ruddymane with a sharper sense of the rift between "vertuous lore" and the "revenge" deemed necessary to the commonwealth as well as the inadequacy of wardship to bridge that rift. It is recognition that once again draws together instructively Ruddymane and Hamlet. Commanded by his ghost of a father, released nightly from Purgatory, to "remember" him, Hamlet vows to do so, saying "from the table of my memory/I'll wipe away all trivial fond records,/All saws of books, all forms, all pressures past,/That youth and observation copied there;/And thy commandment all alone shall live within the book and volume of my brain" (I.v.98–103).[16] Hamlet knows immediately that all his humanist learning—his speech is informed throughout with the practices of the schoolroom and the commonplace book—must yield to this new imperative, not simply to remember his father (he has already been doing that) but to remember the horrifying details of his father's murder and unspeakable suffering in Purgatory, and to be incited to revenge by this memory. He knows instantly that the action demanded of him by his father is contrary to all the "vertuous lore" of his education, that all that must be erased from the "tables" of his memory. He is mistaken, however, in thinking that his memory can continue to work in the same way to fit him to his new task. Remembering his father on his father's terms will not only displace the contents of Hamlet's memory, but will also reform its processes. It will take him the whole of the play to realize that the trauma represented to him by his father completely and violently reconfigures his personal memories, his understanding, his values, his desires, his sense of himself.

Hamlet's case helps us to predict what awaits Ruddymane "so soone as ryper yeares" he reaches when "for memory of that dayes ruth" he shall "Be called *Ruddymane,* and thereby taught,/T'avenge his Parents death on them, that had it wrought" (II.iii.2.6–9). Ruddymane will be wrenched violently from the "truth" of Medina's middle way and from the moral bearings provided by "vertuous lore," from the sense of himself that he will have built up through years of the creative imitation at the heart of humanist education. Guyon's using the verb "conjure" (II.iii.2.3) when he gives Ruddymane to Medina in wardship provides another measure of the violence needed in melding personal and public, familial and national, other-worldliness and this-worldliness to forge heroic agency in the service of the commonwealth. It is a measure that is all the more exact because the word "conjure" looks back to Guyon's going beyond due observance to perform those extra, incantatory, funeral rites at the graves of Amavia and Mortdant. Spenser uses the verb "conjure" sparingly in his poetry, always in highly charged contexts, usually to do with magic and sorcery, once to do with political upheaval. The implication here is not only that Ruddymane, like Hamlet, will have to deal with ghosts. The implication is also that Ruddymane's memory of that day's ruth—the portion allotted to him by Guyon's executorship, we recall—will be haunted also by the legacy *not* passed on to him by Guyon, that is, his mother's virtue, courage, and moral certainty. The heroic agency forged out of these terms can only be impoverished.

University of Manitoba

NOTES

1. Edmund Spenser, *The Faerie Queene,* ed. A. C. Hamilton (Harlow: Pearson Education, 2001), II.Proem.1. Subsequent references are to this edition and will be indicated in the body of the essay.

2. Andrew King's emphasis on "the matter of just memory" in his "*The Faerie Queene" and Middle English Romance* (Oxford: Clarendon, 2000) stems particularly from his interest in tracing the influence of native English romance in Spenser's poem; accordingly, he construes the "matter of memory" as "physical and textual" (1).

3. See *OED Online* ed., Def. 1, 2, 2b, 3a, 3b.

4. Mary Carruthers, *The Book of Memory: A Study of Memory in Medieval Culture* (Cambridge: Cambridge University Press, 1990), emphasizes that memory is creative in terms of intertextuality; she observes also of *memoria* that "it was in trained memory that one *built* character, judgement, citizenship, and piety" (9; my emphasis). For a philosopher's lively defense of "theories of autobiographical memory, both historical and contemporary, which view memories as dynamic rather than static archives," see Paul Sutton, *Philosophy and Memory Traces* (Cambridge: Cambridge University Press, 1998), xiii.

5. Developments in Renaissance historiography lie beyond the scope of this paper, but for compelling arguments that Spenser was attuned to these debates, see Andrew Escobedo, *Nationalism and Historical Loss in Renaissance England: Foxe, Dee, Spenser, Milton* (Ithaca: Cornell University Press, 2004) and Bart Van Es, *Spenser's Forms of History* (Oxford: Oxford University Press, 2002).

6. For readings of the proem that encourage us to see expansionist and colonialist gestures, toward the Americas, Ireland, and India, in the proem and book, see Maureen Quilligan, *Milton's Spenser: The Politics of Reading* (Ithaca: Cornell University Press, 1983) and "On the Renaissance Epic: Spenser and Slavery," in *Edmund Spenser: Essays on Culture and Allegory,* ed. Jennifer Klein Morrison and Matthew Green (Aldershot: Ashgate, 2000); rpt. from *SAQ* 100:1 (Winter 2001): 15–39; Elizabeth Jane Bellamy, "Spenser's Faeryland and the Curious Genealogy of India," in *Worldmaking Spenser: Explorations in the Early Modern Age,* ed. Patrick Cheney and Lauren Silberman (Lexington: University Press of Kentucky, 2000), 177–92; David Read, *Temperate Conquests: Spenser and the Spanish New World* (Detroit: Wayne State University Press, 2000); Willy Maley, *Salvaging Spenser:Colonialism, Culture and Identity* (London: Macmillan, 1997); Christopher Highley, *Shakespeare, Spenser, and the Crisis in Ireland* (Cambridge: Cambridge University Press, 1997).

7. Alan Stewart and Garrett Sullivan, " 'Worme-eaten, and full of canker holes':
Materializing Memory in *The Faerie Queene* and Lingua," *Spenser Studies* 17 (2003):
215–38, identify as detrimental to heroic fashioning the contemporary fascination
with minutiae demonstrated by antiquarians and in the chronicles, contending that
such predilections interfere with memory's function in the formation of heroic
agency by filling up memory with "forgettable" details and so leaving no room in
memory for "historical" and cultural "exemplars"—what I would label with what
Spenser will call "vertuous lore" in II.iii.2. Like Stewart and Sullivan, Chris Ivic
and Grant Williams, eds. *Forgetting in Early Modern Literature and Culture: Lethe's
Legacy* (London: Routledge, 2004), are interested in the possibilities afforded by
forgetting. The emphasis of these critics on forgetting provides an extremely valuable
counterpoint to the myriad studies of memory.

8. Houlbrooke, *Death, Religion, and the Family in England, 1480–1750* (Oxford:
Clarendon, 2000). On changing practices in wills, funerals, and commemorative
events, see also Virginia Bainbridge, *Gilds in the Medieval Countryside: Social and
Religious Change in Cambridgeshire c.1350–1558* (Woodbridge: Boydell Press, 1996),
chaps. 4 and 5.

9. John Swinnerton, writing his will on September 7, 1616, shortly before his
death, does not mince his words about one unruly son, determining to give to son
Henry an additional 500 pounds "being that legacie which I had once determined
to have given to the said Richard Swinarton my second sonne but that I have been
justlie moved to alter my intent therein by the irregular course which my said sonne
Richard hath taken greatlie to my mislike" (PRO, Prob II/128); John Huchenson
(d. 1600) commits to his wife's "good care" the "custodie and governance both for
their personnes and portones of my children before named desiring her for godes
cawse . . . to see that they be brought up in gods feare and in such honest and lawfull
vocation of lyfe as they shall seeme meetest" (PRO, Prob II/98).

10. William Shakespeare, *Hamlet*, in *The Complete Works of Shakespeare*, ed. Hardin
Craig and David Bevington (Glenville: Scott, Foresman, 1973). Subsequent references are to this edition and will be indicated in the body of the essay.

11. Gittings, *Death, Burial, and the Individual in Early Modern England* (London:
Routledge, 1988), 87.

12. For a substantially different interpretation of the uses of affect in this episode,
see Joseph Campana, "On Not Defending Poetry: Spenser, Suffering, and the Energy
of Affect," *PMLA* 120:1(2005): 33–48, who in the course of distinguishing Spenser's
poetics from Sidney's by stressing Spenser's "interest in poetry's capacity to commu-
nicate the painful vitality of lived experience" (35), reads Guyon's intercessions with
Amavia and Ruddymane as an attempt to "contain the flood of affect"; he contends
that Guyon "remains oddly unmoved by" Amavia (42).

13. Joel Hurstfield, *The Queen's Wards; Wardship and Marriage under Elizabeth I*,
2nd ed. (London: Frank Cass, 1973), remains the most thoroughgoing study of
wardship to date. Interest in the implications for our understanding of early modern
literature is starting to grow; see, for example, B. J. Sokol and Mary Sokol, *Shakespeare, Law, and Marriage* (Cambridge: Cambridge University Press, 2003), chap. 3.

14. Smith, *De Republica Anglorum,* ed. Mary Dewar (Cambridge: Cambridge University Press, 1982), 128–29. Subsequent references are indicated by page number
in parentheses immediately following the quotation.

15.   Bradbrook, "No Room at the Top," *Stratford-Upon-Avon Studies* 2. Elizabethan Poetry. (London: Edward Arnold, 1960), 95.

16.   On the ways in which Purgatory informs *Hamlet* without ever even being named, see Anthony Low, "*Hamlet* and the Ghost of Purgatory: Intimations of Killing the Father," *ELR* 29:3 (Autumn 1999): 443–67. See also Stephen Greenblatt, *Hamlet in Purgatory* (Princeton: Princeton University Press, 2001).

RICHARD A. McCABE

"Thine owne nations frend/And Patrone": The Rhetoric of Petition in Harvey and Spenser

This essay examines the topos of friendship in the rhetoric of Early Modern petition and patronage. Concentrating upon the works of Harvey, Spenser, Churchyard, and Ralegh, it seeks to analyze the various ways in which the Horatian paradigm of an idealized, if far from ideal, relationship between poet and patron is used to negotiate problems of social inequality and to attempt to resolve the perceived conflict between artistic independence and political obligation. It demonstrates how the fabrication of complex fictions of "amicitia" functions to manipulate the reader's apprehension of authorial personae, arguing that suggestions of mutual reciprocity are designed both to exploit and to palliate the self-serving economy of poetic service, political clientage, and material reward.

I have chosen the quotation in my title, Contemplation's description of St. George in the first book of *The Faerie Queene* (x.61), because the idealized association it makes between friendship and patronage raises questions about Spenser's personal expectations in a matter that exercized him throughout his career.[1] It is richly indicative of the centrality of patronage to the canon that the relationship between *The Faerie Queene*'s questing knights and the virtues they espouse is characterized in the *Letter to Ralegh* in patronal terms.[2] It is not merely a letter to a patron but a letter than embeds the ideal of patronage in the structure of epic, and even in the nature of "heroism."[3] The very

Spenser Studies: A Renaissance Poetry Annual, Volume XXII, Copyright © 2007 by AMS Press, Inc. All rights reserved.

format of the poem hereby endorses the principle of gracious reciprocation advanced in the dedicatory sonnet to Northumberland which
asserts that because the Muses function as "the Nourses of nobility"
it behoves the aristocracy "t'embrace the service of sweete Poetry"
and "patronize the authour of their praise."[4] As *The Ruines of Time*
suggests, the relationship thus established stretches beyond "service"
to a form of amity: "Provide therefore (ye Princes) whilst ye live,/
That of the *Muses* ye may friended bee" (365–66). The association
of friendship and patronage in the person of St. George is therefore
particularly suggestive in its overtly nationalist dimension. As early
as the "October" eclogue of *The Shepheardes Calender*, Spenser implies
that the state of the literary arts reflects that of the nation. Cuddie is
"the perfecte paterne of a Poete, which finding no maintenaunce of
his state and studies, complayneth of the contempte of Poetrie." It
is made clear, however, that this lack of patronage is symptomatic
of a lack of national fiber, of that species of heroism that characterized
former ages: "For ever, who in derring doe were dreade/The loftie
verse of hem was loved aye" (65–66). When urged to write of "fayre
Elisa" or "the worthy whome shee loveth best" (45–47)—presumably
the earl of Leicester—Cuddie replies that the great exemplars of
courtly patronage have no modern equivalents, "But ah *Mecœnas* is
yclad in claye,/And great *Augustus* long ygoe is dead" (61–62). Writing some seventeen years later, Spenser has the narrator of *Prothalamion* revert to Cuddie's mood of cultural pessimism—brought on,
significantly, "through discontent of my long fruitlesse stay/In
Princes Court, and expectation vayne/Of idle hopes, which still doe
fly away" (6–8)—and characterize his condition quite precisely, in
the wake of Leicester's death, as "freendles" (140). By contrast,
Suetonius relates that Horace held a prominent place not just in
the service but in the "friendship" ["amicitia"] of Maecenas and
Augustus.[5] It is the problematical relationship between friendship and
patronage that concerns the present essay. If Alan Bray has identified
the "gift of the friend's body," in all of its various senses, as central
to amicitia, we are dealing here with the gift of the body textual,
the literary corpus that embodies the "service" and "affection" commonly proffered by an author to a social superior. The extent to
which literary "authority" is compromised by its political or social
equivalents remains a moot point.[6]

In *Promised Verse: Poets in the Society of Augustan Rome* (1993), Peter
White classified patronage as a species of amicitia and drew heavily
on the Horatian canon to support this contention.[7] However, his
admission that the vocabulary of friendship functions to mask both

the social inequality of the parties involved, and the element of "exchange" or reciprocation that is expected, exposed him to the criticism that he had mistaken literary construction for social fact. Poets have an interest in representing themselves as friends rather than clients, and their poetry, however flattering, as independent art rather than mercenary propaganda.[8] The implications for political and artistic "libertas" were recognized at least as early as Servius's commentary on Virgil and have remained evident ever since.[9] In fact, as Phebe Lowell Bowditch pointed out in *Horace and the Gift Economy of Patronage* (2001), publication renders patronal relationships "triangular" rather than bilateral in that it involves poet, patron, *and reader*.[10] It is important to Horace, for example, that the gift of his Sabine farm be seen by the reader as the product of altruistic generosity rather than as payment for political services poetically rendered. Without the element of "friendship," his service to Maecenas and the regime might, metaphorically at least, be seen to return him to the status of bondsman from which his father had been liberated.[11] Spenser's contemporaries were no less circumspect. Indeed, Peter White has gone so far as to suggest that the notion of Augustus orchestrating a political campaign through literature originated in the Early Modern period in response to the acute political censorship of the times.[12] This is certainly to overstate the case but it does call attention to an important element in the Early Modern reception of Augustan literature. Spenser's contemporaries had every reason to imagine an interventionist Augustus because, as Wallace MacCaffrey has pointed out, "patronage" of one sort or another was endemic to the political and social system of Elizabethan England.[13] For figures such as Lord Burghley literary patronage certainly formed part of a wider patronal culture premised upon notions of service and reward.[14] For this reason Louis Montrose has described the practice of literary "prestation" or gift-giving as "a tacitly coercive and vitally interested process predicated on the fiction that it is free and disinterested."[15]

When deployed in such a context the theme of friendship becomes ever more crucial as a marker of social and artistic independence. The problem with the quest for patronage is that it threatens to compromise the moral integrity of its chief vehicle, praise. Because eulogy written with an eye to reward might easily be perceived as suspect eulogy, the language of friendship afforded a preemptive defence against accusations of flattery and bribery. We therefore need to be wary of the role that professed "amicitia" plays in the rhetoric of petition. While critics such as Eleanor Rosenberg frequently allude to the "obligations" of patronage, it is important to recognize that

in England no formal obligations ever existed.[16] Each patronal relationship was to this extent sui generis, a matter of negotiation between the parties involved. As Frank Whigham rightly observes,
much of the rhetoric of petition was designed to manipulate the
prospective patron into a sense of mutual obligation.[17] What Bowditch describes, drawing upon Mauss and Bourdieu, as "the gift economy of exchange" entails not just the "obligation" to reciprocate,
but the need to characterize that reciprocation in a particular way.[18]
And one of the best ways of characterizing the business of reciprocation was to transpose it into the theme of friendly exchange. This is
not to deny that in the Early Modern period the concept of friendship
was every bit as problematic as that of patronage. Quite the opposite,
it is to acknowledge the many ways in which writers exploited the
ambiguity of "friendship" to their own advantage. According to Cicero's seminal *De Amicitia*, friendship was a species of "amor" or love
and sprang rather from nature ["natura"] than from need ["indi-
gentia"].[19] While he acknowledged that great material advantages
["utilitates"] might arise from friendship, he regarded them as by-
products rather than motives because we are drawn to friendship by
the need for love rather than the hope of gain ["spe mercedis"] (8–9).
Hence, perhaps, the concluding words of *The Shepheardes Calender*
"merce non mercede"—"for reward not hire." But Cicero admits
that he speaks of an ideal, that "ordinary" friendship was often characterized by baser motives (21). Whereas ideal friendship created an
"equality" between "inferior" and "superior" thereby transforming
the conferring of "utilitates" into tokens of affection, in "ordinary"
relationships social disparity commonly led to the commercializing of
"officia" or "service" (19–20). The ramifications of such distinctions
were endlessly debated in the Early Modern period.[20] To cite but
one example, in his wonderfully shrewd essay "Of Followers and
Friends" Lord Bacon asserts that "there is little friendship in the
world, and least of all between equals, which was wont to be magnified. That that is, is between superior and inferior, whose fortunes
may comprehend the one the other."[21] For the professional writer
the advantages of such an "unequal" but mutually "comprehensive"
Baconian relationship were many.

   An exemplary illustration of this was supplied in 1588 by Thomas
Churchyard. By way of return for benefits received, Churchyard
dedicated the aptly entitled *A Sparke of Frendship* to "My Honorable
Frend Sir Walter Ralegh Knight" (fig. 1). Although Ralegh's position is noted to be that of a social superior, he is addressed as "friend"
throughout the work, and he is said to have proven his friendship
by speaking "good speeches to the Queen's Maiestye in my behalfe,

Fig. 1. *A Sparke of Frendship and Warme Goodwill, that shewes the effect of True Affection and unfoldes the finenesse of this world* (London, 1588), sig. A1r. Courtesy of the Bodlein Library, University of Oxford.

by which I got some comfortable recreation to comfort my spirits
and keep me in breath." It is therefore by careful design that the
initial letter of the dedicatory epistle encloses an image of the queen,
Ralegh's own socially superior "friend" and the patron to whom he
owed all of the titles employed in Churchyard's address (fig. 2). By
professing friendship to the queen's favorite, Churchyard affords himself the vicarious satisfaction of friendship with the queen—and it
was possibly through such a connection that he received the rare
accolade of a royal pension in 1592.[22] The key point being made in
1588, after all, was that Ralegh's patronage was effective. By contrast,
Churchyard tells us that he has dedicated no fewer than sixteen other
works to "severall men of good and great credite" yet "not one
amongst them all, from the first day of my labour and studies, to this
present yeere and hower, hath anie waye preferred my sutes, amended
my state, or given me anie countenance." To these he feels himself
to be in no sense "indebted."[23] That necessarily implies that he feels
indebted to Ralegh, but he negotiates that sense of indebtedness
through strict adherence to what he regards as an established code of
decorum. He notes in the dedicatory letter that patronage is central
to courtly life, and that he merely follows "the gravest sort of sage
and wise personages, that will not blush nor thinke scorne, to learne
a lesson of their forefathers, that got all their good fortune by following the flood, where we fish for preferment."[24] Some years later in
a letter of petition to Sir Christopher Hatton he states that "I blush,
being old, to beg; and yet not ashamed to crave, being a courtier."[25]
The reference to blushing in both passages is telling. It is potentially
embarrassing to beg, but the patronal economy of the court makes
it perfectly respectable to "crave" without any loss of status. The
concluding page of *A Sparke of Frendship* sees Churchyard "craving"
Ralegh's further support, yet the verso of the title page bears the
petitioner's coat of arms. The implication is clear: this is a work in
which one gentleman "craves" assistance of a well placed "friend"
in accordance with received courtly conventions. The difficulties of
social disparity are elided through a sense of shared gentility that
facilitates equality among unequals. Spenser's self-representation as a
"gentle poet" is of the same stamp—a prophylactic against the dual
stigmas of beggary and the "ungentle" practice of publishing for
profit. By adopting a highly Ciceronian view of friendship in a work
dedicated to a courtly friend, Churchyard implies that any and all
"utilitates" that might be derived from the relationship are incidental
to the "affection" that motivates it for, as the title page asserts, "there
can be no felicity in the absence of friendship" ["nulla potest esse
iucunditas, sublata amicitia"].

TO MY HONORABLE

Frend Sir Water Ralegh Knight,

Seneſhall and Chancelor of the Duchie of
Cornwal & Exon, Lord Warden of the Stan-
neries, and her Maieſties Lieffetenant of
the Countie of Cornwall,
&c.

 *NFORCED*
by affeƈtion (that
leades the mindes
of men to a mul-
titude of cauſes)
J ſtood ſtudying
howe to requit a
good turne recei-
ued, and confeſ-
ſing that no one
thing is more mõ-
ſtrous in nature than an vnthankefull minde, I ſaw
my ſelf in debt, & bound either one way or other to
pay that I owe, but not in ſuch degree as I receiued,
but in ſuch ſort as my abilitie ſerueth, & as a man
might ſay to make a cunning exchange, inſteed of
due payment, to offer glaſſe for gold & bare words

A 2   *for*

Fig. 2. *A Sparke of Frendship*, sig. A2r. Courtesy of the Bodlein Library, University of Oxford.

Strategies comparable to those employed in *A Sparke of Frendship* are operative in Spenser's early work. *The Shepheardes Calender* is dedicated on its title page to Philip Sidney and the envoy anticipates Churchyard's vocabulary by advising the book "when his honor has thee redde, / *Crave* pardon for my hardyhedde" (my emphasis). There is good reason for such circumspection: Sidney is not addressed as a friend but as a superior and the dedication might seem to entail an element of social hubris. In 1579, Sidney was the presumptive heir to both the earls of Leicester and Warwick. The title page chooses its words, and its word-play, very carefully when it states that the work is "entitled" to "the noble and vertuous Gentleman most worthy of all titles both of learning and chevalrie."[26] A mere "shepeheards boye" has dared to append the title of his "little booke" to the great social titles that will inevitably attach to Sidney's name in the future. But the facing page to Immerito's envoy confronts the contemporary reader with a dilemma. E. K's epistle contrarily commits "the patronage of the new Poete" to "*the most excellent and learned both* / Orator and Poete, Mayster Gabriell Harvey" on the grounds that E. K. is Harvey's "verie special and singular good frend." We are here presented with two quite distinct species of patronal authority: on the one hand there is the well positioned Sidney who may "succoure" the poet from "ieopardee" under "the shadow of his wing," and on the other there is the friendly Harvey whose scholarly reputation attests to his literary status. In terms of the gift economy of patronage it is noteworthy, however, that Colin Clout conspicuously refuses Hobbinol's "gifts" in "Januarye," "Aprill," and "Iune." The point becomes intelligible at *September* 176 when Hobbinol is expressly identified by E. K. as Harvey, and we learn of "his late *Gratulationum Valdinensium* which boke in the progresse at Audley in Essex, he dedicated in writing to her Maiestie. afterward presenting the same in print vnto her Highnesse at the worshipfull Maister Capells in Hertfordshire."[27] What this tells the reader is that Harvey had precious few "gifts" of any commercial value to bestow but was himself in desperate pursuit of patronage from the queen and her courtiers. His unexpected appearance as "patron" of the *Calender* works as much to his own advantage as to that of the "new Poet." As E. K. notes, Harvey presented his literary gift to the queen twice, once in manuscript at Audley End, and then in print at Hadham Hall. The printed version served to make public what Harvey took to be the new familiarity he had established with the queen and her principal courtiers at Audley End. It was the tactless laboring of this theme of familiarity that later supplied Thomas Nashe with such a rich vein of satire. As Nashe points out, it was huge blow to Harvey that the *Gratulationes Valdinenses* secured him neither a permanent place in

Leicester's entourage nor the public oratorship at Cambridge, the office for which E. K.'s reference to his skills as *"both / Orator and Poete"* single him out as a prime candidate. By making the "bilateral" relationships of patronage "triangular" the printed version ultimately publicized Harvey's failure. In a very literal sense familiarity bred contempt.

But such disappointment lay in the future. In 1579 there was everything still to play for and Hobbinol, fresh from the self-proclaimed triumph of kissing the queen's hand at Audley End, is appropriately allowed to present Colin's April encomium to Eliza and the world. Fully to understand the strategy employed here we need to locate *The Shepheardes Calender* in the context of a series of "promotional" publications that began in 1577 with Harvey's *Ciceronianus* and *Rhetor*, continued in 1578 with *Smithus; vel Musarum Lachrymæ* and the *Gratulationes Valdinenses*, and culminated with the publication of the *Calender* in 1579 and the Harvey-Spenser *Letters* in 1580. Although these six publications differ widely in genre, style, and theme, they are all deeply implicated in the search for patronage and such evidence as survives suggests that this common thread was obvious to contemporary readers. In his satirical attacks upon Harvey, written most probably in 1581, William Wythie interweaves allusions to all six works as though they were component elements of some great master-text.[28] Harvey's *Letter-Book* suggests that the sequence was intended to continue with the supposedly unauthorized publication of his own English "Verlayes" by an "unfrendly frende," "Signor Benevolo" otherwise known as "Immerito."[29] To read the draft of the verbose letter in which Harvey deplores the publication of a project he simultaneously promotes is to realize the full extent of the calculation employed in the production of all of these works. The *Letter-Book*, in the state in which it has come down to us, affords a glimpse into the literary tiring house in which Harvey and Spenser donned their various personae. It also indicates the extent to which both were indebted to George Gascoigne for expert lessons in the manipulation of the authorial voice.[30] "E. K." carefully paved the way for the publication of the "Verlayes" in the "postscript" to his dedicatory epistle when he urged Harvey to follow the example of his "speciall frends and fellow Poets doings" and "pluck out of the hateful darknesse, those so many excellent English poemes of yours, which lye hid, and bring them forth to eternall light." In this manner "friendship" acts as the midwife to publication and the service is essentially one of courteous reciprocation because Harvey had similarly acted as harbinger to Spenser by concluding his list of famous amatory poets in the *Gratulationes Valdinenses* with the apparently

innocuous words "if perchance a new Cupid [love poet] should arise
let him hold the first place" ["novus et si forte Cupido/Prodeat , o
primum vendicet ille locum"].[31] When, by no great coincidence, the
"new poet" whose "unstayed yougth had long wandred in the common Labyrinth of Love" (29) duly arose the very next year, "E. K."
naturally dedicated his work to its herald. Such "friendly" intertextuality turned poet into patron and patron into poet.

The sequence of works we are considering began, as I have said,
with the publication of Harvey's *Ciceronianus* and *Rhetor* in 1577.[32]
Although it ranks as Harvey's first major literary effort, the *Ciceronianus* is in many respects characteristic of his entire canon. Its publication is wholly attributed to Harvey's friend and mentor William
Lewin, the distinguished scholar and lawyer. According to this elaborate fiction, Harvey sent the manuscript to Lewin as a private new
year's gift but Lewin, recognizing its public utility, dispatched it to
the printer Henry Bynneman—the printer responsible for the *Rhetor*,
Gratulationes Valdinenses, and the Spenser-Harvey *Letters*. The work
is structured as an intellectual autobiography charting Harvey's development from youthful enthusiasm for Cicero's style to mature ap-
preciation of his "consular and senatorial wisdom."[33] In other words,
Harvey represents himself as discovering that eloquence is valuable
primarily as an instrument of public affairs, thereby insinuating that
he is peculiarly suited to public life. What this might entail in practice
is revealed in the *Rhetor*. Harvey is fascinated by Bartholomew
Clerke, its dedicatee, precisely because his career described the trajectory Harvey wished for himself, that of transformation from "scholar"
into "courtier" ("factus deinde ex Academico Aulicus").[34] Clerke
had attained this transformation in both a literary and a literal sense,
the first by translating Castiglione's *Courtier* into Latin, the second
by securing a public niche as a civil lawyer and proctor of the arches.
In this second capacity he was elected to parliament (most probably
through the influence of his patron, Lord Buckhurst), and was en-
trusted by Archbishop Parker and Lord Burghley with the refutation
of Nicholas Sander's *De Visibili Monarchia Ecclesia* (1571).

It is essential to recognize, however, that Harvey regarded Clerke's
literary and public functions as symbiotic. As he well knew, Buckhurst himself was a poet turned courtier and had recently combined
both roles in exemplary fashion by writing a commendatory letter
for the Latin version of Castiglione which Clerke dedicated to their
common patron, the queen. It is no mere coincidence that the *Gratulationes Valdinenses*, in which Harvey celebrates his first audience with
Elizabeth, ends with a pair of poems on the perfect male and female
courtier that are heavily indebted to Castiglione, Della Casa, and

Guazzo.[35] From Harvey's point of view his presentation to the queen at Audley End was a vital stage in the desired transition from "academicus" to "aulicus," and his poems on court *mores* were designed to emphasize his suitability. To write eloquently of the court was to write oneself into a courtly role. The *Rhetor* ends by suggesting that the rhetorical and dialectical arts recommended by Harvey will usher his audience—originally Cambridge undergraduates—into the palace of Eloquence, a "majestic" figure among whose attendants are "Glory, Praise, Honour, Fame, Magnificence . . . Money, Gold, Silver and Opulence."[36] At Audley End, I would suggest, that metaphor was realized in the person of Elizabeth, the efficacy of whose language is repeatedly praised throughout the first book of the *Gratulationes Valdinenses*. Indeed many of the key epithets used of Eloquence are simply transferred to the queen. In political terms she *is* eloquence, the royal logos whose "word" has the power to transform the humble scholar into the gilded courtier: "royal words create nobility, distinguished knight and potent lord. . . . great is the power of the sovereign tongue" ["Generosum Regia verba/Efficiunt: Equitem auratum; Dominumque potentem. . . . multum est regali ponderis ore"].[37]

Harvey is here writing in the direct tradition of Abraham Hartwell's *Regina Literata* (1565), a poem written on the occasion of the queen's visit to Cambridge in 1564 to celebrate her avowed intention of promoting learning and the literary arts.[38] Hartwell's writings were well known to Harvey and are quoted quite frequently throughout the *Gratulationes Valdinenses*. Indeed *Regina Literata*'s employment of the nine Muses to praise Elizabeth's devotion to the Humanities provides a likely subtext for Harvey's own *Smithus; vel Musarum Lachrymæ* and Spenser's *Teares of the Muses*. As the former indicates, the death of Sir Thomas Smith, the principal grandee of Saffron Walden and a figure who had risen from an academic background to the office of secretary of state, was a severe blow to Harvey's hopes of advancement. Smith was not merely a patron and "friend" but also a kinsman, a vital link between the unknown scholar and the glittering world of the court. *Smithus* therefore adumbrates the *Teares of the Muses* in lamenting the apparent death of patronage itself, even as its slippery dedication seeks to substitute Sir Walter Mildmay for the deceased. It is noteworthy that Spenser makes no such substitution. In Harvey the concluding lamentations of Polyhymnia are followed by a vision of Smith's reception into divine grace;[39] in Spenser they are followed by *Virgils Gnat*, and the gnat, unlike Smith, is in Hell. Leicester's patronage, the fable suggests, has failed the poet. The textual and social reminiscence of *Smithus* in *Teares* is doubtless quite intentional since it was probably around 1577 or 1578 that Harvey's and Spenser's hopes of preferment began to center upon Leicester and his circle.[40] In the first book of the *Gratulationes Valdinenses* it is Leicester who introduces Harvey to the queen as one of his (by Harvey's account) intimate servants. Their relationship is therefore marked by "friendly words" ("amicis . . . verbis").[41] Yet such suggestions of intimacy are flatly belied by circumstance. Harvey was wholly unaware that Leicester had secretly married Lettice Knollys and his relentless insistence on the prospect of the earl's marriage with the queen can only have been profoundly embarrassing.[42] The text's clumsy descent to the erotic, that most "familiar" of all modes, exposes its real nature. Harvey was privy to none of Leicester's personal secrets and, when read in the cold light of retrospect, every word of self-proclaimed "familiarity" only serves to demonstrate how much of an outsider he actually was.

The *Gratulationes Valdinenses* may best be described as four books in search of a patron. And Harvey cast his net widely: the first book is addressed to the queen, the second to Leicester (addressed as Muse and patron), the third to Burghley, and the fourth to Oxford, Hatton, and Sidney. What the collection primarily demonstrates, therefore, is the perceived association between patronage and literary status. Harvey begins by telling the queen that he is "not yet a poet," by which he means that his poetic gifts have not yet been publicly recognized in his home country despite (allegedly) widespread recognition abroad. His *Smithus*, for example, is claimed to have won singular admiration in Italy and two adulatory poems are quoted in evidence, the latter declaring Harvey to be worthy of a "laurel crown."[43] But Harvey realized that such an accolade lay solely in the queen's gift, a point made even more forcibly in H. B.'s commendatory verses to *The Faerie Queene*:

> Desertes findes dew in that most princely doome,
> In whose sweete brest are all the Muses bredde:
> So did that great *Augustus* erst in Roome,
> With leaves of fame adorne his Poets hedde.

The turn of phrase here is of considerable interest: the notion that poets confer fame on patrons is a standard, not to say hackneyed, topos; less familiar is the notion that sufficiently elevated patrons can reciprocate in kind, that imperial recognition confers not merely financial security but "fame." For this reason, as Alessandro Barchiesi

has argued, a great poem needs a great addressee, and eulogy is somehow integral to epic—if only because praise of the insignificant or
the mediocre generates bathos unless it is consciously deployed in
the service of mock-epic.[44] Poets confer "kleos" or fame but Spenser's
Gloriana is located in the city of Cleopolis not solely as the recipient
of praise but because her service confers fame on those who perform
it (I.x.58). Similarly, by allowing Harvey to kiss her hand, and re-
marking on his "Italian" appearance (events celebrated in the twin
poems "De Regiæ Manus Osculatione" and "De Vultu Itali"), the
queen is presented in the *Gratulationes Valdinenses* as taking the first
steps towards Harvey's elevation. The process is proleptically enacted
within the text. Acknowledging that he is "not yet a poet" in the
dedicatory verse epistle, Harvey begs the queen to confer such status
upon him by recognizing him as "a new poet" ["novus poeta"]. By
the close of book one, however, he refers to himself almost en passant
as "your poet."[45] When read in context, the poem on his Italian
appearance serves merely as the prelude to asserting his reputation
among the Italians—although it should be noted that "Strozza" and
"Roselettus," his alleged admirers, appear to be otherwise unknown
to literary history and may well have been invented for the occasion.
Such a device would be quite in keeping with Harvey's methods.
His scholarly "fame" was largely the creation of his own *Ciceronianus*,
Rhetor and *Smithus*. As he explains in the *Rhetor*, he was at his most
Ciceronian in this act of self-creation. Cicero, like Harvey himself,
was a "novus homo," a "new man" blowing his own trumpet with
swollen cheeks ["pleno, ut sic dicam ore, et quasi sufflatis buccis
decantare"]. "Read his oration against Lucius Piso," he told his undergraduates, "and as frequently as you encounter 'I', 'I', 'I' you will
hear him speak reverently and vauntingly of himself."[46] By according
to Harvey the status of patron, E. K. suggests that the *novus homo* has
arrived. As the lengthy annotation at *September* 176 indicates, he is a
figure of sufficiently established reputation to introduce E. K.'s "new
poet" to the senate of letters.

The problem from Harvey's viewpoint, however, was that E. K.'s
strategy succeeded all too well. The impact of *The Shepheardes Calender* was far greater than that of any of his own publications and
the new poet quickly eclipsed the new man. Their shifting status is
perceptible even in the Spenser-Harvey *Letters* of 1580.[47] As the situation is presented there, it is Immerito who is "familiar" with the
great and the good and who labors to recommend Harvey to them
for friendship's sake: "your desire to heare of my late beeing with
her Maiestie, muste dye in it selfe. As for the twoo worthy Gentlemen, Master *Sidney*, and Master *Dyer*, they have me, I thanke them,

in some use of familiarity: of whom, and to whome, what speache
passeth for youre credite and estimation, I leave your selfe to conceive, having always so well conceived of my unfained affection,
and zeale towardes you" (6). Yet, as we now know, publication of
the *Letters* proved to be highly counterproductive for Harvey if not
for Spenser. The academic skit *Pedantius* (1581) testifies to the ridicule
his contributions engendered. Cambridge took grave offence at the
way in which he had portrayed it, criticism he directed at Dr. Andrew Perne was interpreted as an attack on Sir James Croft, and his
satirical "Speculum Tuscanismi" was taken to reflect upon the earl
of Oxford. Ironically, credence was doubtless lent to such accusations
by the *Letters'* own inflated claims of familiarity with Sidney. Since
the publication of the *Gratulationes Valdinenses*, Sidney and Oxford,
who are honored together in the fourth book, had fallen into acrimo-
nious dispute and accusations of partiality were all the more liable
to be credited.

In the long term Harvey gained little from the publication of
the *Letters* beyond the cultural capital of his avowed friendship with
Spenser. Had his "Verlayes" reached print under Immerito's sponsor-
ship, as originally intended, cultural capital might well have translated
into capital proper—a point he doubtless recognized since he reflects
quite ruefully in the *Letters* on the financial success of *The Shepheardes
Calender*. Not surprisingly he clung tenaciously in the aftermath to
the little that remained. In *The Shepheardes Calender* E. K. uses his
"friend" Harvey to endorse the "new poet," but in the *Foure Letters
and Certaine Sonnets* (1592), published during the protracted controversy with Nashe, Harvey uses his "friend," now a famous poet, for
the purposes of self-endorsement.[48] "Signior Immerito (for that name
will be remembred)," he writes, "was then, and is still, my affection-
ate friend." To prove the point he ends the *Foure Letters* with Spenser's "overlooving" sonnet, "Harvey, the happy above happiest
men." In fact, the text Harvey produces is as much over-determined
as "over-loving." The sonnet is entitled "To the right Worshipfull,
my singular good frend, M. Gabriell Harvey, Doctor of the Lawes"
and endorsed "Your devoted frend, during life, Edmund Spencer."[49]
It is carefully positioned so that the last word of Harvey's pamphlet
(prior to the word "Finis") will be "Spencer." Here was cultural
patronage on a grand scale and nobody recognized its value better
than Nashe. In *Strange Newes, of the Intercepting Certaine Letters* (1592)
he lands perhaps the heaviest blow of the controversy when he alleges
that the much vaunted "friendship" between Harvey and Spenser is
a fraud. Maliciously focussing on Harvey's reflections on *Mother Hubberds Tale* he remarks, "a *pure sanguine* sot art thou, that in vaine-
glory to have *Spencer* known for thy friend, and that thou hast some

interest in him, censerest him worse than his deadliest enemie would do . . . Immortal *Spencer*, no frailtie hath thy fame, but the imputation of this Idiots friendship."[50] But by being seen to defend Spenser Nashe was pursuing a self-promotional strategy of his own. Following the publication of the first three books of *The Faerie Queene* in 1590, the cultural capital of Spenser's name was ripe for appropriation and what we are watching at this point in the controversy is a contest between *two* would-be appropriators. Nashe duly addresses Spenser in a spirit of "friendship" even in the act of reminding him that he has forgotten to include an (ironically unspecified) "piller of Nobilitie" among the patrons of *The Faerie Queene*.[51] Similarly, in dedicating *Christs Teares over Ierusalem* to Lady Elizabeth Carey he is careful to remind her how "Maister *Spencer*, in all his writings hie prizeth you."[52] By allying himself to Spenser, he seeks to ally himself to Spenser's patrons—and particularly those patrons with whom Spenser claimed kinship. "Spenser" is not just a name in the Harvey-Nashe controversy but a brand name, a marketable commodity. And "friendship" is the currency in which the trade is conducted.

Recent criticism has recognized the crucial role of "paratexts" —dedications, commendatory epistles, authorial prefaces and such like—to the interpretation of any literary work, yet the very term "paratexts" still sets them apart from the "text" proper. Walter Ong was surely correct when he argued that what we term "paratexts" frequently function to condition, or to attempt to condition, the readers' response to a work.[53] In that sense they often need to be recognized as integral parts of the main text—a point most wittily made by Jonathan Swift when fashioning his *Tale of a Tub*.[54] Unlike *The Shepheardes Calender*, the Harvey-Spenser *Letters* carry no formal dedication except, of course, for the anonymous preface by a "Welwiller of the two Authours" who addresses himself, quite tellingly, to "the Curteous Buyer" (447–48). In *Have with You to Saffron-Walden* (1596), Nashe claims that this preface was delivered to the compositor in Harvey's own hand.[55] Given the wealth of self-laudatory materials to be found in draft form throughout the *Letter-Book* this claim may well be true, but true or false it serves to highlight contemporary awareness of the nature of the enterprise on which Harvey was engaged. "Friendship" is undoubtedly the defining concept of the Harvey-Spenser *Letters*. All five of the epistles breathe, not only in their modes of address and endorsements, but throughout the body of their texts, the spirit of an intimacy that has, paradoxically, been carefully honed for public consumption. By reminding us that the correspondents are, as they repeatedly proclaim themselves to be, the associates of "courtiers," the anonymous "Welwiller" endorses the cumulative impact of all of the dedications reaching back to the *Ciceronianus* to suggest that his two scholarly friends are well on their way to becoming public figures in their own right.

Yet, as Nashe later suggests, all was not as it seemed. The new sense of "familiarity" with Sidney that Immerito expresses in the *Letters* was calculated to imply that his gift of dedication had been rewarded with the gift of friendship, and the point is driven home by contrast with the less fortunate Stephen Gosson who "writing a certaine Booke, called *The Schoole of Abuse*, and dedicating it to Maister *Sidney*, was for hys labor scorned" (6).[56] Yet this contrast is by no means purely triumphalist. Rather, I would suggest, it encodes a very deep anxiety. Throughout the *Letters* Immerito's acutely self-conscious air of "familiarity" with the members of the "Areopagus" contrasts markedly with the reserve detectable in his enigmatic allusions to Leicester.[57] He reveals at one point that he decided not to dedicate an unspecified work, possibly the *Calender* itself, to "his excellent Lordship," and that he hesitates to make any future dedications within the same circle "leaste by over-much cloying their noble eares, I should gather a contempt of my self, or else seeme rather for gaine and commoditie to doe it, for some sweetnesse that I have already tasted" (5). The recurrence here of the term "contempt," so prominent in the opening sentence of the argument to "October" where Cuddie complains of "the contempte of Poetrie," illustrates how intensely personal a poem that eclogue actually is. Hence perhaps the elaborate stratagem of substituting Cuddie for Colin while simultaneously proclaiming "that some doubt, that the persons be different." Similarly, the letter's references to "gaine" and "commoditie" seem to echo the debate between Piers and Cuddie on material reward: "*Cuddie*, the prayse is better, then the price,/The glory eke much greater then the gayne" (19–20). The fact that the letter is addressed by Immerito from "Leycester House" and is (pre)dated to October of the preceding year is richly suggestive. It would indeed be a piece of matchless Spenserian wit if an October letter were expressly designed to comment upon an October eclogue.

"Familiarity" is the key to the *Letters*, and in his annotation to "October" 65 E. K. recalls how "the worthy Scipio . . . had evermore in his company, and that in a most familiar sort the good olde Poet Ennius." It is a relationship celebrated in the fourth book of Horace's *Odes*—the book that, according to Suetonius, was commissioned by Horace's imperial "friend" Augustus—in a poem that identifies poetry as the only gift a poet has to offer in return for patronal generosity, although it is a gift that guarantees posthumous fame

(IV.8.11–20).[58] A Horatian subtext is glimpsed again in the annotation to line 105 where E. K. quotes Horace's *Epistles* 1.5.19 on the inspirational effects of wine, but the reference to Bacchus in Spenser's succeeding line might well be seen to suggest a very different Horatian reminiscence. Cuddie is once again contemplating the poetics of state:

> Who euer casts to compasse weightye prise . . .
> Let powre in lavish cups and thriftie bitts of meate,
> For *Bacchus* fruite is frend to *Phœbus* wise. (103–06)

The recurrence of the friendship topos here is telling. In the twentieth ode of the first book Horace invites his friend and patron Maecenas to partake of his modest cellar while in the *Epistles* he alleges that Scipio's friend and protégé Ennius depended on wine for inspiration (I.19.7–8)—a matter to which Spenser directly alludes in the Latin poem dispatched to Harvey from Leicester House (10). Wine, patronage, and inspiration were thus linked. Horace's most famous apostrophe to Bacchus comes not in the epistle cited by E. K. but at *Odes* 3.25: "Whither, O Bacchus, dost thou hurry me, o'erflowing with thy power . . . In what caves shall I be heard planning to set amid the stars, and in Jove's council, peerless Caesar's immortal glory" (1–6).[59] Even in his hymn to Bacchus, I would suggest, Cuddie implicitly reverts, through Horatian reminiscence, to the major theme of the "October" eclogue, the desire to sing of state affairs and the need for friends at court to enable him to do so. Horace had his wish: he "sang" for Augustus and, as he tells us at the outset of *Sermones* 2.6, gained everything he desired through the gift of his Sabine farm. In fact, the "gods" had given him even more than he had requested.[60] It was well understood that the term "gods" frequently served as code for patrons in Roman poetry. In Bynneman's 1570 edition of Virgil's *Opera*, for example, the editor remarks that Augustus "was called a god by Tityrus [in the first eclogue] on account of his great munificence and not, as Servius imagined, because he was venerated in dedicated temples at Rome."[61] But would Spenser's divinity also deliver? "Shee is my goddesse plaine," says Colin, "And I her shepherds swayne,/Albee forswonck and forswatt I am" ("April," 97–99). It is all the more significant, then, that E. K.'s concluding note on "Colins Embleme" cites both Horace and Ovid, generally regarded as Augustus's most favored and most ill used poets.[62] In 1579 it remained quite unclear which would prove to be Spenser's case.

Suetonius records that Augustus invited Horace to become his personal secretary.[63] Horace declined, but the offer was traditionally regarded as an expression of extraordinary trust between poet and prince, and Spenser's secretaryship to Lord Grey repays consideration in this light.[64] The role of secretary was universally seen as particularly intimate not merely despite social inferiority but even because of it.[65] According to Angel Day, for example, secretarial service united two socially disparate people in a common cause, "wherein what the one coveteth, the other desireth." "Being in one condition a *Servant*," the secretary, "is at the pleasure and appoyntment of another to be commaunded: and being in a second respect as a *friend*, hee is charely to have in estimate, the state, honor, reputation and beeing, of him whom he serveth."[66] In becoming secretary to Lord Grey Spenser could be seen as having gained a potentially powerful "friend" and if the appointment was secured through the influence of the Sidneys it may well have seemed like an answer to "October" eclogue's transparent call for patronage. However, when Lord Grey was re-called in the summer of 1582 under Burghley's displeasure, the situation would have looked very different. Spenser's Munster plantation, appropriately known as "Haphazard," fell far short of Horace's Sabine farm—as the representation of Ireland in *Colin Clouts Come Home Againe* makes quite clear. That work, like Churchyard's *A Sparke of Frendship*, is dedicated to Ralegh but the approach is far more subtle. Ralegh is not here addressed as "friend" but as "Sir" and the work is offered "in part of paiment of the infinite debt in which I acknowl-edge my selfe bounden unto you, for your singular favours and sun-drie good turnes shewed to me at my late being in England." The dating of the dedicatory letter to December 1591 (in a work pub-lished in 1595) may be intended to suggest that one of the "singular favours" was the granting of Spenser's royal pension—"yet found I lyking in her royall mynd," says Colin, "Not for my skill, but for that shepheards sake" (454–55)—but it also recalls the period that saw the calling in of the *Complaints* when, according to Sir Thomas Tresham, the emergent "Poett Laurall" proved no more than a "Poett Lorrell" and fled to Ireland in danger of losing his newly granted pension.[67]

In other words, part at least of the public perception of Colin's homecoming was of Spenser's flight. The poem's dedication never expressly claims Ralegh as a friend yet encourages the reader to think of him as such by the simple expedient of alleging that its pastoral fiction agrees "with the truth in circumstance and matter." That fiction offsets social disparity through shared vocation: the Shepheard of the Ocean is portrayed as a fellow poet who "gan to cast great lyking to my lore" (180) and consequently encouraged Colin to seek Cynthia's "bounty" (187). Yet, at the same time, by recalling the Shepheard of the Ocean's social superiority at strategic moments the work underscores the importance of having such very unequal, Baconian "friends" at court. A signal problem, however, was that the Shepheard of the Ocean was currently out of favor with the queen, "which from her presence faultlesse him debard" (167)—and "faultlesse" is left to hover ambiguously between "presence" and "him" in a very noncommittal way. It by no means coincidental that a fictive resolution to their differences is presented the following year in *The Legend of Friendship* because "friendship" had by now become the rubric of choice for discussion of Ralegh's relationship to the queen.[68] In the *Booke of the Ocean to Scinthia* Ralegh notes how his fall from grace drove him, literally and metaphorically, "to kyngdomes strange, to lands farr of addrest" and left him "alone, forsaken, frindless onn the shore" (88–89). The cause of this friendlessness was the change in Elizabeth's personal attitude towards him: "a Queen shee was to mee, no more Belphebe/a Lion then, no more a milke white Dove" (327–28).[69] The proem to Spenser's *Legend of Friendship* duly asks Elizabeth to put off the "use of awfull Maiestie" and "hearke to love"(5), and it is by means of a compassionate "turtle dove" that the lost "Belphoebe" is restored to "Timias" in place of the imperious queen. The eighth canto sees him "receiv'd againe to former favours state" (IV.viii.17).[70] At the time of publication this was, of course, premature. Even as Spenser wrote, Ralegh was desperately trying to regain Belphoebe's "love" by offering the disaffected queen an empire in the New World. His *Discoverie of the Large, Rich, and Bewtiful Empyre of Guiana* (1596) may be dedicated to Lord Howard of Effingham and Sir Robert Cecil but it is directed through them to another patron:

> But I hope it shall appeare that there is a way found to answere every mans longing, a better Indies for her majestie then the King of Spaine hath any, which if it shall please her highnes to undertake, I shall most willingly end the rest of my daies in following the same. . . . The west Indies were first offered her Majesties Grandfather by *Columbus* a straunger, in whome there might be doubt of deceipt. . . . This Empire is made knowen to her Majesty by her own vassal, and by him that oweth to her more duty then an ordinary subject, so that it shall ill sort with the many graces and benefites which I have receaved to abuse her highness, either with fables or imaginations.[71]

Ralegh's contemporary correspondence with Burghley testifies to his very real fear that the whole account of Guiana might be dismissed "for a history or a fable"—as it appears to have been by some.[72] He was anxious at this juncture to present himself not as a poet but as a man of action, to suggest that the "gifts" he now offers in the hope of renewed patronage are more than mere words. "They have grosly belied me," he asserts in the dedicatory epistle, "that forejudged that I would rather become a servant to the Spanish king, then return, and the rest were much mistaken, who would have perswaded, that I was too easeful and sensuall to undertake a jorney of so great travel."[73] The message is clear: if Ralegh's habitual use of "love" as a metaphor for political courtship had exposed him to the accusation that his clandestine marriage to Elizabeth Throckmorton was tantamount to treason, he would now rewrite that metaphor to relocate sensuality in military, rather than amorous, "service." Since "*Guiana* is a Countrey that hath yet her Maydenhead," he may safely satisfy his "lust" there while remaining true to Cynthia.[74] In this manner a way will be found "to answer every man's longing" and reciprocal friendship will function as a sublimation of unrequited "love." The better to further such an aim, mention of the Orinoco and the Amazon in the eleventh canto of *The Legend of Friendship* is used to promote Ralegh's projected enterprise in South America. Indeed the passage eloquently epitomizes the burden of *The Discoverie*:

> And shame on you, ô men, which boast your strong
> And valiant hearts, in thoughts lesse hard and bold,
> Yet quaile in conquest of that land of gold.
> But this to you, ô Britons, most pertaines,
> To whom the right hereof it selfe hath sold;
> The which for sparing litle cost or paines,
> Loose so immortall glory, and so endlesse gaines. (22)

The phrasing is careful and deliberate. The insatiable thirst for "gold" was commonly blamed for the brutality of the Spanish enterprize in the New World, but in the case of England the "gaines" will be "endlesse" precisely because the "glory" will be "immortall." Or is it the other way around?

The hope encoded in the tale of Timias and Belphoebe is that Ralegh's erstwhile patron will once more become his "friend," a development that had far-reaching implications for Spenser himself. It is also in the proem to *The Legend of Friendship* that the poet turns directly to the queen in response to Burghley's perceived hostility. Burghley had long been a problem. All of Spenser's would-be patrons—Leicester, Sidney, Ralegh, and Essex—at various times professed their "love" to the queen and claimed to enjoy some form of special relationship with her, yet it is arguable that no one was ever closer to her than Burghley.[75] If the role of secretary was especially valued as a form of amicitia, that of secretary of state was its apogee. Sir Robert Cecil, Burghley's son and successor in that office, would later compare the relationship between the secretary of state and the monarch to "the mutual affecion of two lovers."[76] The crippling problem at the outset of the *Legend of Friendship*, therefore, is that Spenser has fallen foul of Elizabeth's most long-standing and most trusted "friend"—and it is this that renders his task so rhetorically delicate. In order to solve the problem he would appear to return to Horace. The assertion that "the rugged forhead that with grave foresight/Welds kingdomes causes, & affaires of state,/My looser rimes (I wote) doth sharply wite" (IV.Proem.1) might well spark a subtextual reminiscence in the classically educated reader. Suetonius records that Horace addressed *Epistles* 2.1 to Augustus in response to the emperor's complaint that he had been omitted from the *Sermones*: "are you afraid," Augustus is alleged to have asked, "that your reputation with posterity will suffer because it appears that you were my friend?" ["quod videaris familiaris nobis esse"].[77] In *Epistles* 2.1 Horace defended himself by stating that: "seeing that you alone carry the weight of so many great charges, guarding our Italian state with arms, gracing her with morals, and reforming her with laws, I should sin against the public weal if with long talk, O Caesar, I were to delay your busy hours."[78] In other words, Spenser addresses the politically busy and morally scrupulous Burghley in a manner strongly reminiscent of the way in which Horace addresses the politically busy and morally scrupulous Augustus, and the transposition is intensely ironic. It momentarily raises the uncomfortable specter of the "regnum Cecilianum" but only to dismiss it as political fantasy.[79] Horace hesitates to waste the busy emperor's time but Spenser has, all unwittingly it seems, wasted Burghley's. Yet the solution is simple: "To such therefore," says the narrator, "I do not sing at all,/But to that sacred Saint my soueraigne Queene" (IV.Proem.4). She, not Burghley, is all that really matters, politically, morally, and aesthetically. In the commendatory sonnets to the 1590 edition of *The Faerie Queene*, Ralegh had predicted that Eliza's praise would eclipse that of Laura and by implication that the laurel crown would pass from Petrarch to Spenser through a grateful queen's good offices. By way of reciprocation the 1596 edition promotes the imperial agenda that promises

to see Ralegh "receiv'd againe to former favours state." In this manner the Shepheard of the Ocean might finally come home again
and, in Baconian terms, the fortunes of poet and patron be made to
"comprehend the one the other"—at least ideally. Because of the
lack of any formal system of patronage in Elizabethan England each
patronal relationship remains very largely a construction of the poetry
that supposedly depends upon it. Patronage is indeed a species of
"amicitia" but only to the extent that amicitia itself is a species
of fiction.

Merton College, Oxford University

NOTES

1.   All quotations of Spenser's poetry are from *The Faerie Queene*, ed. Thomas P.
Roche, Jr. (Harmondsworth: Penguin Books, 1978) and *Edmund Spenser: The Shorter
Poems*, ed. Richard A. McCabe (Harmondsworth: Penguin, 1999). The prose is
quoted from *The Works of Edmund Spenser*, ed. Edwin Greenlaw et al., Variorum
Edition, 11 vols. (Baltimore: Johns Hopkins University Press, 1932–58), *Spenser's
Prose Works*, ed. by Rudolf Gottfried, IX (1949). References in the text are by page
to this volume.
2.   For the letter, see Gordon Tesky, "Positioning Spenser's 'Letter to Raleigh,' "
in *Craft and Tradition: Essays in Honour of William Blissett*, ed. H. B. de Groot and
Alexander Leggatt (Calgary: University of Calgary Press, 1990), 35–46.
3.   See also Craig A. Berry, "The Quest for Authority in *The Faerie Queene* I and
Chaucer's *Tale of Sir Thopas*," *Studies in Philology* 91 (1994): 136–66.
4.   For Spenser's pursuit of patronage see Muriel Bradbrook, "No Room at the
Top," in *Elizabethan Poetry*, ed. J. R. Brown and B. Harris, Stratford-upon-Avon
Studies, 2 (London: Edward Arnold, 1960): 91–109; Richard Helgerson, "The New
Poet Presents Himself: Spenser and the Idea of a Literary Career," *PMLA* 93 (1978):
893–911; "The Elizabethan Laureate: Self-Presentation and the Literary System,"
ELH 46 (1979): 193–220; *Self-Crowned Laureates: Spenser, Jonson, Milton and the
Literary System* (Berkeley: University of California Press, 1983); Carol A. Stillman,
"Politics, Precedence, and the Order of the Dedicatory Sonnets in *The Faerie
Queene*," *Spenser Studies* 5 (1984): 143–48; Jon A. Quitslund, "Spenser and the
Patronesses of the *Fowre Hymnes*: 'Ornaments of all True Love and Beautie,' " in
*Silent But for the Word: Tudor Women as Patrons, Translators, and Writers of Religious
Work*, ed. Margaret P. Hannay (Kent: Kent State University Press, 1985), 184–202;
Jean R. Brink, " 'All his minde on honour fixed': The Preferment of Edmund
Spenser," in *Spenser's Life and the Subject of Biography*, ed. Judith H. Anderson, Donald
Cheney, and David A. Richardson (Amherst: University of Massachusetts Press,
1996), 45–64; Lin Kelsey and Richard S. Peterson, "Rereading Colin's Broken Pipe:
Spenser and the Problem of Patronage," *Spenser Studies* 14 (2000): 233–72; Judith

Owens, *Enabling Engagements: Edmund Spenser and the Poetics of Patronage* (Montreal and Kingston: McGill-Queen's University Press, 2002). For the nature of Early Modern patronage generally, see Phoebe Sheavyn, *The Literary Profession in the Elizabethan Age*, ed. J. W. Saunders (Manchester: Manchester University Press, 1967); Guy Fitch Lytle and Stephen Orgel, ed. *Patronage in the Renaissance* (Princeton: Princeton University Press, 1981); Mary Ellen Lamb, "The Countess of Pembroke's Patronage," *ELR* 12 (1982): 162–79; French R. Fogle and Louis A. Knafla, *Patronage in Late Renaissance England* (Los Angeles: William Andrew Clark Memorial Library, University of California, 1983); Michael G. Brennan, *Literary Patronage in the English Renaissance: The Pembroke Family* (London: Routledge, 1988); Alistair Fox, "The Complaint of Poetry for the Death of Liberality: The Decline of Literary Patronage in the 1590s," in *The Reign of Elizabeth I: Court and Culture in the Last Decade*, ed. John Guy (Cambridge: Cambridge University Press, 1995), 229–57.

5. See *The Life of Horace* in *Suetonius*, trans. J. C. Rolfe, 2 vols. (Loeb Classical Library [1913; 1997]), II: 460.

6. Alan Bray, *The Friend* (Chicago: Chicago University Press, 2003), 140–76.

7. Peter White, *Promised Verse: Poets in the Society of Augustan Rome* (Cambridge, Mass: Harvard University Press, 1993), 3–34.

8. Howard Erskine-Hill, *The Augustan Idea in English Literature* (London: Edward Arnold, 1983), 16, 18.

9. Servius Grammaticus, *Servii Grammatici qui feruntur in Vergilii Carmina Commentarii*, ed. G. Thilo and H. Hagen, 3 vols. (Leipzig: Teubner, 1878–87), III: 8, 11. See Annabel Patterson, *Pastoral and Ideology: Virgil to Valéry* (Oxford: Clarendon Press, 1988), 35–36, 41, 77.

10. Phebe Lowell Bowditch, *Horace and the Gift Economy of Patronage* (Berkeley: University of California Press, 2001), 3, 6–7.

11. The bond between a freedman and his former owner constituted a peculiar form of Roman "patronage."

12. White, *Promised Verse*, 100.

13. Wallace T. MacCaffrey, "Place and Patronage in Elizabethan Politics," in *Elizabethan Government and Society: Essays Presented to Sir John Neale*, ed. S. T. Bindoff, J. Hurstfield and C. H. Williams (London: Athlone Press, 1961), 95–126.

14. Richard C. Barnett, *Place, Profit, and Power: A Study of the Servants of William Cecil, Elizabethan Statesman* (Chapel Hill: University of North Carolina Press, 1969). 12. See also J. A. van Dorsten, "Mr Secretary Cecil, Patron of Letters," *English Studies* 50 (1969): 1–9. For the wider extent of Cecil family patronage, see Pauline J. Croft, ed., *Patronage, Culture and Power: The Early Cecils*, Studies in British Art, 8 (New Haven: Yale University Press for the Paul Mellon Centre for Studies in British Art, Yale Center for British Art, 2002).

15. Louis Adrian Montrose, "Gifts and Reason: The Context of Peele's *Araygnement of Paris*," *ELH* 47 (1980): 433–61, 454.

16. Eleanor Rosenberg, *Leicester: Patron of Letters* (New York: Columbia University Press, 1955), 323–28; Spenser found the position different in Gaelic Ireland. See Richard A. McCabe, *Spenser's Monstrous Regiment: Elizabethan Ireland and the Poetics of Difference* (Oxford: Oxford University Press, 2002), 28–56.

17.   Frank Whigham, "The Rhetoric of Elizabethan Suitors' Letters," *PMLA* 96 (1981): 864–82. For the generation of friendship through "the exchange of persuasive texts" see Lorna Hutson, *The Usurer's Daughter: Male Friendship and Fictions of Women in Sixteenth-Century England* (London: Routledge, 1994), 2–3, 52–85.

18.   See Marcel Mauss, *The Gift: The Form and Reason for Exchange in Archaic Societies*, trans. W. D. Halls (London: Routledge, 1990); Pierre Bourdieu, *Outline of a Theory of Practice*, trans. Richard Nice (Cambridge: Cambridge University Press, 1977).

19.   Cicero, *De Senectute, De Amicitia, De Divinatione*, trans. W. A. Falconer (Loeb Classical Library, 1923), 139, 143, 179, 181, 187.

20.   See Catherine Bates, *The Rhetoric of Courtship in Elizabethan Language and Literature* (Cambridge: Cambridge University Press, 1992) 6–24; Laurie Shannon, *Sovereign Amity: Figures of Friendship in Shakespearean Contexts* (Chicago: University of Chicago Press, 2002), 17–53.

21.   *Francis Bacon*, ed. Brian Vickers (Oxford: Oxford University Press, 1996), 437.

22.   R. A. Geimer, "Spenser's Rhyme or Churchyard's Reason: Evidence on Churchyard's First Pension," *RES* 20 (1969): 306–09.

23.   *A Sparke of Frendship and Warme Goodwill, that shewes the effect of True Affection and unfoldes the finenesse of this world* (London, 1588), sig. A3r.

24.   Ibid., sig. A4r.

25.   Quoted in Whigham, "Rhetoric of Elizabethan Suitors' Letters," 872.

26.   The use of the term "entitled," which also had the meaning of authored by, probably misled William Webbe into attributing the *Calender* to Sidney. See *Elizabethan Critical Essays*, ed. G. Gregory Smith (Oxford: Oxford University Press, 1971; first pub. 1904), I: 245.

27.   See Virginia F. Stern, *Gabriel Harvey: A Study of his Life, Marginalia, and Library* (Oxford: Oxford University Press, 1979), 39–47. For the progress of 1578 see Zillah Dovey, *An Elizabethan Progress: The Queen's Journey into East Anglia, 1578* (Stroud: Alan Sutton Publishing, 1996).

28.   Warren B. Austen, "William Wythie's Notebook: Lampoons on John Lyly and Gabriel Harvey," *RES* 23 (1947): 297–309.

29.   *Letter-Book of Gabriel Harvey*, ed. E. J. L. Scott (London: Camden Society, 1884), 58–68.

30.   For Gascoigne see Katherine Wilson, *Fictions of Authorship in Late Elizabethan Narratives: Euphues in Arcadia* (Oxford: Clarendon Press, 2006), 19–51.

31.   *Gabrielis Harveii Gratulationum Valdinensium Libri Quatuor* (London, 1578), Book IV, 22 (sig. L2v). I have also consulted "The *Gratulationes Valdinenses* of Gabriel Harvey," ed. Thomas Hugh Jameson, unpublished dissertation, Yale University, 1938.

32.   See H. S. Wilson, "Gabriel Harvey's Orations on Rhetoric," *ELH* 12 (1945): 167–82.

33.   *Gabriel Harvey's Ciceronianus*, ed. Harold S. Wilson, trans. Clarence A. Forbes, Studies in the Humanities, 4 (Lincoln: University of Nebraska Press, 1945), 79.

34.   *Gabrielis Harveii Rhetor, vel duorum dierum Oratio, De Natura, Arte, et Exercitatione Rhetorica* (London, 1577) sig. aiir.

35.   See G. L. Barnett, "Gabriel Harvey's *Castilio, sive Aulicus* and *De Aulica*," *SP* 42 (1945): 146–63.

36.   *Rhetor*, sigs. P2r–P3r.

37.   *Gratulationes Valdinenses*, Book I, 21 (sig. C3r).

38.   See James Binns, "Abraham Hartwell, Herald of the New Queen's Reign. The *Regina Literata* (London, 1565)," in *Ut Granum Sinapis: Essays on Neo-Latin Literature in Honour of Jozef IJsewijn*, ed. Gilbert Tournoy and Dirk Sacré, Supplementa Humanistica Lovaniensia, 12 (Leuven: Leuven University Press, 1997), 292–304.

39.   *Gabrielis Harveii Valdinatis, Smithus; vel Musarum Lachrymæ* (London, 1578) sigs. G1r–G2r.

40.   In both cases the sequence of Muses is indebted to Ausonius, *De Musarum Inventis*, attributed to Virgil in the Dumaeus edition of 1542 from which Spenser translated *Virgils Gnat*.

41.   *Gratulationes Valdinenses*, Book I, 19 (sig. C2r).

42.   See T. H. Jameson, "The Machiavellianism of Gabriel Harvey," *PMLA* 51 (1941): 645–56; Sydney Anglo, *Machiavelli: The First Century* (Oxford: Oxford University Press, 2005), 446–52.

43.   *Gratulationes Valdinenses*, Book I, 28 (sig. D2v).

44.   Alessandro Barchiesi, *The Poet and the Prince: Ovid and Augustan Discourse* (Berkeley: University of California Press, 1997), 15–44.

45.   *Gratulationes Valdinenses*, Book I, 23 (sig. C4r).

46.   *Rhetor*, sigs. Iv–I2r.

47.   See Jon A. Quitslund, "Questionable Evidence in the *Letters* of 1580 between Gabriel Harvey and Edmund Spenser," in *Spenser's Life and the Subject of Biography*, 81–98.

48.   For the perceived benefits of association with Spenser and his works, see Joseph Black, " 'Pan is Hee': Commending *The Faerie Queene*," *Spenser Studies* 15 (2001): 121–34, 131.

49.   *Complete Works*, ed. A. B. Grosart, 3 vols. (London: privately printed for Huth Library, 1884–85), I: 180, 253–54.

50.   Thomas Nashe, *Works*, ed. R. B. McKerrow, rev. ed. 5 vols. (Oxford: Oxford University Press, 1958), I: 281–82. For the Mother Hubberd controversy, see Andrew Hadfield, "Robert Parsons/Richard Verstegan and the Calling-in of *Mother Hubberds Tale*," *Spenser Studies* 17 (2003): 297–300.

51.   Nashe, *Works*, I: 243–44.

52.   Nashe, *Works*, II: 10.

53.   W. J. Ong, "The Writer's Audience Is Always a Fiction," *PMLA* 90 (1975): 9–21, 18.

54.   For the centrality of paratexts see Randall Anderson, "The Rhetoric of Paratext" in *The Cambridge History of the Book in Britain*, vol. IV (1557–1695), ed. John Barnard and D. F. McKenzie (Cambridge: Cambridge University Press, 2002), 174–188.

55.   Nashe, *Works*, III: 127. There appears to be some confusion here, however, since Harvey seems to associate the epistle with the *Foure Letters* (1592), which contains no such preface.

56.   For Sidney's assessment of *The Shepheardes Calender* see *The Apology for Poetry* in *Elizabethan Critical Essays*, I: 196.

57.   The Areopagus is noticeably referred to as "their" rather than "our," and Daniel Rogers's near contemporary poem on the personal and literary associations

of himself, Sidney, Greville, and Dyer makes no mention of Spenser or Harvey. For Rogers's poem, see J. A. van Dorsten, *Poets, Patrons, and Professors: Sir Philip Sidney, Daniel Rogers, and the Leiden Humanists* (London: Oxford University Press for the Sir Thomas Browne Institute, 1962), 61–67.

58.   Horace, *Odes and Epodes*, ed. and trans. C. E. Bennett, rev. ed. (Loeb Classical Library, 1968), 314.

59.   Horace, *Odes and Epodes*, 258.

60.   Horace, *Satires, Epistles and Ars Poetica*, ed. and trans. R. H. Fairclough, rev. ed. (Loeb Classical Library, [1926; 1929]), 210.

61.   *Virgilii Maronis Opera cum doctissimis scholiis et annotationibus Pauli Manutii in margine ascriptis, illustrata* (London, 1570) 5. See also Bowditch, *Horace and the Gift Economy*, 125, 139, 144.

62.   *Edmund Spenser: The Shorter Poems*, 155–56, 574.

63.   *Suetonius*, II: 460–63.

64.   See generally Richard Rambuss, *Spenser's Secret Career* (Cambridge: Cambridge University Press, 1993), 25–48.

65.   See Alan Stewart, *Close Readers: Humanism and Sodomy in Early Modern England* (Princeton: Princeton University Press, 1997), 161–87.

66.   *The English Secretorie* (London, 1595), 111–112. See the discussion in Stewart, *Close Readers*, 174–75.

67.   Richard S. Peterson, "Laurel Crown and Ape's Tail: New Light on Spenser's Career from Sir Thomas Tresham," *Spenser Studies* 12 (1991, but pub. 1998): 1–35, 8.

68.   For Ralegh's attitude to Spenser see James P. Bednarz, "The Collaborator as Thief: Ralegh's (Re)Vision of *The Faerie Queene*," *ELH* 63 (1996): 279–307.

69.   *The Poems of Sir Walter Ralegh*, ed. Agnes M. C. Latham (London: Constable, 1929), 80, 88.

70.   See Jean R. Brink, "The Mask of the Nine Muses: Sir John Davies's Unpublished 'Epithalamion' and the 'Belphoebe-Ruby' Episode in *The Faerie Queene*," *RES* 23 (1972): 445–47.

71.   *The Discoverie of the Large, Rich and Bewtiful Empyre of Guiana*, ed. Neil L. Whithead (Manchester: Manchester University Press, 1997), 123, 198.

72.   Hatfield, Cecil MS 36/4. Cited in NDNB.

73.   *Discoverie*, 121.

74.   *Discoverie*, 196. For Ralegh's use of the vocabulary of love to sublimate issues of patronage, see Leonard Tennenhouse, "Sir Walter Ralegh and the Literature of Clientage," in *Patronage in the Renaissance*, 235–59, 246.

75.   For this relationship, see Conyers Read, *Mr. Secretary Cecil and Queen Elizabeth* (London: Jonathan Cape, 1955) and *Lord Burghley and Queen Elizabeth* (London: Jonathan Cape, 1960).

76.   For this metaphor see Stewart, *Close Readers*, 176–80, 176.

77.   *Suetonius*, II: 462.

78.   Horace, *Satires, Epistles and Ars Poetica*, 396.

79.   See Natalie Mears, "*Regnum Cecilianum*? A Cecilian Perspective of the Court," in *The Reign of Elizabeth I: Court and Culture in the Last Decade*, 46–64.

JAMES M. NOHRNBERG

Alençon's Dream/Dido's Tomb: Some Shakespearean Music and a Spenserian Muse

The essay visits Spenser's poetical fictions for some themes of Elizabethan marital politics and the dialectic of Accession and Succession: as they might be refashioned and refigured in Shakespeare's epithalamic *A Midsummer Night's Dream*, with its dialectic of Nature and Culture. Malecasta's court and the contretemps during Britomart's adventure there are compared to the shenanigans at the court of Elizabeth's rival the Queen of Scots and the Northern rebellion, and Busirane's tyranny over Amoret is compared to Queen Elizabeth's anxieties over the French marriage. Received identifications of Braggadocchio and Trompart with Alençon and Simier, in their assault on Belphoebe (and of the fox and ape in their assault on the sleeping lion), are applied to the liaison of Bottom and Titania. And the virtual kidnapping of Shakespeare's Indian boy by the dramatist's royal fairies is read as an allusion to the dynastic replacement of the Tudors on the English throne by the Scottish Stuart known as the Cradle King.

> You that with allegorie's curious frame,
> Of other's children changelings use to make,
> With me those paines, for God's sake, do not take;
> I list not dig so deepe for brazen fame.
> —Sir Philip Sidney, *Astrophil and Stella* 28

*W*hy, in Shakespeare's *Macbeth*, does the succession of Duncan's son Malcolm to the Scottish throne result in the latter-day offspring of Banquo's son Fleance becoming kings? The play's central scene has

Spenser Studies: A Renaissance Poetry Annual, Volume XXII, Copyright © 2007 by AMS Press, Inc. All rights reserved.

Macbeth hallucinating Banquo's ghost on the bench (banquette) once occupied by the murdered Duncan, since the witches have predicted that Banquo's progeny will inherit the seat in question. But since the play's action enthrones Malcolm in Fleance's place, Shakespeare obliquely asks why the royal heir of Elizabeth's dead rival, the Queen of Scots—a.k.a. Spenser's Duessa—occupied the English throne.[1] "Lineally extract" from neither Shakespeare's English queen nor Spenser's Elvish one, Elizabeth's successor was nonetheless provided to her people by a genealogical substitution that turned Scotland's James VI into England's James I. Such topical allusions in familiar and apparently complementary texts of Shakespeare and Spenser are a means to elicit a poetically enriched account of the various dynastic designs that had the English monarchy as their cynosure. In the following essay we equate an exchange between sovereignties with comparable literary-allegorical translations and transfers that also work among themselves: transmutatively.

I. COLIN CLOUT CELEBRATES THE SHEPHERDS' ELIZA: ACCESSION AND SUCCESSION AS MONARCHIC AND CAREERIST DIALECTIC IN THE CALENDER

Elizabeth's reign takes its Janus-like structure from the two occasions legitimatizing any royal's occupation of the throne: accession and succession. Thus, the two lyric highpoints in Spenser's *Shepheardes Calender* are the months framing the warmer part of the English year, "April" (just after the first month of the old style calendar) and "November" (just before the last month of the new style calendar). In "April" the celebrated Elisa is the daughter of "Pan the shepheards God," in "November" the mourned Dido is "the great shepeherde his daughter." E. K. explains the second sire as "some man of high degree, and not as some vainly suppose God-Pan," this revealing the great one is the same Henry VIII who fathered Elisa nine months earlier, in an analogous gloss to "April" ("Pan is here meant the most famous and victorious King, her highnesse Father, late of worthy memorye K. Henry the eyght").[2] "Elisa" would become the last and greatest of the five Tudor monarchs, the heir to all their ages, and Spenser, the prince of poets in his time, his monarch's Virgil. Thus we can explain Elizabeth's funeral in "November" by means of the eulogized, apotheosized queen who succeeds to the lamented, deceased one. Tying his career to that of his prince at both ends, Colin has spoken prophetically indeed, if Belphoebe is born in "April" and Gloriana pre-enshrined in "November." The debut and the canonization of the queen boldly announce the poet's own.

Where Colin aspires to secure early, earthly honors for Elisa in "April," his Dido posthumously succeeds to equivalent heavenly ones in "November": for unless Elizabeth married there would be no Tudor successor reigning over the English. Lynn Staley Johnson observes that "April" decks out Elisa not only as the virgin princess, but also Canticles' bride.[3] But "April" may also pre-offer a floral tribute for the Virgin Queen's bier, as the "ensample dead" Spenser celebrates Belphoebe as, just before his Garden of Adonis canto, where seed sown in the "genial bed" is "by succession made perpetuall" (FQ III.v.54, vi.47).[4] Thus "April" is potentially elegiac, while "November"—which prematurely (or preemptively) mourns the queen, or her virginity, patronage, or death—is potentially epithalamic: Elizabeth's coronation day was celebrated in November.[5] The elegy's defunctive music celebrates a funeral that must bring on a succession, yet also its subject's own accession to the thrones of heaven: conveyance to those fields bearing her "Elisian" name, where the shepherds' erstwhile earthly "saynt" "raignes a goddess now emong the saints" that are heavenly (175–76).

Dido in "November" is the noble, civic, royal, and maritally chaste queen of one strand of a tradition recently elicited by Deanne Williams, writing on Marlowe's play.[6] The other strand made Dido the slave of violent and destructive passions. Marlowe's argument is perhaps deliberately and topically premonitory: the noble and devoted Dido's collapses into her unchaste and maddened other when she takes a foreigner for a lover and tragically destroys herself. Thus Colin's verse mourning and celebrating "Dido" might also lament the failure of a queen who could have kept her faith—or exorcise an ignoble ruler who, marrying away her heritage, would dissipate Colin's tribute to her persona Elisa in "April."

If "November" celebrates the apotheosis of a childless maid— "Dido the great shepehearde his daughter [. . .]:/The fayrest May she was that euer wente,/ Her like shee has not left behind" (38–40)—it may also lament the demise of a virgin's eligibility for matrimony, the making of a mother. "November," as Paul McLane explained, can fore-lament the death of the civic Dido, should she end her singularity by marrying an attractive foreign prince, namely the Duc d'Alençon.[7] But the eventual unmaking of Elizabeth's match, upon the "French Marriage" plans' miscarrying, confirmed the queen would die a virgin, sharing neither bed nor throne with a Catholic or Frenchman. E. K. reports that "November" imitates Marot's eclogue mourning the death of the French queen Louise. In allegorical mirror-speech, Marot's pastoral persona might enshrine a French suit to espouse a sainted English Elisa, while a more Skeltonic Colin would simultaneously decry the suit's result as mortal or fatal.[8] Balancing his "November" lyric with his "April" one internally, Spenser's Colin treats the celebrated Dido's apotheosis as weightily as the lamentable/lamented one's decease. "Dido" is bewept by domestic animals (citizens) and bewailed by wild ones (nobles), "[e]xcept the Wolues": because, upon the demise of the Protestants' protector, Catholic priests (or Jesuits) would likelier rejoice than grieve. But if "November" laments the demise of the queen's Protestantism through marriage to a Catholic, it may also celebrate the demise of the French marriage as making for the rehabilitation or apotheosis of the queen's English virginity or political integrity.

"November" treats its topical matter obliquely, for the accession and succession were polarized precisely by the amount of publicity they were allowed to generate: the country was enjoined to celebrate the accession every year, while ignoring the succession every day. Roy Strong proposes that the annual celebrations were initiated by Thomas Cooper in Oxford around 1570.[9] If those celebrations are thus to be tied to the suppression of the Northern rebellion in the fall of 1569, as might appear from the dates, it follows that the exclusion of Mary Stuart from the Succession is their secret burden—if not indeed their original occasion. Mary is, so to speak, the wrong Dido, and the unsucceeding one. Yet she was the one who had issue.

II. BRITOMART'S BEDMATE: THE DYNASTIC DUESSA

In the first canto of Book III of *The Faerie Queene* Gardante manages to wound Britomart with a glancing love-shaft that betokens something like the onset of the menses; in the last canto Busirane does a similar thing with a circumcising blade that draws the blood denoting the maiden's biological readiness for maternity. The second wound indicates Britomart's vicarious participation in Amoret's impending defloration in the nuptial bed. But the nocturnal, erotic experience of Britomart in the opening and closing cantos of Book III also bookends the narrative with an analogy between the two major events in Elizabeth's reign involving marital politics. The first was the suppression of the Northern rebellion sponsored by the duke of Norfolk, which re-secured Elizabeth's accession, as observed annually in poetical and dramatic tributes featuring mythography like that of "April."

The second was the queen's protracted but unfulfilled engagement to marry Alençon; had she proved fertile, this match could have secured the succession. Britomart bleeds cyclically, and she expects to bear children (note her "bleeding bowels" at *FQ* III.ii.39, and compare Amoret's "riven bowels" at xii.38), but in "November" "the greate shephearde his daughter [. . .] *Her like* has not left behinde." — No issue.

Britomart's narrative begins at Malecasta's castle, where the martial British virgin is greatly troubled by a lascivious lady whom the rubric doubles with a discomfited Duessa: "Duessa's traines and Malecastaes/champions are defaced." The Scottish queen is identified with Duessa at the two key scenes of judgment on her in *The Faerie Queene*: her unveiling in Book I and her conviction in Book V. They are virtually the same scene, since Arthur's exposure of Duessa's baldness in Book I reveals her as the malefactor Artegall sentences to death in Book V—the headsman lifted Mary's severed head by the hair, and was left holding only her shaved head's wig. Few readers, however, trouble with the rubric's leaguing of Malecasta's gang with Duessa's designs, because the imposter's name never appears in Book III's text again. At the opening of Spenser's second installment and Book IV, Duessa returns as the fellow-traveler of the False Florimell and Ate; they and their paramours have replaced Malecasta and her cadre of champions (and the chaste/chased Florimell) in the same canto of Book III. Ate is the "mother of debate/And all dissention" (IV.i.19), and Elizabeth's reign virtually re-began with her triumph over "the daughter of debate," in the words of the queen's own poem on the defeat of the Northern rebellion and the scotching of Norfolk's intrigue: Norfolk planned to wed the Queen of Scots himself. Elizabeth warned her cousin of her duty of bringing the murderers of Mary's husband Darnley to justice, after having perhaps contrived in the marriage herself—and then disowning it. But the wayward woman had instead wed the principal conspirator Bothwell. Thereafter she became the ambitious Norfolk's object; his schemes threatened the destruction of the precarious union of England itself.

But why read Malecasta's Duessan approaches to Britomart's bed politically as well as sexually? At the start of her reign Elizabeth received marriage proposals from various ambitious European dynasts and would-be dynasts. If Britomart is tempted to be like Malecasta politically, rather than merely to favor or like her socially, or follow her lead sexually, she would still be drawn towards operating like Mary Stuart. Mary was a marriageable female sovereign like Elizabeth, but in her own way: thanks to the successive demises of three husbands. Duessa's avatar in Revelation says "I am no widow," and

Mary wasn't one for long: like the adulterously inclined Malecasta, she kept bringing lovers into her bedroom. Since Malecasta molests Britomart's sleep with echoes of both Ovid's incestuous Myrrha and the *Ciris*'s love-smitten Scylla approaching their fathers' beds, and of Britomart tossing in bed with her nurse (after entering her father's closet and before approaching Merlin's cave), Malecasta and Brito-mart *each* appear in "the mirrours more than one" in Book III's proem (5).[10]

"Mirror, mirror, on the wall,/Who's the fairest of them all?" — Elizabeth put the question to the Scottish ambassador; Sir James Melville's *Historic Memoirs* reports her having tried very hard to betray him into saying "which of the [two] women was the fairer one. 'You are the fairest Queen in England,' [Melville] answered diplomatically, 'and ours is the fairest in Scotland.' "[11] Confronted by Malecasta's champions, Britomart will solve an analogous conundrum quite as diplomatically:

> Then spake one of those sixe, There dwelleth here
>   Within this castle wall a Ladie Faire,
>   Whose soueraine beautie hath no liuing pere,
>   Thereto so bounteous and so debonaire,
>   That neuer any mote with her compaire.
>
> (*FQ* III.i.26)

— Just what Elizabeth was intensely curious and insecure about, the celebrated beauty of her royal rival in Scotland. The stanza then suggests the adoration that Elizabeth, like the "Ladie faire," compelled from her own courtiers, especially bachelors:

> She hath ordained this law, which we approue,
>   That euery knight, which doth this way repaire,
>   In case he haue no Ladie, nor no loue,
> Shall doe vnto her seruice neuer to remoue.
>
> (*FQ* III.i.26)

Malecasta is the reward for a knight's defeating her champions; successfully defending his lady's beauty, a knight forfeits his fidelity. In reply, Britomart's gender-dissembling riddle finesses the Duessan catch-22:

Loue haue I sure, (quoth she) *but Lady none*;
Yet will I not from mine owne loue remoue,
Ne to your Lady will I seruice done,
But wreake your wrongs wrought to this knight alone,
And proue his cause.

                                                    (*FQ* III.i.28)

Merlin's incubus-impregnated mother was "a faire ladie Nonne" (III.iii.13), "but Lady none."

But why bring sexual types for the two ladies into the same bedroom and under the same sheets in Book III, versus bringing political types for the two queens into the same courtroom in Book V? — Partly because Redcrosse in disarray seconds the assaulted Britomart: he is unprepared because the Northern rebels plotting to put a Catholic queen on England's throne quickly adopted the restoration of the Old Religion as their pretext and justification. Britomart vindicates Redcrosse's "cause," loyalty to Una: an Englishman's faith in a national church headed by a Protestant sovereign devoted to its unity ("alone" = "all one"). Duessa puts her hand in for the Englishman's at the end of Book I, alluding to Mary's political ambitions in despite of the triumph of Protestantism in the English Church and the likely failure of the Counter-Reformation in Elizabeth's England—Archimago's reintroduction of Duessa in Book II doesn't get very far, though her gallivanting about with adulterous Paridell and fickle Blandamour in Book IV is eventually applied to Mary's proclivities on Scotland's throne at Duessa's trial in Book V.

What "Duessa" might be up to in the guise of Britomart's hostess in Book III concerns not only Elizabeth's sexual and religious ambivalence, but also her marital situation. The queen was much in love with her long-time friend Robert Dudley, and suddenly his wife died. Four days before the fatal accident's removing the impediment, Elizabeth told the Spanish Ambassador that Mrs. Dudley was as good as dead already. The new widower, however, was no mate for the queen—quite the contrary. The British sovereign could hardly marry an alleged wife-murderer:

[. . .] Elizabeth and Mary [. . .] both had to face a similar situation. A lover whose partner — in Elizabeth's case a wife [Dudley's], in Mary's a husband [Darnley] — must be eliminated in order to make marriage possible. [In contemporary opinion]

[b]oth [women] were besmirched by the crime of murder. Either could have been guilty of complicity. And this rocked the thrones of both [queens]. Their different methods of dealing with a similar situation give a revealing indication of their characters. [. . .] Newly come to the throne at the time, Elizabeth was in dire danger of losing it and wise enough to realize this, for whether [Mrs. Dudley's] death was due to accident, suicide or murder made little difference to the Queen's position. [. . .] The Queen knew that she must act with the utmost caution, and she did. She gave up all idea of marrying Dudley, because to have done so could have been construed as an admission of guilt. [. . .] Mary showed no such political wisdom. She married the murderer [Bothwell], and so brought down on herself the terrible years of retribution. [12]

Mrs. Dudley's demise effectively committed Elizabeth to a lifelong union with her virginity.

And what was the queen to do with her favorite, "Robin"? — Make him an earl in front of the Scottish ambassador, while offering to marry him to Mary Stuart. Why give away her own favorite? — So Mary, in avoiding the offer, would be driven into the arms of a rival candidate, the young Darnley? Elizabeth herself saw something in him—but perhaps guessed he would be a disastrous consort. If such machinations are the invisible strings controlling the principals in Britomart's first night out, Malecasta could represent "Evil Incest" because "[r]umours were set in motion by the Queen [of Scot]'s enemies that [she] was a wanton woman who had had many lovers, the Cardinal of Lorraine, Chastelard and Rizzio being but a few of them. It was said that she was Darnley's mistress already and that she was insatiable in her sexual desires [. . .]. Opposition only increased Mary's determination to marry Darnley as soon as possible, and although a dispensation from the Pope was necessary because of the blood relationship between the two, she would not even wait for this."[13] She married while still dressed in mourning for her last husband. And when the new mate was murdered "in house," probably with her collusion, she succumbed to a man assumed to be among the conspirators. Mary lost much of her moral innocence, but retained her political naïveté to the end.

Malecasta's misguided motions are in Mary's unhappy style. Politically, Mary seems never to have quite understood whom she was getting into bed with. If Elizabeth also had her swains, it was virtuously, virtually, and vicariously: in contrast to Mary, she retained her sexual virginity to the end, as opposed to her political naïveté. The latter was early disposed of: in the Tower. From imprisonment there Elizabeth successfully denied charges of treasonously contriving to overthrow her Catholic half-sister; Mary Stuart proved unable to refute like charges regarding her Protestant cousin. Elizabeth left the Tower in one piece; Mary ended up a prisoner in Fotheringhay, and was decapitated. Duessa enters Book I and beweeps the faith's demise with crocodile tears (ii.22 with v.17–18); Mercilla leaves Book V beweeping Duessa's demise with tears equally suspect (ix.50): the throne of Britomart's divine patroness, Isis, harbors a crocodile.

At Malecasta's castle, Britomart accommodates castle custom, as Elizabeth dealt with the importunities of marriage. Unlike Mary Stuart, she had no laddie, nor a succession of them, but she would requite the wrongs to chastity in her loyalty to singularity and enmity to lust, and prove her country's cause. She did not fear Malecasta's six champions: even if Darnley might have had a glancing interest for her, and Dudley much more than that, the result of any such males' amorous glances was a comparatively superficial scratch. Mary, in contrast, was not the Dido who maintained a lifelong integrity and faith with her people, but the one forced into liaisons that tended to her and her people's destruction.

Since they both reflect Ovid's Myrrha, Britomart has a double in Malecasta, and each can stand for one of the queens. Malecasta's unchaste castle can refer to Mary Stuart's: Princess Mary was the daughter of Marie de Guise, and Malecasta's great chamber displays rich French tapestries—"costly clothes of *Arras* and of *Toure*"—and its "sumptuous *guise*" dissimulates a "Princes place": furnished in "the antique worlds guise" with many couches (III.i.32, 34, 33, 39). The luxurious Malecasta is ensconced on a "sumptuous bed" (41). Approaching Britomart's "bowre," she is covered with a "scarlot mantle / That was with gold and Ermines faire enveloped" (st. 60, 59): these "traines" are the trademark colors and garments of royalty (see "April," 57–58, "Yclad in Scarlot like a mayden Queene, / And Ermines white"), not the iconic ermines of chastity on Artegall's shield in Merlin's mirror (ii.25: emblematically mirroring Britomart's virtue, as the lion on her shield reflects Artegall's martial power [i.4; cf. Mercilla's enthroned lion at V.ix.33, with III.i.4]).

Among the Queen of Scot's most celebrated possessions were her French tapestries; wherever Mary went, the tapestries were sure to go. Construed as Mary Stuart's royal apartment, Malecasta's hall, with its "superflous riotize" (III.i.33) and its tragic Adonis tapestry, might well host the masque that issued in the Chastelard incident. The French courtier-poet was enamored of the Queen, and the evening's performance fatally emboldening him featured eight ladies dressed as men, and eight men dressed as ladies. Chastelard's masque-partner proved to be Mary herself, from whom as her lady he extracted a kiss: "So did she steale his heedelesse hart away" (III.i.37). At bedtime he concealed himself in her room but attendants discovered and prevented him. He tried again later, and Mary's call for help brought to her side her Protestant half-brother James. The arrested intruder's "defense was that he had acted foolishly on the first occasion and on the second he had come to the Queen's chamber to ask her forgiveness," but he was sentenced to die.[14] John Knox rejoiced in such scandals; they became commonplaces in Protestant diatribe against Mary's court and religion. Elizabeth favored the dynastic principles that brought both her and Mary to their respective thrones, but Cecil and his agent Walsingham only favored them when they kept a Protestant in power; thus Redcrosse's makeshift defense of Britomart in Book III hardens into Zeal's unrelenting prosecution of Duessa in Book V.

III. Entertaining the Offered Fantasy: The Suit of
Monsieur in Spenser and Shakespeare

The wound to Britomart's bodily integrity in the first canto of Book III recurs in the last. If the first episode suggests life in the court of Elizabeth's promiscuous rival Mary Stuart, the last may suggest her own enchantment with the Duc d'Alençon, by way of Britomart's resolve to relieve the distressed Scudamour, stymied champion of Cupid as depicted on his shield, and lover of Amoret whose heart is pierced by the dart that arms that Cupid. Elizabeth was also smitten, and moreover in conjunction with the celebration of her accession, when the Duc d'Alençon, otherwise duke of Anjou, was (for a second time) Elizabeth's guest:

> He was received with the greatest curtesie he could hope for, and no arguments there were of honour and love which shee did not shew him to the full. In so much as in the moneth of November, as soone as shee had with great pompe celebrated her coronation day, the force of modest love amongst amorous talke carried her so farre that shee drew off a ring from her finger and put it upon the Duke of Anjou's, upon certaine

conditions betwixt them two. The standers by tooke it that the marriage was now contracted by promise [. . .].[15]

The "November" fatality perpends.

In the second canto's "prequel" to the narrative begun in Canto i of Book III, Britomart has discovered her own "stout" lover in the rotundity of a global mirror that she finds in her father's wardrobe, as if Elizabeth were finding her image as a sovereign in Holbein's famous painting of the overdressed and bejeweled Tudor monarch who was her sire. While it would not do for her to be married to her philandering parent, armchair psychologists will nonetheless guess that Elizabeth idolized him; and she could join with him only by retaining her virginity while uniting herself with the ideal of power and authority he embodied and symbolized for her. Given such competition, Alençon hardly stood a chance.

The queen may have surrendered her heart to Monsieur, but she kept a firm grip on her father's scepter. She was not going to hand her title over to a Frenchman (the adventurer Bothwell, in contrast, had virtually ordered Mary Stuart to make him king). Elizabeth had denied herself marriage with either subject or stranger, yet expected to retain the attentions of her devotion-professing courtiers, as if they were engaged to the throne, not married to their wives. The court rejected the Alençon suit, the last formal courtship Elizabeth entertained. Any possibility of the match ended with Alençon's death, in the queen's fifty-first year. The chances are, Elizabeth now knew herself past childbearing. In 1579, when the dalliance began, she at 46 was twice her suitor's age, but it had been communicated to the French that she was still able to have children.

Alençon's suit is found in *Mother Hubberds Tale*, where the fox and the ape are adventurers and opportunists chronically on the make, like Braggadocchio and Trompart in *The Faerie Queene*: courtiers in search of the ultimate in courtly preferment. Elizabeth called Simier, the duke's envoy, her ape (Lat. *simia*); Alençon himself she called her frog. While Burghley can be the fox, manipulating any royal match to his own advantage and successfully promoting his candidate, Reynaldo can be the frog if there is room for a bilingual pun on the Latin *ranis* and Reynaldo, which the fox is called six times. Reynaldo plots to steal the skin of the sleeping lion, with the fearful ape effecting the design. Elizabeth flirted indecorously with the Frenchman, and allowed Simier—the Master of Alençon's Wardrobe—to raid her bedchamber and filch her nightcap as a love token.[16]

In the view of the present essay, Spenser's "April" and "November" are analogized not only generically—like Shakespeare's *Midsummer Night's Dream* and *Romeo and Juliet*—but also symbolically: like the erotic flower "of [. . .] purple dye" in *Midsummer Night's Dream* (III.ii.102) and the elegiac one in the Ovidian story of Pyramus and Thisbe (where "The blood out of the wounde as brode sterte / As water whan the conduyt broken is" [Chaucer, *Legend of Thisbe*, 850–51].) The arching path of the arrow that empurples Shakespeare's erotic flower is like that of the spurting blood that dyes Ovid's elegiac mulberry and Thisbe's nightgown the same color, when Thisbe is "deflowered" (as Pyramus reports [*MND* V.i.287]) by the lion—and as Elizabeth would also have been, had she taken a mate with pretensions to Hercules' lionskin.

That Shakespeare's epithalamic play refers extensively to the queen's long-proposed French marriage—the decade-late allusion being recognizable partly because of Spenser's own belated allegories for it—is a notion fully developed in Marion Taylor's book, *Bottom, Thou Art Translated* (1975).[17] Spenser's Gloriana has visited the sleeping Arthur, whose sleep is characterized by an echo from its original in Chaucer's Sir Thopas, just before Chaucer quits his tale—his helmet was his pillow—but Arthur's suit for Gloriana becomes as fruitless a dream as that of Sir Thopas. Applying this Spenserian key to its Shakespearean lock releases a full-fledged allegorical allusion that translates the playwright's central fantasy into Elizabeth's marital politics.

Taylor's demonstration starts from Peele's and Sidney's topical drama, and bypasses Spenser's House of Busirane. But Spenser's championess of chastity is also brought upon the theatrical scene of her capacity for love or commitment, and this lonely vigil may be compared to the sleepless night of Elizabeth, who commented in a well-known poem on her love-life, "I dote, but dare not what I meant; [. . .] I am, and am not [. . .] Since from myself my other self I turn." This dotage was Elizabeth's infatuation with Le Duc; the dotard's divided person is Elizabeth as private mistress or public paragon:

She told the French Ambassador he could write to Paris with the news 'the Duke of Alençon shall be my husband', and then turning to her suitor 'kissed him on the mouth, drawing a ring from her own hand and giving it to him as pledge', while Alençon gave her a ring of his in return. [. . .] The story goes that the same evening her ladies [. . .] 'wailed and by laying terrors before her did so vex her mind with argument' against marriage that she had a sleepless night. The following morning she sent for the Duke and told him that two more such nights and she would be in the grave, but in the long silent watches, torn between her duty as a Queen and her feelings as a woman, she had decided to sacrifice her own happiness for the welfare of her people [. . .].[18]

Neville Williams's account is based on Camden for 1581. Its telling gloss on Britomart's vigil at the House of Busirane reminds us that Britomart can do for Amoret what she cannot do for herself: consummate a marriage contract. Britomart is vulnerable, but not devirginated; the fiancée dotes, but the sovereign turns from what she dotes upon.

IV. DYNASTICS, EROTICS, AND POETICS: PLUMBING BOTTOM'S DREAM

In Shakespeare's play the equivalent fantasy for the ape and fox's royal endowment is Bottom's dream; it hath no Bottom in it, but in Bottom's place it has an ass. Similarly, in the passage quoted below, Puck saw no Cupid, because in Cupid's place is the knavish enchanter Puck. Entertaining the enchanted buffoon, the enchanted Titania both encourages and infantilizes him, but it would hardly do for her to marry the gross and hairy fellow, who may have some of the proclivities, as perhaps the shape, of Elizabeth's lustful progenitor; but he's not the Oberon to whom she's joined dynastically. Yet in the fairy chronicle in Spenser's Book II, "Oberon" stands for Henry VIII (FQ II.x.75–76). Bottom is king-for-a-night or knight-for-a-queen, and in the amour one recognizes the foolish pretensions of the Alençon suit. In Peele's Endymion, on related marital themes, Cynthia arranges a lesser marriage for the enchanted Sir Tophas, a buffoonish Braggadocchio type. In history, however, Elizabeth arranged for Alençon's severance gift and war-loan, and sent him packing.

There are two queens in Shakespeare's play: the fairy Titania and her human counterpart the Amazon Hippolyta. Titania is mated with Oberon, with whom she quarrels; Hippolyta is engaged to marry Theseus, with whom the Amazons have fought. Hippolyta has lost the war, but perhaps won the battle to preserve her own royal status by making a marriage of political convenience—one way of seeing Elizabeth's devotion to her virginity and her people. Elizabeth's "Oberon" was England or Albion, the corporation to whom she was virtually wedded from her accession.

Theseus's re-commissioning of Shakespeare's play, from within, rejects Spenser's embittered Muse in favor of the "tedious brief scene" of Pyramus and Thisbe (*MND* V.i.56). Yet the matrimonial music for which a Spenserian Muse might stand remains notably present, if marital eligibility is a main motif in *The Faerie Queene*, and likewise, as in the *Epithalamion*, propitious timing of nuptials. Shakespeare's play also knows the inspired devices of entertainments like those at Kenilworth, where a statue of a mermaid on a dolphin sang in a pool. Oberon once sat on a promontory and heard such a mermaid singing so sweetly she calmed the waters: while also precipitating astral fireworks. The Queen of Scots is possibly betokened by the mermaid, as may be Rizzio's and Darnley's deaths by the fireworks.[19] But while the mermaid as Siren and love-in-idleness as sex might draw eyes to Mary Stuart, Cupid had also shot off proposals to Miss Tudor. Titania's erotic vulnerability, however, is averted by the "imperial vot'ress [. . .]/In maiden meditation, fancy-free"—the young Elizabeth who had translated *A godly meditation of the soule*.[20]

Sanguinary effects comparable to those Britomart suffers recur when Oberon tells Puck about witnessing a theater-like spectacle in the mundane sphere:

> That very time I saw, but thou couldst not,
> Flying between the cold moon and the earth,
> Cupid all armed. A certain aim he took
> At a fair vestal thronèd by the west,
> And loosed his love shaft smartly form his bow,
> As it should pierce a hundred thousand hearts.
> But I might see young Cupid's fiery shaft
> Quenched in the chaste beams of the wat'ry moon,
> And the imperial vot'ress passèd on,
> In maiden meditation, fancy-free.
> Yet marked I where the bolt of Cupid fell.
> It fell upon a little western flower,
> Before milk-white, now purple with love's wound,
> And maidens call it love-in-idleness.

(*MND* II.i.155–68)

Oberon's agent Puck doesn't see his own knavish and folkish activity as the cosmos's supernatural machinery. Love is blind, therefore Puck does not see himself as Cupid, any more than the self-centered, self-pleasing lovers contemplate their own foolishness.

The play-as-masque begins from the commissioning of entertainment for royal nuptials and ends with the blessing of the bridal chamber: therefore the symbolic flower is potentially hymeneal. The passage implies the vulnerable but Diana-esque English queen might have entertained a marriage-suit favorably, but wisely thought better of granting it; instead she deferred it. Spenser's romance abounds in delayed or unconsummated nuptials, and Shakespeare's play begins from the waning of an old moon lingering Theseus's desires, "Like to a stepdame or a dowager/Long withering out a young man's revenue" (*MND* I.i.4–6). The comparison attracts a double allegorical tenor, the long delayed Alençon match, or the future James I's accession—the stepdame being James's aging royal godmother Elizabeth. Moreover, James is another such vehicle's tenor, namely the changeling boy's.

The murder of David Rizzio in the chambers of the pregnant Scottish queen, with her husband Darnley present as one of the conspirators, took the scandal surrounding the Northern monarchy to new levels. James was latterly said to be as wise as Solomon, because David was his father. Yet Elizabeth once averred Mary was her likely successor, and she was one of James's godparents. When Mary was forced to abdicate, James at thirteen months was crowned Scotland's new monarch. He was called the Cradle King, and also a changeling, it being alleged Mary had miscarried at the time of Rizzio's murder and substituted another woman's child for her own. Yet it had Elizabeth's blessing.

While Theseus rejects for his evening's entertainment a piece apparently based on Spenser's *Teares of the Muses*, an earlier example of the tearful Muse is "November": "The gaudie girlonds deck her graue, [. . .]/Morne nowe my Muse, now morne with teares besprint./O carefull verse" (109–12). This Muse sheds tears over Dido, or Dido's tomb. In the *Aeneid* itself it is only Dido's pyre: in Shakespeare's play, it is something for star-crossed lovers to exchange vows by. Thus Hermia and Lysander plan to elope:

Hermia.   My good Lysander,
I swear to thee, by Cupid's strongest bow,
By his best arrow with the golden head,
By the simplicity of Venus' doves,

By that which knitteth souls and prospers loves,
And by that fire which burned the Carthage queen,
When all the vows that ever men have broke,
In number more than ever women spoke,
In that same place thou hast appointed me,
Tomorrow truly will I meet with thee.

(I.i.169–78)

The play's actual site of disappointed rendezvous is the one where
Pyramus and Thisby swear to meet: in place of Dido's pyre—or
Juliet's bier—"Ninny's" or "Ninus' tomb" is four times cited.

At King Ninus's grave, Chaucer's Pyramus apostrophizes the missing Thisbe:

Allas, to bidde a woman goon by nyghte
In place theras peril fallen myghte,
And I so slowe! Allas I ne hadde be
Here in this place a furlongwey or ye!

(*Legend of Thisbe*, 838–41)

Thus lovers' commitments fall under the shadow of missed chances
for love—torch-bearing Romeo coming upon the comatose Juliet,
passionate Pyramus coming upon the bloodied relictae of the fugitive
Thisbe, cold-hearted Aeneas parting from Dido going up in flames,
and Cupid's erotic arrow doused by the icy virgin enthroned in the
west. The lovers are in effect engaged for eternity by the defaulted
assignations in time.

It is Puck as Cupid who drives girls mad—and makes them err,
even as he causes Titania to dote on a rude mechanical. Yet Bottom
speaks with a surprisingly deft and gentle tongue when addressing
Mustardseed, Peaseblossom, Cobweb, and Moth—Titania's sounding
of these names translates the roll call of Quince's cast, Bottom, Flute,
Robin, and Snug (Snout is omitted). The fairies are assigned to cosset
and attend an ass: feast him with apricots, berries, and honey; light his
progress with torches; fan him with wings; treat him with ingratiating
courtesies (III.i.159–69). The favor dissimulates the mismatch it reveals: all Bottom wants is dry oats, or hay and dried peas. The fairy
offices are lost on him—yet found in translation: cobwebs for styptic,
mustardseed for greens and fodder, blossoms for squash and pea production, and moths for not much of anything: pure ephemera of the
night, yet pollinating those flowers that open in the dark.

Bottom could play his part as Pyramus in an "orange-tawny beard" (I.ii.85); as a lover he describes "The ouzel cock so black of hue,/ With orange-tawny bill" (III.i.120–23). One of the Frenchmen in Alençon's crew was named Le Bec, "the beak," proportionable to Snout. For the forms Master and Mistress which Bottom uses in the fairies' first appearance get translated at their second: to Monsieur (for both Cobweb and Mustardseed)—the French king's brother's title is employed repeatedly, and moreover in an orthography peculiar to this usage.[21] In Chapman's two plays on his protégé Bussy D'Amboise, D'Alençon is Monsieur. Such a clue recurs in Bottom's readiness to play "Erecles." Both of Bottom's references to Erecles's part or vein (I.ii.25, 35) use the aspirated or French form of the name—the only cases in Shakespeare. Both Titania and Oberon have accompanied the real Hercules, and they use the typical Latin–English form of the name, as otherwise found throughout the canon. Alençon had been christened with the name Hercule. The lion-skin his Spenserian counterparts steal animadverts upon the pretentious name. Monsieur was actually a shrimp: Elizabeth's frog.

Titania's infatuation with the Hairy Fairy is ended by an herb causing not infatuation but disenchantment: the force of "Dian's bud o'er Cupid's flower" (IV.i.72), or Chastity over Promiscuity, Maidenhead over Womanhood, and the queen's actual Virginity or Celibacy over her potential for Matrimony or Maternity. Apart from the blind bowboy's ineffectiveness regarding sworn Vestals, and this antidote of Dian's bud, Cupid's operation certainly serves to make parties fall in love. But do they make a match? — That's the question. Regarding *biological* readiness, the answer starts from Flute: "Let me not play a woman. I have a beard coming" (I.ii.41). "Most brisky juvenal [bristly juvenile]," as Thisby says to Pyramus (III.i.90). Again, the prematurely dead corn—thanks to the discord among those nature spirits of the corn and wild who are its parents and original—"hath rotted ere its youth attained a beard" (II.i.117, 95), thus sharing its fate with Bion's perished Adonis. Undertaking the male lead in Quince's drama, Bottom expands the motif:

What beard were I best to play it in? [. . .] I will discharge it in either your straw-color beard, your orange-tawny beard, your purple-in-grain beard, or your French-crown-color beard, your perfit yellow.

(I.ii.81–87)

He shortly discovers his face is marvelously itchy. But only on awaking does he express awareness of the ass's head itself. This he ascribes to a dream; we attribute it to an unconscious monitoring of that change whereby boys and girls are translated into men and women: when they can reproduce themselves as infants in the cradle.

Some principal objections to the Alençon match were purely physical: the suitor's size, age, and complexion. He was too small, too immature, and too disfigured in his face. If the actor playing Bottom were Will Kemp, he would have been exceptionally small. But the negotiations over the candidate's face seem even more relevant, since Alençon's oversized nose and uncomely complexion were being treated like Bottom's ass's head. The French's go-between—La Mothe Fenelon—claimed first to Burleigh and then Elizabeth that Alençon's scars could be remedied by a physician in London who had accomplished such a cure twice already. But

> The Earl of Lincoln, on his arrival from Paris, spoke very favourably of the young prince, and settled the two great objections, that were constantly urged against the marriage, in an off-hand way, by saying, 'that his youth need not be any impediment, as he was growing older every day, and as for the scars of the small-pox, they were of no consequence, as he would soon have a beard to hide them.'[22]

The metamorphic alteration caused by puberty—the female flower ensanguined, the male countenance becoming hirsute—reappears in the mutual interference of alternate worlds, Puck intervening in the humans', Nick Bottom in the fairies'. Puck among mortals compares with Bottom among sprights: with Puck all experience is preposterous or fantastical; with Bottom the fantastic is just another experience. On this antithesis the play turns, yet the dream-bound Bottom sings the play's most delicate verses, and the mischievous Puck tricks Titania into the basis for its grossest jokes: about kissing uncouth things in the dark, lime and hair instead of "Limander." Bottom rises to Ariel's pitch in *The Tempest*; Puck sinks to the crudities of the Miller in Chaucer's *Tales* (where the pranks turn on God's eschatological secrets, a female's unexpected beard, and gaseous Nicholas's bottom).

The two operant forces here are Nature (rustic, like coupling), and Culture (refined, like courtship and marriage). The poet hybridizes them; each serves as a metaphor translating the other. Bottom is a product of Athenian society, but he is a natural, as much beast as man. Puck is a nature spirit, but practices jokes depending on culture, like yeast making cakes rise.

The means to natural reproduction is the "genial bed." Its genius is Puck, a four-letter word for the catalytic converter letting bread puff up, cream curdle, pots boil, and jokes and conceits go over: the last metaphorically significant on wedding night, in rising above an activity otherwise merely frictional, hydraulic, and glandular. Without the language of love, the physiology of congress could hardly be human at all. Culture is nature's changeling, or nature culture's. And this argues for the centrality—versus a marginal decorativeness—of the dispute over the changeling. He is translated, from human mother and royal father, to fairy godparents; and from Titania's parental surrogacy for her vot'ress, to Oberon's dynastic surrogacy as the Indian king. If the females are nature, the males are culture; if the humans are culture, the fairies are nature. Oberon claims the privileges of an early-rising forester, shortly before Theseus arrives on the woodland scene with a hunting party and twice summons the local forester. Theseus has been moonlighting as Oberon, now Hobgoblin turns back into Apollo.

How do the dialectical metaphorics—puberty and marriage, nature and culture, "her" and "me" (Hermia/Helena), nighttime fairy self and daytime mundane self—map onto the dynastic translations swirling around the royals and their objects? In *Mother Hubberds Tale* the two adventurers allegorically advancing the plans for the French marriage only manage to steal the lionskin thanks to the lion's shameful and unnatural sleep. This truancy the messenger Mercury uncovers and indicts:

At last he found, where sleeping he did ly:
The wicked weed, which there the Foxe did lay,
From vnderneath his head he tooke away,
And then him waking forced vp to rize.
The Lion looking vp gan him auize,
As one late in a traunce, what had of long
Become of him: for fantasie is strong.
Arise (said Mercurie) thou sluggish beast,
That here lies senseles, like the corpse deceast,
The whilest thy kingdome from thy head is rent,
And they throne royall with dishonour blent:
Arise, and doo thy self redeeme from shame,
And be aueng'd on those that breed thy blame.

(1320–32)

"The wicked weed" can be identified. Camden (*Annales*, 1579) reports that Spenser's patron "Leicester (who from his heart opposed the marriage) and others spred rumours abroad that by amorous potions and unlawfull arts (*phyltris et illicitis artibus*) hee [Simier] had crept into the Queenes mind and intised her to the love of Anjou [= Alençon]."

Awakening from his fantasy or trance, or a stupor deeper than common sleep, one resulting from contact with a narcotic, the king of the beasts discovers his lion-skin is missing: "Therewith he began full terribly to roar" (1337). Bottom, in the part of the lover Alençon, began by wanting to play the lion's part: "I will roar that I will do any man's heart good to hear; I will roar, that I will make the duke say 'Let him roar again, let him roar again' " (*MND* I.ii.64–67). But out of consideration for Athens's new duchess, Bottom changes his tune: "I will aggravate my voice so that I will roar you gently [. . .] and 'twere any nightingale" (I.ii.74–76). In *Mother Hubberds Tale* the lion roars his head off, at the discovery of the plot on his perquisites of power; nor does he moderate his rage until he has cleansed the royal house and reduced the fox to a whimper. Elizabeth certainly did not turn against the French match in complete fury, but the French crown's part in the St. Bartholomew's Day massacre did throw a large wrench into the earlier negotiations for it.

Bottom's delicate song about the birds shows he can turn a tyrant's stridency into a lover's dulcet tune. Quince's casting has some merit. Taylor suggests Quince's name is that of Alençon's agent Du Quincé, who made many of the arrangements for the staging of the Frenchman's courtship.[23] Shakespeare's audience, with Lysander, might observe the play's actual lion "is a very fox for his valor" (*MND* V.i.228), while Bottom commands the lion's share of the audience's attention. But Englishmen would have thought the "lion vile," as per Quince's script, if he is the French fox who would have "deflow'red [their] dear" Elizabeth in place of Thisbe (V.i.42, 287).

Elizabeth's court was full of courtiers who had offended Belphoebe, wounded or deflowered Amoret, and committed love-in-idleness with sometimes extramarital paramours. The court also entertained many courtiers who dreamed of making a royal match. Spenser's presumptuous ape and fox steal the lion's skin, and the self-pleased and self-Tromparting Braggadocchio appropriates both Arthur's sword and Guyon's mount: but the thieves are hardly allowed to steal the queen's glory or make her match. Where Spenser is sardonic, however, Shakespeare is sympathetic; for the author of the plays and the author of *The Faerie Queene* have unlike analyses of the sameness of the self and of humankind, and contrary opinions of the dignity of the commons. Thus the playwright's exceedingly self-pleased and self-taken Bottom and his gloriously unchivalric and vain-glorious Falstaff—the dramatic equivalents of Spenser's aspiring buffoons—are positively encouraged to steal their respective shows. The harsh trumpet that gives the sign of gory war in the *Aeneid* (XI, 474–75) resounds in the "trumpets sterne" that announce *The Faerie Queene*, while Shakespeare, like Prince Hal, was half in love with Vanity. England's Virgil certainly was not, but the Virgin Queen herself would ask to see Falstaff in love. Perhaps she already had.

V. AND A NEW HENCHMAN FOR OBERON-AS-ALBION

If the queen would not in fact be deflowered, the Tudor rose would die out; if she married Monsieur, the Protestant monarch would deeply compromise the integrity of her position as the head of the Anglican Church, and adulterate her figurative marriage to the English. And the popular cult of her virginity, her self-chosen singularity, would expire. Elizabeth might die politically (by marrying the wrong suitor) or dynastically (by failing to marry at all). She told Parliament she planned to marry only to have children. The Alençon match would have been critical to begetting an heir to the English throne. Parliament had urged the queen to produce a successor, or designate one. But it was better balance-of-power politics for her not to marry, and likewise the better part of political calculation not to settle the succession question—keep 'em guessing. (She'd been successor-designate herself and knew the perils from inside.) Discussion of the matter was made illegal. But people will talk, and the talk turned to James Stuart. James banned *The Faerie Queene* in Scotland because of the prosecutor Zeal's unsavory charges against his mother. Perhaps both acts of censorship favored his chances of succeeding in England.

The English queen's scotched maternity was compensated for by the Scottish king's English blood. Mary Stuart led troops in battle and in the fifth canto of Spenser's fifth book she figures as the embattled and enamored Amazon queen who seizes on Artegall. It may be that Shakespeare's fairies can only secure progeny by adoption, and the Amazons—those devoted to their unmarrying order—by bastardy.

Shakespeare's play casts two queens: one an Amazon, the other maternal. It cites two vot'resses; one a Vestal, the other pregnant.

The changeling boy is fairy in one context, human in the other. He is either the offspring of the Indian monarch, or the issue of Titania's vot'ress. In the "maternal" account, the mother died in childbirth: Titania has *adopted* the newborn of a human mother (as Titania avers herself). Or else she's *kidnapped* the seed of foreign royalty, as Oberon's servant Puck reports: this is the "paternal" account. Kidnapping is crossed with adoption. Oberon being the name of a legendary fairy royal in the East, it's as if the child were taken from an Eastern Oberon to be apprenticed to a Western monarch. Superimposing the two stories, we could say Titania kidnapped the son of a dead foreign royal and presented it to her people as the heir to Oberon's throne—or the Tudors's.

Embodying the archetypal custody battle, the child's origins correspond to the duality of all parentage: father-love vs. mother-right, as Malinowski would say. The Fairy King, like Henry VIII and Elizabeth's Parliament, wants a boy—a male heir. Give me a son, Oberon is saying to Titania, as "Albion" was saying to Elizabeth, Provide us a Prince. Hermia's father evidently has no son; he has chosen Demetrius, and threatens Hermia with a nunnery if she does not oblige him. Hermia's friendship with Helena, Titania's relation with her "vot'ress," and Hippolyta's status as an Amazon, challenge patriarchy's right to determine the female's fate as wife and mother, and conscript her womb for the purposes of patrilineal pedigree-making. But Titania finally submits, or delivers; after dallying with an inappropriate or taboo consort, she yields up the boy to become Oberon's henchman. Evidently besotted with her boy, she once calls him her squire (the father of Chaucer's Squire is the Knight whose *Tale* features Theseus). Bottom replaces Titania's boy, and she gets something out of her system. She surrenders the child to Oberon's care, as Elizabeth gave up on childbearing and left the determination of her successor to her people, in the menopausal juncture when she parted from Alençon. Comparably, Mary consented to abdicate in the knowledge that making James king in Scotland brought the Stuarts closer to becoming monarchs in England.

In the dynastics of Spenser's *Faerie Queene*, the lineage that leads up to Prince Arthur, in the archives of memory, can only be continued by means of the substitution of Artegall, in the prophecy of Merlin; analogously, the monarchy must substitute Stuarts for Tudors. Like the changeling's mother, Mary Stuart proved mortal, but she had a son who could become an Elvish king, or English Oberon. In the end of Mary's reign in Scotland was the beginning of her son's in England. A year after Alençon's death, Elizabeth began corresponding with James, the heir apparent to Scotland's throne. In the sudden development of their royal colleagueship and "contract of amity," James even addressed his correspondent as mother. Janel Mueller believes the words of the letters imply not only support for James's Scottish kingship, but also her promising him the English throne.[24]

Not only would people talk about the succession, they also dreamt of it: famously, through an article by Louis Montrose quoting the astrologer Simon Forman:

> I dreamt that I was with the Queen, and that she was a little elderly woman in a coarse white petticoat all unready [. . .] we came over a great close where there were many people, and there were two men at hard words. One of them was a weaver, a tall man with a reddish beard, distract of his wits. She talked to him and he spoke very merrily unto her, and at last did take her and kiss her. So I took her by the arm and did put her away; and told her the fellow was frantic. [. . .] She had a long, white smock very clean and fair, and it trailed in the dirt [. . .]. I told her she should do me a favour to let me wait on her, and she said I should. Then said I, 'I mean to wait *upon* you and not under you, that I might make this belly a little bigger to carry up this smock [. . .] out of the dirt.' And so we talked merrily; then she began [. . .] to be very familiar with me, and methought she began to love me. And when we were alone, out of sight, methought she would have kissed me.[25]

To judge by the dream's report, Bottom the weaver decided to play his part in the orange-tawny beard, not the French one. Contrary to the biological reality, the dreamer fantasizes an old lady with an advanced pregnancy, with either the weaver or the dreamer himself presenting the means to achieve it. But the conjunction is like Oberon's design for Lysander's memory of the night in the woods, or like the dynastics of Spenser's epic-romance, "a dream and fruitless vision" (*MND* III.ii.371); for Simon awakened before the queen could consummate their relation. A month later Forman dreamed of Elizabeth again, coming to him to "all in black, with a French hood."[26] That England would be widowed by the French marriage confirms the alleged conceit of "November."

Dreams allow us to go insane every night: it was a little crazy to imagine the old maid was fertile. But Shakespeare's play has shown

another way of conceiving the succession. While sitting on a promontory with Puck, Oberon observed the de-enamoring of "western"
Queen Elizabeth. Meanwhile the Amazon queen's fairy counterpart
Titania sat on a beach with other "vot'ress" reported in the play,
"Marking th' embarkèd traders on the flood" (*MND* II.i.127). This
woman "laughed to see the sails conceive/And grow big-bellied with
the wanton wind" (II.i.128–29), she herself being pregnant, in the
same way that the flower to which Cupid's glancing arrow is de-
flected is ensanguined with love's wound—a "western" flower one
could identify with it the rival Queen of Scots herself. India gets into
this because a fairy king named Oberon haled from India, and the
changeling boy's father is an Eastern version of Oberon himself. As
for the "embarkèd traders," the Indian air is "spicèd" (II.i.124) with
a whiff of the spice trade.[27] The Honorable Company of Merchants
and Traders to the East Indies (following on the Muscovy, Levant,
and Venice companies) is a-borning in a play about "trading places,"
as if "trading spices" were a metaphor for even that.

The changeling's parentage is presented both equivocally and spic-
ily. Nobody knew if Scotland's cradle prince was actually Darnley's
son. But here culture trumps nature. Elyot's *Book of the Governor*
recommends taking a seven-year-old boy away from his mother, and
giving him to a male tutor to preclude effeminization by women.
The metaphors informing Shakespeare's play conform to Elyot's rec-
ommendation about male upbringing, and the reorientation of the
court—no longer seeking a royal consort like Alençon—on a Scottish
heir to the English throne. As a twelve-month-old boy, James had
been virtually kidnapped from his papistical mother, to be trained
up by Presbyterians and educated by Protestant Humanists like Bu-
chanan. The fairies adopt progeny from human parents in India;
Tudor and Anglican England recruits a new dynasty from Stuart and
Presbyterian Scotland. James VI became James I. He was the changeling boy, even if in 1596 it was no fair guessing.

And surely such guessing had taken place. Here is Camden on
ideas that occurred to "very many" a year before the one in which
Accession Day may have been instituted:

> Certainly very many which saw the Queene averse from mar-
> riage, and that forraine Princes, enemies to England, cast their
> eyes and mindes upon the Queene of Scots as the most un-
> doubted heire of England, thought it would make more for the
> settling of quiet, and the restraining of the Queene of Scots
> within her limits, if she were joyned in marriage to the Duke

of Norfolke, the greatest and Noblest man of all the Nobility of England, a man in great favour with the people and bred up in the Protestants Religion, then if she were marryed to a forraine Prince, which might by her endanger both Kingdomes, and come to the inheritance of both, which they hartily wished might be conjoyned in a Prince of the English blood, *in case any thing other then well should befall the Infant King of Scots. And him also they propounded to draw into England, that he being the true heire of England, brought up amongst the English, might be the more deare to the English, all scruple concerning the succession might be taken away,* and Queene Elizabeth might be freed from feare of any thing to be attempted against her by the Duke or Queene of Scots, when she had him in her owne power. [28]

Oberon's kidnapped and appropriable squire embodies the divination of Shakespeare and the "very many" that the Prince of Pictland would succeed Elizabeth to become the King of England.

That same monarch would one day honor his mortal mother's remains with a white marble monument placed exactly parallel to the Virgin Queen's: at the center of Westminster Abbey, over the Henry VII chapel in which both women are buried. Many years ago my wife and I took our children to see such things, but I did not bother them with the observation that here lies Britomart beside Malecasta, at the instance of the changeling boy who could not altogether choose between his natural mother Mary, and his cultural mother Elizabeth.

University of Virginia

Notes

1. As Malcolm substitutes for Fleance, and Banquo's and Fleance's seed in turn replace Duncan's and Malcolm's seed, so Stuarts replaced Tudors: because the wife of a Stuart/Stewart royal *was* a Tudor: Margaret Tudor was both Elizabeth Tudor's and Mary Stuart's grandmother. Both grandchildren are buried in Westminster Abbey in the tomb of Margaret Tudor's husband, Henry VII, the first Tudor monarch.

2. All passages from Spenser are cited from *Spenser: Complete Poetical Works*, ed. J. C. Smith and E. De Selincourt (Oxford: Oxford University Press, rpt. 1970). Shakespeare is cited from *The Complete Pelican Shakespeare*, ed. Stephen Orgel and A. R. Braunmuller, 2nd rev. ed. (London: Penguin, 2002).

3. Lynn Staley Johnson, *The Shepheardes Calender: An Introduction* (University Park: Pennsylvania Sate University Press, 1990), 164, 170.

4. No fewer than five of the "vernal flowers" named in the catalogue in Milton's "Lycidas" previously featured in Spenser's "April." For "genial bed," see: "The bridale bowre and geniall bed" in Spenser, *Epithalamion* 399, "the genial bed" in Milton, *Paradise Lost* VIII.584, and Ben Jonson, *Hymenaei*, "The genial bed, where Hymen keeps/The solemn orgies, void of sleeps:/And wildest Cupid, waking hovers/With adoration 'twixt the lovers," and *New Inn*, V.iv, "A bed, the Genial Bed, a brace of Boys/To night I play for." See Servius *in Aen.* VI.603 (= 603f., "Genialibus [. . .] toris"): "Nam geniales proprie sunt, qui sternuntur puellis nubentibus: dicti à generandis liberis" [for they (beds) are properly *geniales*, which are lain upon by married girls: spoken about the generating of children]; Horace, *Epistles* I.i.87, "lectus genialis" (the marriage-bed honored by the family man: opposed to a celibate's bed). The garden's creatures "daily forth are sent/Into the world, it to *replenish* more" (III.vi.36), *re* the injunctions (Gen. 1:28, 9:1) "Be fruitful, and multiply, and *replenish* [fill] the earth" (KJV, following the Bishops Bible [1568]; see Chaucer, *Parson's Tale, sub* "Remedium contra peccatum Luxurie": "Trewe effect of mariage [. . .] replenysseth Hooly Chirche of good lynage").

5. Pagan elegy can end in apotheosis, and therefore Christian elegy leads to an epithalamium, if, as pastoral, it celebrates the marriage of the Lamb: see Bruce Boehrer, " 'Lycidas': The Pastoral Elegy as Same-Sex Epithalamium," PMLA 117:2 (March 2002): 222–36.

6. Deanne Williams, "Dido, Queen of England," *English Literary History* 73:1 (Spring 2006), 31–59. On the larger question, see Carole Levin, "Can a Woman Rule? Can a Woman Rule Alone?: Elizabeth's Courtships," a lecture presented at Grasselli Library and Breen Learning Center, John Carroll University, March 15, 2006. See also Donald Stump, "Marlowe's Travesty of Virgil: *Dido* and Elizabethan Dreams of Empire," *Comparative Drama* 34:2 (Spring 2000).

7. See Paul MacClane, *Spenser's "Shepherd's Calender": A Study in Elizabethan Allegory* (Notre Dame: University of Notre Dame Press, 1961), 47–60; Barbara J. Bono, *sub* "Dido," in A. C. Hamilton, gen. ed., *Spenser Encyclopedia* (Toronto: University of Toronto Press, 1990), 218, cols. 2–3, on the fictive, "civil," and allegorical character of the death of Dido (= Elissa = Eliza = Elizabeth I); cf. John Watkins, *The Spectre of Dido: Spenser and Virgilian Epic* (New Haven: Yale University Press, 1995), passim. The following historical reversal is a curiosity of our subject here: "Elizabeth was greatly grieved when she heard of Anjou's [Alençon's] death [in 1584], and wept in public every day for three weeks [. . .]. The court was put into mourning, the Queen herself wearing black for six months [. . .] Elizabeth told the French ambassador, 'I am a widow woman who has lost her husband.' " (Alison Weir, *The Life of Elizabeth I* [New York: Ballantine Books, 1998], 350.) Dido, of course, was also a widow.

8. See E. K. in "January": "the word Colin is Frenche, and vsed of the French Poete Marot in a certain Æglogue": vs. his recognizing in Colin Clout's name "a poesie of M. Skeltons vnder that title." The parenthetical rhetorical question in *FQ* VI.x.16, " [. . .] *Colin Clout* (Who knowes not *Colin Clout?*)" was answered, before its being asked, in Skelton's poem at "Who brought this rhyme about,/My name

is Colin Clout." (Spenser's question and anadiplosis both recall Ovid, *Fasti* II, 83, "What sea does not renew, what land not know Arion?"). Curiously, Marot and his Protestant opinions had been under the protection of Marguerite d'Alençon.

9. Roy Strong, *The Cult of Elizabeth* (London: Thames and Hudson, 1977), 118:

> It is impossible to get to the bottom of how it all started, although the belief late in Elizabeth's reign was that Oxford was the place of origin. In his sermon in defence of the annual celebrations, preached in 1599, Thomas Holland said that the first public observance of that day had been instituted by Thomas Cooper, then Vice-Chancellor of the university, and later Bishop of Winchester. Before his translation to the latter, he had held the see of Lincoln, and it was within his diocese that Accession Day coincided with the feast of the patron saint, St. Hugh of Lincoln. ¶ The Accession Day festivities were thus an adaptation of an old Catholic festival to the ethos of Protestantisms—how typically Elizabethan!

The connection of Accession Day to the suppression of the Northern rebellion in 1569 (and the popular reaction to the excommunication of Elizabeth by the pope in the next year) is found in William Camden, *Annales* (1570: sec. 23), in Dana E. Sutton's e-text edition at http://www.philological.bham.ac.uk/camden/157ol. html:

> The twelfth yeare of the Reigne of Queene Elizabeth beeing nowe happily expired, wherein some light beleeving Papists expected according to the prediction of certaine Wizards [it would be] their golden day, as they termed it, all good men throughout England joyfully triumphed, with Thanksgivings, Sermons in Churches, Prayers multiplied, joyfull ringing of Peels, running at Tilt, and Festivall mirth beganne to celebrate the 17th day of November, being the anniversary day of the beginning of her reigne, and in testimony of their obsequious love towards her, gave it not over as long as she lived.

I owe both the reference to Strong and the idea of the day's contemporary significance to the generosity of David Galbraith.

10. For Malecasta and Britomart as Myrrha-esque and Scylla-esque in Book III, see Nohrnberg, *Analogy of "The Faerie Queene"* (Princeton: Princeton University Press, 1976), 442–43, 445–48, 450.

11. After Jean Plaidy, *Mary Queen of Scots: The Fair Devil of Scotland* (London: Robert Hale; New York: Putnam's, 1975), 106.

12. Plaidy, 104.

13. Plaidy, 108–09. Henry Stuart Darnley's mother was Margaret Douglas, the daughter of Archibald Douglas; the latter's descent from Margaret Tudor gave Darnley, like Mary, a claim to the English/Tudor throne. Some allege Elizabeth therefore condemned the match.

14. Plaidy, 93. Similarly, though without the description of the masque itself, Antonia Fraser, *Mary Queen of Scots* (New York: Dell, 1971 [rpt. of London: Weidenfeld and Nicolson, 1969]), 233–38. See also Fraser, 236: "The ugly speculation arises

whether [the poet's being discovered in the bed-chamber] was not in fact Châtelard's intention, and whether his ultimate aim was to blacken Mary's reputation rather than win her love. According to Maitland, Châtelard had confessed to Mary that he had been despatched by persons in a high position in France expressly to compromise her honour, and the duchess of Guise hinted at the same thing to the Venetian ambassador. [. . .] The nuncio at the French court heard that the incident had been arranged to give Mary a bad name."

Note in passing that architectural interiors decorated with erotically and epithalamically suggestive mythological programs had a very real, material existence, Agostino Chigi's rooms at Rome's Farnesina Palace being an eminent example. For phallic/genital imagery comparable to Shakespeare's in Helena's longest and most longing speech in *A Midsummer Night's Dream* II.iii—"a double cherry, [. . .] an union in partition, / Two lovely berries molded on one stem"—see the priapic cucumber and vulval fig painted among the fruited festoons in the Farnesina's Loggia di Psiche, in Julian Kliemann and Michael Rohlmann, *Italian Frescoes: High Renaissance and Mannerism, 1510–1600* (New York: Abbeville Press, 2004), 198, 202 (plate 67, bottom).

15.   Camden, *Annales*, is taken from Sutton's e-text edition, at 1581e: "He was received with the greatest curtesie he could hope for, and no arguments there were of honour and love which shee did not shew him to the full. In so much as in the moneth of November, as soone as shee had with great pompe celebrated her coronation day, the force of modest love amongst amorous talke carried her so farre that shee drew off a ring from her finger and put it upon the Duke of Anjou's, upon certaine conditions betwixt them two. The standers by tooke it that the marriage was now contracted by promise [. . .]."

16.   This is borrowed from Nohrnberg, "Britomart's Gone abroad to Brute-land," in *Edmund Spenser: New and Renewed Directions*, ed. Julia Lethbridge (Madison: Fairleigh-Dickinson University Press), 214–85, 262. For the French marriage generally, a full account is Alison Weir, *The Life of Elizabeth I* (New York: Ballantine Books, 1998), 278–79, 284–88, 292–94, 311–12, 318–30, 331–34, 335–41, 350. For the Frenchified flirtation leading to the "trophies" incident, see 319–20.

17.   Marion A. Taylor: *Bottom, Thou Art Translated. Political Allegory in* A Midsummer Night's Dream *and Related Literature* (Amsterdam: Rodopi, 1973). See also Maurice Hunt's critical review of the case, "A Speculative Political Allegory in *A Midsummer Night's Dream*," *Comparative Drama* 34:4 (Winter 2000–01). Hunt's own theory (like mine) extends to King James. For the French marriage itself, besides the accounts in Camden's *Annales*, and Weir as cited in the preceding note, see also Agnes Strickland, *The Life of Queen Elizabeth* (London: Dent, 1906): for Henry of Anjou as proposed consort, 288–92, 296–310, 315–16; for Hercules-Francis of Valois, duke of Alençon, later duke of Anjou, 316–17, 322–26, 330–35, 337–39, 341–42, 346–47, 352–54, 364–69, 392–93, 401–08, 414–24 (with terminal quotes from both *Midsummer Night's Dream* on the "imperial votaress," and Elizabeth's verses "On Monsieure's Departure"), 509. Also see Wallace MacCaffrey, *Elizabeth I* (Edward Arnold, 1993), 178–80, 198–217 (chapter 16, "The Anjou Match"),

Mary M. Luke, *Gloriana: The Years of Elizabeth I* (New York: Coward-McCann & Geoghegan, 1973), esp. 408–09, 444–55; Elizabeth Jenkins, *Elizabeth The Great* (New York: Coward-McCann, 1958), 238–51, 258–61, 271–75, with the same terminal quotes as in Strickland).

18.   Neville Williams, *Elizabeth, Queen of England* (London: Weidenfeld & Nelson, 1967), 210.

19.   Mary's consort was literally blown up. Plaidy, 140, prints the "satirical placard" of Mary as Siren: "posted in Edinburgh in March 1567." For the relation to Shakespeare's play, see Antonia Fraser, *Mary Queen of Scots* (New York: Dell, 1969), 352, 357 ("The stars were intended to represent Bothwell").

20.   I.e., Elizabeth's translation of Marguerite of Navarre's *Mirror of the Sinful Soul* (*Miroir de l'âme pécheresse*). See *The Mirror of the Sinful Soul: A Prose Translation from the French of a Poem by Queen Margaret of Navarre*, 1544. Trans. Queen Elizabeth. Reproduced in facsimile. Ed. P. W. Ames (London, 1897).

21.   Taylor, 198–202 (on Le Bec = Snout); 136–38 (on Monsieur's name).

22.   Strickland, 333. For the impish Kemp as Bottom, see Taylor, 209–14. In Chaucer's *Miller's Tale* the bestial male beard seems to be found at a hirsute private aperture ("At the window out she putte hir hole [. . .] He kiste hir naked erse [. . .] Wel he wiste a woman hath no berd./He felte a thyng al rough and long yberd" (*Canterbury Tales* I.3732–39).

23.   Taylor, 192–98, 216 (on [Peter] Quince's name as the Frenchman's De Quincé's); see also, ibid., 41. Alençon himself visited England twice in pursuit of his match, first semi-secretly in 1579 for twelve days, and then openly and with great fanfare in 1582, preceded by the French embassy, 500 dressy Frenchmen strong, in 1581. (Camden places the original proposal of the French match of Elizabeth with Henry duke of Anjou, Alençon's older brother, in 1568, and he shows the match with Alençon himself more formally propounded in 1571.) It may be that the medicinal attention Belphoebe affords Timias in *FQ* III.v reflects not only Elizabeth's tender-hearted practice of visiting and ministering to the sick, but also her dramatic and prompt attention to the wounds of the oarsman accidentally shot through the shins while she was on a boat with Simier in 1579. (She refused to believe the shot was intended for the Frenchman, and her pardon saved the trigger-happy disturber of the royal peace from hanging.) Titania's entertainment of the enchanted Bottom seems recognizable in Elizabeth's public fuss over Alençon upon his second visit, and seems, moreover, especially pertinent, in light of the queen's private ministrations to her lover on that occasion, as detailed in Weir, 339: e.g., she herself brought him a cup of broth each morning (see *MND* III.i.165–75: "Feed him with [. . .] dewberries, [. . .] and do him courtesies").

24.   See *Elizabeth I: Collected Works*, ed. Leah S. Marcus, Janel Mueller, and Mary Beth Rose (Chicago: University of Chicago Press, 2000), 383 (Letter 91, Elizabeth to James, June or July 1594: "your bond of firm and constant amity"); and ibid., 265 (Letter 58, Additional Document B, James to Elizabeth, August 19, 1585, "Madame and mother"), with Mueller, " 'To my Very Good Brother the King of Scots': Elizabeth I's Correspondence with James VI and the Question of the Succession," *PMLA* 115:5 (October 2000): 1063–71.

25.   A. L. Rowse, *Simon Forman: Sex and Society in Shakespeare's Age* (London: Weidenfeld and Nicolson, 1974), 20. See Louis Montrose, "*A Midsummer Night's*

Dream and the Shaping Fantasies of Elizabethan Culture: Gender, Power, Form,"
Representations 8 (Fall 1984): 1–13.
26.   Rouse, 20–21.
27.   In 1583 Edmund Fenton of the Muscovy Company (one of the earliest adventurer companies founded in London for purposes of trade and exploration) visited the Moluccas and Spice Islands with the backing of Sidney and Lord Burghley. In 1592 Sir John Burrough captured an East Indian carrack laden with 900 tons of spices, cloth, and treasure from the orient. In the same year the Levant Company was created and permitted to trade with Turkey, and in 1592 or 1593 it combined with the Venice company. At the same time—1592—the plague struck London, for which Titania may take the blame in her speech on the causes of a weather in which "rheumatic diseases do abound": "We are their parents and original" (*MND* II.i.115, 117). In 1595 Cornelius de Houtman reached Java via the Cape of Good Hope—and thus began the Dutch exploration of the East Indies, in the wake of the Portuguese. England would not be far behind.
28.   Camden, *Annales*, 1569; text from Sutton, at 1569.1. To the same end, see Strickland, *Life of Queen Elizabeth*, 323: "Walsingham and Smith were recreated with another diplomatic walk in the garden of the castle of Blois with the scheming queen-mother of France. Some curious conversation occurred, relating to the mutual jealousies felt by England and France, at the Ridolfi plot, the gist of which was to steal young James of Scotland from his guardians, and deliver him to Philip II. in order that marriage might be contracted between him and the young infanta." ("Letter of Smith to Burleigh, Complete Ambassador, p. 167, dated March 22, 1571–2"—Strickland's note for her source.)

GORDON TESKEY

Thinking Moments in *The Faerie Queene*

To ask how Spenser thinks in *The Faerie Queene* is to look past traditional notions of what the poem is—on the one hand, pure poetry, on the other hand, moral allegory—and also to look past familiar notions of thinking, e.g., thinking having an end outside itself, such as wisdom; and thinking as pure cerebration apart from the material world. Developing by *entanglement* and progressing through *moments*, in the Hegelian sense of the term, thinking in *The Faerie Queene* is not an answering but a searching of questions initially asked, leading to the totally unexpected, the new.

*P*OETIC THINKING IN SPENSER'S *Faerie Queene* is not what it would be for poets in a later age. Even Donne, who was of the next generation, made thinking differently from Spenser the intellectual program of his verse, brittle where Spenser is supple, caustic where Spenser is cool, fiercely articulate where Spenser is mythopoeic and obscure. We might ask, brittle, caustic and articulate at what? Supple, cool and obscurely mythopoeic at what? What is this poetic thinking? The grammar of the phrase, "poetic thinking," in which *poetic* is the modifying adjective, suggests one is speaking of a nonstandard, dubiously legitimate species of thinking that is peculiar to poetry. It would seem reasonable to proceed by defining unmodified, proper thinking first, philosophical thinking. Only when that has been done will we be ready to examine its impure imitation in verse: *poetic* thinking. But as readers of *The Faerie Queene* know, the obvious starts are often the false ones, leading to early and easy but unfruitful conclusions. The early and easy conclusion is that the philosophy of *The Faerie Queene* is a bastard blend of inexactly-remembered Aristotle, crude, Calvinist polemic, vacuously complicated star-lore and

Spenser Studies: A Renaissance Poetry Annual, Volume XXII, Copyright © 2007 by AMS Press, Inc. All rights reserved.

second-rate Neoplatonism, which as its prefix suggests is already second-rate. That, or something like it, is what we get by supposing
that thinking is not proper to Spenser's poetry, is not its very substance, but finds its way into the poetry in a secondary way—on the
grey wings of the owl of Minerva.

"The poet's poet," as Leigh Hunt called Spenser, is hardly someone we are likely at first to regard as a thinker, as we might, say,
George Chapman, or Sir John Davies, neither of whom one would
ever call a poet's poet.[1] There is in them too much admixture of
prosaic thinking for us to regard their works—as Spenser's are so
often regarded—as effusions of the purely poetical. A poet's poet, we
suppose, doesn't think, for thinking is something that may be *in*
poetry but is always other with respect *to* poetry. Because there can
be no identity of poetry and thinking, a poet may indulge in the one
to the neglect of the other. Like the composer of *musique concrète* or
the painter of color field paintings, Spenser's pursuit of his art is so
pure that there can be no place in it for pedestrian discursiveness.
His feet are never on the ground, or in the world. Such is the Spenser
who is unjustly but very beautifully evoked by Wordsworth in the
third book of *The Prelude*: "that gentle Bard,/Chosen by the Muses
for their Page of State—/Sweet Spenser, moving through his clouded
heaven/With the moon's beauty and the moon's soft pace."[2]

The unthinking aesthetic purity that is still associated with Spenser
today was fastened on him by William Hazlitt in the second of his
Lectures on the English Poets (1818), when he says that "of all poets
[Spenser] is the most poetical" because "the love of beauty . . . and
not of truth, is the moving principle of his mind."[3] Spenser "takes
us and lays us in the lap of a lovelier nature . . . He waves his wand
of enchantment—and at once embodies airy beings, and throws a
delicious veil over all actual objects." The wish to free Spenser from
the burden of philosophic song (and from the more onerous burden
of commentary on the song) motivates Hazlitt's famous attack on the
allegory of *The Faerie Queene*. After an enthusiastic litany of splendid
pageants and mysterious, symbolic *loci*, Hazlitt says, "But some people
will say that all this may be very fine, but that they cannot understand
it on account of the allegory. They are afraid of the allegory, as if
they thought it would bite them: they look at it as a child looks at
a painted dragon, and think it will strangle them in its shining folds.
This is very idle. If they do not meddle with the allegory, the allegory
will not meddle with them. Without minding it at all, the whole is
as plain as a pike-staff." Hazlitt does not deny that *The Faerie Queene*
is an allegory, or at least that it has allegory in it. But he does greatly
demote the importance of the allegory so that he might emphasize

the purity of Spenser's poetical vein: "Spenser was the poet of our waking dreams, lulling the senses into a deep oblivion of the jarring noises of the world, from which we have no wish to be ever re-called."

Why does the poet do this, instead of striving to improve us by improving our understanding of the ethical life as that life must be lived: not in oblivion of the jarring noises of this world but in the midst of them? Twentieth-century criticism has taken the allegory of *The Faerie Queene* very seriously indeed and has had little time for Hazlitt's pages on Spenser, except as the most eloquent example of a wrong-headed but persistently romantic conception of the poet. But perhaps we should be cautious about slighting a great critic who, in castigating mystagogic suppositions about Spenser as an excuse for not reading him, can write the following sentence about *The Faerie Queene*, capturing one of its moments of Botticellian glory: "Is there any mystery in what is said of Belphoebe, that her hair was sprinkled with flowers and blossoms which had been entangled in it as she fled through the woods?" Well, yes, there is, although we have little hope of unveiling it by direct exegesis. It is drawn from the long and complex blazon with which Belphoebe is introduced into the poem:

> And whether art it were, or heedlesse hap,
> As through the flouring forrest rash she fled,
> In her rude haires sweet flowers themselves did lap,
> And flourishing fresh leaves and blossomes did enwrap.
>
> (II.iii.30)

Hazlitt's question certainly seems a rhetorical one. But perhaps he really does want to know if there is any mystery in these lines, and to raise the question for us. If that is what he is doing, then perhaps he has caught something vital to the way *The Faerie Queene* thinks, which is why I shall return to Belphoebe, and perhaps also to the flowers entangled in her hair.

Inasmuch as Spenser was regarded by the romantics as being even learned, he is learned in the quaint way Southey describes, or rather the fictional Southey we encounter in Landor's *Imaginary Conversations* relishing Spenser's allegory, though with much condescension, as a spacious but low-ceilinged chamber copiously furnished in charming disarray, a cabinet of curiosities. Southey's interlocutor, who serves as the mouthpiece for Landor's own tastes, is the great classicist, Richard Porson: "*Porson*. But your great favourite, I hear, is Spenser, who shines in allegory, and who, like an aerolite, is dull and heavy when he descends to the ground. *Southey.* He continues a great favourite with me still, although he must always lose a little as our youth declines. Spenser's is a spacious but somewhat low chamber, hung with rich tapestry, on which the figures are mostly disproportioned, but some of the faces are lively and beautiful; the furniture is part creaking and worm-eaten, part fragrant with cedar and sandalwood and aromatic gums and balsams; every table and mantelpiece and cabinet is covered with gorgeous vases, and birds, and dragons, and houses in the air." This is marvelous (although that house in the air is in Ariosto, not Spenser), but it is not long before Porson has badgered Southey into admitting Spenser's "vast exaggeration and insane display"—the inevitable result of great poetical power ungoverned by truth.[4] As to the allegory, it sparkles like a meteor descending through the atmosphere, but is dull and heavy when it reaches the ground.

If Milton inhibited the romantics as a towering fortress of thought, Spenser was to them a friendly, enabling presence, like Keats's teacher, Charles Cowden Clarke, "who had," as his grateful pupil said, "by Mulla's stream/Fondled the maidens with the breasts of cream."[5] No one ever compared reading the sage and serious Milton to fondling maidens with breasts of cream. But still we should recall that "sage and serious" were his epithets for Spenser.

Finally, there is the Spenser who is a friend to the romantics because he makes it easier for them to write, inspiring rather than intimidating them, and this power to aid and to inspire is the best reason for calling Spenser "the poet's poet." This Spenser is evoked in an aside in the introduction to *The Revolt of Islam*, where Shelley states that he composed that enormous poem in Spenserian stanzas because they caused the poem more or less to write itself without forethought, whereas you can't write blank verse—and by "blank verse" Shelley really means "Milton"—unless you know what you are going to say: "I have adopted the stanza of Spenser (a measure inexpressibly beautiful), not because I consider it a finer model of poetical harmony than the blank verse of Shakespeare and Milton, but because in the latter there is no shelter for mediocrity; you must either succeed or fail. This perhaps an aspiring spirit should desire. But I was enticed also by the brilliancy and magnificence of sound which a mind that has been nourished upon musical thoughts can produce by a just and harmonious arrangement of the pauses of this measure."[6]

"A mind that has been nourished upon *musical thoughts.*" At first, we may suppose Shelley is falling in with the rest of our romantics, reducing Spenser not only to a poet who offers pure imagination without thought but almost to one who offers sound for sense. But in the phrase *musical thoughts* Shelley means us to hear the full, Greek sense of *mousikê*: deep learning, bright inspiration, agile and various rhythm—all moving together into the discovery of what has not been thought before, and of what is thinkable only through Spenser's "harmonious arrangement of pauses." In such thinking, as James Merrill said of verse, the feet go bare.

If it is still a popular error (one hears it among students) to suppose Spenser is purely poetical, where poetry has nothing to do with thinking, the opposite error, into which specialists are in more danger of straying, is to suppose the thinking in Spenser's *Faerie Queene* consists of the philosophical content that went into the poem and that can be led out again by *exegesis*, which means "a leading out." I have mentioned a Platonism that is already *neo-neo* before Spenser takes it in hand, to which may be added—from the *Letter to Ralegh*—an Aristotelian poetics so much mediated by Italian critical theory that the Stagirite would hardly recognize it as his own. In the poem itself we find another Aristotle acquired by Spenser at Cambridge, where he was central to a curriculum that a later graduate of that university, Milton himself, would deride as "an asinine feast of sow thistles and brambles."[7]

This Aristotle, derived from commentary on the *Ethics*, lies behind what we think of as the most simplistic allegorical episodes, such as the House of Alma, wherein the teeth bow to the Soul, or the setup episode for the Legend of Temperance, in which three sisters inhabit the castle of Medina, "an ancient worke of antique fame" (II.ii.12); which is to say, the ancient castle represents the accumulated moral thought, unaided by any Christian revelation, on the wisdom of keeping to the golden mean. The castle is therefore inhabited by Medina herself and the extremes of excess and defect which her sisters represent: her younger sister, Perissa, and her older sister, Elissa, Little Miss Too Much Sex, and Little Miss Too Little:

> Therein three sisters dwelt of sundry sort,
>   The children of one sire by mothers three;
>   Who dying whylome did divide this fort
>   To them by equall shares in equall fee:
>   But striffull minde, and diverse qualitee
>   Drew them in parts, and each made others foe;

Still did they strive, and dayly disagree;
  The eldest did against the youngest goe,
And both against the middest meant to worken woe.

II.ii.13

Elissa and Perissa (we will not learn their names for another twenty
two stanzas) are courted by another pair of opposites: the melancholy
Huddibras, suitably matched with Elissa, she of "froward countenance" and sullenly unassailable virtue (II.ii.35), and Sans Foy, that
"boldest boy," as Spenser calls him, for "warlike weapons" and for
"lawless lust" (II.ii.18), who enjoys Perissa's lavish favors, she being
"quite contrary to her sisters kind" (II.ii.36): "a mincing minion,/
Who in her loosenesse tooke exceeding joy." Even at table, she is
to the eager hands of Sans Loy a "frank franion," or wanton sharer,
"of her lewd parts," which spectacle is grievous to the unrelieved
Huddibras, who "hardly could . . . endure his [Sans Loy's] hardi-
ment,/Yet still he sat, and inly did him selfe torment" (II.ii.36).[8]

The moral setup in the castle of Medina is permutatively unstable
and mindlessly repetitive, like the game of scissors, paper, and rock.[9]
After all, the advice, "not too little, but not too much!", which leaves
us still unable to tell whether we are nearer the Gulf of Greediness
or the Rock of Vile Reproach, is about as useful in any particular
situation as "buy low and sell high!" It is true in theory, but it is
nearly useless in practice, and starts us oscillating between extremes
as we search for the nonexistent middle. Circumstances in the Castle
of Medina are so hermetically sealed, like the Second Empire décor
of the infernal room in Sartre's *Huis Clos*, where alliances likewise
continually change with vicious alteration, that when Guyon arrives
and Huddibras and Sans Loy rush out to fight him, urged thereto by
their ladies, they fail to reach Guyon because they start fighting each
other instead:

    But when they heard,
  How in that place straunge knight arrived late,
  Both knights and Ladies forth right angry far'd,
And fiercely unto battell sterne themselves prepar'd.

But ere they could proceede unto the place,
  Where he abode, themselves at discord fell,
  And cruell combat joynd in middle space:
  With horrible assault, and furie fell,
  They heapt huge strokes, and scorned life to quell,

That all on uprore from her settled seat
The house was raysd, and all that in did dwell;
Seemd that lowd thunder with amazement great
Did rend the rattling skyes with flames of fouldring heat.

(II.ii.19–20)

When the "straunger knight," Guyon, hears the uproar, he rushes
to the scene and attempts by "goodly meanes" to pacify the combat-
ants, who immediately turn on him "without remorse,/And on his
shield like yron sledges bet" (II.ii.22). Guyon defends himself so well
that Huddibras and Sansloy must take out their frustration on each
other; but when Guyon again tries to make peace, they turn again
on him:

. . . Whose grieved minds, which choler did englut,
Against themselves turning their wrathful spight,
Gan with new rage their shields to hew and cut;
But still when *Guyon* came to part their fight,
With heavie load on him they freshly gan to smight.

(II.ii.23)

"Straunge sort of fight," Spenser says, as well he might, after three
more stanzas of inextricable altercation between parties whose alliances continually change. It is evidently intended as psychological
allegory, but if we think of the stages of the fight as unfolding over
decades instead of minutes, and between nations instead of individuals, it begins to look less strange. It begins to look rather like Europe
from the seventeenth century to the twentieth or, in Spenser's day,
like the continually changing alliances of two parties against one in
the foreign relations of France, Spain, and England, it being Elizabethan policy wherever possible to keep the other two at each other's
throats, and always to side with the weaker. In any event, it appears
at this moment as if nothing can ever enter into the Castle of Medina
and alter the structure of its interlocking, violent compulsions. The
changes are rung endlessly, but the situation remains the same.

Yet simple as it appears (and I confess to taking much pleasure
from the mechanics of this episode and others like it), it is richly
entangled in its widening contexts and flows into them like the ripples
from a stone dropped in a pool. It is entangled with the earlier history
of Sansloy, who in the Legend of Holiness attacks Una. It is entangled

with the brothers of Sans Loy, especially Sans Joy, whose character is recapitulated in Huddibras. It is entangled, moreover, with what we suppose lies outside it, the history of the English Church and of the Elizabethan *via media*, not to mention the permutations of foreign alliance, which I have already mentioned. The episode is, of course, entangled with Guyon himself, with Guyon's Palmer and perhaps even with Guyon's hobbled horse and the events of the canto to follow, in which the thief of Guyon's horse, Braggadocchio, showing defect and excess, is terrified of Belphoebe at first, and yet attempts to rape her. The episode is most peculiarly entangled with Ruddy-mane, the child Guyon and the Palmer leave at the castle, whose hands cannot be cleansed of his father's blood, even by water from the fountain of the maiden turned to stone. The child is a vision of original sin, caught red-handed at his very birth, and is left with Medina to be trained up "in virtuous lore . . . And all that gentle noriture ensu'th" (II.iii.2).

Inserted into the episode of the Castle of Medina at its conclusion, almost as an afterthought, Ruddymane nevertheless symbolizes the problem to which mediation between extremes at the Castle of Medina is supposed to be the classical solution: "virtuous lore" manages the consequences of original sin, even if it cannot eradicate them. Despite this normalizing interpretation, however, Ruddymane continues as a foreign element, a negative presence, a moment in the shape of the situation as a whole which cannot be assimilated to its existing moral structure. For whatever the problem is with the blood that sticks to Ruddymane's hands, moderation isn't going to solve it. The episode at the Castle of Medina is therefore strangely entangled with the preceding episode, in which Ruddymane's parents, Mortdant and Amavia, die. Dying is neither a moderate nor an immoderate act: it is incommensurable with moderation. Yet temperance is entangled with somatic death, for it is the means of putting death off as long as possible by keeping the body in balance, and so achieving what the gerontologists call—in a wonderful, Borghesian phrase—"compression of morbidity."[10] But is that what temperance is for, shortening the period of helplessness in extreme old age? That is an eminently sensible aim, but it hardly makes temperance a heroic virtue.

For the allegory of Temperance in the Castle of Medina is still more strangely entangled with events in the following canto, when Braggadocchio, who seems to have been assembled from warring elements in Sansloy and Huddibras, encounters that paragon of moral completeness, Belphoebe. I leave aside Belphoebe's blood-lust and its possible relevance to the blood on Ruddymane's hands. I leave it aside because I don't understand it. What I think I do understand is that Belphoebe, who represents the perfection of the body, shows us how the virtue with which Spenser is truly concerned in Book II is not Temperance after all but rather something that is sublimely in excess of that simple moderation for which we strive throughout life and for which Medina, not Belphoebe, is the model. In the very effort to think Temperance as moderation, something far beyond moderation is revealed when Belphoebe unexpectedly enters the tale, though she has little to do there except to be gazed on in wonder. She is gazed on because she is what, by moderation, we hopelessly aspire to be, or to attain, although the one thing she does in the episode is indicate another path altogether from that of moderation: "Who seekes with painfull toile," she says, "shall honor soonest find" (II.iii.40). The thrusting yet cowardly Braggadocchio, burning in "filthy lust" (II.iii.41) as he reaches for what he knows he is unworthy of, yet comically terrified of it, too, is a devastating moral parody of our own aspiring moderation.

As I hope this example has shown, in Spenserian allegory matters become complicated and deepened not by looking farther into them where they are and analyzing them microscopically, by close reading. There is no poet for whom the techniques of close reading are more unsuitable if relied on exclusively, or more likely to mislead if mechanically applied. When we read *The Faerie Queene* we need a long memory and a distanced, somewhat relaxed view of its entanglements even more than we need the capacity for paying minute attention. Matters are complicated and deepened in Spenser's verse by continually widening contexts and by what I have called *entanglement*, a term I prefer to the medieval, hermeneutic notion of *polysemy* "having many significations," and to Bishop Butler's term, *analogy*, which has so much enriched Spenser studies in the work of James Nohrnberg.[11] But like *polysemy*, *analogy* suggests an harmoniousness and logocentric order, like combed as opposed to tangled hair, that is not true to the real conditions of thinking in *The Faerie Queene*. The conditions of thinking in *The Faerie Queene* are more material, and therefore more complex, than abstractions such as *polysemy* and *analogy* allow. Meaning in *The Faerie Queene* is like meaning in life: it is always entangled with the real. Such entanglement in Spenser is the condition of the possibility of meaning. It may therefore be asked, what larger, more flexible concept of system could embrace both the scale of *The Faerie Queene*, its sheer bigness, and the noetic entanglement of the episodes in it? How may we speak of the poem thinking?

In attempting to answer such a question I wish to turn first to one of the most celebrated passages of critical writing on Spenser's *Faerie Queene*:

> The clashing antitheses which meet and resolve themselves into higher unities, the lights streaming out from the great allegorical *foci* to turn into a hundred different colours as they reach the lower levels of complex adventure, the adventures gathering themselves together and revealing their true nature as we draw near the *foci*, the constant re-appearance of certain basic ideas, which transform themselves without end and yet ever remain the same (eterne in mutability), the unwearied variety and seamless continuity of the whole—all this is Spenser's true likeness to life.[12]

This is, of course, C. S. Lewis, in *The Allegory of Love* (1938), from the chapter on Spenser, which I suspect did more than any other single text outside *The Faerie Queene* to draw three generations of Spenserians into the study of their poet. That attractive force may be especially strong when Lewis says, just before the passage quoted, that "[t]he things we read about in [*The Faerie Queene*] are not like life, but the experience of reading it is like living." Or, perhaps, thinking. In an entertainingly evasive remark following the passage I have quoted, Lewis seems at once to acknowledge and to deny the Hegelian inspiration of his vision of *The Faerie Queene* when he says that reading it affords "a sensation akin to that which Hegelians are said to get from Hegel, a feeling . . . that this is not so much a poet writing about the fundamental forms of life as those forms themselves spontaneously displaying their activities to us through the imagination of a poet."

Lewis began his career not as an English but a philosophy tutor with an interest in Hegel, English Hegelianism being the dominant school of philosophy at Oxford at the time, although the logical positivists had appeared on the scene and Lewis himself was meditating a thesis on Russell. Writing about this period in his life, Lewis is fairly ironical about his youthful, "watered Hegelianism," but leaves no doubt whatever that the thrilling "sensation which Hegelians are said to get from Hegel" is a thrill he experienced himself.[13] Even so, the distance is real. Where Lewis speaks of Spenser's "images of life," the title of another book by him on Spenser, Hegel would have said "the forms of consciousness, or of self-knowing"—*die Gestalten des Bewusstseins*.

The difference is captured in the emphasis on unthinking, exuberant life. For the Hegelian, Spirit, or Mind, envelops and informs life, directing life towards its consummation in the Mind, when the rational and the real coincide. For the Christian, life, the gift of God, informs and envelops our capacity for thought, which is but a small and, finally, uncomprehending part of life's force. Thought does little more than collect shells along the shore of the sea of life. Lewis wished through literature to put thought back in its place, as what Hotspur called "the slave of life," and he is fond of showing how the most cerebral pretensions turn out to be either grossly sensual or maniacally arrogant in their underlying motivation. Note the irony with which he speaks of a *"sensation* akin to what Hegelians are said to get from Hegel"—as if the Hegelian philosophy were not about transcending the illusion of sense-certainty, which affords what Hegel calls the most impoverished, because the most abstract form of knowing.[14] From Lewis's fiction we know how well he thought of the senses and of the pleasures of the senses, to which he accords something like a moral force. For him, simple folk who enjoy a good breakfast are in this wiser than all the philosophers in the world.

I am myself favorably inclined to Lewis's robust preference for images of *Life* over some watery neo-Hegelian *Spirit*, which in Spenser studies has its analogue in Neoplatonism. But there is danger in this position as well, for it moves back in the direction of what we have seen in the romantics, that is, in the direction of an unthinking Spenser whose poetry indulges, albeit at the highest level of art, the very sensationalism Lewis sees as Hegelianism's opposite danger. After all, Spenser's images of life must mean or teach something, and not only because they are deployed in an allegorical poem. In the first instance, they mean or teach something simply by their being in the plural: we are not dealing with a unified spectacle, a panoramic mimesis of life such as we get, for example, in a great realist novelist like Tolstoy. We are dealing with images or forms, in the plural, and images must be taken in combination. We need to be able to speak, therefore, not only of those images but of the relations between them, and these relations, considered apart from the bare narrative from which they so casually emerge, can only be relations of thought. How are they connected?

Thus far the term, or the image (it is a little of both), which I have used for these relations is noetic entanglement. But if we zoom in, so to speak, on these entanglements and examine them closely we begin to see them as what in my title I have called *moments*, thinking moments. *Moment* is, admittedly, an Hegelian term, but it belongs to Hegel's logic and not his metaphysics. It is not the Absolute or anything like it, such as Spirit, and we can use it in the plural without ever supposing that this plurality would be better if it would lead us to the One. In fact, the logic of the entangling of the moments is a plurality that leads away from the one, branching out unexpectedly in all directions, but re-entangling with one another later on, in fantastic complexity, and with no common destination in view— indeed with no destination for any particular filiation or path, like the vast entanglement of neuronal dendrites in the brain. This is thinking that does not try to get out of itself at its destination, disembarking, so to speak, on an answer to thought that is not itself part of the thinking, that is, of continual questioning. The entangled moments are on paths that lead nowhere because the idea of a destination to thinking is foreign to the wisdom that is gathered on these paths.

By "thinking *moments* in *The Faerie Queene*" I mean *moment* in the two meanings of the word that are distinguished in Hegel's German by the use of the neuter and the masculine articles: first, there is a moment in our usual sense of the word, a *moment* of arrest, an instant within which, so long as it lasts, nothing seems to move or change, inviting us to grasp some state of affairs before it slips away, and to subject it to careful analysis. "Just a moment!" we say, when we are in the heat of discussion, "Hold on! Not so fast! Let's look carefully at what you just said." We wish to make time stand still (and in a sense we do) so that we may examine the argument synchronically at one of its stages, its moments. This arresting moment is, of course, not peculiar to Hegel but rather to philosophy: it happens all the time in Plato's dialogues, which is why Socrates was compared to the torpedo fish, with its paralyzing sting. Reading philosophy is unlike other kinds of reading because it is discontinuous: we have to keep stopping to think, and this thinking is the grasping of a structure we conceive to stand out of time.

It is the other sense of *moment*, the more technically philosophical term for a destabilizing element in a totality, which has peculiar force in the Hegelian philosophy. For it derives from the Latin *moveo* and implies motion or development within a larger whole, effecting some change in that whole. The two meanings of *moment* twist together opposite things in a dynamic situation: instability and stasis, movement and arrest. This is hardly peculiar to Hegel's philosophy. It is what every moment in any poem feels like, where each image, each word, each moment, may seem to be perfectly itself even as it is becoming something other than itself. But it is especially true of

The Faerie Queene, with its continual oscillation between narrative movement and symbolic tableau. What does it mean to say Spenser thinks in this way or, more strangely still, to say that *The Faerie Queene* thinks in and through such pulsatile moments? These moments may be reducible as far down as the stanza, with its longer final line forcing us to pause and hear each passing stanza as a unit, in contrast with the headlong rush of the ottava rima used by the Italian narrative poets. This brings us back to the question raised at the outset. Does it make sense to say that poets think as poets and not in some secondary, decorative way?

To put the question more fully, how may it be possible to speak of a poet "thinking" in a way that is different from scientific thinking and from philosophic, or conceptual thinking? The problem of the relation of poetry to philosophical knowledge goes back to Plato. (It may go back farther than Plato, but my point is that in Plato it becomes a *problem*: in Pindar, for example, poetry, knowledge and wisdom are unproblematically one and the same.) But the question of the relation of poetry to philosophical knowledge was revived in the mid-twentieth century by Heidegger and Adorno and has recently become a subject of interest again in literary criticism.[15] Heidegger and Adorno come to different conclusions about the relation of poetry to philosophy. Heidegger says that the philosophers are too busy doing philosophy to "think," in his primordial sense of the word, which is related to *thanking* the gods and *dwelling* on earth, and that it is only the poets who think. Adorno holds that although philosophy and art are different things, with neither being subordinate to the other, Hegel's subordination of art to the theory of art shows "prophetic" understanding of "art's need of philosophy for the unfolding of its own content."[16]

Both these writers were concerned with German lyric poetry in the tradition of Hölderlin, that is, with dithyrambic poetry for which the great and inimitable model is Pindar. The case is much altered with Spenser, and perhaps the first thing that alters the case is length. A long poem, and certainly a very long poem, allows freedom of movement and room for development. A long poem forces the poet to work on the poem from within, without being able ever to consider the poem as a whole in a moment out of time, like a well-wrought urn. *The Faerie Queene* is very much in time and its "form" is of continual, dynamic adjustment to its changing understanding of itself. If the experience of *The Faerie Queene* is like Hegel's thought thinking itself, it is thought thinking itself while continually changing its mind and giving itself ampler room in which to explore. When I speak of thinking in Spenser, therefore, I mean a kind of work that is the opposite of the concept, or *Begriff*, which grasps things, like tools, and holds things together. Spenser's thinking is more in the nature of a "letting-go," or what Heidegger called *Gelassenheit*.[17]

Such "letting-go" is also a probing of mystery that approaches the strange, treating the strange not as it is treated in mathematics, or physics, or biology: as an object that fully exists but is yet to be known. In the sciences, the strangeness of any manifestation must be reduced to an abstract but persisting object, such as a number, a force, or an organ. But in poetry the strange manifests itself as another consciousness the very strangeness of which—or, to speak allegorically, the "otherness" of which—must be respected. Spenser's poetic thinking works away from its original questions: what is holiness? What is temperance? What is chastity? What is friendship? What is justice? What is courtesy? What is constancy? The form of these questions is the philosophically traditional one of definition—"ti esti?"—treating the things questioned as things that already exist, rather than as thought still in motion. Spenser's poetic thinking does not strive to make the questions disappear into answers telling us what these things are. Instead, it strives to make those questions even more strange than we had ever supposed.

Let me attempt an overview of the themes of the seven books and of some of the transformations of those themes, transformations which make us feel by the end of a book that we know less, rather than more, about the virtue in question, but that the impoverishment we suffer at Spenser's hands has also made us wiser about the questions he asks. What begins as thinking about holiness becomes thinking about substance, purity, and danger. What begins as thinking about temperance as a middle way becomes thinking about the mysterious boundary between the living and the dead. What begins as thinking about chastity becomes thinking about sexual violence but also, more importantly, about the paralyzing fear of all sexual feeling, indeed of all touching, as violence. What begins as thinking about friendship becomes thinking about nature, exchange, and ecology. What begins as thinking about justice becomes thinking about what we would suppose to be quite irrelevant to justice, courtesy. What begins as thinking about courtesy becomes an anthropological thinking about culture. What begins as thinking about constancy and mutability—the two senses of *moment*—becomes thinking about thinking itself.

We commonly suppose two things about thinking. The first thing we suppose, as I suggested earlier when I spoke of a destination to thinking that is not itself thought, is that thinking is about something outside itself; thinking is orientated towards that which is not itself thought. The second thing we suppose is that thinking takes place in the head, from which executive commands are sent through un-thinking nerves to mechanical organs and limbs. When we consider Spenser's poetic thinking both these statements must be reversed so as to affirm, first, the identity of the poem with its thinking and, second, the identity of this identity with the movement of thinking in circuit between the head, the hand, the text, the material remains appropriated by this text, and ultimately with the thinking of readers. How could Spenser's thinking be confined to his head if the poem he is making is not a representation of his thinking but simply *is* his thinking?

A still more important issue follows from this circulatory move-ment of Spenserian thought through its moments. It is that Spenser's poetic thinking is *material*, in the sense that everything the poet tears apart and subsumes in his poem is composed of the material remains of the past. What I would call "the objectifiable, but non-objectified other" in Spenser's creative process is composed of all previous poems, commentaries, and historical documents—in short, *texts*—with which the poet is concerned. I have used the term, *texts*, but Spenser's word for them was *ruins* and, later, *moniments*, a word that makes the passage of time visible in the materials with which the poet is engaged. The material remains of the past with which Spenser worked included classical and medieval poetry, the spiritual and intel-lectual culture of the Christian tradition, and the imaginary, Arthu-rian lore of Britain. By deploying those materials kaleidoscopically to represent such abstract ideas as holiness, temperance, chastity, friend-ship, and so on, Spenser repeatedly found his dead materials seeming to take on a life of their own and speaking to him, driving his thoughts into unexpected channels. Spenser was a prophetic poet because he was willing to listen to the voice of a material other emerging from the process of making his poem. This voice told him more than he expected to hear, and almost certainly more than he wished to hear, about the emerging conditions of human existence in the built environment of a post-civilized world.

I have said that Spenser's poetic thinking is self-identical and that it is material. We may see Spenser's manner of thinking more clearly when we contrast it with Milton's, first because Milton worked out everything he would ever think before he wrote *Paradise Lost*. This claim is not always heard favorably by Miltonists. But it does him no discredit and is perhaps the reason he is presently regarded as more intellectually serious than Spenser. The thought of *Paradise Lost* is not created in and through the poem: it is represented in the poem. But Spenser in *The Faerie Queene* does his thinking as he goes along, arriving often, as it seems, by accident, as a result of some particular instance he has seized on, at a deeper formulation than that with which he began, but also a stranger formulation. You cannot run Spenser's thinking backwards. Milton can see farther than Spenser into any question set before him and defined for him. Spenser takes us into regions of thought the existence of which Milton would never have suspected—nor would we have suspected them, either. And to Spenser himself they come as a surprise.

Milton thinks by going back to first principles, to the *archai* or, as Samuel Barrow called them, in a dedicatory poem to *Paradise Lost*, the *primordia rerum*, those first causes by which all things are determined, so to speak, in advance of themselves. That is why Milton's great epic looks back behind divine Creation to its very substance, or *ousia*, in the body of God, and that is why Milton's epic explains the catastrophe of human history—more particularly the failure of the English revolution—by going back to the Garden of Eden. He does not go back to the weakened Protectorate of Richard Cromwell or to the dictatorial Protectorate of Oliver Cromwell. He does not go back to the Barebones parliament, to the Rump Parliament, or to the Long Parliament. He goes back to the Garden of Eden. The scriptural account of the Fall is for Milton an axiomatic primal scene and his view of the Fall is not obscured by anything between him and that event, that is, it is not obscured by history. As in linear perspective, where the glance of the eye seems to travel across an empty distance, all of human history between Milton and the Garden of Eden becomes perfectly transparent. History does not appear until the end of the poem, after the Fall, so that it can be shown to derive from the Fall as from a first principle, its *archê*.

Spenser, by contrast, is not an archaic but an *archeological* thinker. He is temperamentally an investigator and a haunter of ruins, the remains of high cultures, marked, and indeed half-effaced with the passage of time. I don't believe Spenser ever held a book—whether it was Homer, or Petrarch, or Sidney—without thinking of it as an index of the passage of time, and without finding the poetical spirit in this temporal aura that the book seems to exhale.

Spenser is not a seeker of origins, therefore, but a seeker without a definite goal. Starting from where he is, he works patiently through the strata of historical remains because turning them over and meditating upon them stimulates his thinking and sends it down unexpected, improvisatory and even supernatural paths, to places where he encounters in the deposits a consciousness that is hard to distinguish from his own—so it seems, for example, in *The Ruins of Time*, when the genius of a place—of Verulam and Troynovant and Rome—appears among its ruins, and speaks. The overriding tone of lament—Spenser published an entire volume called *Complaints*—is the registration in consciousness of the passage of time. The tone of lament is also the registration in consciousness of the material remains of the past, for it is by lament that those remains are made conscious and so absorbed into thinking. In such thinking Spenser does not direct his eye to an object set at a fixed distance across which nothing intervenes. There is for him no "object," no thing impinging on consciousness from without (which is what the very word *object* implies), because the material remains of the past already belong to consciousness. What consciousness? We may call it the consciousness of the Muses, who are daughters of Memory, the mind of the poetic tradition into which Spenser's mind enters and with which it blends.

There is one especially conspicuous thinking moment in *The Faerie Queene*. It comes at the end. Mutabilitie is winding up her spectacular case against Jove, in which she has shown us the pageant of the seasons and months, followed by a survey of changeableness in the heavenly bodies, in the planetary spheres, and in the sphere of the fixed stars, which "even itself is mov'd, as wizards saine" (VII.vii.55). Mutabilitie could have read about those wizards in the proem to the fifth book of the very poem she is in: "those Egyptian wizards old,/ Which in Star-read were wont have best insight" (V.Proem.8). In every motion—and I remind you that this word, from Latin *moveo*, lies behind the word *moment*—Mutabilitie spies a moment of arrest, where her trophy might be raised:

Then since within this wide great *Universe*
  Nothing doth firme and permanent appeare,
  But all things tost and turned by transverse:
  What then should let, but I aloft should reare
  My Trophee, and from all, the triumph beare?
  Now judge then (o thou greatest goddesse trew!)
  According to thy self doest see and heare,
  And unto me adoom that is my dew;
That is the rule of all, all being rul'd by you.

(VII.vii.56)

Mutabilitie wants a swift, unthinking, favorable decision from Dame
Nature, having told the goddess not only what to think but how to
think: judge from what you see, from what appears, and you will see
that appearance itself is uncertain and wavering: "within this wide
great *Universe*/Nothing doth firme and permanent appeare." Such a
statement would seem to discredit seeing, but for Mutabiltie seeing
is the guarantee of truth: "But what we see not, who shall us per-
swade?" (VII.vii.49).

Now, Spenser is the greatest poet of appearances, of manifestation.
He is, for example, the poet who brings before our eyes as vivid
personifications all the rivers of the world, "Great Ganges, and immortall Euphrates,/Deep Indus, and Maeander intricate,/Slow Pene-
us, and tempestuous Phasides,/Swift Rhene, and Alpheus still
immaculate" (IV.xi.21). Even so, I am hardly the first to notice that
from the earliest episodes in *The Faerie Queene*, certainly from the
introduction of Archimago, Spenser harbors a distrust of his own as
well as of others' power to make manifest.[18]

In another thinking moment in *The Faerie Queene*, the episode of
the giant with the scales, the giant repeatedly urges Artegal to see,
to judge with his eyes. The scales with which the giant tries to
weigh all things are a means of verifying what is observed before it
is corrected. In this sense, the giant is the moral and epistemological
opposite of Mutabiltie, who thinks the wavering unsteadiness and
inequality of all things is delightful—because it is the manifestation
of her power. Artegal challenges the giant, in beautiful verse, to
"weigh the winde, that under heaven doth blow;/Or weigh the light,
that in the East doth rise;/Or weigh the thought which from man's
mind doth flow" (V.ii.43). Notice that this thought, "which from
man's mind doth flow," flows *from* the mind rather than within the
mind. It is thought that moves through the world, rather than thought
that, being confined to the head, can act outside itself only by moving
the limbs in the arena of unreflecting matter and motion. It is true
that Artegal summarizes his argument with the giant by stating that
"in the minde the doome of right must bee" but it is the thought,
not that mind, that flows out of itself. The mind remains in itself, in
the head, but thought flows into the world to animate and transform
it creatively.

Especially striking is Artegal's statement that "the eare must be the
balance, to decree/And judge" (V.ii.47). The ear as a balance, or a
set of scales, is a wonderful image because it cannot be visualized as
such. It requires thinking about the balance as a symbol of creation
by God—as it is in Isaiah—and of judgment by men. Dame Nature
herself will use it as such when she speaks of "all things" being

"rightly waid." When Artegal says "the ear must be the balance," he means that the ear is a true test, a means of verifying or of falsifying what only appears to be true. We remember from Blake's *Jerusalem* that the ear is a labyrinth (4.Pl.94), and this labyrinth is not so much an image of lost directions as it is of intricacy, like a neural net. That is why we must not think of Nature gazing on the pageant brought before her with the same rapt attention we give it. I suppose Nature's head is turned very slightly to the side, so that she can attend to how Mutabilitie speaks, leveling her ear and catching the insolence with which Mutabilitie says "*Now!*": "Now judge then (o thou greatest goddesse true.)" For Spenser, it is listening, not seeing, that is the privileged index for judging what flows into the mind; and it is speaking, not physically acting, that is the means through which thought flows out again into the world. Dame Nature's judgment, as it is pronounced in words, is what Spenser means when he speaks of "the thought which from man's mind doth flow."

When Mutabilitie concludes her harangue there is a protracted and tense moment of silence: "silence long ensewed, Ne *Nature* to or fro spake for a space,/But with firme eyes affixt, the ground still viewed." Of course, Nature is not *viewing* the ground at all; she is turning her eyes to the ground so that her ear will be turned toward what, as in a balance, she will weigh, which is not the spectacle she has seen but the voice she has heard: "What then should let, but I aloft should reare/My Trophee, and from all, the triumph beare?" In aristocratic cultures, with their indirect and even unconscious systems of signaling, close attention is paid to how things are said, to what we call *tone*, and the tone of Mutabilitie, as we should expect of a titaness, is pushy. She's a thruster. In the face of such pushiness, deliberate and unhurried calm must be shown. It is not a question of justice, in our more egalitarian sense of the word, but of desert: Mutabilitie doesn't deserve to rule all things. I would go so far as to say that it is also a question of aesthetics: for Mutabilitie to rule all things would be nauseating, arousing what the poet will call, in the first of the two stanzas of the "canto unperfit," *loathing*. So Nature, looking down, is not doing what Mutabilitie tells her to do. Nature is not thinking about the visual spectacle of the whirling motions of the stars or of the tormented gyres of the planets, or of the waning of the moon, or of the turning of the year, or of growing things fading in autumn and flourishing in spring, or even of the fish wavering in the currents of the sea as grass wavers in an uncertain wind. Nor is Nature thinking of the pageant of the life of man from birth to death and of the labors and terrors between. Nature is doing something that takes a moment: she is absorbing and testing, weighing in the balance of the ear the tone with which Mutabilitie speaks, which is why, when Nature answers at last, she does not say, "I well consider all that ye have *shown*"; she says, "I well consider all that ye have *sayd*" (VII.vii.58). She's considering *how* it was said, too.

During Nature's thinking moment, when "silence long ensewed," all the creatures present look anxiously at Nature's downturned face, impatiently awaiting what will follow, like the birds in Chaucer's *Parlement of Foules*: "Meanewhile, all creatures, looking in her face,/ Expecting th'end of this so doubtfull case,/ Did hang in long suspence what would ensew" (VII.vii.57). I am struck by the repetition of the word *ensue* because, although Dame Nature seems to consider the matter in a state of calm arrest that could continue indefinitely, she is also doing something from which something must *ensue*. I mean that there resides in her very stability and calm a moment of instability that necessitates development from one state to another. This is not a question whether or not the moment of arrest could ever be broken, although it is interesting to imagine the action stopping here, in this moment, for ever, so that centuries would pass as the creatures stare fixedly at Nature as she stares at the ground. The creatures would be blanketed by leaves falling in autumn and by the snows of innumerable winters, and like statues, their very forms would erode in the wind and rain until Arlo Hill itself, on which they stand, is washed down into the valley and carried off in Mulla or Bregog, or the silver, shining Shure, in which, even in that future epoch, when human beings have disappeared from the earth and their ruins are no longer haunted, "are thousand Salmons bred" (VII.vi.55).

We should imagine such a scene of arrest as part of the anxiety that the creatures feel: they're worried that Mutabilitie may be right, but they are also worried about the opposite condition of the world, which is the giant's unacknowledged goal: that nothing may ever change again, that everything will freeze. It's therefore not so much a question about change as it is a question of time signature—and of tempo. It is above all a question of who is in control of the tempo of thought, which is why it is important that Nature not be seen to be forced to give an answer in any fixed period of time, still less that she answer when Mutabilitie says she should, which is immediately. The very silence that ensues, in that moment of thinking, is like an isolating, transparent container. That is why Nature must *break* it, like a foetus in its caul: "At length, she looking up with chearefull view,/ The silence brake, and gave her doome in speeches few" (VII.vii.57).

In a classic article on "Mutabilitie," William Blissett draws attention to the importance of Nature's face at this moment, which having been formerly downturned and thoughtful now looks up with "chearfull view."[19] The purport of her answer is there, in that look. It is a *view* in the active, not the passive sense of the word: Nature is viewing her audience, which she is happy to see, since she has been gone for a moment, and her cheerfulness is part of the thought that will flow from her mind when she speaks.

We know what she says. It's one of the most famous stanzas in *The Faerie Queene*, as perfect in its musical organization as that other little masterpiece of sound, from a different thinking moment, the numerological stanza describing the House of Alma. Indeed, it says much the same thing as that other stanza, impelling the flow of a new kind of mutability, of kinetic transformative difference through which thinking moments blend with one another in what Hegel calls the bacchanalian whirl. Listen to how the rhymes come chiming in on one another at the end, imitating the effect of a sestina:

> I well consider all that ye have sayd
>   And find that all things stedfastnes doe hate
>   And changed be: yet being rightly wayd
>   They are not changed from their first estate;
>   But by their change their being doe dilate:
>   And turning to themselves at length againe,
>   Doe worke their owne perfection so by fate;
>   Then over them Change doth not rule and raigne;
> But they raigne over Change, and doe their states maintaine.
>
>   (VII.vii.58)

So intense is this moment, occurring but a handful of stanzas from the end of *The Faerie Queene*, that the poet feels impelled to take up its stance in the final two stanzas, each of which has the word *think* in its first line, and each of which is an instance of thought thinking itself in the world. Why then, we might ask, are there two?

Some of the language I have used to describe the convergence of consciousnesses in reading will recall the phenomenological approaches to literature, but I would emphasize the difference between consciousness and thinking. Both are important to the experience of the poem, but thinking is a peculiar kind of work that is done with consciousness—if consciousness is involved in it at all. Where consciousness modulates and changes, thinking advances. Where consciousness is passive, thinking is active and vigilant, perhaps most of all when it seems to be relaxed, tentative, or playful. Poetic thinking does this work, which is at once relaxed in its attentiveness to the other and rigorous in its attention to itself, to accomplish several things: to find something out about our moral nature; to enrich the wisdom we bring to reflection on that nature; to be in communion with the presences in the earth where we live—we might now say, to be "ecologically aware"—and to build a temple of song to the gods, whether or not there are, objectively speaking, any gods to sing to. For it is of our thinking nature to do so. Doing this asks much more of the poet, and of the poet's audience, than merely being conscious in a poetical way. It demands the tougher work of the thinking Spenser does in every moment of *The Faerie Queene*.

Harvard University

NOTES

1.   Paul Alpers, "The Poet's Poet," *The Spenser Encyclopedia*, ed. A. C. Hamilton et al. (Toronto: University of Toronto Press, 1990), 551b.

2.   *The Prelude* (1850), book 3, lines 281–84. In *The Prelude, 1799, 1805, 1850*, eds. Jonathan Wordsworth, M. H. Abrams, Stephen Gill (New York: W. W. Norton, 1979).

3.   *The Complete Works of William Hazlitt*, ed. P. P. Howe, vol. 5 (London: Dent, 1930). The quotations from Hazlitt are taken from the discussion of Spenser on pp. 34–44. See David Bromwich, "Hazlitt, William," *Spenser Encyclopedia*, 349–50.

4.   *Complete Works of Walter Savage Landor*, ed. Earle Welby, vol. 5 (London: Chapman and Hall, 1927), 204–05.

5.   "To Charles Cowden Clarke," line 33–34. See Greg Kucich, *Keats, Shelley, and Romantic Spenserianism* (University Park: State University of Pennsylvania Press, 1991), 142.

6.   Percy Bysshe Shelley, "Preface to *The Revolt of Islam*," in *Complete Poems of Percy Bysshe Shelley* (New York: Modern Library, 1994), 37–38.

7.   John Milton, "Of Education," in *The Complete Prose Works of John Milton*, vol. 2 (New Haven: Yale University Press, 1959), 277.

8.   *Franion* usually means a wanton male companion (OED). Spenser applies it to a woman here and also, as OED notes, at V.iii.22, where it refers to the False Florimell.

9.   Sean Kane, *Spenser's Moral Allegory* (Toronto: University of Toronto Press, 1989), 57–59.

10.   Sherwin B. Nuland, *The Art of Aging: A Doctor's Prescription for Well-Being* (New York: Random House, 2007), 230. Nuland attributes "compression of morbidity" to the Stanford gerontologist, James Fries.

11.   James Nohrnberg, *The Analogy of "The Faerie Queene"* (Princeton: Princeton University Press, 1976). Joseph Butler, *Analogy of Religion, Natural and Revealed* (1736), in which it is argued that there is "a general analogy between the principles

of divine government, as set forth by the biblical revelation, and those observable in the course of nature," warranting the conclusion "that there is one Author of both."

12.   C. S. Lewis, *The Allegory of Love: A Study in Medieval Tradition* (Oxford: Oxford University Press, 1938), 358.

13.   C. S. Lewis, *Surprised by Joy: The Shape of My Early Life* (London: Geoffrey Bles, 1955), 198, on the religious quality of the Hegelian Absolute, and 210–11, on Lewis's teaching: "I was now teaching philosophy (I suspect very badly) as well as English. And my watered Hegelianism wouldn't serve for tutorial purposes." One side of Lewis's nature was strongly attracted by the uncompromising rationalism of logical positivism, the other by the spiritual character of an unsatisfactory Hegelian-ism—Lewis actually preferred Berkeley—which would be given its quietus by A. J. Ayer's *Language, Truth and Logic*. It was with the poets, especially Spenser, that Lewis supplied his loss of faith in Hegelianism, and at this juncture Lewis's old English tutor at University College, F. P. Wilson, urged him to turn from philosophy to English, in response to which Lewis proposed "a study of the romantic epic from its beginnings down to Spenser," the first indication of what would become *The Allegory of Love*. A. N. Wilson, *C. S. Lewis: A Biography* (London: Collins, 1990), 85–89.

14.   "Those who put forward such an assertion also themselves say the direct oppo-site of what they mean." *Phenomenology of Spirit*, trans. A. V. Miller (Oxford: Oxford University Press, 1977), 65. This is section 3.4; paragraph 109.

15.   See Simon Jarvis, *Wordsworth's Philosophic Song* (Cambridge: Cambridge Uni-versity Press, 2007), a rich meditation on the ways in which Wordsworth's poetry effects a kind of thinking that is not "philosophical" in any formal sense of the word (as Coleridge had expected) but rather in a manner that is peculiar to poetry itself.

16.   Theodore W. Adorno, *Aesthetic Theory*, trans. Robert Hullot-Kentor (Minne-apolis: University of Minnesota Press, 1997), 91.

17.   Martin Heidegger, *Discourse on Thinking* (German title, *Gelassenheit*), trans. John M. Anderson and E. Hans Freund (New York: Harper and Row, 1966).

18.   The ambiguity is the theme of Kenneth Gross's *Spenserian Poetics: Idolatry, Iconoclasm, and Magic* (Ithaca: Cornell University Press, 1985).

19.   "Spenser's Mutabilitie," in *Essays in English Literature from the Renaissance to the Victorian Age, Presented to A. S. P. Woodhouse* (Toronto: University of Toronto Press, 1964), 39–40.

REBECA HELFER

Remembering Sidney, Remembering Spenser: The Art of Memory and *The Ruines of Time*

This article explores the art of memory in *The Ruines of Time*, especially in its memorial to Philip Sidney. The art of memory here represents not only the use of places and images as an aid to recollection, but also a story of history—a narrative about building upon the ruins of the past—drawn from the art's origin as told in Cicero's *De oratore*: the tale of the poet Simonides, which Cicero uses as a frame tale for his recollection of Rome's ruin. Spenser's poem marks his and Sidney's dialogue about the Ciceronian art of memory and its relation to England's collective memory, articulated in Sidney's *Defense of Poetry* and its response to *The Shepheardes Calender* and then continued in *The Ruines of Time*.

> It chaunced me on day beside the shore
> Of silver streaming *Thamesis* to bee,
> Nigh where the goodly *Verlame* stood of yore,
> Of which there now remaines no memorie,
> Nor anie little moniment to see,
> By which the travailer, that fares that way,
> This once was she, may warned be to say.[1]

*T*O SEE RUIN IS TO SEE DOUBLE: both a broken, irretrievable past and the desire for its repair. But what if there are no ruins to

Spenser Studies: A Renaissance Poetry Annual, Volume XXII, Copyright © 2007 by AMS Press, Inc. All rights reserved.

see? This dilemma confronts the speaker of *The Ruines of Time*, an accidental tourist of sorts who "chaunced . . . on day" to meet the unhappy spirit of Verulamium, a former Roman outpost in Britain whose ruins do not exist—not in stone, anyway. "There now re-maines no memorie,/Nor anie little moniment to see," the speaker warns, lest travelers miss the invisible Verlame whose ruins exist only memorially. This potential confusion of material and memorial ruin (inscribed in the title itself) points to the poem's central paradox: poetic monuments, like material ones, fall to ruin. Yet rather than repairing "the ruines of time," Spenser locates immortality in ruin itself—in poetry's ruins—and the process of recollection.

Modern visitors don't always notice the lack of Verlame's physical ruins, though this absence figures centrally in how Spenser reimagines the architecture of poetic immortality. "The ruins of Rome and of Verulam as the visible and material signs of the past introduce the problem which the immortality-of-poetry *topos* solves as a national key," Anne Janowitz writes, adding that "the lesson Spenser intends to teach . . . is that the image of the nation is made in poetry, and that poetry can ensure national immortality, repairing the ruins of previous empires and shifting the locus of the *translatio imperii* into the domain of poetic structure."[2] These remarks gesture to an opposition between empire and poetry. By this account, empire falls to ruin but monuments of poetry resist ruination; poetry thus achieves the permanence denied to empire. Indeed, Verlame seems to make this very case for poetic immortality. Spenser, however, makes a more subtle one.

The impulse to substitute literary for imperial immortality seems a natural solution for the dilemma faced by early modern authors. All of poetry's roads led to Rome—to Virgil's promise of endless empire—and Rome's fall to ruin produced a conflicting desire to repair this ruin for new nations and would-be empires, coupled with the acute knowledge that Rome's reputation had fallen beyond re-pair, its Babylonian church no longer welcome in England.[3] Spenser's *Complaints* volume, published in 1591 soon after the first three books of *The Faerie Queene*, acknowledges this problem, in part by appearing when it does, at an odd moment for a poet ostensibly following the path of the Virgilian *rota*.[4] Why would a poet apparently fashioning himself as England's "new Virgil" interrupt his praise of Gloriana and her burgeoning empire to reassert the presence of ruin in cultural memory—or, for that matter, to criticize the very court where we imagine Spenser hoped to find a home? One answer relates to Spen-ser's skepticism about reproducing an historical fiction of perma-nence, a complaint he makes in his epic and then underscores in *The*

Ruines of Time. Rather than substituting poetry for empire, Spenser illustrates how his fiction is like history: poetry participates in cycles of ruin and re-edification within time.

In effect, Spenser looks to another Rome to reform the architecture of immortality. That "where the goodly *Verlame* stood of yore" is no longer visible matters less than the fact that she lacks a location for memory—a problem which finds an answer, appropriately enough, in locational memory. Critics such as Millar Maclure have long seen the *ars memorativa* at work in this poem; as he suggests, *The Ruines of Time* evokes the "art of memory [as] a process of imprinting on the mind virtues, vices, states of being, as in the tradition described by Frances Yates."[5] Yet Spenser engages with this art not only as a technique—the use of imaginary places, often buildings, filled with vivid images that orators and poets would mentally traverse when remembering a speech or a poem—but also in a far more expansive way: as a narrative of ruin and re-edification based upon the art's origin as told in Cicero's *De oratore*. A recounting of the tale of the poet Simonides, who discovers the importance of location to memory when remembering a ruined edifice, frames Cicero's story of Rome's history.

This article traces a dialogue within *The Ruines of Time* about Cicero's art of memory, a dialogue that reforms fictions of permanence through a narrative of change, contingency, and continuity. This conversation turns on Verlame's remembrance of Philip Sidney, whom in death she venerates as the epitome of deathless poetry. While she appears to make utterly conventional claims for the immortality of Sidney's poetry, Spenser finesses these claims, in part by virtue of having Verlame make them; she is, after all, the poem in ruins that aspires to permanence. More broadly, the disparity between how the poem seems to define immortality and how it demonstrates immortality matters a great deal: rather than portraying poetic endurance as a monument that resists ruin, *The Ruines of Time* suggests that its immortality lies in the ongoing process of recollecting "ruines." This vision of immortality as an art of memory emerges fully in the context of Sidney.[6] *The Ruines of Time* looks back to Sidney's *Defense of Poetry*, which itself looks back to Spenser's *The Shepheardes Calender* and its implicit defense of poetry. Through these intertexts, *The Ruines of Time* marks a dialogue about the art of memory and the location of poetry in culture, the conclusions of which the progress of the poem itself serves to demonstrate. So even as Spenser subverts the poem's ostensive ideal of permanence as stasis, he nevertheless creates a place in poetry's ruins where England can remember itself perpetually.

The Ruines of Time reimagines poetry's ability to translate the past for the present in part through translation. By retranslating Du Bellay's seminal ruins poetry as the *Ruines of Rome* for the *Complaints*, Spenser effectively replies to Du Bellay's own ambivalence about emulating Virgil's authority.[7] Exploiting his ambivalent response to the ruins of Rome, Du Bellay creates an internal dialogue about Virgil's legacy. He expresses both longing to recreate Virgil's Rome—"that at least I could with pencill fine,/Fashion the pourtraicts of these Palacis;/By paterne of great *Virgils* spirit divine"—and despair at this impossibility: "To builde with levell of my loftie style,/That which no hands can evermore compyle" (*RR* 25). Du Bellay's sequence thereby vacillates between a longing to recover a Rome buried in ruins, what he calls "*Rome in Rome,*" expressed through necromantic and archaeological metaphors, and his sense that history matters as much as fiction, even if it contradicts his own desire for a lost Rome (3). Countering the fantasy of Rome's endless empire, the "*Rome in Rome*" Du Bellay seeks, he explores its infinite regress into ruin: "Alas, by little ye to nothing flie,/The people's fable, and the spoyle of all," concluding: "though your frames do for a time make warre/Gainst time, yet time in time shall ruinate/Your workes and names, and your last reliques marre" (7). Rome's empire was built not upon the legendary ruins of Troy, Du Bellay reminds himself, but rather upon the spoils, or ruins, of war and conquest. Moreover, Rome's ruin does not mark the end of history; instead, it reflects historical cycles until time's end. Most significantly, Du Bellay realigns poetry and history not through permanence but rather through ruin. Rome's fiction mirrors its history: the same cyclical edification Du Bellay sees in the rise and fall of the Roman empire he also finds, by analogy, in the process of literary imitation and creation. In other words, both memory and monuments fall to ruin and need to be remembered. The memorial ruins of Rome are now available for France's new cultural edifice, represented not least by Du Bellay's own architectural poetry. In neither heroic nor defeated terms, he describes himself less as a new Aeneas than as one of many pilgrims who gather Rome's memorial remains:

So grew the Romane Empire by degree,
Till that Barbarian hands it quite did spill . . .
Of which all passers by doo somewhat pill:
As they which gleane, the reliques use to gather,
Which th'husbandman behind him chanst to scater.

(30)

The transmission of culture figured here in agricultural terms as the mundane, incidental scattering of Rome's "reliques" nevertheless provides the foundation for Du Bellay's poem: Rome's rise and fall—from agriculture to culture and back again—parallels the speaker's artistic endeavor. When Du Bellay invokes the immortality of poetry *topos*, his hope for immortality has a ring of hopelessness to it. More accurately, he qualifies this conventional boast about poetic permanence by placing his poetry within history's cycles. "If under heaven anie endurance were," he writes, "These moniments, which not in paper writ,/But in Porphyre and Marble . . . / Might well have hop'd to have obtained it" (32). Instead of a memorial edifice that will resist ruination, these monuments remain in ruins. "Cease not to sound these old antiquities," he charges, intimating that future remembrance, gleaning, represents the only immortality possible.[8] By the end of the "Ruines of Rome," Du Bellay's ambivalence—always rhetorical as well as psychological—leads him to a new end: away from epic aspirations of endlessness and toward a georgic sense that immortality lies in the endlessly renewed labors of reading and recollection.

Spenser's response in *The Ruines of Time* registers the significance of Du Bellay's resolution. The English poet sees what lies beneath a Virgilian fiction of permanence: ruin capable of translating the past for the present not permanently but perpetually, insofar as ruin summons the reading and remembering of readers. Spenser begins where Du Bellay leaves off, with a city that "time in time" has ruined completely, its memory as well as its monuments:

> I was that Citie, which the garland wore
> Of *Britaines* pride, delivered unto me
> By *Romane* Victors, which it wonne of yore;
> Though nought at all but ruines now I bee,
> And lye in mine owne ashes, as ye see:
> *Verlame* I was; what bootes it that I was,
> Sith now I am but weedes and wastefull gras?
>
> (36–42)

Verlame comes by her ambivalence naturally, for she is simultaneously the spoil of "*Romane* Victors" and "that Citie . . . of *Britaines* pride," both the civic spirit of ancient Rome to whom Du Bellay beckons and Spenser's reply from ancient Britain. "*Verlame* I was," she declares in the past tense, and thus describes her present paradoxical state: "nought at all but ruines now I bee,/And lye in mine owne ashes, as ye see." The speaker, like the reader, sees nothing of Verlame "but weedes and wasteful gras." Verlame laments the loss of memory more than the loss of empire, though. Bemoaning the decay of her city into an empty, undemarcated space where memory once re-sided—"Where my high steeples whilom usde to stand," she com-plains, "There now is but an heap of lyme and sand,/For the Schriche-owle to build her balefull bowre" (127–30)—she also points to the broader implications of her decimation within the context of history. "Where be those learned wits and antique Sages," she asks, "Where those great warriors, which did overcomme/The world with conquest of their might and maine,/And made one meare of th'earth and of their raine?" (59–63). Time has taught Verlame that earthly monuments inevitably fall: "They all are gone, and all with them is gone,/Ne ought to me remaines, but to lament/My long decay, which no man els doth mone" (155–58). Only poetry, she asserts, persists.

The temptation to view *The Ruines of Time* as a corrective to Du Bellay's ambivalence makes sense, since Verlame positions poetry as the key to recovering her memory. Janowitz argues that for the Spenser of the *Complaints,* as "the lineage of poets—from Roman to Du Bellay to Spenser—is established . . . so the fame of empire is also preserved"; "thus the immortality of the nation is ensured by the *topos* of the immortality of poetry" (24). Poetic immortality would seem to repair, if only symbolically, the transmission of em-pire. As A. Leigh DeNeef suggests, "a metaphoric line much like . . . [a] conception of Troy-Rome-Troynovant corrects Verlame's notion that her city is simply and literally destroyed."[9] Certainly, Verlame despairs of the fall of Rome's empire; as she exclaims, "O *Rome* thy ruine I lament and rue/And in thy fall my fatall ov-erthrowe" (78–79). Yet by virtue of writing about Verlame, a city famous not only for resisting Roman conquest but also for sacking London-as-Troynovant, Spenser clearly avoids reproducing a Trojan lineage. Verlame stands de facto as the "anti-Troynovant": "In *Britan-nie* was none to match with mee," she boasts, "Ne *Troynovant,* though elder sister shee" (100–02).

Further, Spenser's distance from the Trojan legend—and his repre-sentation of the art of memory as a model of cultural transmission in *The Ruines of Time*—emerges from Verlame's defense of poetic immorality. Even if she has no desire to rebuild fallen empires, Ver-lame nevertheless seeks to repair the ruin of her memory, as well as England's, through poetry:

> Provide therefore (ye Princes) whilst ye live,
>   That of the *Muses* ye may friended bee,
> Which unto men eternitie do give.
>   For deeds doe die, how ever noblie donne,
>   And thoughts of men do as themselves decay,
>   But wise wordes taught in numbers for to runne,
>   Recorded by the Muses, live for ay;
>   Ne may with storming showers be washt away,
>   Ne bitter breathing windes with harmfull blast,
>   Nor age, nor envie shall them ever wast.
>
>   (365–406)

This conventional boast about the immortality of poetry—offering an escape from "deeds" and "thoughts" that inevitably "decay," providing a place where "wise words" can never "be washt away," an "eternitie" where neither "age, nor envie shall them ever wast" —finds a focus in the poem's memorializing lament for Sidney. Verlame rejoices that Sidney has joined "that blessed throng/Of heavenlie Poets and Heroes strong," contending his poetry is immortal on heaven and earth: "So there thou livest, singing evermore,/And here thou livest, being ever song/ . . . So thou both here and there immortall art" (337–43). "I will sing" Sidney's praises, she promises,

> . . . but who can better sing
> Than thou thy selfe, thine owne selfes valiance,
> That whilest thou livedst, madst the forrests ring,
> And fields resownd, and flockes to leap and daunce . . .
> To runne thy shrill *Arcadian* Pipe to heare.
>
>   (323–28)

Turning Sidney into an exemplar of the immortality of poetry *topos*, Verlame asserts that Sidney himself needs no memorial—unlike his family, particularly Leicester, who have been forgotten: "His name is worne alreadie out of thought,/Ne anie Poet seekes him to revive:/Yet manie Poets honourd him alive" (222–24). Verlame accuses Spenser's poetic persona of guilt in this regard, exemplifying England's amnesia: "Ne doth his *Colin*, carelesse *Colin Cloute*, Care now his idle bagpipe up to raise/ . . . Wake shepheardes boy, at length awake for shame" (225–31).

But Spenser undercuts Verlame's idealization of Sidney's poetic immortality, not least of all by providing Sidney with a memorial that he ostensibly does not need. This points to a larger contradiction: this invocation of the immortality of poetry *topos* ultimately does not accord with how the poem memorializes Sidney and his clan. Despite Verlame's apparently straightforward arguments for Sidney's "immortal art," Spenser counterpoints this simplicity, suggesting instead that immortality resides in a complex process of remembering that the ruins of poetry themselves elicit. That Verlame charges Spenser's poetic persona Colin Clout with the task of remembering Sidney's family matters not only because the *Calender* is dedicated to Sidney, but also because its model of poetry as an art of memory finds an elaborate reply in Sidney's *Defense of Poetry*.[10] This next section digresses—moving from Sidney's *Defense*, to Spenser's *Calender*, to Cicero's *De oratore*, and then back again—but with a clear end: in order to reveal the art of memory's role in *The Ruines of Time* as a *topos*, a location itself, for a dialogue about remembering the past.

II.

At the end of the *Defense*, Sidney serves up a malediction against poetry-haters that Spenser transforms into a wry commentary on poetic immortality. "Thus much curse I send you in behalf of all poets," Sidney declares, "that while you live, you live in love, and never get favor for lacking skill of a sonnet; and when you die, your memory die from the earth for want of an epitaph."[11] Spenser's epitaph for Sidney, *The Ruines of Time*, implies that "skill of a sonnet" alone cannot guarantee immortality. Rather, Spenser memorializes him through Sidney's own definition of poetry in the *Defense of Poetry*—as an art of imitation and an art of memory:

> . . . even they that have taught the art of memory have showed nothing so apt for it as a certain room divided into many places, well and thoroughly known. Now that hath the verse in effect perfectly, every word having his natural seat, which seat must needs make the words remembered. But what needeth more in a thing so known to all men? Who is it that ever was a scholar that doth not carry away some verses of Virgil, Horace, or Cato, which in his youth he learned, and even to his old age serve him for hourly lessons?

(54)

Sidney briefly describes the art of memory as a technique, suggesting that poetry's pretty rooms naturally provide such a place for memory: "seats" in the double sense of locations and topics. Yet even as he coyly asks, "what needeth more in a thing so known to all men?", Sidney points to the art's greater potential with another question: "Who is it that ever was a scholar that doth not carry away some verses of Virgil, Horace, or Cato" from "youth" to "old age?" With this query, Sidney suggests that poetry's art of memory provides a vehicle for cultural transmission. Crediting the "fitness it [poetry] hath for memory" to the "delivery of arts—from grammar to logic, mathematics, physic, and the rest"—he explains that "the rules chiefly necessary to be borne away are compiled in verses" (55). Sidney's expansion of the *ars memorativa* from "rules" to "verses" depends upon transmission, learning being "borne away" and reborn within the space of poetry, on poetry's ability to convey the past toward the present. This seems obvious to Sidney, who concludes "that verse, being in itself sweet and orderly, and being best for memory, the only handle of knowledge, it must be in jest that any man can speak against it" (55).

To understand poetry as an art of memory requires taking seriously the conceptual jest that underlies the *Defense*.[12] Sidney recalls *The Shepheardes Calender* and its apology for poetry through a witty parody of Spenser's first literary critic, E. K. This parody, a witty play on E. K.'s rhetoric of ruin, reflects a genuine response to Spenser's poetry and its reformation of the art of memory. Lamenting the state of poetry in England, Sidney says things could be worse but not much. "Why," he has demanded, should "England . . . be grown so hard a step-mother to poets, who certainly in wit ought to pass all other," why "poesy, thus embraced in all other places, should only find in our time a hard welcome in England?" (68–70). Poetry has enemies, but the real enemy lies within poets. Whither England's laureates? "I think the very earth lamenteth their absence, and therefore decketh our soil with fewer laurels than it was accustomed" (71). This neglect "should seem to *strew the house* for poets," he writes, figuring English culture as a ruined house of fame. Yet when Sidney famously cites *The Shepheardes Calender* as an exception to England's sad decline and fall, he proceeds *serio ludens* into Spenser's use of the art of memory:

> *The Shepheard's Calender* hath much poetry in his eclogues, in-
> deed worthy the reading if I be not deceived. That same framing
> of his style to an old rustic language I dare not allow, sith
> neither Theocritus in Greek, Virgil in Latin, nor Sannazzaro in

Italian, did affect it. Besides these, do I not remember to have
seen but few (to speak boldly) printed that have poetical sinews
in them . . . for proof whereof, let but most of the verses be put
in prose, and then ask the meaning, and it will be found that
one verse did but beget another, without ordering at the first
what should be at the last; which becomes a confused mass of
words with a tingling sound of rhyme, barely accompanied
with reason.

(74)

Sidney's model for this passage is E. K.'s introductory letter to *The
Shepheardes Calender* defending its poetry (16). E. K. attempts to justify
the author's apparently rough literary style by arguing that "this kind
of wryting, being both so base for the matter, and homely for the
manner," has been used by "young birdes . . . by little first to prove
theyr tender wyngs, before they make a greater flyght": "So flew
Theocritus . . . So flew Virgile . . . . Sanazarus, and also divers others
excellent both Italian and French Poetes, whose foting this Author
every where followeth" (18). Like Sidney's criticism of poets who
produce a "confused mass of words with a tingling sound of rhyme,
barely accompanied with reason," E. K. makes Spenser an exception
to "the rakehellye route of our ragged rymers," who "without learning boste, without judgement jangle, without reason rage and fome,
as if some instinct of Poeticall spirite had newly ravished them above
the meanenesse of commen capacitie" (17). Yet whereas Sidney rejects Spenser's *"framing of his style"* because it lacks classical precedent,
E. K. defends Spenser's style—"his dewe observing of Decorum every where, in personages, in seasons, in matter, in speach, and generally in al seemely simplycitie of handeling his matter, and *framing his
words*"— for the opposite reason: in order to give the "new Poete"
an old pedigree (13–14, my emphasis).

Sidney's criticism of *The Shepheardes Calender*'s style points us back
to E. K.'s own defense of Spenser's style in the *Calender*, a crucial
topic for understanding the functions of ruin and memory in Spenser's later *Complaints*. E. K. defends Immerito's strange "choyse of
old and unwonted words" (16) in an attempt to give the "new Poete"
a new name: "The Roman Tityrus Virgile" (13). Portraying Spenser
as a skilled literary architect, E. K. contrasts him with earlier poets
who "patched up the holes with peces and rags of other languages,
borrowing here of the french, there of the Italian, every where of
the Latine, not weighing how il, those tongues accorde with themselves, but much worse with ours: So now they have made our

English tongue, a gallimaufray or hodgepodge of al other speches"
(16). Spenser repairs this ruin, E. K. repeatedly argues, "For what in
most wryters useth to be loose, and as it were ungyrt, in this Authour
is well grounded, finely framed, and strongly trussed up together"
(17). Yet even as he strives to make a name for Immerito, E. K.
hints at his anxiety about Virgil's influence: rather than an immortal
monument that repairs the ruins of the past, E. K. worries, the *Calender* appears to be in ruins due to Immerito's archaic style. To bolster
his argument, E. K. turns to Cicero's authority on matters of style,
in order to demonstrate how these "olde and obsolete wordes" create
in Immerito's "worke an eternall image of antiquitie": "For if my
memory fayle not, Tullie in that booke, wherein he endeavoreth to
set forth the paterne of a perfect Oratour, sayth that ofttimes an
auncient worde maketh the style seeme grave, and as it were reverend," and "yet nether everywhere must old words be stuffed in, nor
the commen Dialecte and maner of speaking so corrupted therby,
that as in old buildings it seme disorderly and *ruinous*" (15).

But E. K.'s memory *does* "fayle" because he only half-remembers
the context for Cicero's discussion of style in *De oratore*: the art of
memory. As I have argued elsewhere, at stake is a disagreement between E. K. and Spenser about who (and what) builds immortality.[13]
For E. K., literary immortality requires an heroic poet, like Virgil,
who refashions cultural remains into an immortal monument, epitomized by the promise of Rome's "empire without end"; for Spenser,
immortality lies in ruins, in an ongoing renovation of poetry's figurative ruins. The difference between E. K. and Spenser amounts to
how they imagine poetic structure: whereas E. K. believes that poetry
represents an individual mnemonic, Spenser suggests that a literary
edifice is created through collective memory in the form of dialogue.
This disagreement points up an alternative interpretation of influential Ciceronian ideas of style and memory in *De oratore*. In effect,
Sidney's verbal echoes of E. K. in his *Defense* reminds readers of this
disagreement between Spenser and E. K. in *The Shepheardes Calender*
about the architecture of immortality. Yet Sidney also suggests what
he and Spenser share: a rhetoric of ruin, a sense of poetry as a Ciceronian art of memory. By wittily imitating E. K.'s style, Sidney
reverses E. K.'s defense of Spenser's style.

Although long viewed as an historical source for the *ars memorativa*,
Cicero's *De oratore* also transforms the art of memory into a tale about
cultural transmission, a story of Rome's history.[14] Moreover, Cicero
expands what this art means in the context of style—language and
decorum. When the speaker Antonius describes the art of memory
in Book II, he does so in perfunctory terms, not wanting to be "prolix

and impertinent upon so well-known a subject" (188), offering the story of the art's origin, the tale of Simonides, in the same winking fashion. After delivering a poem praising his patron, Simonides leaves the building when it falls to ruin:

> the apartment in which Scopas was feasting fell down, and he himself, and his company, were overwhelmed and buried in the ruins; and when their friends were desirous to inter their remains, but could not possibly distinguish one from another, so much crushed were the bodies, Simonides is said, from his recollection of the place in which each had sat, to have given satisfactory directions for their interment.
>
> (186)

Simonides, the story goes, is saved by the twin gods Castor and Pollux, who call him away from the banquet hall before it falls to ruin. "Simonides, or whoever else invented the art," Antonius concludes, gently dismissing the fiction, "is reported to have discovered that it is chiefly order that gives distinctness to memory," and that "certain places must be conceived in the mind, and ranged, as it were, in those places" (187). For Antonius, the fanciful story of Simonides's discovery matters far less than the techniques of artificial memory and its practical applications.

Book 2 ends with the art of memory's perfunctory treatment and Crassus's complaint that Antonius has left him only the insubstantial topic of style to speak about the following day. But style meets substance when Cicero begins Book III by describing a Rome in ruins—in terms clearly meant to evoke the tale of Simonides. Describing his "bitter remembrance" to his brother Quintus, Cicero recounts the death of Crassus and decline of the other interlocutors: "such misfortunes afterward fell upon the commonwealth, that life does not appear to me to have been taken away from Lucius Crassus by the immortal gods as a privation, but death to have been bestowed on him as a blessing," for Crassus "did not live to behold Italy blazing with war, or the senate overwhelmed with popular odium, or the leading men of the state accused of the most heinous crimes . . . or, finally, that republic in every way disgraced, in which, while it continued most flourishing, he had by far the pre-eminence over all other men in glory" (194). Counting Crassus's death as a gift from the gods, Cicero writes, "if any fortune had rescued you from so barbarous a death, the same fortune would have compelled you to

be a spectator to the ruins of your country" (195). Cicero *was* a
spectator to Rome's ruin and remembers it by rewriting the tale of
Simonides as a frame tale for *De oratore*'s book-cum-edifice: "For I,
who was not present at this dialogue, and to whom Caius Cotta
communicated only the topics and heads of the dissertation, have
endeavored to shadow forth in the conversation of the speakers those
particular styles of oratory, in which I knew that each of them was
conspicuous" (196). As a new Simonides, Cicero recollects the ruins
of Rome for his dialogue, remembering the discourse according to
the topics of the dialogue—like the seats or heads at Simonides's
banquet table.

De oratore functions as an art of memory. Yet Cicero's confession
that his recollection comes secondhand, that he "was not present at
this dialogue" and thus can only "shadow forth" the dialogue from
"topics," indicates the art's limits: it can neither rebuild the past nor
revive the dead. Instead, it can speak to the topics of Book III: style,
language, and decorum. By introducing the subject of style with the
art of memory, Cicero suggests that decorum applies as much to
culture as language. Without referring to decorum per se, he writes
that "it is . . . clear that no single kind of style can be adapted to
every cause, or every audience, or every person, or every occasion";
rather, Crassus argues, "on this head . . . no direction seems possible
to be given but this, that we adopt a character of style, fuller, plainer,
or middling, suited to the subject on which we are to speak" (255).
The pure Latin that he promises to delineate turns out to be a fiction
itself, and he struggles to find the right word to describe decorum,
calling it alternately "aptitude," "congruity," "eloquence," which
he sums up as speaking "gracefully" (203, 207). Similarly, the immortality Cicero promises turns out to be something of a fiction. Cicero
writes this dialogue "while we still retain a lively remembrance of
them, to render their fame, if I could, imperishable" (85). At the
same time, nothing is written in stone: "I publish an account to be
read by those who have frequently heard the men themselves of
whom I am speaking, that I may commend those two illustrious men
to such as have never seen either of them from the recollection, as
a testimony, of those to whom both those orators were known, and
who are now alive and present among us" (85). Cicero thus aims
to create an ongoing dialogue: those alive are free to challenge his
representation, but his hopes are directed toward posterity—inviting
future readers to engage in dialogue with writing. "Let us deliver
[*De oratore*] as a memorial to posterity," he declares, though this
edifice remains in ruins, a locus for future recollection (196).

Accepting Cicero's invitation, Sidney frames poetry as an expansive art of memory, a perspective that proceeds through his debate with E. K. (and Spenser) about issues of style. When Sidney complains that too many similitudes produce an over-wrought style, "a most tedious prattling, rather over-swaying the *memory* from the purpose whereto they were applied" (84), he turns to *De oratore* for support:

> For my part, I do not doubt, when Antonius and Crassus, the great forefathers of Cicero in eloquence, the one (as Cicero testifieth of them) *pretended not to know art, the other not to set by it*, because with a plain sensibleness they might win credit of popular ears; which credit is the nearest step to persuasion; which persuasion is the chief mark of oratory; I do not doubt (I say) but that they used these knacks very sparingly.
>
> Undoubtedly (at least to my opinion undoubtedly) I have found in divers smally learned courtiers a more sound *style* than in some professors of learning; of which I can guess no other cause but that the courtier, following that which by practice he findeth fittest to nature, therein (though he know it not) doth according to art, though not by art: where the other, using art to show art, and not to hide art (as in these cases he should do) flieth from nature, and indeed abuseth art.
>
> But what? Methinks I deserve to be pounded for straying from poetry to oratory.
>
> (84, my emphasis)

With characteristic *sprezzatura*, Sidney reveals and conceals what he means by *ars celare artem*: by "art" he refers to style and its relation to the art of memory. The act of hiding the art of memory in plain sight, a gesture inscribed within *De oratore* and *The Shepheardes Calender*, emerges as Sidney's jest.

Indirectly Sidney challenges E. K.'s views on language and poetry, engaging him in a way that emulates Spenser. On one point, Sidney and E. K. agree: the English language has been underestimated. E. K. argues that "our Mother tonge, which truely of it self is both ful enough for prose and stately enough for verse, hath long time ben counted most bare and barrien of both" (16). Sidney concurs: "For the uttering sweetly and properly the conceits of the mind, which is the end of speech," he writes, English should be regarded "equally with any other tongue in the world" (85). But here they part company. E. K. and Sidney fundamentally disagree about what style and Ciceronian decorum mean. E. K. denies that English should be a "mingled language" and his praise of Spenser never attempts to conceal this desire for linguistic purity: "we speak no English, but gibbrish," he argues, praising Immerito's use of "old words" as a return to real English and an heroic act of Renaissance: "he hath laboured to restore as to theyr rightfull heritage such good and naturall English words, as have ben long time out of use and almost cleare disherited" (16). Conversely, Sidney praises the eclecticism of the English language. "I know some will say it is a mingled language," he confesses, but "why not so much the better, taking the best of both the other?" (85). Making good use of the mingled English language, Sidney contends, represents a matter of artistic decorum: "we may bend to the right use both of matter and manner; whereto our language giveth us great occasion, being indeed capable of any excellent exercising of it" (84).

By contrasting the courtier's style with the professor's, Sidney challenges E. K.'s authority.[15] Although a "professor of learning," E. K. clearly knows less then he professes, for he asserts that his glosses reveal what the author "him selfe," Spenser, is "labouring to conceale" (19): "Hereunto have I added a certain Glosse or scholion for the exposition of old wordes and harder phrases" so "we might be equal to the learned of other nations," for "I was made privie to his counsell and secret meaning in them" (19). E. K. implies that his glosses justify the "old words" marring the *Calender*, as if repairing its ruins. Yet E. K.'s glosses almost always get things wrong or only partially right, and nowhere more poignantly than in his final gloss to the *Calender*. The final emblem has gone missing, but E. K. nevertheless glosses the blank space where the emblem should be with a declaration of the immortality of poetry *topos*: "The meaning whereof is that all things perish and come to theyr last end, but workes of learned wits and monuments of Poetry abide for ever," adding that Immerito "Hath made a Calender, that shall endure as long as time, etc. folowing the ensample of Horace and Ovid in the like" (212). The absence of Spenser's poetry offers a sly, silent riposte to E. K.'s intimations of immortality. By seeming to enact E. K.'s fear that the *Calender* already lies in ruins, Spenser implies that ruins function as the location for poetic immortality. Spenser's poetry as ruins provides a place for recollection for readers who, inevitably, will change the *Calender* through their interpretations.

Sidney gets the joke and locates this paradox at the very heart of his *Defense of Poetry*. Playing a game of hide-and-seek with the art of memory allows Sidney, like Spenser, to recuperate its use for poetry, not only as a poetic technique but as a way to imagine poetry as an agent of cultural transmission. In reversing E. K.'s defense of Spenser's style, Sidney emulates Spenser's implicit defense of poetry as a place of continuing dialogue and renovation. Sidney also joins Spenser in reforming the art of memory for poetry, less by replacing the rhetorical art of memory than by translating it into English, adapting its memorial *ruinae* for new edifices. As a technique, mnemonics has limits, as Sidney agrees: a "gorgeous palace, the architecture, with declaring the full beauties, might well make the hearer able to repeat, as it were by rote, all he had heard," but it "should never satisfy his inward conceits with being witness to itself of a true lively knowledge" (28). Still, he suggests this same art can do more than build castles in the air:

> if the saying of . . . *Tully* be true, that who could see virtue would be wonderfully ravished with the love of her beauty, this man sets her out to make her more lovely in her holiday apparel, to the eye of any that will deign not to disdain until they understand. But if anything be already said in the defence of sweet poetry, all concurreth to the maintaining the heroical, which is not only a kind, but the best and most accomplished kind of poetry. For as the image of each action stirreth and instructeth the mind, so the lofty image of such worthies most inflameth the mind with desire to be worthy, and informs with counsel how to be worthy.
>
> (48–49)

In this passage, Sidney illustrates his accommodation of the rhetorical art of memory to poetry. Just as Cicero "taketh . . . pains and [not] without poetical helps to make us know the force love of our country hath in us" (28), so Sidney adapts Cicero's fiction of the art for his own theory of poetry. Using misdirection, Sidney "directs" the architectural mnemonic "to the highest end of the mistress knowledge, by the Greeks called *architectonike*," the "end" of which is "well doing and not of well knowing only," "so that the ending end of all earthly learning, being virtuous action" (23). This "virtuous action" involves translating learning from poets to princes, past to present. He exemplifies this 'virtuous action' through poetry, specifically Virgil's *Aeneid*: "Only let Aeneas be worn in the tablet of your memory, how he governeth himself in the ruin of his country; in the preserving

his old father and carrying away his religious ceremonies, in obeying
the god's commandment to leave Dido" (48–49). For Sidney, epic
poetry—Virgil's—answers the need for the "heroicall," the quality
which Sidney argues makes poetry memorable and valuable.

Sidney thus answers E. K.'s (and perhaps Spenser's) anxieties about
Virgilian authorship by returning the art of memory to poetry while
also giving Virgil pride of place in a new context. Yet Sidney ultimately historicizes Virgil's legacy throughout his *Defense*, thereby
revising the role of ruin in cultural transmission. Without saying so
directly, Sidney deflates the Trojan legend as a model of *translatio*.
He tacitly denies the legend of Brutus when he describes how "In
Wales, the true remnant of the ancient Britons," poets called bards
survived despite invaders who "did seek to ruin all memory of learning"—yet, Sidney writes, "their poets even to this day last" (10).
The past survives in ruins, he acknowledges, specifically the ruins of
poetry. Sidney also winks at the godless tradition of Virgilian *sortes*,
"when by the sudden opening Virgil's book they lighted upon any
verse of his making, whereof the Histories of the Emperors' Lives
are full" (11). Albeit in passing, Sidney acknowledges the difference
between Virgil-the-Author and his historical reception. Rather than
epitomizing the Trojan legend, Aeneas becomes an exemplar of poetry as an art of memory—a model of cultural transmission. When
Sidney asks, "Who is it that ever was a scholar that doth not carry
away some verses of Virgil, Horace, or Cato, which in his youth he
learned, and even to his old age serve him as hourly lessons?" he
argues that poetry effects the transmission of culture (54–55). Poetic
memory forms the symbolic ruins that readers "carry away" from the
past, "verses" that continue the process of edification.

III.

In *The Ruines of Time*, Spenser demonstrates poetry as an art of memory, building the poem's memorial edifice within the place of
ruin—Sidney's as well as Verlame's—yet less as a new Virgil than as
a new Simonides, for even his own poetic monument is not "without
end." At the same time, Spenser replies to Sidney's return to the
heroic with Sidney's own life story: just as Sidney has Aeneas exemplify poetry as an art of memory, so Spenser has Sidney exemplify
the role of Aeneas, the heroic figure whom England needs to impress
upon its memory. *The Ruines of Time* thus continues a conversation

about the kind of cultural transmission that poetry can achieve. Spenser remembering Sidney remembering Spenser creates a dialogue about their arts of memory, a dialogue that Spenser then incorporates into his memorial. Together, they suggest that poetry creates the best location for memory in culture; and together they reform poetry's place in cultural transmission through locational memory. *The Ruines of Time* presents the art of memory in the broadest possible terms, offering readers multiple ways of thinking about locational memory. The oratorical display by which Verlame reconstructs her "High towers, faire temples, goodly theaters," demarcating spaces "with faire pillours," and filling them with "fine imageries" can be seen as a literary art of memory: spaces and images designed to aid to the recollecting of key topics (92–96). Similarly, the final visions produce a kind of emblematic memory theater.[16] But Spenser also suggests that the art of memory functions as a story of ruin and recollection. Sidney's life story not only dovetails with his theory of poetics; it also provides England with a history to remember. Through Verlame's and Sidney's stories, Spenser expands the art of memory from its limited pictorial sense into narrative: a story that translates the past for the present, that continues to build upon the ruins of time.

This art of memory creates an undercurrent in *The Ruines of Time*, offering a more complex view of immortality than Verlame's praise of Sidney's poetry would seem to suggest. As with E. K., we might imagine that Spenser creates a tacit dialogue with Verlame about his own poetry, that Spenser and Verlame disagree about what immortality looks like. Ultimately, though, Spenser makes her claims about poetic permanence deeply ambiguous, such that they can be read in two different ways: as either an absolute statement of poetic incorruptibility or as a qualified assertion of perpetuation. The purpose of this anamorphic image becomes clear. The shape immortality takes—whether whole or ruined—depends upon location and locational memory. When Verlame asserts that "deeds do die, how ever noblie donne,/And thoughts of men do as themselves decay,/But wise wordes taught in numbers for to runne,/Recorded by the Muses, live for ay," she suggests the absolute intransience of poetry (399–403). Yet when comparing those who "live for aye above" with "the Gods" and "on Nectar and Ambrosia do feede" and those "soules" or "mortall wreakes" who live "in foule forgetfulnesse, and nameless lie," Verlame also implies that place matters to memory. Poetry may be immortal in heaven—on the "golden throne" of Jove, "the father of eternitie"—but not necessarily on earth, as the title of Spenser's poem suggests (365–70). As such, Verlame's claim that "fame with golden wings, aloft doth flie,/Above the reach of ruinous

decay" should be taken literally; immutable immortality heads to
heaven, but poetry remains in ruins within time (421–22). Within
the earthbound world of England, immortality needs to be retrieved
from oblivion. Verlame's final invocation of the immortality of poetry *topos* clarifies poetry's ability to translate between places and
times:

> The seven fold yron gates of grislie Hell,
> And horrid house of sad Proserpina,
> They able are with power of mightie spell
> To breake, and thence the soules to bring awaie
> Out of dread darknesse, to eternall day,
> And them immortal make, which els would die
> In foule forgetfulnesse, and nameles lie . . .

> So raisde they eke faire *Ledaes* warlick twinnes,
> And interchanged life unto them lent,
> That when th'one dies, th'other then beginnes
> To shew in Heaven his brightnes orient.

(372–89)

As this description of poetry suggests, poetry both bestows immortality and partakes of it, creating exchange between past and present,
the living and dead. Poetry makes immortal what otherwise would
"in foule forgetfulnesse, and nameles lie," not because it creates a
monument that never falls to ruin but because poetry's ruins create
a place for a process of recollection.

Through a series of images, Spenser illustrates poetic immortality
as a kind of reciprocity. In each case, recalling the dead to life occurs
temporarily: Persephone must return to the underworld, Eurydice to
death, and in the case of Castor and Pollux, "when th'one dies,
th'other then beginnes" (388). Through the example of Castor and
Pollux, "faire *Ledaes* warlick twinnes," who play a key role in the
tale of Simonides, Spenser suggests how poetry acts as an art of memory: poetry recalls the dead from the ruin of forgetfulness, but returns
to this state as well. Adapting the story of Castor and Pollux, Spenser
indicates that this relationship mirrors his relationship with Sidney:
by remembering one another, Sidney and Spenser create an exchange
between heaven and earth (or England), continuing the cycle that
constitutes immortality.[17]

Ruin can now function as a place for recollection rather than a reminder of forgetfulness. But if we have trouble crediting the poem's idiosyncratic theology, Spenser draws attention to the fact that his primary aim is cultural rather than religious.[18] Bringing heaven down to earth, so to speak, and paying homage with the art of memory, Spenser makes Sidney into both subject and text. Indeed, Sidney's apotheosis evokes his description of the proper location of wit: in the heavens. As he writes in the *Defense*, "The grammarian speaketh only of the rules of speech" and "theron gives artificial rules, which are still compassed within the circle of a question," whereas "only the poet . . . goeth hand in hand with nature, not enclosed within the narrow warrant of her gifts, but freely ranging only within the *zodiac of his own wit*" (14; my emphasis). Spenser translates the association of fame with the stars into a memory theater that remembers Philisides: Sidney-as-Star-lover exemplifies how ruin translates into immortality.

Remembering *is* immortality, and remembering Sidney's life story illustrates this notion; the state of Sidney's memory, whether whole or ruined, depends upon its location. Poetry can translate immortality from heaven to earth not permanently but rather contingently, a process of exchange illustrated by Sidney's and Spenser's remembrances of each other's arts of memory. Through Sidney's apotheosis in the poem's final visions, which depict the ruins of time while remembering his role in England's nation and culture, Spenser teaches his art of memory. Verlame concludes her complaint by drawing attention to her paradoxical state: "Let them behold the piteous fall of mee . . . / And his owne end unto remembrance call; / That of like ruine he may warned bee, / And in himselfe be moov'd to pittie mee" (461–69). Readers are once again asked to see her absent presence—her invisible ruin. "Thus having ended all having ended all her pitious plaint, / With dolefull shrikes she vanished away," Spenser's narrator explains, though "Looking still, if I might of her have sight" (470–71). The fact that Verlame remains in a state of memorial ruin ultimately becomes the point of the poem, the lesson that Spenser offers. Busy recalling her "passion strong" and "renewing her complaint," the speaker is presented with a series of visions appear which, in effect, offer a double vision of poetic immortality (479–81). "Before mine eies strange sights presented were," he says, "Like tragick Pageants seeming to appeare" that enact the drama of cultural recollection in a theater of memory (489–90). The first set of emblems portrays images of destruction: an "Image, all of massie gold, / Placed on high upon an Altare faire/ . . . Then downe it fell, and low in ashes lay"; "a stately Towre" that falls "sodainlie to dust," a "Bridge

made all of golde . . . that down shortly fell" (546–48), a giant who
falls into "the deepe Abisse" (491–558). Crucially, though, poetry
falls to ruin in the same way: "I did see a pleasant Paradize / . . . Made
for the gentle squire, to entertain, / His fayre *Belphoebe* . . . / But o
short pleasure bought with lasting paine, / . . . I saw this gardine
wasted quite" (519–29). With this vision of *The Faerie Queene* itself
falling to ruin, Spenser suggests that his own monument of poetry
cannot stand permanently, marking his path as different from Virgil's.

   With the next set of emblems, Sidney's apotheosis demonstrates
how the past translates into the future not whole but in ruins. The
speaker looks heaven-ward to see the process by which Sidney's remains translate into immortality: a swan who becomes "an heavenly
signe" (601); "th'Harpe of Philisides . . . / beside the Northern
Beare" (609, 616); "A curious Coffer . . . / . . . transform'd into that
starre, / In which all heavenly treasures locked are" (618, 629–30):

A Knight all arm'd, upon a winged steed . . .
Fully mortally this Knight ywounded was,
That streames of blood foorth flowed on the gras.

Yet was he deckt (small joy to him alas)
With manie garlands for his victories,
And with rich spoyles, which late he did purchas
Through brave atcheivements from his enemies:
Fainting at last through long infirmities,
He smote his steed, that straight to heaven him bore,
And left me here his losse for to deplore.

                                                    (646–58)

Spenser allows Sidney to translate his "manie garlands" to heaven (as
the memory of Sidney's "brave atcheivements") and, by extension,
to offer England these "victories" to remember. With this image of
Sidney's apotheosis, the material remains or "rich spoyles"—the stuff
of history—are transformed into the "ruines of time," the stuff of
immortal memory.

   By calling his poem *The Ruines of Time*, Spenser emphasizes the
work's location within time and history. The struggle to retrieve
Sidney's heavenly memory continues even for Spenser, who concludes that he has built this poetic edifice by recollecting the "riche
spoyles" of memory:

Immortal spirite of *Philisides*,
Which now art made the heavens ornament,
That whilom wast the worlds chiefst riches;
. . . with last duties of this broken verse,
Broken with sighes, to deck thy sable Herse.

. . . Vouchsafe this moniment of his last praise.

(673–82)

As Spenser directs Sidney's sister to "vouchsafe this moniment of his last praise" in part as a bid for further patronage, he reminds readers that *The Ruines of Time* must be remembered to live on after the death of its author. Clearly, Spenser's own immortality depends not only upon his ability to remember others but also upon being remembered himself. With his final tentative invocation of the immortality of poetry *topos*, Spenser makes his poem the place or location that Verlame claims England lacks. This poetic edifice, both built from ruin and destined to return to ruin, encloses Spenser's vision of immortality as ongoing remembrance. Spenser intimates that his "broken verse" will be ruined and recollected again.

The status of the poem matters. *The Ruines of Time* remains in ruins, a contingent edifice meant to be renovated in future dialogue. In this regard, the process of recollecting matters more than the product, the poetic monument less than what remains of it, for these ruins will translate to new times and places. Spenser thus creates a memory theater for Sidney and England which explores how poetry builds and rebuilds immortality from and within the ruins of time. Poetry would seem to offer no guarantee of memorial permanence, witnessed by the ostensibly ruinous state of the poem itself. Yet while Spenser never invests his or any other poetic structure with static immortality, he still champions poetry's ability to translate the ruins of the past for new memorial edifices. Perhaps the pathos and ambivalence associated with ruin in the Renaissance—the impossibility of rebuilding cultural or imperial permanence in Virgil's image—also provided an impetus for creativity. After all, to complain of ruin was one way to make space for authors like Spenser, who could gather the ruins and make something new of inevitable decay.

University of California, Irvine

NOTES

I am grateful to David Galbraith and Theresa Krier for their intellectual engagement and support. This article is dedicated to Ian Andrew Munro and Anne Lake Prescott, two souls of wit.

1.   *The Ruines of Time*, 1–7, *The Yale Edition of the Shorter Poems of Edmund Spenser*, ed. William Oram et al. (New Haven: Yale University Press, 1989). All citations of *The Ruines of Time*, *Ruines of Rome*, and *The Shepheardes Calender* are from this edition.

2.   Anne Janowitz, *England's Ruins: Poetic Purpose and National Landscape* (Oxford: Basil Blackwell, 1990), 21. I am building upon Janowitz's argument that *The Ruines of Time* responds to the anxiety of influence with novelty: "Spenser's version of continuity points his own nation and its poetry in the direction of futurity" (27). My thinking here is indebted to David Galbraith's *Architectonics of Imitation in Spenser, Daniel, and Drayton* (Toronto: University of Toronto Press, 2000), which examines the complex relation between poetry and history.

3.   They also led to Ovid and to metamorphosis as a model of imperial and cultural edification. But Ovid's assertion of change without end provides a different kind of answer to Virgil's empire without end than the art of memory. On Ovid and Virgil in Spenser, see Theresa Krier, *Gazing on Secret Sights: Spenser, Classical Imitation, and the Decorums of Vision* (Ithaca: Cornell University Press, 1990).

4.   As Richard Rambuss argues, "By publishing these corrosive poems between the installments of his epic, and hence interrupting in midcourse his path along the *rota Virgilii*, Spenser is also staging an implicit challenge to the example of Virgil as the normative model for the poetic career"; see Rambuss, *Spenser's Secret Career* (Cambridge: Cambridge University Press, 1993), 87. See also Patrick Cheney, *Spenser's Famous Flight: A Renaissance Idea of a Literary Career* (Toronto: University of Toronto Press, 1993).

5.   "Spenser and *The Ruines of Time*," *A Theatre for Spenserians*, ed. Kennedy and Reither (Toronto: University of Toronto Press, 1973), 7. For work on *The Ruines of Time*, see, for example, Deborah Cartmell, " 'Beside the shore of silver streaming Thamesis': Spenser's Ruines of Time," *Spenser Studies* 6 (1985): 77–82; and Lawrence Manley, "Spenser and the City: The Minor Poems," *Modern Language Quarterly* 43 (1982): 203–27.

6.   On Sidney and Spenser, see S. K. Heninger, Jr., *Sidney and Spenser: The Poet as Maker* (University Park: Pennsylvania State University Press, 1988). In his letters to Gabriel Harvey, Spenser describes his literary relationship with Sidney: they have "drawen mee to their faction," Spenser writes, intimating his involvement in reforming English verse—the "silenc[ing] of balde rymers"; see *The Works of Edmund Spenser*, v. 6, ed. Greenlaw et al. (Baltimore: Johns Hopkins University Press, 1949), 6. Still more compelling is the way that the art of memory frames Harvey's letters to Spenser. Harvey first letter begins with reference to the art: "*Immerito*, in good soothe my poore Storehouse will affourd me nothing" as your "large, lavish, Luxurious, Laxative Letters," but he writes, "I shall be faine to supplye the office of the Arte Memorative, and putte you in minde of a pretty Fable in *Abstemio*" (441–42). Harvey concludes his final letter with a reference to the art of memory in the context

of Spenser's poetry: "I dare saye you wyll holde your selfe reasonably wel satisfied, if youre *Dreames* be but as well esteemed of in Englande, as *Petrarches Visions* be in Italy . . . But, see, how I have the *Arte Memorative* at commaundement. In faith, I had once againe nigh forgotten your *Faerie Queene*" (471), which Harvey suggests does not follow classical or current precedents as well as it might. Harvey's strange, fascinating recollection of the 1580 earthquake, which affords him an opportunity to reflect upon ruin and its significance throughout history, might be taken as a rewriting of the tale of Simonides. In any case, their letters strongly suggest their mutual interest in the art of memory.

7.   Spenser revisited his youthful translations of ruins poetry for Jan Van der Noot's Protestant polemic-cum-emblem book, *Theatre for Worldlings*, which extended Virgilian golden-age rhetoric to England's empire. On Van der Noot's *Theatre*, see Carl Rasmussen, "Quietnesse of Minde: *A Theatre for Worldings* as a Protestant Poetics," *Spenser Studies* 1 (1980): 3–27.

8.   On Du Bellay, see Thomas Greene, *The Light in Troy: Imitation and Discovery in Renaissance Poetry* (New Haven: Yale University Press, 1982); Anne Lake Prescott, *French Poets and the English Renaissance: Studies in Fame and Transformation* (New Haven: Yale University Press, 1978); and Margaret Ferguson, "The Afflatus of Ruin: Meditations on Rome by Du Bellay, Spenser, and Stevens," in *Roman Images*, ed. Annabel Patterson (Baltimore: Johns Hopkins University Press, 1982).

9.   A. Leigh DeNeef, *Spenser and the Motives of Metaphor* (Durham: Duke University Press, 1982), 35. Sidney's family tree seems to provide an historical alternative to the legendary Trojan genealogy. DeNeef makes the key point that though Spenser praises Camden for remembering Verlamium, Camden's history itself does not secure Verlame's memory; see "The Ruines of Time: Spenser's Apology for Poetry," *Studies in Philology* 76 (1979): 262–67.

10.   On Sidney's legend and multiple personalities, see Alan Hager, *Dazzling Images: The Masks of Sir Philip Sidney* (Newark: University of Delaware Press, 1991); and Lisa Klein, *The Exemplary Sidney and the Elizabethan Sonneteer* (Newark: University of Delaware Press, 1998).

11.   Sidney, *An Apology for Poetry*, ed. Robinson (New York: Macmillan, 1970), 88.

12.   For a discussion of Sidney's playful side, see "Play and the Courtly Maker," in Dorothy Connell, *Sir Philip Sidney and the Maker's Mind* (Oxford: Clarendon Press, 1977).

13.   See my article, "The Death of the 'New Poete': Virgilian Ruin and Ciceronian Recollection in *The Shepheardes Calender*," *Renaissance Quarterly* 56 (Fall 2003): 723–56.

14.   On Cicero's *De oratore* and the art of memory, see Frances Yates, *The Art of Memory* (Chicago: University of Chicago Press, 1966); Mary Carruthers, *The Book of Memory: A Study of Memory in Medieval Culture* (Cambridge: Cambridge University Press, 1990); and my forthcoming article, "Arts of Recollection and Cultural Transmission," in *Translatio, or the Transmission of Culture*, ed. Laura Hollengreen, *ASMR* 13 (Turnhout: Brepols, 2007).

15.   Sidney also seems to allude to Castiglione's rewriting of *De oratore* in *The Courtier*. Further, the English translator Thomas Hoby writes an introductory letter in which he sounds not unlike E. K.: "As I therefore have to my smal skil bestowed

some labour about this piece of woorke, even so coulde I wishe with al my hart . . . that we alone of the worlde maye not be styll counted barbarous in oure tunge, as in time out of minde we have bene in our maners. And so shall we perchaunce in time become as famous in Englande, as the learned men of other nations have ben and presently are"; see *The Courtier*, ed. Virginia Cox (London: Everyman, 1994), 7.

16.   On the relation between the art of memory and emblematics, see Rosemary Freeman, *English Emblem Books* (London: Chatto & Windus, 1970); Michael Bath, *Speaking Pictures: English Emblem Books and Renaisance Culture* (New York: Longman, 1994); John Bender, *Spenser and Literary Pictorialism* (Princeton: Princeton University Press, 1972). On theater and the art of memory, see Yates, *Theatre of the World* (London: Routledge & Keegan Paul, 1969).

17.   In the account in *The Odyssey*, Castor and Pollux exchange places endlessly: "both buried now in the life-giving earth though still alive. Even under the earth Zeus grants them that distinction: one day alive, the next day dead, each twin by turns, / they both hold honors equal to the gods' " (XI.344–47); *The Odyssey*, trans. Robert Fagles (New York: Penguin, 1996).

18.   How do we reconcile these secular and sacred portraits of immortality? Verlame can sound both self-pitying, her lamentation for former empires and confidence in poetry's immortalizing abilities an articulation of her flawed pagan perspective, and strangely Christian: a theology buttresses her complaint when Verlame lambastes this "vaine world" and "sinfull earth" (43–44), warning against the "trustless state of miserable men, / That builde your blis on hope of earthly thing, / And vainly thinke your selves halfe happie then" (197–99). Richard Brown Danson argues that the mingling of sacred and profane ideas of immortality relates to Spenser's desire to accommodate the two: "In transforming the didactic form of the vision into something more symbolic, Spenser effects and accommodation between Christian and humanist ideas of immortality through the transcendent Sidney"; Danson's *'The New Poet': Novelty and Tradition in Spenser's Complaints* (Liverpool: Liverpool University Press, 1999), 127. But their irreconcilability seems to be the point: fact and fiction mingle because Spenser is not offering religious truths but cultural—poetic and historical—ones. I would argue that Spenser complains throughout his work about imitating Virgil *because* this involves turning fiction into theology.

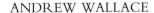

ANDREW WALLACE

Edmund Spenser and the Place of Commentary

The paper argues that the enigmatic commentator E. K.'s often baffled, often baffling engagement with Spenser's pastoral poems generates problems which gradually become integral to Spenser's art. It argues, further, that the scholarly apparatus that brackets each of the New Poet's pastoral poems in 1579 becomes internal to the rhetorical and narrative mechanics of *The Faerie Queene*. As if reflecting on the particular encounter between commentator and text that gives material form to *The Shepheardes Calender* (a book in which poetry constantly rubs elbows with commentary), Spenser adopts as one of his chief intellectual preoccupations the encounter between puzzled, desiring observer or interpreter and the baffling, recalcitrant spectacle or work of art. These preoccupations reemerge forcefully during Britomart's sojourn in the House of Busirane, which the essay reads as an allegory of the practice and position of commentary.

*T*HIS ACCOUNT OF THE PLACE of commentary in Spenser's poetry is grounded in three related intuitions: first, that Spenser's poems everywhere give evidence that their maker delights in fashioning encounters between mysterious or enigmatic scenes or tableaux and their would-be interpreters; second, that the frequency with which Spenser stage-manages those encounters bespeaks the poet's all but overwhelming appetite for commentary; and third, that the practice of commentary is for Spenser charged with desire and couched in the language of sexual intimacy.

My understanding of the intellectual stakes of Spenser's fascination with these obscure encounters is guided in part by Paul Ricoeur's

Spenser Studies: A Renaissance Poetry Annual, Volume XXII, Copyright © 2007 by AMS Press, Inc. All rights reserved.

insistence that "Enigma does not block understanding but provokes it."[1] Ricoeur advances this assertion while studying the process by which "the problem of symbols enters into the wider problem of language"; my own more modest goal, however, is not to study or define the symbolic but rather to measure the intensity with which Spenserian agents seem haunted by the suspicion that there is always something (to borrow another of Ricoeur's phrases) "to unfold, to 'dis-implicate' " in what Spenser has set before them.[2] This is, as I will call it, the critical moment to which Spenser returns again and again in what amounts to an insistent preoccupation with the encounter between puzzled, desiring observers or interpreters and the baffling, recalcitrant spectacle or work of art. Throughout his career Spenser vacillates between the possibility that such moments breed an overwhelmed silence, on the one hand, and an overwhelming desire to speak on behalf of the silent aesthetic object, on the other. With these dynamics in mind, Ricoeur's emphasis on the ways in which enigmas seem to solicit interpretation provides a compelling gloss on a pair of remarks that are much closer to Spenser's historical moment. George Puttenham, for instance, speaks of the ways in which enigmatic or riddling speech generates a particular kind of interpretive labor: "we dissemble againe under covert and darke speeches, when we speake by way of riddle (Enigma) of which the sence can hardly be picked out, but by the parties owne assoile."[3] Here, the interpretive field imagined by Puttenham contains an auditor who strives "hardly" to pick out a solution, and a solution that may belong to the enigmatic speaker alone. Puttenham's definition magnifies the vexatious quality of Henry Peacham's description of "Aenigma" as "a kind of Allegorie, differing only in obscuritie, for Aenigma is a sentence or forme of speech, which for the darknesse, the sense may hardly be gathered."[4]

The encounters in which I am interested recur with special frequency in the narratives of *The Faerie Queene*. One representative moment might be Spenser's framing of Calidore's ardent desire to find words for the spectacle he secretly observes and then shatters when he steps from his hiding place on Mount Acidale. Britomart's silent interpretive work in the final cantos of Book III offers an even more suggestive example, however, and I will argue that her sojourn in the House of Busirane, along with the dark arts of Busirane himself, constitute something like an allegory of the practice of commentary. On this account, the material forms in which commented texts reached their early modern readers—that is, with their margins and back pages swimming with interpretation and controversy—are subjected to narrative scrutiny in Busirane's rooms.

Spenser's assiduous fashioning of these encounters, and his practice of continuous commentary on them, help account for the alluring reticence of so much of the poetry of *The Faerie Queene*. Seeing these moments or encounters as conditions of Spenser's art helps explain his eagerness to revisit again and again the gap that separates his narrators (his poems, his knights, etc.[5]) from the scenes, figures, and images with which they interact and whose interpreters Spenser compels them to become. One thinks in this context of the almost outrageously offhand manner in which *The Faerie Queene* records Archimago's curiosity about the allegory in which he somehow knows himself to be an agent. Disguised as Red Cross, Archimago sidles up to Una and her lion, takes stock of this odd couple, and is said by the narrator to have asked Una "what the lion ment" (I.iii.32.8).[6] If there is a lesson here, it is that Spenser's allegories hunger for commentary.

As I have suggested, these issues will pull my argument towards the House of Busirane, but a more natural point of entry into the mechanics of commentary is *The Shepheardes Calender*, a volume whose consumption by inquisitive readers is thematized in the interpretive labors of E. K., the New Poet's apparently self-appointed commentator. My desire to establish a set of connections between what E. K. does to Spenser's pastoral collection in 1579 and what Busirane is doing to Amoret at the end of the 1590 *Faerie Queene* is rooted in a conviction that the alternating spatial disposition of poem and commentary in *The Shepheardes Calender* is reimagined as a constitutive element of the rhetorical texture of Spenser's later poetry. To put this another way, the formal scholarly apparatus that brackets each of the twelve poems of *The Shepheardes Calender* becomes internal to the rhetorical and narrative method of *The Faerie Queene*. This sense that the practice of commentary infiltrates narrative structures is in many ways a ripe old epic convention. Andrew Ford, for example, has offered an illuminating reconstruction of the history of the relationship between riddling, enigmatic speech and the practice of epic allegoresis.[7] Ford notes that Homer's heroes already "exhibit an aptitude for the allegoresis of divine and heroic names,"[8] and argues that the practice of interpreting epic allegorically is born of a desire to apply to epic interpretive strategies developed to decode riddles. Returning to the Spenserian problems at hand I want to suggest that Spenser's career might be described as a series of attempts to make the formal interpretive postures that bracket and cluster around the poems of *The Shepheardes Calender* flash within the later poems, as if the later poems were always actively seeking to open up and study their own secret declivities.

The Shepheardes Calender establishes a problematic that will exercise Spenser's attention for the rest of his poetic career.[9] The enigmatic commentator E. K.'s often baffled, often baffling engagement with Spenser's pastoral poems generates problems which gradually become integral to Spenser's art. As if reflecting on the particular encounter between commentator and text that gives material form to *The Shepheardes Calender* (a book in which formal poetry constantly rubs elbows with formal commentary), Spenser labors to explore in increasingly adventurous ways different material and theoretical relationships between text and commentary. Seminal work on the history of the glossed page in England by William W. E. Slights, Evelyn B. Tribble, and others always pauses at *The Shepheardes Calender* as at a pilgrimage site.[10] This, I take it, is due not only to the fact that the volume is such a famously and complex specimen, but also to the fact that it seems self-consciously to theorize the traditions in which it participates. For Slights, who notes that "Fully half of Spenser's one-hundred-eleven-page book is by someone else—unless the elusive E. K. is actually Spenser engaging in a highly self-reflexive form of glossarial play," the question of the extent to which the glosses are self-reflexive is inseparable from the vexed question of E. K.'s identity.[11] And yet, it is not clear to me why self-reflexiveness or glossarial play cannot equally be undertaken by an E. K. who is not Spenser.

I am interested here not so much in the ways in which E. K.'s individual glosses mount what Tribble suggestively calls their "festival of insinuation,"[12] or in Tribble's and Richard Rambuss's illuminating assertions that E. K.'s obsession with "secrecy" can be read as "a code to signal the urgent presence of hidden referents."[13] Instead, I will remain at arm's length from E. K.'s individual readings of individual eclogues, preferring instead to dwell on what the commentator has to say about the nature of his critical practice and about the nature of his relationship to the text he is glossing. These issues cluster in and around E. K.'s prefatory epistle "To the most excellent and learned both Orator and Poete, Mayster Gabriell Harvey," a document which calls attention to E. K.'s conception of commentary as a practice that is shot through with desire.[14] Indeed, E. K. seems to suggest that there is a decidedly intimate dimension to the interpretive labor of commentary. This understanding of exegesis is deeply implicated in what E. K. and Spenser have to say about the sounds produced by their curiously noisy book of pastoral poems.

1. THE NEW POET'S MAIDENHEAD

The book's capacity to make noise—that is, its capacity to speak for itself—is emphasized even before E. K. sets about making noise on its behalf. The poet's opening verse address "To His Booke" specifically imagines a speaking text, describing a scene in which the anonymous *Shepheardes Calender* presents itself to (and is then questioned about its origins by) its explicit dedicatee, Philip Sidney. Spenser—or as he calls himself here, "Immerito," as if the volume's anonymous maker were some undeserving Petrarchan lover—instructs the book to articulate a series of apologies and evasions: "A shepheards swaine saye did thee sing," "Crave pardon for my hardyhedde," "Say thou wert base begot with blame," "Come tell me, what was sayd of mee" (12). The trope of the speaking book is here put to a characteristically Spenserian use, in that *The Shepheardes Calender*'s capacity to speak for itself becomes a sign of its capacity for reticence or evasiveness. How do we know that Spenser's poem can speak for itself and that it has secrets to tell? Not because it reveals those secrets, but because it prevaricates, equivocates, and refuses to answer the questions it ascribes to its addressee. "Immerito" thus instructs his book to withhold rather than deliver the truth about its undeserving and unworthy creator. As the oft-noted etymological connection between glossing and glozing suggests, E. K.'s project, with all its indirection and dilation, continues precisely the patterns of behavior in which Immerito instructs his book.[15] At this particular scene of instruction, Immerito ensures that the book's inaugural words will withhold rather than deliver the truth about its undeserving or unworthy maker.

Speech and noise are relevant here because E. K. seems to be guided by the conviction that critical practice is prosopopoeic. He speaks, for instance, of his hope that the publication of *The Shepheardes Calender* will entice the New Poet to "put forth divers other excellent works of his, which slepe in silence" (19–20). To be unknown, to be unpublished and unread, is thus figured as a kind of silence—the very silence from which *The Shepheardes Calender* has already emerged in its passage into print and commentary. (It is, of course, a modest irony that E. K. has chosen to dedicate himself to speaking on behalf of the only text by the New Poet that is already speaking on its own behalf.) E. K.'s understanding of the nature of poetic influence further amplifies his sense of the volume's noisiness. Justifying the volume's "strange" and "hard" words on the grounds that their "rough sound" has been deliberately cultivated, E. K. explains that his poet has acquired his taste for archaic diction from the ancients, and that he has composed his pastoral poems with "the sound of those auncient Poetes still ringing in his eares" (14). E. K.'s and Immerito's shared emphasis on noise—ancient noise, at that—is at once an instance and a theory of the Spenserian critical encounter. What we have here is an image of commentary as clamor.

E. K. is in this sense already walking the path traced by Anthony Grafton, who has emphasized that the glossed humanist page, with its constellation of warring critical voices, is indeed a prosopopoeic space in which interpretations and methodologies collide.[16] In Grafton, Slights, Tribble, and others, the play of voices on the humanist page is described as an agonistic struggle for authority, and recent approaches to the glossed page have described it as a network of power relations within which poetic and exegetical authorities are at once constructed and contested. One of the quintessential forms of the commented text was of course the schoolbook, and there is a sense in which any encounter with a commented edition of a school text—a Virgil, say, or an Ovid—was also an encounter with the pedagogical legacies of those authors. Those pedagogical legacies were legible on the printed page, where competing late antique and early modern voices actively turned ancient poets into schoolbooks by debating the function of a preposition, clarifying geographical or mythological terms, or reordering poetic syntax for the benefit of their readers. It is in this sense that the practice of commentary in early modern editions of classical texts (where the competing voices of several commentators, collected together over the centuries and then accumulating with increasing rapidity during the early decades of the sixteenth century) is inherently competitive. It is a turf war waged at the level of syntax in the volume's white margins and back pages.[17] The territory to be won and lost is finite, and the great folio Virgils and Ovids are blackened with commentary in such a way as to have finished by commenting on almost every particle and preposition. E. K. is of course in charge of a different kind of volume. His commentary does not swim in the margins of the New Poet's pastoral poems; rather, it crowds in on the heels of those poems in a way that reminds us that to have the last word is a commentator's dream.[18] I want to suggest, however, that the sometimes wild variation in E. K.'s tone and interests is an attempt to anticipate the kind of broad tradition just described. Far from simply commenting on the New Poet's pastoral poems, E. K. is attempting to ventriloquize an entire tribe or crowd of commentators.

Without denying the agonistic dimension of this play of voices on the glossed humanist page, it bears emphasizing that E. K. glosses his text under the sign of eros and intimacy. At times these governing terms erupt into E. K.'s commentary with an energy that forges bonds between the specific verses, topics, and problems under examination and the more general mechanics of commentary itself. The most pregnant instance of this bond is also perhaps the most notorious of E. K.'s notes. Glossing Colin Clout's scorn for the naïve advances of the lovesick Hobbinol ("It is not *Hobbinol*, wherefore I plaine, / Albee my love he seeke with dayly suit: / His clownish gifts and curtsies I disdaine, / His kiddes, his cracknelles, and his early fruit" ["January," 55–58]), E. K. notes:

Hobbinol) is a fained country name, whereby, it being so commune and usuall, seemeth to be hidden the person of some his very speciall and most familiar freend, whom he entirely and extraordinarily beloved, as peradventure shall be more largely declared hereafter. In thys place seemeth to be some savour of disorderly love, which the learned call pæderastice: but it is gathered beside his meaning. For who that hath red Plato his dialogue called Alcybiades, Xenophon and Maximus Tyrius of Socrates opinions, may easily perceive, that such love is muche to be allowed and liked of, specially so meant, as Socrates used it: who sayth, that in deede he loved Alcybiades extremely, yet not Alcybiades person, but hys soule, which is Alcybiades owne selfe. And so is pæderastice much to be præferred before gynerastice, that is the love whiche enflameth men with lust toward women kind. But yet let no man thinke, that herein I stand with Lucian or hys devilish disciple Unico Aretino, in defence of execrable and horrible sinnes of forbidden and unlawful fleshlinesse. Whose abominable errour is fully confuted of Perionius, and others.

(33–34)

E. K.'s response to this "savour of disorderly love" is not so much a piece of exegesis as it is a set of unruly equivocations, as if frenzied speechifying were the natural response to Colin's intimations, or as if the note itself had been conceived in self-defense and iterated in the voice of an embarrassed Hobbinol. Tribble acutely observes that the note "seems deliberately to court an interpretation which the gloss denies," and that "the relationship between verse and gloss is almost one of flirtation."[19] If Colin has transformed Hobbinol's "clownishe gifts and curtsies," "His kiddes, his cracknelles, and his early fruit" into the stock-in-trade of his own flirtations with Rosalind ("Ah foolish *Hobbinol,* thy gifts bene vayne:/*Colin* them gives to *Rosalind* againe" ["January," 59–60]), then E. K.'s note seems to venture its equivocations in the name of tenderly recuperating Hobbinol's misplaced affections and slotting whatever hint of "disorderly love" the poem might contain into a specific philosophical genealogy of intellectualized erotics. The note's ambivalence, its capacity to both foster and hold at bay this "savour" of physical intimacy, is the means by which the practice of commentary is itself eroticized.[20]

Tribble's sense that the relationship between verse and gloss can be described, however tentatively, as a kind of flirtation is compelling enough to warrant further scrutiny. Seminal work by classicists on scholia and commentaries has called attention to what might be described as the commentator's flirtations with the spaces above, below, between, around, and behind the words that have cast their spell on him. J. E. G. Zetzel describes the elusive processes by which ancient commentaries on authors, which originally circulated as independent books, were abridged, divided, recombined, reexpanded, corrupted, emended, and reinvented as they found their way into and out of the manuscripts of the works upon which they exercised their attentions.[21] The history of commentary, according to Zetzel, is the history of its vexed negotiations with the space occupied by the words that elicit it. Even in early modern printed editions of Virgil, the commentary of Servius does not immediately occupy its familiar position around Virgil's poems. Instead, it is a separate animal that finds its way onto the page; its presence there marks a particular innovation in the history of early printed books.[22] There are, then, particular historical moments at which ancient commentaries find their way into what now looks, from our historical perspective, like their overdetermined position either in the margins or simply between the covers of classical poems.

What does a gloss do to the text? In the context of a long chapter on schoolroom "inconveniences," and "friendlinesse between parentes and maisters," Richard Mulcaster's *Positions Concerning the Training Up of Children* ventures some comments on discipline that conclude in an enigmatic reference to glossing:

The second remedie to helpe schoole *inconveniences* was to set downe the schoole *ordinaunces* between the maister, and his scholars in a publicke place, where they may easily be seene and red: and to leave as little uncertaine or untouch, which the parent ought to know, and whereupon misliking may arise, as is possible. For if at the first entry the parent condiscend, to those orders, which he seeth, so that he cannot afterward plead eitheir ignorance, or disallowing, he is not to take offence, if his childe be forced unto them, when he will not follow, according to that fourme, which he himselfe did confirme by his owne consent. And yet when all is done the glosse will wring the text.[23]

The paragraph in which this remark appears concludes by insisting that "a certaintie resolveth, and preventes douting" (269), so that the earlier promise that "the glosse will wring the text" seems to stand on the notion that the gloss is a mechanism for quelling doubt. It operates, however, in the context of a paragraph that strives to keep parents reconciled with their child's schoolmasters. That the posting of binding regulations, the prospect of punishment or compulsion, and the eliciting of implied consent (here taking the form of the parent's silent assent to posted "ordinaunces") should somehow conclude in a statement about what glosses do to texts is a curiosity worthy of E. K. himself. And yet, Mulcaster is not alone in locating the practice of commentary within this coercive economy. In a powerful, belated reprisal of Mulcaster's image, Thomas Watson, an ejected Puritan minister (d. 1686), condemns in his *Body of Practical Divinity* those "Abusers of Scripture" "who do mud and poison this pure Chrystal Fountain with their corrupt Glosses," complaining that their perverse efforts "wring the Text so hard as they make the Blood come."[24] It is not difficult to perceive that these remarks imagine commentary as visiting a vivid form of violence on the text; what is perhaps more difficult to see, however, is that an implied eroticism is bound up in the practices described by Mulcaster and Watson. To pose this as a question, what image of exhausted, eroticized emptying is being figured under the rubric of the capacity of glosses to "wring the text so hard as they make the Blood come"?

A preliminary answer to this question can be sketched in relation to E. K.'s assertion that his anonymous poet is "Uncouthe unkiste" (13). The reference is to Chaucer's *Troilus and Criseyde*, and it hints that a sexualized note of "pandering" inhabits the labors of this particular commentator. E. K. boasts: "But I dout not, so soone as his name shall come into the knowledge of men, and his worthines be sounded in the tromp of fame, but that he shall be not onely kiste, but also beloved of all, embraced of the most, and wondred at of the best" (13).

E. K. will continue to explore this vocabulary as he proceeds in his labors, but this is a key example of the ways in which reading, commentary, and publication inaugurate forms of exchange that are rendered in quasi-erotic terms, as the poet is kissed, beloved, and embraced first by his commentator and then by his eager readers. A remark by Marshall Grossman seems perfectly to capture the equations and transformations at hand: "Intercourse is merely the horizon of discourse." In its original context Grossman's assertion caps an argument concerning desire, mutuality, and conversation in Book III of *The Faerie Queene*:

> Spenser's exploration of the vagaries of desire and its reciprocal satisfactions and common frustrations appears to be driven thematically by the complexity of what Milton would later call "collateral amitie," the necessary conversation of equals, in which the term conversation grafts the Aristotelian model of friendship and the carnal relations of conjugal pairs to evoke the nascent Protestant ideal of companionate marriage.[25]

It would be perverse to suggest that E. K.'s commentary explicitly theorizes companionate marriage. And yet we will see that under its most optimistic construction the practice of commentary can indeed yearn to locate such erotic energies in its procedures.

At times E. K.'s descriptions of his critical practice are positively underwhelming:

> Hereunto have I added a certain Glosse or scholion for thexposition of old wordes and harder phrases: which maner of glosing and commenting, well I wote, wil seeme straunge and rare in our tongue: yet for somuch as I knew many excellent and proper devises both in wordes and matter would passe in the speedy course of reading, either unknowen, or as not marked, and that in this kind, as in other we might be equal to the learned of other nations, I thought good to take the paines upon me, the rather for that by meanes of some familiar acquaintance I was made privie to his counsell and secret meaning in them, as also in sundry other works of his.
>
> (19)

And yet, the "familiar acquaintance" upon which E. K.'s knowledge of the collection's "secret meaning" stands repeatedly acquires more surprising forms. The hint that poet, commentator, and poem are experiencing an inaugural moment that is in some sense figured as being erotically charged emerges forcefully at the end of E. K.'s prefatory epistle:

> These my present paynes if to any they be pleasurable or profitable, be you judge, mine own good Maister Harvey, to whom I have both in respect of your worthinesse generally, and otherwise upon some particular and special considerations voued this my labour, and the maydenhead of this our commen frends Poetrie.
>
> (20)

To speak of glossing this poem as handling "the maydenhead of this our commen frends Poetrie" is to step into the sensual postures which scholars such as Leonard Barkan, Anthony Grafton, Kenneth Gouwens, and others discern in the humanist desire for antiquity.[26] "Renaissance intellectuals did not only meet the classical world when having their noses ground into the *Catilinarians* at school," writes Grafton; Rome's humanists "pursued jobs and love affairs amid classical ruins, which they explored as eagerly as the bodies of their lovers."[27] It is also the case, however, that Renaissance intellectuals could describe the textual legacy of the classical world (the *Catilinarians*, Virgil's *Eclogues*, Ovid's *Metamorphoses*, the wrecked and ruined single manuscript of the poems of Catullus) as if they were exploring the bodies of their lovers. If, as Gouwens argues, humanists can be characterized as programmatically nurturing an "intellectual and affective encounter with the past,"[28] then it seems possible to think about the ways in which this program colors the commentary structure most closely associated with early modern editions of classical texts. E. K.'s "New Poet" is being cast (or, to borrow an appropriate phrase from the print shop, cast off) as an Old Poet, and E. K.'s preoccupation with Immerito's "maydenhead" is part of his general attempt to find language for an affective encounter with an alluring author and text from the present.

I would argue that this is a trick learned in the humanist schoolroom, where assertions of the schoolboy's love for the master, and of the master's love for the schoolboy, made it possible for humanist pedagogical theorists to imagine that the objects of knowledge (a rule, a grammatical exception, a maxim, one of Virgil's *Eclogues*) might somehow reciprocate the student's ardent attentions and desires. (Alan Stewart has called attention to the fact that the discourse of love and affection is even native to the study of grammar: "Amo magistrum" ["I love the Master"] is the first example of an accusative noun in John Colet's *Rudimenta grammatices*.[29]) In the schoolroom the impossibility of eliciting a response from the desired schoolbook is rearticulated under the sign of the responsiveness of the master, as if the text's unresponsiveness could be channeled through and corrected by the master. This emphasis on the master's affection for the student is, in effect, the only means whereby the student's love of learning can be figured as something other than a dead end in a mute schoolbook. The practice of humanist pedagogy sees the master striving to embody a particular experience of the text by becoming the object of the student's zeal—or better yet, by speaking on behalf of the recalcitrant text, the object of the student's attentions. The loving masters who populate schoolbooks thus embody in a more modest form the fantasy that a schoolbook might reciprocate the schoolboy's desires. Similarly, the speaking book is no mute object of the commentator's attentions, but rather an intimate participant in relations that both Immerito and E. K. want to imagine as a kind of dialogue—or, for E. K., as a loving handling of the New Poet's maidenhead. These arguments about the place of commentary in *The Shepheardes Calender* have skirted the entire question of Spenser's complicity in E. K.'s commentary. I will continue to skirt that question, but if Spenser is hiding behind E. K.'s mask, then the intimacies described here are in some sense autoerotic, and this autoeroticism may fuel E. K.'s rather utopian image of interpretation as intercourse.[30]

2. THE PLACE OF COMMENTARY

By way of conclusion, I want to suggest that in its dark, menacing way, Britomart's visit to the House of Busirane sets out to explode the fantasy that a text might somehow reciprocate its interpreter's desires. As Jeff Dolven has noted, the scene in Busirane's torture chamber enacts "a strategic perversion of the dream of mutuality."[31] Britomart's progress through the ornate rooms of the House of Busirane is structured to call attention to (and indeed to spatialize) the silence that precedes commentary. Gazing upon the tapestries and the golden "image" of Cupid, Britomart is forever staring and silent, and her inability to make sense of what she sees is imagined as a form of thwarted satisfaction (in its full semantic range): "That wondrous sight faire *Britomart* amazd,/Ne seeing could her wonder satisfie,/But evermore and more upon it gazd,/The whiles the passing brightnes her fraile sences dazd" (III.xi.49.6–9). Casting her "busie eye,/To search each secret of that goodly sted," she catches sight of the famous directive to "*Bee bold*" (III.xi.50.2–4). She is, however, always short of words and understanding: "she oft and oft it over-red,/Yet could not find what sence it figured:/But what so were therein, or writ or ment,/She was no whit thereby discouraged,/From prosecuting of her first intent,/But forward with bold steps into the next roome went" (III.xi.50.4–9). To the extent that a single temptation is hanging in the balance here, it is perhaps the temptation to over-read. In the next room, surrounded by Busirane's golden "wilde Antickes" (III.xi.51.5–6), another "solemne silence" (III.xi.53.7) dominates the place in which Britomart gazes in insatiable wonder: "The warlike Mayd beholding earnestly/The goodly ordinaunce of this rich Place,/Did greatly wonder, ne could satisfy/Her greedy eyes with gazing a long space" (III.xi.53.1–4). A new message ("*Be not too bold*" [III.xi.54.8]) also leaves her mute and always just short of understanding: "whereto though she did bend/Her earnest minde, yet wist not what it might intend" (III.xi.54.8–9). At the beginning of Canto xii, the Mask of Cupid fills her yet again with silent wonder: "The noble Mayd, still standing all this vewd,/And merveild at his straunge intendiment" (III.xii.5.1–2).

This episode has enjoyed influential extended commentary by scholars such as Susanne Wofford, Lauren Silberman, and Judith Anderson, all of whom have argued that the responsibilities of right reading, Petrarchan poetics, and rhetorical abuses are under examination in the House of Busirane.[32] William Oram's remarks are useful: "Critics are right to see in Busirane an image of a male poet, busily consigning women to an imprisoning fantasy, so long as they allow Spenser's characteristic multiplicity of reference."[33] Oram's own project is to emphasize that "Busirane lies in Britomart's imagination as well as Amoret's," and it is upon this pivot that my understanding of the episode turns.[34] Here, I wish only to add to the increasingly wild multiplicity of reference to which Oram refers, and to stress that Spenser is here concerned with this particular observer or interpreter's capacity for marvel and wonder, and on her incapacity for speech as she emerges from and retreats once again into the "secret shade" (III.xii.27.5) from which she observes the Masque of Cupid. Britomart is as silent as the dark night and empty room in which she finds herself surrounded by erotic "Anticke" figures. When the lead masquer, Ease, is described "beckning with his hand,/In signe of silence" (III.xii.4.3–4.), he can only be hushing his own special effects: Britomart cannot possibly be more silent during the entire episode. What that long description of the masque of Cupid does is to amplify our sense of the time and space in which Britomart is silent, marveling, wondering, unable to find words (or even ideas, it seems) for what she sees. Once again, after the first night's Masque of Cupid, Britomart (compulsively, it now seems) wanders her chamber: "All that day she outwore in wandering,/And gazing on that Chambers ornament" (III.xii.29.1–2).

When we join Britomart as she steps through that final door into Busirane's inner sanctum, we are stepping into the domain not so much (better yet, not only) of the crazed Petrarchan poet or of abusive rhetoric, but into the domain of a crazed commentator who is at once discovering and demonstrating that the humanist fantasy of reciprocity and responsiveness is, well, a very dark fantasy. In this final view, the body of Amoret is the body of the text itself in the act of being violently wooed and violently glossed. Reading this scene back against E. K.'s engagements with *The Shepheardes Calender*, it is as if Britomart has caught Busirane in the act of reading Amoret as the "secret person" lurking behind or beneath the generalized narratives of the tapestries and images in Busirane's outer rooms.[35] The point here is that it becomes possible to see Busirane not just as the abusive image of the Petrarchan poet, but as laboring assiduously (and in sinister fashion) to perform the work of commentary. He is, as is often noted, seated before Amoret, "Figuring straunge characters of his art," and laboring with "charmes" in such a way as to appear to be the very type of the poet. And yet, when Busirane is compelled by Britomart to reverse his spell he is said to have "red, and measur'd many a sad verse" (III.xii.36.4), as if the disciplines of prosody and exegesis—rather than "making"—were his business. To read, to measure: this is the business of the commentary.

Coming last, and hot on the heels of a series of protracted descriptions of works of art (tapestries, golden images, a masque) that are desperately in need of exegesis and illumination, Busirane's erotic torture chamber occupies the position of a commentary on all that precedes it; indeed, Busirane's "utmost roome" (III.xi.27) is the place of commentary itself. All is silence in the rooms through which Britomart wanders, always face-to-face with the sensuous making of some anonymous artist or artists. Not until we step into Busirane's torture chamber do we step into the place of commentary on all that Britomart has silently registered. In keeping with Spenser's conception of the place of commentary, that is where all the action is.

Carleton University

NOTES

1. Paul Ricoeur, *Freud and Philosophy: An Essay on Interpretation* (New Haven: Yale University Press, 1970), 18.

2. Ricoeur, 18.

3. George Puttenham, *The Arte of English Poesie*, ed. Gladys Willcock and Alice Walker (Cambridge: Cambridge University Press, 1936), 188.

4. Henry Peacham, *The Garden of Eloquence* (Gainesville: Scholars' Facsimiles and Reprints, 1954), 27.

5. I am tempted to include Spenser's great weaver in this list, given the astonished silence in which Arachne is said to stare at Minerva's tapestry in *Muiopotmos*. There, however, envy and metamorphosis stand in the place of commentary.

6. Edmund Spenser, *The Faerie Queene*, ed. A. C. Hamilton with text by Hiroshi Yamashita and Toshiyuki Suzuki, rev. 2nd ed. (Harlow: Longman, 2007). All citations from *The Faerie Queene* are from this edition.

7. Andrew Ford, "Performing Interpretation: Early Allegorical Exegesis of Homer," *Epic Traditions in the Contemporary World: The Poetics of Community*, ed. Margaret Bessinger, Jane Tylus, and Susanne Wofford (Berkeley: University of California Press, 1999), 35–53.

8. Ford, 36. Ford cites Glenn Most, "Die früheste erhaltene griechische Dichterallegorese," *Rheinisches Museum* 136 (1994): 209–12. See also the essays contained in *Homer's Ancient Readers: The Hermeneutics of Greek Epic's Earliest Exegetes*, ed. Robert Lamberton and John J. Keaney (Princeton: Princeton University Press, 1992).

9. To the extent that Spenser's contributions to Jan van der Noot's *Theatre for Worldlings* provide a kind of commentary on that volume's woodcuts, his immersion in the problematic in which I am interested could be said to predate *The Shepheardes Calender*.

10. See especially Slights's influential essay, "The Edifying Margins of Renaissance English Books," *Renaissance Quarterly* 42 (1989): 682–716. See also Slights, *Managing Readers: Printed Marginalia in Renaissance Books* (Ann Arbor: University of Michigan Press, 2001); Tribble, *Margins and Marginality: The Printed Page in Early Modern England* (Charlottesville: University of Virginia Press, 1993).

11. On the subject of E. K.'s identity see below, n.30. See also, Slights, "Edifying Margins," 704n.45. Further studies of the volume's canny engagement with the commentary tradition have been undertaken by, among others, S. K. Heninger and Richard McCabe. See Heninger, "The Typographical Layout of Spenser's *Shepheardes Calender*," *Words and Visual Imagination: Studies in the Interaction of English Literature and the Visual Arts*, ed. Karl Josef Höltgen et al. (Erlangen: Universitätsbund Erlangen-Nürenberg, 1988), 33–71. Heninger argues that *The Shepheardes Calender* explicitly rewords the visual layout of a 1571 edition of Jacopo Sannazaro's *Arcadia* printed at Venice by Francesco Sansovino. For an extremely fine discussion of *The Shepheardes Calender* and the commentary tradition see Richard A. McCabe, "Annotating Anonymity, or Putting a Gloss on *The Shepheardes Calender*," *Ma(r)king the Text: The Presentation of Meaning on the Literary Page*, ed. Joe Bray, Miriam Handley, Anne C. Henry (Aldershot: Ashgate, 2000), 35–54.

12. Tribble, 77.

13.   Tribble, 81; Richard Rambuss, *Spenser's Secret Career* (Cambridge: Cambridge University Press, 1993).

14.   Citations from *The Shepheardes Calender* are drawn from *The Yale Edition of the Shorter Poems of Edmund Spenser*, ed. William A. Oram et al. (New Haven: Yale University Press, 1989). References to the volume's poems will be keyed to month and line number; references to E. K.'s glosses are keyed to page numbers.

15.   On glossing/glozing see especially Tribble, "Glozing the Gap: Glossing Traditions and *The Shepheardes Calender*," *Criticism* 34 (1992): 155–72.

16.   Anthony Grafton, "Renaissance Readers and Ancient Texts: Comments on Some Commentaries," *Renaissance Quarterly* 38 (1985): 615–49.

17.   Such turf wars are arguably most violent in printed editions of the Bible. I am deliberately echoing Slights's and Tribble's recourse to martial metaphors in their accounts of the commentary tradition. Slights speaks of Biblical glosses as "preemptive strikes," and of the commentator's desire "to defend the perimeter of Scripture from the unholy attacks of contending sects" (" 'Marginall Notes that Spoile the Text': Scriptural Annotation in the English Renaissance," *Huntington Library Quarterly* 55 [1992]: 255–78). Tribble describes the glossed page as a "battleground" (*Margins and Marginality*, 43). In a very different vein, see Lawrence Lipking, "The Marginal Gloss," *Critical Inquiry* 3 (1977): 609–55.

18.   McCabe suggests that this arrangement "promotes the commentary from a position of marginality to one of centrality, problematising the very distinction between text and 'scholion' " (41), and that it marks the volume's chief departure from one of its apparent models, Abraham Fleming's translation of *The Bucolikes of Publius Virgilius Maro, with Alphabeticall annotations upon proper names of Gods, Goddesses, men, women, hilles, flouddes, cities, townes and villages etc. orderly placed in the margent. Drawne into plaine and familiar Englishe, verse for verse by Abraham Fleming. Student.* (London, 1575).

19.   Tribble, *Margins and Marginality*, 77.

20.   E. K.'s indirection mimics Erasmus's instructions for schoolmasters who find themselves having to teach and discuss Virgil's Second Eclogue, in which the lovesick shepherd Corydon yearns for the boy Alexis: *The Collected Works of Erasmus*, ed. Peter Bietenholz et al. (Toronto: University of Toronto Press, 1974–), 24: 685–87. On Erasmus's strategies see also Alan Stewart, *Close Readers: Humanism and Sodomy in Early Modern England* (Princeton: Princeton University Press, 1997), 122–25.

21.   See J. E. G. Zetzel, "On the History of Latin Scholia," *Harvard Studies in Classical Philology* 79 (1975): 335–54; Zetzel, "On the History of Latin Scholia II: The *Commentum Cornuti* in the Ninth Century," *Medievalia et Humanistica* 10 (1981): 19–31. Zetzel emphasizes that "no single pattern of development is correct for all scholia. There was a continuous flow of ancient scholarship into and out of variorum commentaries, margins, glossaries, and the like" ("On the History of Latin Scholia," 354). Freestanding commentaries were abridged in individual notes that found their ways into margins, and these individual notes were often re-expanded into freestanding commentaries that thus bear a distinctly problematic relationship to their originals. "Of Latin commentaries now extant dealing with a literary text, Servius is the only one which is complete: all of the others have been through various processes of expansion and contraction, of separate transmission and marginal excerpts" (Zetzel, "The History of Latin Scholia," 339). See also Gerald Snare, "The Practice of

Glossing in Late Antiquity and the Renaissance," *Studies in Philology* 92 (1995): 439–59; Zetzel, *Latin Textual Criticism in Antiquity* (New York: Arno Press, 1981). Michael D. Reeve asserts that "even after the adoption of the codex no Latin scribes before the Carolingian revival surround the text with commentary" ("Scholia," *The Oxford Classical Dictionary*, ed. Simon Hornblower and Antony Spawforth, 3rd ed. rev. (Oxford: Oxford University Press, 2003), 1368.

22.   In the case of Virgil this happens in a 1475 Venetian edition of the *Opera* printed by Jacobus Rubeus.

23.   Richard Mulcaster, *Positions Concerning the Training Up of Children*, ed. William Barker (Toronto: University of Toronto Press, 1994), 269.

24.   Thomas Watson, *A body of practical divinity consisting of above one hundred seventy six sermons on the lesser catechism composed by the reverend assembly of divines at Westminster: with a supplement of some sermons on several texts of Scripture* (London: 1692), 17.

25.   Marshall Grossman, "Spenser's Middle Voice: The Grammar of Jouissance in *The Faerie Queene* III," Spenser's Civilizations: The Fourth International Spenser Society Conference, May 18–21, 2006. I thank Professor Grossman for permission to quote from his paper.

26.   See especially Barkan, *Transuming Passion: Ganymede and the Erotics of Humanism* (Stanford: Stanford University Press, 1991); Grafton, "The Revival of Antiquity: A Fan's Notes on Recent Work," *American Historical Review* 103 (1998): 118–21; Gouwens, "Perceiving the Past: Renaissance Humanism after the 'Cognitive Turn,' " *American Historical Review* 103 (1998): 58–82; Findlen, "Possessing the Past: The Material World of the Italian Renaissance," *American Historical Review* 103 (1998): 83–114.

27.   Grafton, "The Revival of Antiquity," 118.

28.   Gouwens, 56.

29.   See Stewart: "the two cases nominative and accusative—forming the basic social transaction—are demonstrated through the love of the master for his scholars, and the love of the scholars for their master" (95).

30.   McCabe emphasizes that a translation given by E. K. in his glosses on "Maye" are attributed to the author of *The Shepheardes Calender* in the Spenser-Harvey letters of 1580: "Part of the 'text' that apparently establishes E. K.'s autonomous identity is hereby assigned to the very author from whom he is supposed to be distinct" (36). "Edward Kirke" no longer seems to be a sure expansion of the initials "E. K." See, most recently, D. Allen Carroll's ingenious "The Meaning of 'E. K.,' " *Spenser Studies* 20 (2005): 169–81. On the subject of E. K.'s identity, I will only say that I do not see why there should be any necessary reservations about seeing Spenser as fully complicit in the commentary *even if* E. K.'s work is being performed by the elusive "Edward Kirke" rather than by Spenser and Gabriel Harvey, by Harvey alone, or by Spenser himself under an enigmatic imprimatur. For different versions of these permutations see Louis Waldman, "Spenser's Pseudonym 'E. K.' and Humanist Self-Naming," *Spenser Studies* 9 (1988): 21–31; Heninger, 43–51; Louise Schleiner, "Spenser's 'E. K.' as Edmund Kent (Kenned/of Kent): Kyth (Couth), Kissed, and Kunning-Conning," *ELR* 20 (1990): 374–407.

31.   Jeff Dolven, "When to Stop Reading *The Faerie Queene*," *Never Again Would Birds' Song Be the Same: Essays on Early Modern and Modern Poetry in Honor of John Hollander*, ed. Jenn Lewin (New Haven: Beinecke Library, 2002), 443.

32.   See Wofford, "Gendering Allegory: Spenser's Bold Reader and the Emergence of Character in *The Faerie Queene* III," *Criticism* 30 (1988): 1–21; Silberman, *Transforming Desire: Erotic Knowledge in Books III and IV of* The Faerie Queene (Berkeley: University of California Press, 1995), 63–67; Anderson, "Busirane's Place: The House of Rhetoric," *Spenser Studies* 17 (2003): 133–50. Anderson's wonderful intuition is to extend the semantic range of Busirane's name to include "*abusio*, the familiar Renaissance word for catachresis, a wrenching of metaphor or an extravagant use of it, in any case, a violent (mis)use of language" (141). See also Harry Berger Jr., "Busirane and the War Between the Sexes: An Interpretation of *The Faerie Queene* III.xi–xii," *Revisionary Play* (Berkeley: University of California Press, 1988), 172–94.

33.   Oram, "Spenserian Paralysis," *Studies in English Literature* 41 (2001): 60.

34.   Oram, 60. Thomas P. Roche, Jr.'s extremely influential reading of the episode underlies many of the attempts to emphasize Britomart's implication in everything she sees. See Roche, *The Kindly Flame* (Princeton: Princeton University Press, 1964), 75–77.

35.   E. K. continually hungers after such identifications. See his labors in this line of work at *Shepheardes Calender* 33 (on Colin, on Hobbinol, on Rosalind), 49 (on Phyllis), 63 (on the harlot lurking behind Flora), 77–78 (on Rosalind again), 80 (on Pan as Henry VIII), 163–64 (on Colin and Hobbinol again), 187 and 195–96 (on Dido), and 209 (on Virgil's Tityrus). Spenser's narrator is prompted to a similar reflection when imagining a response to the sight of Amoret and Scudamour's melting embrace at the end of the 1590 *Faerie Queene*: "Had ye them seene, ye would have surely thought,/That they had beene that faire *Hermaphrodite*,/Which that rich *Romane* of white marble wrought,/And in his costly Bath causd to bee site" (III.xii.46.1–4). Here, Amoret and Scudamour somehow become the "secret" couple whose identities are hidden and unified in the name of Hermaphroditus.

LINDSAY ANN REID

Certamen, Interpretation, and Ovidian Narration in *The Faerie Queene* III.ix–xii

Considering the "vile Enchaunter" Busirane as an Ovidian author, and using his tapestries as a point of reference, this paper probes the dynamics of Ovidian discourse in *The Faerie Queene* III. Cantos ix–xii form a discrete narrative unit within the larger book, and, in these cantos, we find three distinct Ovidian voices: those of Paridell, Busirane, and the narrator. These voices—which compete both against one another and their literary precedents for hermeneutic supremacy—contribute to the poem's tangible Ovidian spirit. Using Ovid's character-author and textual critic Arachne as a model for all later interpreters of Ovidian text, this paper investigates the idea that interpretation necessarily relies upon *certamen*. A consideration of Paridell's and Busirane's literal responses to and reproductions of mythological *caelestia crimina* helps to elucidate not only how Ovidian irony works in Book III's narrative polyphony, but also how the ostensibly discordant Ovidian voices in Cantos ix–xii cumulatively contribute to Book III's metaliterary self-consciousness.

*W*HEN BRITMART ENTERS THE HOUSE of Busirane and encounters a sumptuous set of tapestries in *The Faerie Queene* III.xi, she enters an Ovidian world dominated by an *ekphrasis* describing the textiles, an *ekphrasis* that draws heavily upon Ovid's *Metamorphoses*. The content, if not the flavor, of Busirane's images is almost identical to the subject matter of the weaving which Arachne produces in Book VI of Ovid's poem.[1] Thus Busirane's tapestries constitute one of the most explicit literary allusions in a poem full of

---

intertextual moments. These wall-hangings and the descriptions of the mythological rapes portrayed in them reflect more than the enchanter's lewd taste in interior decor. Busirane has not merely *selected* the tapestries. Rather, he is their creator; they are a product of the "thousand charmes" issued from his pen (III.xii.31).[2] On the basis that he has rewritten a well-known Ovidian *ekphrasis* in Amoret's blood, we might say that Spenser's Busirane is an artist with a distinct literary genealogy. Modeled upon Ovid's Arachne, he is a reader and interpreter of Ovidian text. Moreover, along with fellow character-author Paridell and the narrator of *The Faerie Queene*, he serves as one of Book III's major Ovidian voices. As such, he is one of the key figures in a complex narrative configuration in which polyphonic Ovidian interpreters play both with and against each other—and their Ovidian precedents.

Like Lauren Silberman, I read the events in the House of Busirane as a battle of interpretation.[3] But rather than focusing upon the more frequently invoked gender politics of this interpretative battle, I point to the ways in which diverse modes of reading and adapting Ovidian poetry contend for dominance in the final cantos of Book III. So as to address Busirane's particular hermeneutic position and investigate how his artistry contributes to Book III's Ovidian discourse, I first examine Arachne, whom I read not only as Busirane's most immediate literary precedent, but also as a paradigm for all later interpreters of Ovidian text. Giving particular consideration to the use of ironic distance as it relates to Ovidian artistry, I then consider the Ovidianism of Busirane's fellow character-author Paridell, for in light of Arachne and Paridell we can begin to characterize accurately the Ovidianism of Busirane and understand how the various Ovidian voices in Cantos ix–xii cumulatively contribute to Book III's metaliterary self-consciousness.

In Ovid's version of the Arachne and Minerva story, the mortal girl, an extraordinarily skilled weaver, attracts the hostility of the goddess, and their clash results in a *certamen* to determine which of the two is the superior craftswoman. Predictably, their competition ends badly. Ovid's narrative implies that Arachne's artistry is as good as, and perhaps even better than, that of the goddess. As a result, Minerva vindictively rends the *infelix* girl's tapestry and beats her mortal opponent with her weaving shuttle. In a final demonstration of what has been called "greater power if not superior *ars*,"[4] the goddess transforms her proud rival and prohibits Arachne's attempted suicide; in an act of putative mercy, she forces her rash opponent to live forever as a spider attached to her rebellious text.

The story of Arachne and Minerva is not simply, as Brooks Otis once suggested, a morality tale about pride and punishment.[5] It is also a reflection on the dynamics of authorship and adaptation and, furthermore, a meditation on contest and interpretation. Playing upon Greco-Roman associations between weaving and poetic production, the Ovidian episode investigates the open-ended nature of hermeneutics as it relates to webs of textual reception.[6] If we examine the substance of Arachne's entry in the weaving contest, we find that it is laced with strands of subversive commentary. In contrast to Minerva's symmetrical and balanced weaving, which takes an ostensibly cautionary theme by portraying the authority and justice of the gods and the detrimental ends of those who defy divinity, Arachne's art defiantly depicts "caelestia crimina" [celestial crimes] committed by the deities (VI.131). In a move that mimics the self-referentiality of Ovid's own densely allusive and repetitive narrative "jigsaw puzzle,"[7] the audacious girl weaves a disorderly eddy of rape scenes, most of which echo or restate the violations of mortal women by gods found elsewhere in the *Metamorphoses*. Sympathetically focusing on the mortal victims of the gods, Arachne exposes the brutality and consequences of passion. Thus, by paraphrasing and presenting select Ovidian stories in a new context, Arachne offers a pointed critique of the divine "justice" lauded by Minerva.

Arachne's material critique of and response to Ovid functions as an ironic space within the larger narrative structure of the *Metamorphoses*. By focusing upon the horror of *caelestia crimina* in her redaction, Ovid's character-narrator Arachne deflates and demystifies the amours of the gods. Her weaving devalorizes mythic agency; the gods become the objects of criticism and commentary and her narrative provides a crucial distance from which to view divine transgression. Thus, ironic distance is implied in the fabric of the tapestry as human drama momentarily eclipses the glamour and allure of divine *eros*.

Arachne functions as a proxy Ovidian narrator.[8] Her story literalizes the dynamics of Ovid's own literary production, his figurative weaving of stories into a complex literary web. And her choice of subject matter is particularly apt, for, as Philip Hardie has noted, "many readers' most abiding memory of [Ovid's] poem" is of a "seemingly unending chain of stories of pursuit and rape."[9] However, although she explicitly draws on Ovid, Arachne does not simply recreate the *Metamorphoses* in miniature. Rather, she is a craftswoman with her own agenda who selects, edits, amends, and augments preexisting Ovidian material to fulfill a novel artistic vision. Her figure embodies a dynamic principle of interpretative tension or conflict, and Arachne's tapestry is both a work of art and a discrete article of opposition and criticism. Operating as both an author and critic within Ovid's poem, she provides the original adaptation of Ovid's work. Hence, her artwork can also be seen as a model for *all* later adaptations of the *Metamorphoses*.

Although he functions as an Ovidian interpreter, Paridell, the first of Book III's character-authors, lacks both Arachne's critical sensibility and sense of irony. In Cantos ix and x, we find Paridell busily wooing, and then subsequently rejecting, "a lovely lasse,/Whose beauty doth her bounty far surpasse" (III.ix.4). This episode of "privy lust, and gealous dred" restages the rape of Helen by Paris, using instead the figures of Paridell, a descendant of the passionate Trojan prince, and the "second *Hellene*, faire Dame *Hellenore*" (III.ix.28, x.13); he models his own relationship with Hellenore after Paris's earlier seduction of Helen.

The Ovidian inspiration for Paridell's duplicitous discourse is apparent from the outset of these cantos. Paridell's "messages of loue" to Hellenore, as well as the "close signes," "speaking lookes," and "false belgardes" which he employs in his wooing of her (III.ix.27, 28, 31, 52), are those proscribed by Ovid's amatory texts.[10] Paridell has evidently taken great pains to study and internalize the lessons of the *Amores* and *Ars Amatoria* and is a "learned louer" who is "perfect in that art" (III.x.6, 5).[11] Paridell is also acquainted with Ovid's *Heroides*, for he self-consciously replicates an episode from *Heroides* XVII when he coyly "let[s] his loue be showne" in the "dauncing bubbles" of spilled wine; this diversion is "to him well knowne" (III.ix.30), apparently from his prior reading of Ovid.[12]

As Heather Dubrow has noted, these "preliminary games" played by Paridell and Hellenore "in their *liaison dangereuse* are closely linked to the succeeding accounts of Troy."[13] As Paridell begins to recount the story of the Trojan War, it becomes clear that he regards Ovid's *Heroides* as an historical source as well as an instructional manual in the arts of love. Paridell's rendition of the Trojan saga is part of his larger attempt to seduce Hellenore; it is only one of the many "layes of loue and loues paine,/Bransles, Ballads, virelayes, and verses vaine . . . which flowred in his braine,/With which he fed her fancie" (III.x.8). Consequently, he fashions the substance of epic into Ovidian-inspired romance and "pitifull complaint" (III.ix.40). Paridell glorifies and revises his own Trojan ancestry, recasting characters so that his infamous progenitor Paris becomes the "Most famous Worthy of the world" and the adulterous Helen is smoothed into a "flowre of beautie excellent" (III.ix.34, 35).

The Ovidian raconteur's account of Trojan history reflects his own subjective reading of the *Heroides* in other ways as well. He systematically edits out the distress of heroines abandoned by their lovers. Paridell, who is related to Paris through his first wife Oenone, deliberately downplays the ills done to his ancestress. Noting only that the war "madest many Ladies deare lament/The heauie losse of their braue Paramours," he downgrades Oenone's woeful and impassioned plea to Paris in *Heroides* V to mere "remembraunce of her passed ioy" (III.ix.35, 36). Similarly, Dido's sorrows of *Heroides* VII are glossed over entirely in Paridell's suggestion that Aeneas "weetlesse wandered/From shore to shore, emongst the Lybike sands,/Ere rest he found" (III.ix.41). Given that Paridell is obviously an avid reader of Ovidian texts, these emendations and omissions resonate all the more. Paridell's account of the Trojan War thus reflects what Mihoko Suzuki has termed his "reductive use of Ovid as the advocate of adultery and the progenitor of courtly love."[14]

Caught up in the romance of his own self-characterization, Paridell overglorifies his literary and mythological antecedents. He adheres to the Arachnean hermeneutic prototype only insofar as he re-appropriates Ovidian material and reinterprets it to new ends. In stark opposition to Arachne's art, the creative and ironic tensions of Ovid's poetry are lost in Paridell's discourse. His reading of Ovid is, in this regard, unintentionally subversive, colored by an unquestioning and literal valorization of Ovidian passion. He is uncritically inspired by ostensibly glamorous *crimina*, and he fails as both a lover and interpreter precisely because he has failed to appreciate the ironic structure of Ovid's poetry.

These observations on Arachne and Paridell clarify the nature and function of Busirane's artistry. Along with Paridell, Busirane also seems to have been reading and relishing Ovid's urbane amatory poetry, and this is reflected in the presentation of his "arras made in painefull loom" (III.xi.51). The opening line of *Amores* I.ix could serve as a caption for his artwork: "Militat omnis amans, et habet sua castra Cupido" [Every lover is a soldier, and Cupid holds the fortress].[15] Furthermore, Busirane's gory mode of composition eerily reflects and actualizes another image from the *Amores*, in which the poet conceives of himself as a victim who must suffer the brutality of Love's art and endure the pain of an arrow sticking into his heart:

> an subit et tecta [Amor] callidus arte nocet?
> sic erit: haeserunt tenues in corde sagittae,
> et possessa ferus pectora uersat Amor
>
> (I.ii.6–8)

But has Love entered and deftly hurt me with his art?
Thus it is: there is a slender arrow sticking into my heart
And dreadful Love twists about in my conquered breast.

This description has resonances in the final canto of Book III, where "With liuing bloud [Busirane] those characters wrate,/Dreadfully dropping from her dying hart,/Seeming transfixed with a cruell dart" (III.xii.31). It is as though Busirane, in trying to incite Amoret's affection, artificially uses "strong enchauntments and blacke Magicke leare" literally to reproduce the conditions described by Ovid in his erotic poetry (III.xi.16). It is in this way that, though Busirane lacks the same sense of dynamic human psyche displayed by his fellow character-author, his unironic reading and interpretation of Ovidian text closely resembles Paridell's.[16]

Moreover, the very fact that he reproduces and re-envisions Arachne's art—in much the same way that she earlier filtered and reinterpreted Ovidian text—invites explicit comparisons between Book III's second character-author and the rebellious girl. Busirane's familiar subject matter marks his artwork as highly self-conscious Arachnean and Ovidian imitation; his tapestries are, as Syrithe Pugh has called them, his "selective edition of the *Metamorphoses*."[17] Although the subject matter of Busirane's wall-hangings may be the same *caelestia crimina* taken up by Arachne, the divergences between each character's reinterpretation of the Ovidian source material demonstrate that their respective thematic intents differ radically.

From our first introduction to Busirane's pictures in stanza 28, it is clear that the *ekphrasis* from the *Metamorphoses* has been excerpted and resituated in an entirely new context. Busirane's tapestries are

> Wouen with gold and silke so close and nere,
>   As feigning to be hid from enuious eye;
>   Yet here, and there, and euery where vnwares
>   It shewed it selfe, and shone vnwillingly;
>   Like a discolourd Snake, whose hidden snares
> Through the greene gras his long bright burnisht backe declares.
>
> (III.xi.28)

The golden threads to which the above passage refers are a detail borrowed directly from the corresponding Ovidian *ekphrasis*; however, their further, non-Ovidian comparison to a "discolourd Snake" relates Busirane's images back to the preceding story of Malbecco, who found that, when Hellenore left him, jealousy "as a Snake . . . lurked in his wounded mind" (III.x.55).[18] Similar snake imagery permeates the opening lines of Canto ii, in which we find apostrophized the "Hateful hellish Snake" of "Fowle Gealosie, that turnest loue divine / To ioylesse dread, and mak'st the louing hart / With hatefull thoughts to languish and to pine" (III.xi.1). This change of context is signaled equally in the closing stanza of the description, where we learn that, unlike Arachne's art, which she frames with ivy, Busirane's revisionary tapestry is finished with a border "Of broken bowes and arrowes shiuered short, / And a long bloudy riuer through them rayled" (III.xi.46). As with the imagery of the serpent, this divergence from Arachne serves to recontextualize the tapestry within the world of Book III, a world in which an absentee and war-like Cupid—who is characterized as "the disturber of all civill life, / The enimy of peace, and author of all strife" (III.vi.14) —has managed to exert his influence upon most of the characters. Thus, the tapestries decorating Busirane's house are conspicuously repositioned within a context of love, lust, and jealousy, and the *caelestia crimina* portrayed in them take on new meanings which were absent from their immediate Ovidian and Arachnean precedents. Ovidian art is conspicuously reframed within Spenserian narrative. Much as Arachne paraphrased and appraised Ovid in her own tapestry, Busirane quotes—and misquotes—Ovid, Arachne, *and* Spenser in his own revisionary interpretation of the *caelestia crimina*.

In a sense, Busirane becomes both an Arachne and an alter-Arachne. He produces nearly indistinguishable artwork, but his tapestries do not share in Arachne's critique of divine *eros*. Rather, Busirane glamorizes the loves of the gods and thus fails to problematize lust. Like Paridell, Busirane glorifies the male predator; rather than Arachnean irony, we find a troublesome synthesis between his own project to win Amoret and the *caelestia crimina* of Greco-Roman mythology. Busirane's interpretation conspicuously reverses Arachne's, and his function as an Ovidian narrator becomes polarized from hers.

Implicit to Ovid's story of Arachne and Minerva is the idea that interpretation is, by its very nature, *certamen*. The goddess and the mortal compete not only to determine whose fingers move more deftly at the loom, but also to establish hermeneutic supremacy. Thus the Ovidian rendition of the story explores how prejudice necessarily precedes both dialogue and poetic judgment. The *caelestia crimina* in *The Faerie Queene* are not without these same Ovidian implications of contest, these associations with conflict and interpretation.

Both of Book III's Ovidian character-narrators are challenged by
Spenser's knight of chastity. If we return our attention to Paridell,
we notice that his romantic retelling of the Trojan War does not go
unchecked.[19] It is commented upon, modified, and augmented by
Britomart, who highlights the heroic and imperial dimensions of the
story. Britomart later compels Busirane to draft his own palinode,
ensuring that his textual and visual "charmes" are literally reversed
(III.xii.36). As readers and adapters of Ovid, Paridell and Busirane,
like Arachne before them, are involved in a metaliterary *certamen* of
interpretation. These character-authors' renditions of Ovidian material are competing and at once playing against their own literary
prototypes and against the third Ovidian voice contained within the
final cantos of Book III: the narrator.

Maureen Quilligan has made the argument that the characters in
Book III go astray when they interpret by Petrarchan metaphor and
that Spenser's narrative criticizes the limitations of such interpretations. I suggest a similar dynamic in terms of Book III's Ovidian
discourse.[20] It is through the narrator that we become aware both of
the allure and the menace of Busirane's and Paridell's unironic, literal
readings of Ovidian text. The narrator alerts us that Busirane's art
represents misleading, perhaps even dangerous, interpretations. Busirane's tapestries are arresting; one hundred and fifty lines are given
over to their graphic depictions of "loue, and . . . lusty-hed"
(III.xi.29). They seduce us with their beauty, and it is precisely that
beauty and capacity to entice us that makes them potentially dangerous interpretations.[21] The enchanter's artwork is "So liuely and so
like, that liuing sence it fayld," just like Archimago's false Una and
similar to the false Florimell, who is "So liuely and so like, that many
it mistooke" (III.xi.46, I.i.45, III.viii.5).[22] The narrator effectively
manipulates the fraud and deceit which Arachne attributed to the
gods in her tapestry so that this deception and duplicity is transferred
or extended to Busirane's tapestries. It is through the narrator that
we come to understand that the predatory nature of the caelestia
crimina represented within the weavings is shared by the physical
objects themselves.[23] In an analogous way, Paridell is shown to use
Ovidian storytelling and performance—his so-called "sleights" and
"false engins" (III.x.7)—for purposes of temptation. He is described
as a "crafty Paramoure" who "bayted euery word" as he steals away
Malbecco's wife (III.x.10, 6). "[F]inely did he his false nets dispred"
and spider-like, "through his traines he . . . intrapped" his willing
victim Hellenore (III.x.9, 11).

The narrator of *The Faerie Queene* does not simply represent a
sober, corrective voice in Book III's complex narrative configuration;

he is an Ovidian interpreter in his own right. It is in the narrator that we find Book III's Ovidian spirit. This is comparable in sentiment to what Harry Berger, Jr. has called the "effect of Ovid" in Book III, an impression of Ovidianism which "extends beyond the Ovidian plot and theme to the storyteller's urbane amusement."[24] Berger has examined this with particular reference to the characterization of Florimell and her pursuers, and I would argue that this same dynamic is found in the narration of Cantos ix–xii. It is through the superior narrative voice that Paridell and Busirane become comedic. The true nature of their respective characters and Ovidian adaptations are un-masked. Paridell becomes a ridiculous dandy and a calculating would-be lover, and Busirane is dismissed as a sexually frustrated old man.

The narrator relies on techniques of parody to achieve this tone, and examination of the Paridell and Hellenore episode reveals how the narrator's discursive strategies collapse the quasi-Ovidian performance of the characters. The narrator's deflation of Paridell and Hellenore's romance begins in ix.2, where the narrator makes an incongruous association between the fall of the angels and the impending fall of Malbecco's wanton wife. The narrator's language is similarly inflated as he employs a formal—and highly strained—epic simile to introduce Paridell:

> Tho hastily remounting to his steed,
> He forth issew'd; like as a boistrous wind,
> Which in th'earthes hollow caues hath long bin hid,
> And shut vp fast within her prisons blind,
> Makes the huge element against her kind
> To moue, and tremble as it were agast,
> Vntill that it an issew forth may find;
> Then forth it breakes, and with his furious blast
> Confounds both land & seas, and skyes doth ouercast.
>
> (III.ix.15)

The elevated language of the passage is undercut by the comparison as the effusive Ovidian storyteller is reduced to a "boistrous wind." Even before Paridell begins his literalized performance of Ovidian precepts his heroic stature begins to shrink to mock heroic proportions. The narrator's further invocations of classical precedents, such as the comparison that he makes between Hellenore and Dido (III.ix.52) or the imagery of the Trojan siege which he uses to characterize Paridell's wooing strategies (III.x.10), create an interpretative

contrast. The reader perceives a marked distinction and distance between Paridell's contrived and unironic recital of Ovidianism and
the narrator's classically allusive yet critical commentary.

The narrator's interactions with Busirane are less explicitly critical
or advisory, but the distancing effect is similar. Rather than using an
overburdened explanatory mode to signal discursive remoteness from
Book III's second character-author, the narrator relies on a more
subtle use of Ovidian subtext.[25] At the close of Book III, Busirane's
similarities to Arachne are exploited in ways that extend beyond the
mere substance of his tapestries. I here wish to note the uncanny
resemblance between the narrator's descriptions of Busirane's fate at
the end of the twelfth canto and the punishment of Arachne in the
Metamorphoses. Accused of "huge mischiefe," Busirane is forced to
recant. The enchanter is physically overthrown by "the noble Cham-
pionesse," who "So mightily . . . smote him,/that to the ground/He
fell halfe dead" (III.xii.35, 41, 34).[26] Moreover, like Arachne, though
his "meed . . . Is death" (III.xii.35), he is granted life, and the description of his punishment is drawn out over the course of several cantos until

> With that great chaine, wherewith not long ygo
> He bound that piteous Lady prisoner, now relest,
> Himselfe [Britomart] bound, more worthy to be so,
> And captiue with her led to wretchednesse and wo.
>
> (III.xii.41)

Although the chaining or binding of sinister characters is by no means
an unfamiliar punishment in Spenser's poem, this particular retribution seems to carry a special significance in the case of Busirane. As
Judith H. Anderson has noted, "while Busirane's art works may van-
ish, he must survive, bound by the very chain, or, in terms of traditional iconography, by the rhetorical art, that he has abused."[27] These
parallels suggest that, much as Arachne hangs as a spider from a noose
of her own making, Busirane is caught up in the limitations of his
own hermeneutic web.

By invoking the narrative subtext of the Arachne and Minerva
story to describe the overthrow of Busirane, the narrator not only
manages to draw attention to the "paragone" of narration in preceding cantos and its associations with *certamen,* but also to contrast
the immense disparity between Arachne's ironic reinterpretations of
Ovidian text and Busirane's wholesale identification with and invocation of *caelestia crimina.* By setting up Busirane as both the re-creator

of Arachne's artwork and the sufferer of her punishment, the narrator invites us to contrast and comparatively evaluate the interpretations of the two character-authors. Busirane's Ovidianisms are deflated, then, not by the language of the narrator's commentary so much as the absurdity of the very comparison.

Concerns with competing textual traditions are highlighted throughout Book III, a book which is conspicuously peppered with ideas and instances of intertextuality, recantation, and palinode. This is a subject which first emerges at the outset of the second canto, where the narrator claims that he has "cause, in men iust blame to find" because, unlike the ancients, contemporary authors rarely record "ne maken memorie/Of [women's] brave gestes and prowess martiall" (III.ii.1), and, in contrast, indicates that he means to correct this deficiency in his own work. We sense that the narrator, unlike the book's character-authors, is self-consciously revisionary. It is in this sense that the narrator's commentary is more Arachnean than Paridell's or Busirane's; he shares in Arachne's ability simultaneously to adapt and critique existing material to new ends.

In the final cantos of Book III, as the narrator participates in an interpretative *certamen*, a peculiar narrative gap emerges. This space is defined by Book III's distinct Ovidian voices, which work both with and against one another and their Ovidian precedents. We find the character-authors in *The Faerie Queene* reading Ovid and unironically glamorizing *caelestia crimina* in a way that is antithetical to Arachne's position. However, though Ovidian irony has eluded both Paridell and Busirane, it is not lost on the narrator, who effectively exercises Arachnean strategies to deflate and critique the interpretations of both character-authors. In Spenser's work, the structural space of irony expands from a physical tapestry to a less easily defined narrative gap, a breach between the puerile and limited interpretations of the character-authors and the commentary of and subtexts evoked by the narrator. Hence, it is in the conflict of interpretations and the narrative space defined by this divergence that we find Book III's clearest manifestation of Ovidian and Arachnean irony. Book III's tangible Ovidian spirit is found in the revisionary abilities, aloof and amused commentary, and metaliterary self-consciousness of the narrator, who conveys the Arachnean nature of his discourse by distancing his own hermeneutic position from the literal and inadequate Ovidian interpretations of Paridell and Busirane. It is a narrative dynamic that creates a peculiar interpretative unity from ostensibly cacophonous and discordant Ovidian voices. The aim of polyphony is not to obscure meaning but to enhance it, and it is in this way that Spenser's poetry, like Ovid's, employs seemingly inharmonious

narrative strands to achieve ironic distance and ultimately to demy-
thologize Ovidian mythology.

University of Toronto

NOTES

1.   I cite from *The Faerie Queene*, ed. A. C. Hamilton (London: Longman, 1977)
and from *Ovid's Metamorphoses, Books 6–10*, ed. William S. Anderson (Norman:
University of Oklahoma Press, 1972). Among studies of Spenser's use of the Arachne
story in *The Faerie Queene* are: Judith H. Anderson, "Busirane's Place: The House
of Rhetoric," *Spenser Studies* 17 (2003), 133–50; Heather James, "Ovid and The
Question of Politics in Early Modern England," *English Literary History* 70:2 (2003),
343–73; Pamela Royston Macfie, "Text and *Textura*: Spenser's Arachnean Art,"
*Traditions and Innovations: Essays on British Literature of the Middle Ages and the Renais-
sance*, ed. David G. Allen and Robert A. White (Newark: University of Delaware
Press, 1990), 88–96; Judith Dundas, *The Spider and the Bee: The Artistry of Spenser's
Faerie Queene* (Urbana: University of Illinois Press, 1985).

2.   Textual and visual artistry seem to be inextricably bound up in Busirane's
tapestries. Adam McKeown raises an interesting question about the nature of Busirane's authorship when he asks: "Are these 'straunge characters' images or words?
'Wrate' would suggest they are words, but 'figuring' connotes the making of pictures
or the use of language to make things seem visible": "Looking at Britomart Looking
at Pictures," *Studies in English Literature* 45 (2005): 55.

3.   *Transforming Desire: Erotic Knowledge in Books III and IV of* The Faerie Queene
(Berkeley: University of California Press, 1995), 58–70.

4.   William S. Anderson, ed. *Ovid's Metamorphoses: Books 6–10*, 151.

5.   *Ovid as an Epic Poet* (Cambridge: Cambridge University Press, 1966), 146.

6.   Betty Rose Nagle has read Arachne's tapestry as metanarrative: "Ovid's *Meta-
morphoses*: A Narratological Catalogue" *Syllecta Classica* 1 (1989): 97–125. Sarah
Annes Brown also explores the Arachne and Minerva episode as a "paradigm of
Ovidian intertextuality": "Arachne's Web: Intertextual Mythography and the Re-
naissance Actaeon," *The Renaissance Computer*, ed. Neil Rhodes and Jonathan Sawday
(London: Routledge, 2000), 120–34.

7.   Ovid's poem is so characterized in L. P. Wilkinson, *Ovid Recalled* (Cambridge:
Cambridge University Press, 1955), 147.

8.   For a lucid reading of Arachne as a surrogate narrator in Ovid, see Lynn
Enterline, *The Rhetoric of the Body: From Ovid To Shakespeare* (Cambridge: Cambridge
University Press, 2000), 33–35. Leonard Barkan similarly claims: "It requires no
great leap of the imagination to see in Arachne's tapestry all the elements of Ovid's
own poetic form in the *Metamorphoses*, which is, after all, a poem that eschews a
clear narrative structure and rather creates a finely woven fabric of stories related via
transformation": *The Gods Made Flesh: Metamorphosis and the Pursuit of Paganism* (New
Haven: Yale University Press, 1986), 4. Feminist scholars such as Patricia Klindienst

Joplin and Nancy K. Miller have focused more specifically upon the implications of Arachne's female voice: "The Voice of the Shuttle is Ours," *Stanford Literature Review* 1:1 (1987): 25–53; and "Arachnologies: The Woman, The Text, and the Critic," *Subject to Change: Reading Feminist Writing*, ed. Nancy K. Miller (New York: Columbia University Press, 1988), 77–101.

9.   *Ovid's Poetics of Illusion* (Cambridge: Cambridge University Press, 2002), 67.

10.   Ovid's *Ars Amatoria* and *Amores* are cited from *P. Ovidi Nasonis: Amores, Medicamina Faciei Femineae, Ars Amatoria, Remedia Amoris,* ed. E. J. Kenney (Oxford: Oxford University Press, 1961).

11.   We further learn that "all that art [Paridell] learned had of yore," and of Hellenore we are told "Ne was she ignoraunt of that lewd lore" (III.ix.28). This may be a reference to Ovid's lines in *Ars Amatoria,* where he suggests that Paris and Helen do not need his advice, as the art of love is already well known to them (III.v.1–4). Such games also seem to have been known by Malecasta, as evinced by her futile attempts to flirt with Britomart earlier in the book (III.i.50–56).

12.   Cf. *Amores* I.iv.17–20 and II.v.15–20; and *Ars Amatoria* I.569–72.

13.   "The Arraignment of Paridell: Tudor Historiography in *The Faerie Queene* III.ix," *Studies in Philology* 87:3 (1990): 320. The Ovidian associations of the episode have also been remarked upon by Mihoko Suzuki, *Metamorphoses of Helen: Authority, Difference, and the Epic* (Ithaca: Cornell University Press, 1989), 159–173; and Helen Cheney Gilde, "Spenser's Hellenore and Some Ovidian Associations," *Comparative Literature* 23:3 (1971), 233–39.

14.   Suzuki, *Metamorphoses of Helen,* 164.

15.   Moreover, his construction of the Arachnean tapestries further demonstrates Busirane's desire to follow Ovidian precepts in his attempt to seduce Amoret. I am reminded of the poet's address to his lover in *Amores* I.iii.19–24, where he wants to insert his own beloved into the poetic realm and use his own art to immortalize her alongside well-known victims of mythological rape.

16.   This similarity between Busirane's and Paridell's "slanted histories" is alluded to in Harry Berger, Jr.'s influential essay on the House of Busirane: "Busirane and the War Between the Sexes: An Interpretation of *The Faerie Queene* III.xi–xii," *English Literary Renaissance* 1:2 (1971), 100.

17.   *Spenser and Ovid* (Aldershot: Ashgate, 2005), 145.

18.   Cf. Ovid, *Metamorphoses,* VI.68–69.

19.   This has been widely noted by commentators. For example, Suzuki writes: "Against Paridell, who trivializes Virgil's hero [Aeneas] through iteration, Spenser sets his own heroine Britomart, who corrects and supplements Paridell's narrative" (165). In a similar vein, David Galbraith claims: "In Paridell's story the rhetoric of complaint modulates into a recasting of Virgil according to the conventions of medieval romance. But in Britomart's response, complaint becomes instead the material of heroic and prophetic vision": *Architectonics of Imitation in Spenser, Daniel, and Drayton* (Toronto: University of Toronto Press, 2000), 65.

20.   *The Language of Allegory: Defining the Genre* (Ithaca: Cornell University Press, 1979), 83–84. On literalized Petrarchanism, particularly as it relates to the House of Busirane, see Mark Rose, *Heroic Love: Studies in Sidney and Spenser* (Cambridge: Harvard University Press, 1968), 121–27. Susanne Lindgren Wofford shows how

The Faerie Queene draws attention to the limitations of Petrarchan—and its own—discourse: "Britomart's Petrarchan Lament: Allegory and Narrative in *The Faerie Queene* III.iv," *Comparative Literature* 39:1 (1987): 28–57.

21.   In this sense, Busirane's tapestries are drawn into Book III in another way as well; they relate to the internal struggle between reflection and desire which Britomart must face when she is confronted with Arthegall's image in the "glassie globe that Merlin made" and her unsubstantiated fears that she will "feed on shadowes . . . And like a shadowe wexe" (III.ii.21, 44). These issues are also worked upon in the form of the virtuous Florimell and her shameless *doppelgänger*; in the representations of Malecasta's "false eyes" with which she views and misapprehends Britomart (III.i.50); and, of course, in Spenser's retelling of Paris and Helen's adultery. It is in Busirane's seductive visual apparitions, however, that Book III's preoccupation with the allurements of beauty and the danger of passion is epitomized.

22.   Similar wording is also used to describe the tapestry at Malecasta's castle (III.i.38).

23.   It is notable that this alluring exhibit of Arachne's artwork in Busirane's "vtmost rowme" is not her first association with Spenser's text. Book II twice refers directly to Arachne, first at the Cave of Mammon where she is associated with the almost fetishized enticement of wealth, and second in the Bower of Bliss, where, following the description of Acrasia "arayd, or rather disarayd,/All in a vele of silke and siluer thin,/That hid no whit her alabaster skin," the narrator remarks, "More subtile web *Arachne* cannot spin" (II.xii.77). Both these earlier references link Arachne's figure with enticement.

24.   " 'Kidnapped Romance': Discourse in *The Faerie Queene*," *Unfolded Tales: Essays on Renaissance Romance*, ed. George M. Logan and Gordon Teskey (Ithaca: Cornell University Press, 1989), 215.

25.   I use the term "subtext" here in Wofford's sense: "a separate text which may or may not have been written by the author of the 'primary' text being interpreted) to which explicit reference is made. It is distinguished from a general allusive context by the fact that the specific concerns of the subtext form an essential part of the meaning of the 'primary' text, whether they are criticized, transformed, challenged, or incorporated with little change" (29).

26.   In the 1596 edition, Britomart is explicitly referred to as Minerva only three cantos prior to this (III.ix.2).

27.   Anderson, "Busirane's Place," 141.

LINDA GREGERSON

Spenser's Georgic: Violence and the Gift of Place

This essay reconsiders the functions of georgic in *The Faerie Queene*, Book I and *A Vewe of the Present State of Ireland*, arguing that Virgil plays a crucial role in Spenser's evolving ethic of human habitation. At the heart of georgic, both Virgilian and Spenserian, lies an ethical conundrum: a double allegiance to peaceful or ameliorative co-existence and to the violent imposition of human will. While he posits what we might call an "ecological" vision of interlocking systems, grounded in affective attachment to abode, Spenser never resolves the violence inherent in human cultivation. Indeed, he offers a further account of its radical persistence.

*I*F THE EXEMPLARY PATH of poetic career dictates a passage from pastoral to georgic to epic, a Renaissance commonplace succinctly rehearsed by Cuddie in the tenth eclogue of *The Shepheardes Calender*, readers may well ask what became of the second, or interim, genre in the course of Spenser's own life in letters. One answer is that georgic was conflated with the third, or epic, phase, in Spenser's *Faerie Queene*, that a single historical allegorical epic romance contrives to work out the legacy of Virgil's *Georgics* as well as his *Aeneid*: a number of commentators have suggested as much.[1] Another possibility is that Spenser's georgic eschewed both the logic of "interim" and the social decorums of poetry, manifesting itself instead in a prose tract and a civil career devoted to the endless, conflicted labor of Irish plantation. I should like in this paper to take both propositions to heart, suggesting in the end that *The Faerie Queene* and *A Vewe of the*

Spenser Studies: A Renaissance Poetry Annual, Volume XXII, Copyright © 2007 by AMS Press, Inc. All rights reserved.

Present State of Ireland work in tandem to contemplate a central georgic, and Virgilian, conundrum: the difficult ethics of habitation in a household or *oikos* built on earth. The problem, and the insight, Spenser borrows from the *Georgics* is the one we have come to call "ecology."

Some years ago, William Sessions argued that *The Faerie Queene*'s chief debt to Virgil's *Georgics* is structural rather than thematic: that the primary lesson Spenser derived from the *Georgics* was how to construct a communal hero by means of plural labors.[2] With deference to this argument, which I find both elegant and convincing, I would like to dwell for a time on a simpler, more naive observation: when Spenser recreates the English patron saint as a ploughman, he insists that the work of civility and redemption be performed by one with dirt on his hands. Redcrosse Knight is described in the *Letter to Ralegh* as a clownish young man who sits on the floor at the court of the Faerie Queene, "unfitte through his rusticity for a better place." True, he will look better once he dons the armor of holiness and, true, he will learn on the eve of his great three-day battle with the dragon that he springs from the blood of Saxon kings, but the hero's second birth, in "an heaped furrow," has arguably proved to be the decisive one, his fosterage "in ploughmans state" a permanent part of his heritage. What Tristram White describes in 1614 as "vulgar errour"[3] Spenser contrives to make a moral argument. Georgos secures the nation as a man of earth.

1.

Civil, civic, civilization, civility: the entire nexus derives from *civis*, citizen. In ancient Rome, explain the editors of the OED, *city* derives from citizen and not the other way around: *civitas* refers in the first instance to the corporate body of citizens, the comprehensive state of citizenship, and only rarely and later to the town or place inhabited by citizens. But in English, as in ancient Greek, the generative logic is reversed: civic identity derives from place, the citizen from the city that grants him rights and privileges. The *Georgics* is profoundly conflicted about its relationship to the city. Virgil associates dense settlements of humanity with divisive agitations and appetites: public honors and the ambition that secures them, purple of kings, strife rousing brother to break with brother, extreme displays of poverty and wealth, the one inspiring pity, the other envy (*Georgics* 2.495–510). But even as he praises, by contrast, the contentments of country life, its sustaining rhythms, its self-sufficiency, its nurturing of virtue and familial affection, the poet reinstates the city as the cynosure of human endeavor, the culmination of the very order he has praised at its expense. "Such a life," he writes, referring to the sheaves of corn, the furrowed field, the fatted goats, the fecund cattle, the material practices and psychic rewards of an idealized rural order, "such a life the old Sabines once lived, such Remus and his brother" (2.532–33). To the extra-urban, even anti-urban, life he sets forth in commendatory detail, the poet grants a venerable genealogy, and then, from this doubly praised and doubly attested rural order he derives the very social formation to which he has opposed it. "Thus surely Etruria waxed strong, thus Rome became of all things the fairest, and with a single city's wall enclosed her seven hills" (2.533–54). In swelling chords at the very center of his treatise, the conclusion to Book 2 of the *Georgics*, Virgil traces the consummate achievement of the city to its wellspring in the well-proportioned rural life and, conversely, proposes that cultivation of the land reaches its natural apotheosis in the city. Throughout its four divisions, Virgil's poem unfolds two different and opposing models of social well-being, two different and opposing patterns of aspiration, and carefully maintains them in dialectical discord.[4]

This same profound ambivalence attends the entire spectacle of productive labor in the *Georgics*. On the one hand, and remarkably, in the midst of a poem devoted to the arts of tillage and domestication, the poet exclaims, "What joy to view fields that owe no debt to the harrow, none to the care of man!" (2.438–39). On the other hand, he admires the very bees as "great-hearted," their industry as a "wondrous pageant" and model for the nation: "Slight," in such a subject, "is the field of toil; but not slight the glory" (4.6). Virgil makes husbandry a model for the human arts in general. "The great Father himself . . . first made art awake in the fields" (1.125). Granted, the incentives to learning were harsh: Jove "in black serpents put their deadly venom, bade the wolves plunder and the ocean swell, shook honey from the leaves, hid fire from view, and stopped the wine that ran everywhere in streams" (1.129–32). But the consequent technological and cultural development amounted to much more than the mere staving off of hunger and cold. By means of the hardships he introduced, Jove purposed that humanity "might little by little hammer out divers arts, might seek the corn-blade in the

furrows, and strike forth from veins of flint the hidden fire"
(1.133–35). According to the georgic account, the painstaking experiment and observation that undergird the work of physical sustenance
lead seamlessly to grander and more speculative labors: "Then first
did rivers feel the hollowed alder" (navigation); "then the sailor num-
bered the stars and called them by name, Pleiades, Hyades, and Arctos,
Lycoan's gleaming offspring" (1.136–38). The vista is both epistemological and political: as the stars are divided and invested with individ-
uating stories and identities, so too are the earth's denizens divided
into master and subaltern; both hunters and the hunted are subdued
to human use. "Then men found how to snare game in toils, to
cheat (*fallere*) with bird-lime, and to circle great glades with hounds"
(1.139–40). The very elements are made to work against one another:
"Then came iron's stiffness and the shrill saw blade—for early man
cleft the splitting wood with wedges; then came divers arts. Toil
conquered the world" (1.142–45). *Labor omnia vicit.* And in a final
turn, one that makes the ambivalence ring like iron, labor's conquest
is made to include the laborer. *Labor omnia vicit.* Labor conquers
everything, "unrelenting toil, and want that pinches when life is
hard" (1.145–46).

Georgic—from *geos*, earth, and *ergon*, labor—involves the imposition of human will on nature, itself a species of violence. If Virgil
encourages his husbandman to "learn the winds and the wavering
moods of the sky, the wonted tillage and nature of the ground, what
each clime yields and what each disowns" (1.51–53), it is so that he
may better harness the elements for his own purposes. He bends the
elm until it assumes the shape of the plow (1.169–70). He breaks the
earth with "sledges and drags, and hoes of cruel weight" (1.162–64).
He prunes and grafts, transplants and "tames" the trees until they
surrender their wild spirit and "readily follow any lessons you would
have them learn" (2.49–52, 61–62). He trains the bullock to the yoke
and the horse to the bit. If the bees swarm aimlessly and neglect the
hive, he tears off the wings of their queen (4.106). His tools are
"rustics' weapons" (1.160). When the poet would teach the grower
of grapes to mete out his vineyard in even and uniform paths, he
compares the desired result to the ranks and files of soldiery: "as
when, in mighty warfare, the legion deploys its companies in long
array and the column halts on the open plain, when the lines are
drawn out, and far and wide all the land ripples with the gleam
of steel" (2.276–87). Nature thrives with discipline: the bees yield
sweetness because they pass their lives "under the majesty of law"
(4.154). The poet pays homage to coercion's gleaming aesthetic, but
also allows the fabric of his poem to register coercion's dubious ethic.

Spenser shares Virgil's sympathy for the legible orders and expertise of settled rural life, construing the farmer's practice of material cultivation as cognate to nurturance of the larger cultural field, the one we call civilization. Spenser also shares the Latin poet's deep unease with civilization's violent entailments, as witness his doomed but valiant efforts to insulate the Knight of Justice from Talus's merciless threshing in Book V of *The Faerie Queene*. But that unease is also unevenly registered. In *A View of the Present State of Ireland*, Irenius discourses lengthily on his objections to the itinerant herding populations of Ireland. They "keepe their cattle, and . . . live themselves the most part of the yeare in boolies, pasturing upon the mountaine, and waste wilde places, . . . driving their cattle continually with them, and feeding onely on their milke and white meats" (*View* 55).[5] Mobility makes the Irish disorderly, ungovernable, and maddeningly resilient in the face of English efforts at colonization. "[T]he people that thus live in those boolies, grow thereby the more barbarous, and live more licentiously than they could in townes" (55). Their elusive and provisional relation to place is abetted by indigenous habits of grooming and dress: the covering glibes (long hair) and the versatile mantles that serve as portable house, bed, and garment all in one.[6] It is the very genius of the mantle, its infinite adaptability, that makes it so objectionable to Irenius, as it is the perfect symbiosis of boolie and mountainous topography that make itinerant pasturage so inimical to settled rule. Expert in their native adaptations, the Irish "think themselves halfe exempted from law and obedience, and having once tasted freedome, doe like a steere, that hath beene long out of his yoke, grudge and repyne ever after, to come under rule again" (56). The yoke that was for Virgil a practical symbol of bullock's conformability is for Irenius a positive figure for the cultural practices he wishes to see inscribed on the landscape and its people. To the frequent discomfort of his interlocutor and, intensely, of Spenser's modern readers, Irenius is unblinking about those violent impositions he construes as necessary to the work of civilization.

In Ireland, however, as Irenius explains to Eudoxus, barbarous habits of land use are reinforced by barbarous systems of tenure and inheritance. Landlords refuse to lease their acreage for extended periods, preferring tenants-at-will or tenants who lease from year to year. Nor are tenants willing to bind themselves to longer terms, for fear of extortionate and arbitrary exactions. As a result, the husbandman has no incentive to build worthy habitations, to "ditch and incluse his ground, to manure and husband it as good farmours use" (83). Instead, he "dayly looketh after change and alteration, and hovereth in expectation of new worlds" (83). This puts him firmly outside the ameliorating habits of civilization: he lives together "with his beast in one house, in one roome, in one bed, that is, cleane strawe, or rather a foul dunghill" (84). The very conditions of ownership and inheritance in Ireland seem to English judgment inimical to stability. "For all the Irish doe hold their land by Tanistrie; which is no more but a personall estate for [a man's] life time" (16). Neither lordship nor property descends from father to son; transmission is governed by tanist election. One generation acknowledges the sovereignty of the English king (of Henry VIII in 1541, for example), and the next brazenly disavows it, asserting that their ancestors had no power to dispose of either land or fealty for any period exceeding their own lifetimes (15–16). And thus, explains Irenius, the Irish evade all durable contract.

Like the booly, tanistry is very well adapted to Irish circumstance and aspiration, as Irenius can only concede: election of the tanist, who serves as second and successor to the present chief, assures that the collective is never without a line of clear succession, never subject to the peril of an underaged or inexperienced heir, and ever vigilant against the encroachments of bordering lords and, especially, against the English, "which they thinke lye still in waite to wype them out of their lands and territoryes" (17). The English do not read these adaptations as conducive to civilization. Unable or unwilling to construe sovereignty in the context of mobile and collective land use, the English, like other European colonizers, furthered a powerful and profitable logic, a logic that was crucial to early modern empire. English law did not acknowledge proprietary rights in land that was not cultivated according to English patterns: when John Eliot in Massachusetts trained his "praying Indians" in the ways of settled agriculture, he did it partly that he might gather his converts into Christian congregations, but also, and explicitly, because he had no other means of helping them secure land rights under colonial administration.[7]

Irenius's plans for reform in Ireland involve new mappings of human population and the land, mappings quite distinct from those he judges to be indigenous. First and foremost, he would "have the land . . . inclused, and well fenced" (84), made legible and subject to survey. He would have broad roadways cut through the woods, highways fenced, bridges built and fords destroyed so that all travelers should have to pass by way of gates and gatehouses (156). And whoever "keepeth twentie kine" should also by ordinance be required to "keep a plough going; for otherwise all men would fall to pasturage, and none to husbandry" (150). "For this keeping of cowes," he says, "is of it selfe a very idle life." (149). "And to say truth, though

Ireland bee by nature counted a great soyle of pasture, yet had I rather have fewer cowes kept, and men better mannered . . . " (150). If husbandmen must graze their cattle in mountain pastures, "let them make some townes neare to the mountaines side, where they may dwell together with neighbours, and be conversant in the view of the world" (150). That is, let them learn the ways and perspectives of settled habitation (the views of the world) and let their conversance and its evolution be subject to surveillance (the view of the world). Irenius sees towns and countryside, trade and agriculture, as natural allies, bringing out the highest potential in one another, "for nothing doth more enrich any country or realme than many townes; for to them will all the people draw and bring the fruites of uses; and the countrymen will also be more industrious in tillage, and rearing of all husbandry commodities, knowing that they shall have ready sale for them at those townes" (157).[8]

The world of the *Georgics* is the world of *homo faber*, the species that distinguishes itself by making, that apprentices itself to the physical world with a specific agenda in mind, a species for whom understanding, even wonder, is never disinterested, a species that fabulously extends, by means of tools, its original powers of observation and material manipulation. In the Golden Age, which Virgil describes as having preceded the present Age of Iron, no tools were necessary because no labor was necessary and therefore no art. In that earlier era, "no tillers subdued the land," the earth yielded her fruits freely, and men made gain for the common store: "Even to mark the field or divide it with bounds was unlawful" (1.125–28). This Golden Age makes a teasing, elliptical appearance in Spenser's Book of Holinesse, where we learn of an Eden in which "all good things did grow,/ And freely sprong out of the fruitfull grownd,/As incorrupted Nature did them sow" (*FQ* I.xi.47). This Eden no longer exists, of course, neither inside the narrative nor without, but even as a lost ideal it differs in crucial respects from the Virgilian ideal: the land that "freely" yields its riches in mythic Faerie Land is imagined as already marked and bounded; it is not and has never been an undivided commonwealth. If many a Renaissance playwright seems to have resonated to that watchword of the fourteenth-century Peasants' Revolt, "When Adam delved and Eva span,/who was then the gentleman?," this is not the perspective from which the author of *The Faerie Queene* derives his Eden. In contrast to the staples of classical myth and medieval uprising, Spenser's originary garden is imbued with hierarchy. The blessings of geographic place—intimacy with the soil, abiding nurture, earthly home—are imagined as inextricably linked with the disciplines of social place, assigned and asymmetrical patterns of allegiance. Georgic values are made to intersect, through the figure of Redcrosse Knight, with dragon fights and the feudal orders of romance. The Garden St. George must violently restore is governed by a king and queen.

2.

The historical St. George has always been an elusive figure. Early evidence includes a church named for him at Thessalonica, considered by some authorities to belong to the fourth century, and dedicatory inscriptions found among church ruins in Syria, Mesopotamia, and Egypt. He appears in narratives of the early pilgrims, Theodosius, Antoninus, and Arculphus, written in the sixth to the eighth centuries; all speak of Lydda or Diospolis in Palestine as the seat of his veneration and the resting-place of his remains (Geyer, "Itinera Hierosol.," 139, 176, 288; *The Catholic Encyclopedia*). The papal or pseudo-papal decree "De Libris recipiendis," probably dating from the sixth century and promulgated to distinguish between church canon and apocrypha, includes St. George among those saints "whose names are justly reverenced among men, but whose actions are only known to God" (*Decretum Gelasianum*, discredited attribution to Pope Gelasius 1, bishop of Rome 492–96). In *The Golden Legend*, the collection of saints' lives compiled by Jacopus de Voragine, bishop of Genoa, in the late thirteenth century, St. George is a nobleman of Cappadocia and a tribune in the Roman army.[9] He delivers the Libyan city of Silena from the dragon who has been devouring a daily offering of sheep and, as the supply of sheep runs low, the city's sons and daughters. He saves in particular the king's fair daughter, and converts the city to Christianity. Twenty thousand people, writes Voragine, were baptized on a single day, "not counting the women and children." This is all commendable, but none of it quite accounts for canonization; the circumstances of George's martyrdom are not part of the narrative that supplies his iconography: the dragon, the spear, the maiden with her jointly sacrificial lamb. The martyrdom is understood to constitute a different, concluding part of the life; accounts are various, obscure, and contradictory. Voragine tries to cover all bases: Saint George of the Golden Legend suffers a veritable anthology of persecutions under one Dacian, who is either the emperor of Persia or a prefect under the Roman emperors Diocletian and Maximian; Voragine calls him one thing, then another. Under the ministrations of this Dacian and amidst the general hostility directed toward the primitive Christian church, the knight who was to become St. George is stretched on a rack and torn limb from limb with hooks; he is burned with flaming torches and his wounds rubbed with salt. He is twice given poison, twice drinks it and suffers no harm. He is bound upon a wheel fitted with sharp knives, but the wheel falls apart. He is plunged into a cauldron of molten lead but emerges as though from a bath, refreshed. He is finally beheaded and his martyrdom, writes Voragine, accomplished.

The legend of St. George enjoyed immense popularity in medieval Europe, where it seems to have served as touchstone for devotional attachment to nation or region, and regional culture, an unfolding and adaptable figure for allegiance to place. Accounts of the dragon-slaying saint appeared in Anglo-Saxon as well as Latin and other European languages. St. George was made a patron saint of Portugal, Germany, Lithuania, and Malta as well as of England. English churches built before the Norman Conquest were dedicated to his memory. In the middle of the fourteenth century, Edward III dedicated the Order of the Garter to his patronage. St. George has been adopted in various domains of Christendom—the Eastern Orthodox, the Roman Catholic, and the Protestant—as patron saint of armorers, archers, butchers, and saddle makers, farmers, field hands, shepherds, sheep, of those who suffer from skin diseases and syphilis, of, in a later era, Lord Robert Baden-Powell's Boy Scouts. By the fifteenth century, St. George was a familiar figure in English mummer's plays, pageants and ridings, a portion of his legacy about which Mary Ellen Lamb has written with great sensitivity.[10] When the feast days of other Catholic saints were removed from the English calendar by Henry VIII, St. George's feast day was retained. During the stricter reforms of Edward VI, Lord Protector Somerset banned images of this favored English saint and eliminated his feast day from the prayer book, but these banishments were short-lived. If the cultural prestige associated with St. George's feast day, April 23, has in the modern era largely been transferred to another English icon, the calendrical coincidence is one of history's wittier commentaries on pride of place. Like William Shakespeare, St. George has long possessed the power to consolidate Englishness in both popular and elite imaginations.

In the Golden Legend, St. George's relation to earth, the very earth built into the etymology of his name, is highly allegorized and abstracted, removed from all the compromising circumstances of material embodiment. The earth, writes Voragine, is his own flesh: Augustine tells us that good earth is found high in the mountains, and George was on the heights because he disdained base things. Or:

George is derived from *gerar*, holy, not from earth at all. Or: George comes from *gero*, pilgrim, for he was a pilgrim in his contempt for the world. That world, the earth, is quickly vaporized in Voragine, subsumed by what the author takes to be more pressing theological matters. But Spenser deliberately forestalls this hasty and seamless subsumption. He carefully restores, which is to say, he *supplies* the literal ground upon which his allegorical knight shall learn to labor. He insists that we, his readers, linger awhile on earth, that George pass through the heaped furrow, that our shared, embodied passage is not nothing. I have been much puzzled by this heaped furrow, since I have always thought of furrows as indentations, and all the dictionaries I have consulted confirm that narrow understanding. I was for a time similarly puzzled by a locution I have come across in Irish sources, where country folk are periodically described as sitting on, not in, a ditch. "Ditch," I now know, can refer to a mounded formation of earth as well as the concavity with which I generally associate the term, but no such help with furrow; indeed, the OED cites a proverbial formula ("to spare neither ridge nor furrow") that confirms the venerable distinction between raised and indented portions of the ploughed field. Spenser's "heaping" is willfully odd, as best I can determine. It calls attention to itself.

Certainly, it stops the hero in his tracks. Why, says Redcrosse to Contemplation in the tenth canto of the Book of Holinesse, did you refer to me as English just now? (It has already been a day of revelations). Because, says Contemplation, "How euer now accompted Elfins son" (I.x.60), you actually spring from a race of Saxon kings, were stolen by a faerie, and hidden where a ploughman would find you: in an heaped furrow. To be planted in a furrow is rather different than appearing on a doorstep or in a cradle of rushes: the ploughman is actively working the earth ("As he his toylesome teme that way did guyde" [I.x.66]), the infant has been placed in the path the plowshare cuts, the furrow is "heaped," as though pregnant. The poet makes much of the infant's oblivion on either side of its momentous passage: "a Faery thee vnweeting reft" from your royal English nursery and hid you in a furrow, "[w]here thee a Ploughman all vnweeting fond" (I.x.65–66); the one world is not consciously available to the other. In other words, the child's unearthing in his second home is attended with all the imagery and mystery of fleshly birthing. And Contemplation, when he greets the changeling, calls him "man of earth" (I.x.52). Redcrosse's second birth thus recapitulates the second version of human creation, as narrated in the Book of Genesis. (And despite Edmund Spenser's unfortunate ignorance of modern textual scholarship, one might also argue that the ambiguous redundancy of double birthing shrewdly recapitulates the ambiguous redundancy of double sourcing in canonical scripture.) "Let vs make man in our image," reads the first, or "Priestly," version of human creation; "let them rule . . . ouer all the earth" (Gen. 1:26).[11] But "made of the dust of the grounde," reads the second, or "Yahwist," account (Gen. 2:7). Which "sheweth," according to the commentary in the Geneva Bible, "whereof mans bodye was created, to the intent that man shulde not glorie in the excellencie of his owne nature." The double vista, of native privilege and humble habitation, of lordly rule and earthly labor, encompasses just those contradictions that inform Virgilian georgic.

3.

Which is the ground, exactly, that makes Redcrosse a man of earth? How does he carry forward Virgil's affective dialectic of tenderness and violence toward the fertile matrix? Redcrosse's human fathers, Saxon kings, are said to have vanquished ancient Britons and conquered British land (I.x.65): heartland of a nation, Arthur's land, but not the earth of tillage. By way of supplement or corrective, Redcrosse's Elfin father brings him up "in ploughmans state" and names him (Georgos) for the ploughman's labor (I.x.66). The champion's double lineage manifests a chronic Spenserian paradox: Redcrosse's most down-to-earth-ly bringing up takes place not in historical England but in the mirroring universe of Faerie Land. And paradox will govern both his coming-into-consciousness and his embrace of knightly action. Grown to manhood, Redcrosse will bind himself to a cause—Contemplation will call it "earthly conquest" (I.x.60) —whose full consequence he begins to apprehend only when he beholds the heavenly goal it requires him to defer. In order to enter the holy city, says Contemplation, you will have to wash your hands "from guilt of bloody field" and "earthly conquest shonne." So Redcrosse pleads with perfect reasonableness, "O let me not . . . then turne againe / Back to the world, whose ioyes so fruitlesse are" (I.x.63). But he is destined to dirty his hands before he can wash them, to plant the seeds of holiness in rocky soil, to labor for a full life term on earth. As soon as I have defeated the dragon according to my bond, he says to his holy tutor, I shall "shortly back returne vnto this place." Having killed the dragon, however, he suffers an apparent loss of memory or motivation; now it is Una to whom he issues a promise, by way of betrothal: I shall return to marry you as soon as I have completed my contracted term of service to the Faerie Queene. Even if marriage to Una and entry into the holy city are versions of a single progress of the soul, and this is not exactly what Contemplation seems to suggest, Redcrosse is bound to a period of indefinite deferral. This pattern of deferral will become one of the most conspicuous dynamics of *The Faerie Queene*, of course, but the pattern accrues an extra layer of resonance in Book I of Spenser's poem, for it links the Knight of Holinesse to another hero of surrogacy. Like the one whose trials and sacrifice are commemorated by the cross Una's champion wears on his breast and on his shield, the one whose earthly incarnation led not to final things but to a baffling interim, whose earthly return is everywhere expected "soon," the exemplary Knight of Holinesse secures a vista of hope by means of serial displacements.

Virgil's catalogue of the trees in Book 2 of the *Georgics* celebrates both the bounty of nature and the discriminating ingenuity of humans: varied aptitudes and varied use. The pine yields timber for ships, the willow supple osiers, the myrtle yields spear shafts, the yews Ituraean bows; smooth lindens and the boxwood are especially suited to the lathe; even the hollow cork tree and the rotting ilex make good lodging for the beehive. Spenser's homage to this Virgilian topos in Book I of *The Faerie Queene* seems at first to exceed its original in confidence and praise: the earth seems made for humans and humans for the earth; there seem to be no limits to nature's hospitality. When Redcrosse and Una seek shelter from a tempest in a "shadie groue," they find a densely planted testament to human industry and cultural meaning:

> The sayling Pine, the Cedar proud and tall,
> The vine-propp Elme, the Poplar neuer dry,
> The builder Oake, sole king of forrests all,
> The Aspine good for staues, the Cypress funerall.

> The Laurell, meed of mightie Conquerours
>   And Poets sage, the Firre that weepeth still,
>   The Willow worne of forlorne Paramours,
>   The Eugh obedient to the benders will,
>   The Birch for shaftes, the Sallow for the mill,
>   The Mirrhe sweete bleeding in the bitter wound,
>   The warlike Beech, the Ash for nothing ill,

The fruitfull Oliue, and the Platane round,
The caruer Holme, the Maple seeldom inward sound.

(I.i.8–9)

But this last must be read as something of a warning, for these woods
are an entangling. Where Virgil's woods were mental survey, trees
assembled in the mind and in the poem but otherwise left to native
soils and dispositions, Spenser's are unnaturally forced together in a
single figurative place, which makes that place, by incremental and
seductive stages, monstrous. The powers of human synthesis and
purview, which seem to be so warmly celebrated, lead to wandering
and to Error's den: these woods are a species of pride. And Errour
is a ghastly parody of intellectual mastery, the technology that is
capstone to them all: she vomits books and papers and ink, great
gobbets of half-digested raw materials. The imposition of human will,
unchecked, is foul deformity.

Spenser has assembled a scene of instruction for his first exemplary
protagonist, the Holiness in which Prince Arthur's comprehensive
virtue, Magnificence, is to be grounded. The poet is teaching his
Knight of Holiness to think ecologically. Ecology: from Gk *oikos*
(house, abode, dwelling) and *logia* (study). Despite the deceptive echoes, eclogue and ecology share no etymological connection. Eclogue
derives from *eklegein* (Gk), "selection," and its natural occasion is
contemplative, or complaining, respite from labor. But ecology, like
husbandry (from Old Norse *hus*) has "house" at its root and labor at
its heart, whether the work is that of tillage or of study (*logia*). Economy (*oikonomia*), from the same root as ecology, means management
of the household or family and, only by extension, administration or
government of the state. Ecological thinking emphasizes system, the
profound interdependence and interrelation of organisms and their
environments. Ecological thinking is divided about the place of the
human: some would still insist upon and privilege a special capacity
for reflection and intervention on the part of homo sapiens, thus
echoing the biblical concept of natural "rule." Others would acknowledge no more than a special capacity for harm. One way or
another, to their credit or discredit, humans are accorded a special
ethical position. But ecology insists that humans understand themselves as one among many biological manifestations.

With all deference to a much-disputed discursive and political
field, I would like to suggest that we lose something important when
we too quickly abandon or correct for the naive understanding of
environment as "house" or "lodging." Redcrosse seeks and must be

taught his proper abode, which is both a genealogy and a telos; Spenser expends considerable energy on this unfolding. Redcrosse discovers a destined abode in Eden, where he shall be joined in marriage to Una and inherit the kingdom, but not yet. He is shown a vision of the holy city, the New Jerusalem, and is told it holds a place for him, his citizenship assured, but not yet. His home is England, where he was born and which he shall exemplify and sponsor as its patron saint. His home is Fairie Land, where he was born a second time, in heaped furrow, and to which he owes the trajectory of quest. The thinking in which he is trained through twelve cantos demands complex suspensions: multiple forms of citizenship, multiple forms of allegiance, multiple forms of ethical obligation, multiple modes of moving through time, both sacred and historical. But complex as are these suspensions and trajectories, the Knight of Holiness is above all, or rather at the foundation of all, required to sustain simplicity of heart. Hence the affective importance of abode: *oikos*. In the Golden Legend, St. George is a nobleman of Cappadocia. He rescues a princess. He converts a kingdom to Christianity. He is able to nullify the power of poisons and boiling lead with the sign of the cross; he survives tortures no earthly body is designed to survive. His body is more important as the token of steadfastness than as flesh and blood; his relation to earth is abstract. But Spenser's St. George is wedded to earth, and the ecological thinking in which he is trained—the system-thinking of intricately balanced interdependent obligations and imperatives—is unified by a homely insight, the affective attachment to habitation.

Contemporary ecological thought has worked hard to correct for the naive assumption of earthly abode, riddled as it is with potentials for abuse. We have been taught that to imagine the earth as mere dwelling place, an inert container, is dangerous oblivion. To understand the earth as living and malleable but made for us, ours to use, ours to use up, is dangerous presumption. To fail to apprehend that we are made of the same stuff as the rest of the earth is to woo both self- and world-destruction. But the homely apprehension, the story told in Genesis about the gift of place, which is at once a habitation and the source of sustenance, an "organism," as later vocabularies will have it, this apprehension still has considerable emotional and ethical power. Stewardship seemed to Spenser a worthy ethical imperative, and stewardship derives from this sense of gift. Stewardship is what Virgil teaches his husbandman, his breeder of cattle, his keeper of orchards and vineyards and bees. Stewardship is what Redcrosse has learned at the plow, at both its handle and its cutting edge; it is what his epic labors sustain. And yes, just as modern ecological critique discerns, those stewardly labors begin in a vision of sovereignty; they shore that sovereignty up, the sovereignties of Eden, of England, and of Faerie Land. Habitation of the planet is incompatible with innocence.

Spenser is by no means an uncritical champion of regnant power. The Rome that was for Virgil the cynosure of human achievement, despite its troubling ethical costs, is for Spenser the site of depravity and spiritual deformation. Among the "caytiue wretched thralls" (I.v.45) Redcrosse discovers in the dungeon of the House of Pride are the legendary agents of empire: Romulus, Tarquin, Scipio, Hannibal, Caesar, Pompey, Antony. But Spenser's figurative vocabulary, the model toward which he gravitates when he wishes to body forth the shapely discipline of appetite, judgment, spiritual and social order, is again and again dominated by the idea of sovereign center. This center gains in density and gravitas through the earthy origins of Redcrosse Knight and his affiliations with georgic husbandry; it gains affective warmth through the very poles of human longing—restored Eden, distant New Jerusalem—it must defer; but it never escapes its problematic legacy of force and subjugation.

The pursuit of virtue in *The Faerie Queene* is governed by the twin poles of rural and imperial cultivation; this mimics a dynamic already present within the *Georgics* and, more broadly, between the *Georgics* and their author's later, "less perfect" *Aeneid*. In Spenser's epic, the root of "civill conversation" (VI.i.1) is the court. No matter that this court is not and cannot be actual. It exists as a gravitational field, a point of origin and return for the distributed consciousness that constitutes *The Faerie Queene*, the distributed labors and variegated fields of knightly quest. The genre of romance takes Spenser's knights abroad in scattered errantry while referring their labors to a sovereign center; the genre of georgic underwrites (and contests) that center in a different key, proposing an earthier vision of rooted belonging. In the *Vewe*, Spenser follows the furrow of georgic from political dominion to patterns of land use and back again, frankly acknowledging the violence required to uproot one system and replace it with another. In *The Faerie Queene*, the multiple vocabularies of literary genre allow the poet more latitude for explicating these tensions within the architecture of hope. He contrives the labors of his allegorical knights, labors georgic in inspiration, chivalric in contour and momentum, soul—and nation-making in consequence, as a kind of groundwork for a new political ecology. The lesson would be much taken to heart by Spenser's most attentive reader, John Milton: when the latter addressed his own pen to the problem of georgic restoration in an epic mold, he gave labor at last its honored place in the prelapsarian garden.

NOTES

I am grateful to the organizers of "Spenser's Civilizations," the Fourth International Spenser Conference, and especially to Elizabeth Harvey, who invited me to deliver a version of this paper as a plenary address at the University of Toronto in May 2006. I am also greatly indebted to Theresa Krier and David Galbraith, editors extraordinaire, for their patience and generosity.

1. See Andrew Ettin, "The Georgics in *The Faerie Queene*," *Spenser Studies* 3 (1982): 57–71; Alastair Fowler, "The Beginnings of English Georgic," in *Renaissance Genres: Essays on Theory, History, and Interpretation*, ed. Barbara Kiefer Lewalski (Cambridge: Harvard University Press, 1986), 105–25; Andrew Wallace, "Norseled up in life and manners wilde': Spenser's Georgic Educations," *Spenser Studies* 19 (2004): 65–92; and especially William A. Sessions, "Spenser's Georgics," *ELR* 10:2 (Spring 1980): 202–38.

2. Sessions, "Spenser's Georgics."

3. White's observation is far from naive: "In S. *Georges* English birth the Poet followes the vulgar errour, of purpose, to fit his fabulous morall argument the rather." (See *Spenser Allusions in the Sixteenth and Seventeenth Centuries*, ed. William Wells [Chapel Hill: University of North Carolina Press, 1972]; see A. C. Hamilton, ed., *The Faerie Queene* [Harlow: Longman, 2001], 136n.) I would only add that Spenser chooses to preserve not only the English birth but the vulgar lineage. All quotations from Spenser's epic are taken from Hamilton's edition. Quotations from Virgil are taken from *Georgics*, trans. H. Rushton Fairclough (Loeb Classical Library, 1974).

4. Warm thanks to my editors David Galbraith and Theresa Krier for suggesting an important conceptual link to Lucretius here. They write: "This is a profoundly Lucretian dialectic; Virgil's exploration of origins and technology itself engages dialectically with the great account of origins at the end of Book V of Lucretius's *De rerum natura*. . . . In their alternative views of prehistory, labor, and technology, Lucretius and Virgil make available to Spenser a complex analysis of hard and soft primitivism, a simultaneously harsh and generous sense of earthly derivation." This is a link I cannot claim to have drawn myself, but it shall certainly be part of the revised thinking in later versions of this essay.

5. Citations are from the Ware edition of *A View of the State of Ireland*, ed. Andrew Hadfield and Willy Maley (Oxford: Blackwell, 1997).

6. For a fuller discussion of the mantle and the glibe, see Ann R. Jones and Peter Stallybrass, "Dismantling Irena: The Sexualizing of Ireland in Early Modern England," in *Nationalisms and Sexualities*, ed. Andrew Parker et al. (New York: Routledge, 1992), 157–71. See also my own discussion in "Colonials Write the Nation: Spenser, Milton, and England on the Margins," in *Milton and the Imperial Vision*, ed. Balachandra Rajan and Elizabeth Sauer (Pittsburgh: Duquesne University Press, 1999), 169–90.

7.   See Eliot's prefatory letter "To the Right Worshipful, the Commissioners of the United Colonies in New England," in *John Eliot's Indian Dialogues*, ed. Henry W. Bowden and James P. Rhonda (Westport: Greenwood Press, 1980). See also Linda Gregerson, "The Commonwealth of the Word: New England, Old England, and the Praying Indians," in *British Identities and English Renaissance Literature*, ed. David J. Baker and Willy Maley (Cambridge: Cambridge University Press, 2002), 178–93.

8.   Recent decades have witnessed a remarkably flowering of scholarship on Spenser's Ireland, and, more broadly, on the Irish colonial ventures of early modern England. See, inter alia, Nicholas Canny, *Making Ireland British, 1580–1650*, 2nd ed. (Oxford: Oxford University Press, 2003); Richard A. McCabe, *Spenser's Monstrous Regiment: Elizabethan Ireland and the Poetics of Difference* (Oxford: Oxford University Press, 2002); Andrew Hadfield, *Spenser's Irish Experience* (Oxford: Oxford University Press, 2001); Willy Maley, *Salvaging Spenser: Colonialism, Culture, and Identity* (New York: Palgrave Macmillan, 1997); Brendan Bradshaw, Andrew Hadfield, and Willy Maley, eds., *Representing Ireland: Literature and the Origins of Conflict, 1534–1660* (Cambridge: Cambridge University Press, 1993).

9.   The *Leganda Aurea*, compiled ca. 1260–75 and first printed in 1470, dominated western hagiographical literature for centuries. It survives in approximately 900 manuscripts and from 1470 to 1530 was the most frequently printed book in Europe. Caxton's English edition was first published in 1483.

10.   See Mary Ellen Lamb, "The Red Crosse Knight, St. George, and the Appropriation of Popular Culture," *Spenser Studies* 17 (2003): 185–208.

11.   Passages cited are from the Geneva Bible, 1560.

ANDREW ESCOBEDO

Daemon Lovers: Will, Personification, and Character

Spenser reveals little interest in the representation of free and independent choice. His characters' choices don't produce narrative consequences so much as the narrative appears to determine their choices. Yet *The Faerie Queene* does show intense interest in the expression of will—Duessa exerts a "cursed" will, Arthur asserts a "will to might," Scudamour's will is "greedy," etc. But what would it mean to say that a character wills, but does not choose? And could we call such a character an agent? To answer these questions, this essay revisits the notion of personification allegory as "daemonic possession" and treats it as a form of inspired motivation, one that achieves not choice but rather something we might call *volitional mastery*. Britomart's erotic adventures in Busirane's castle serve as a primary example.

UNLIKE WRITERS SUCH AS MILTON or Sidney or Shakespeare, Spenser does not conceive of moral action in terms of deliberate choice or free will. This contrast is especially sharp in the depiction of erotic desire. Milton requires his Lady to *choose* not to succumb to Comus's temptations, and the heroes of Sidney's *Arcadia*, although they usually find themselves captured by love, expatiate at length about desire's coöptation of their free will. Such debates hold little interest for Spenser, who nearly always imagines ethical meaning to derive from the (largely unchosen) expression of moral character, especially when such character encounters narrative scenarios already fraught with erotic content. In this respect we can still be instructed by Paul Alpers's brilliant insight of forty years ago, that "the condition of [Spenser's] poetry is the abeyance of will . . . . He seems

---

Spenser Studies: A Renaissance Poetry Annual, Volume XXII, Copyright © 2007 by AMS Press, Inc. All rights reserved.

not to have imaginatively grasped that the potentialities of human nature . . . could show themselves in dramatic actions whose consequences . . . could not be undone."[1] Although subsequent Spenser critics have not liked the idea that their poet might fail to grasp something, Alpers's statement ought to remain the starting point of any investigation of Spenser's characters and their relation to his narrative. Their choices don't produce narrative consequences so much as the narrative appears to determine their choices.

Yet we could also *qualify* Alpers's observation by noting that, if Spenser is largely uninterested in deliberate choice, he nonetheless reveals intense interest in the expression of will—Duessa exerts a "cursed" will, Arthur asserts a "will to might," Guyon "bridles" his will, Scudamour's will is "greedy," and so forth. Such moments of willing do constitute more than the involuntary expression of moral character, yet volition in these cases does not seem to result from conscious deliberation. But what would it mean to say that a character wills, but does not choose? And could we call such a character an agent? I want to try to answer these questions through a consideration of the recent trend to read Spenserian personification and allegory as a form of "daemonic possession"—a reference to the quasi-divine daemon figure of Greek literature—which critics usually see as a form of compulsion that nullifies the will. Yet, although it is true that daemonic possession sometimes results in obsession, and therefore self-dispossession, daemonic possession can also inspire and motivate the heroes. In the latter form, such possession achieves not choice but rather something we might call *volitional mastery*. I'll begin by discussing the problem of character and choice in allegory, move to a consideration of personification and acts of will, and conclude with a brief look at Britomart's and Amoret's behavior in the castle of Busirane.

CHARACTER, CHOICE, AND ALLEGORY

When I say that Spenser is not interested in free will, I mean that he is disinclined to represent characters whose choices imply a self-originating agency for which they could take almost full responsibility. In the work of Shakespeare and Milton, we are invited to contemplate characters whose deliberate actions potentially initiate a new sequence of narrative consequences. They create this effect in part by dramatizing the deliberative process that leads up to a choice.

Shakespeare's Brutus voices dozens of lines of anguished deliberation before he resolves to kill Caesar (2.1.10–58), and even after this he gives us an extraordinary account of his *experience* of choice: "Between the acting of a dreadful thing/And the first motion, all the interim is/Like a phantasma, or a hideous dream" (2.1.63–65).[2] Likewise, Milton makes sure that Eve weighs her options in an extended internal monologue ("yet *first*/Pausing awhile" [9.743–44]) before "she plucked, she ate" (9.781).[3] *Julius Caesar* and *Paradise Lost* go further than indicating mere narrative options, to assassinate or spare, transgress or obey; after all, any story of significant length must allow for the possibility of multiple options. Instead, both narratives dramatically foreground characters making crucial choices that seem to cut through surrounding circumstances and direct the momentum of the story. Foregrounding choice both stems from and reinforces the impression of *character*. Brutus and Eve make apparently free and independent decisions based on the resources of personality more than the coercion of external influence, however daunting this coercion may seem to us. (We need not invoke the modern novel here: "character" in the Renaissance is a category of narrative resource, not an individualized interior.[4])

There are any number of ways to account for this literary impression on the reader. It may owe something to what cognitive psychologists call the Fundamental Attribution Error, the inclination of observers to over-ascribe the behavior of an agent to her internal disposition rather than to the situation confronting her.[5] Or, it may mimic the Aristotelian account of moral will as "desiderative reason," desire-inflected rational volition, in which choice flows from and actualizes the potentialities of moral character: "The origin of action . . . is choice [*proairesis*], and the cause of choice is desire and reasoning with a view to an end. This is why choice cannot exist either without reason . . . or without a moral state; for good action and its opposite cannot exist without a combination of intellect and character [*ethos*]."[6] Yet whatever the psychological or philosophical links between choice and character, it remains the case that some texts take more advantage of these links than do others. *Julius Caesar* and *Paradise Lost* both cultivate the impression of character as something complex (the personality did not simply compel a foregone conclusion) and coherent (the personality helps make a given choice intelligible). The moral responsibility of Brutus and Eve thus resides in the manner in which the narratives encourage us to link what happens to the characters back to what they deliberately chose, however much we allow for extenuating circumstances or the artifice of plot.

The Faerie Queene, by contrast, regularly encourages us to interpret the characters' "choices" as themselves consequences of earlier events. The narrative determines the decision, not the other way around. To say this does not deny that Spenser may rely, for example, on the Aristotelian account of moral action, but it does mean that Spenser emphasizes the extent to which character and desire are, as the *Nicomachean Ethics* claims, the determining "causes" of choice, an emphasis so pronounced in *The Faerie Queene* that choices often seem like effects rather than independent events. (Even Aristotle himself doesn't worry much about whether a choice is "free" or not.) This view comes into conflict with Susanne Woods's resourceful and vigorous account of Spenser's commitment to an "elective poetics," one in which "freedom is mainly conceived as the precondition for human agency, and therefore as the moral and efficient basis for all choices."[7] Yet whatever Spenser's philosophical or political advocacy of liberty, it plays little part in the form and effects of his poetry. *The Faerie Queene* rarely allows us to understand moral culpability in terms of a process that starts with free choice and leads to consequence. Consider an example that Woods herself uses (13), Arthur's deliverance of Mirabella from her tormentors: "Unto your selfe I freely leave to chose,/Whether I shall you leave, or from these villains lose" (VI.viii.29).[8] Remain in bondage or escape? This would seem a clear example of dramatic choice, until one reads Mirabella's response in the following stanza:

> Ah nay Sir Knight (sayd she) it may not be,
> But that I needes must by all meanes fulfill
> This penaunce, which enjoyned is to me,
> Least unto me betide a greater ill;
> Yet no lesse thankes to you for your good will.
>
> (VI.viii.30.1–5)

We could call this a "choice" in the sense that no one forces Mirabella to respond as she does, but Spenser thoroughly declines to dramatize it as a volitional act. There is no deliberation, no weighing of options. Instead, Mirabella automatically responds to a sense of necessity: the "need" to complete a "penance." Indeed, her initial "nay" and her concessive assurance to Arthur that she feels "no lesse thankes" for the offered options signals her perception that free choice was never an issue; it was never really up to her. We will find the same effect with Redcross Knight's "choice" to abandon Una and Arthur's to pursue Florimell instead of the Forester. This pervasive subordination of choice to necessity does not moot the fact of moral responsibility; instead, it makes such responsibility flow from other dimensions, such as the apprehension of poetic justice, the currents of narrative momentum, or the *determinism* of character.

Again, this determinism is distinct from the kind of psychological determinism we find operating in the modern novel. If Anna Karenina or Charles Swann make choices that seem vaguely fated, this impression derives in part from the psychological completeness with which Tolstoy and Proust imbue their characters. Anna's and Charles's personalities, we might say, constantly if unevenly push them from behind into a certain kind of future. Spenser's characters do not possess psychological "backgrounds" in quite the same manner. As William A. Oram has noted, Spenser's characters, unlike modern ones, are "teleologically determined": "the characters we find in the novel have, by and large, a fixed past and an open future; those we find in Spenser have a blank past and a fixed future."[9] In *The Faerie Queene*, then, the futurity of the titular heroes appears gripped by the necessity that they evolve into the kind of exemplar they are meant to become. Whether they *do* in fact achieve this perfected exemplarity by the end of their adventure is another question, one that we could answer variously from book to book. In any case, Oram's fine observation has important consequences for the representation of choice in *The Faerie Queene*: their past may not determine Spenser's characters, but neither does the past open up a space of elective activity. To rely one more time on Aristotle: "It is to be noted that nothing that is past is an object of choice, e.g., no one chooses to have sacked Troy; for no one deliberates about the past, but about what is future and capable of being otherwise, while what is past is not capable of not having taken place."[10] One cannot choose the past, only the future. Yet the future is precisely what Spenser closes off with his emphasis on narrative inevitability. Spenser's heroes do have moments of psychological complexity, and they wander and backslide from their fated exemplarity, but consistently the poem presents *character* as something that evolves toward a telos that already lies waiting for the hero in the future.

Spenser's lack of interest in free and independent volition that might appear to determine a character's future has sometimes created interpretive difficulty for critics who assume that moral culpability depends on choice. Yet, again, such an assumption rarely goes very far in explaining the ascription of culpability in *The Faerie Queene*. Take, as a rather complex example, the wound that Britomart receives from Gardante's arrow, "Which did her lilly smock with staines of vermeil steep" (III.i.65.9). What are we to make of the sense of blame—the intimate red stain on the pure white—that attaches itself to this wound? We could conclude that it's not blame on Britomart, but something more general, say, the "ever present dangers of maintaining chastity unimpaired in the active life."[11] Yet, if so, it is *Britomart's* life and character suffering impairment, she who is "[w]herewith enrag'd" (66.1), and she who specifically wreaks vengeance on Malecasta's knights for this staining. But what did Britomart do or choose to merit this stain? Take off her armor? Fall asleep? Fail to keep an eye on that tricky Gardante? None of these strike us as deliberate choices that would make her responsible for the vermilion consequences, even as the stain stubbornly implies that some kind of blame does impinge on her.

In an episode like this we are obliged to conclude that Britomart is both culpable and not culpable. This claim in no way entails moral relativism, as if Britomart were simply equivalent to Malacasta and Gardante. But in Faerie land innocence and culpability are mixed together, so that one cannot start off on purely neutral ground and choose one *or* the other. Again, this intermixing marks the poem's distance from *Julius Caesar* or *Paradise Lost*, narratives in which a deliberate choice divides the story into a preliminary segment of ethical suspense and a following segment of ethical consequence.[12] *The Faerie Queene* allows choice and consequence to flow into each other, and so requires us to think about Britomart's culpability rather differently: by merit of being alive and traveling the narrative landscape, Britomart has wandered into blame. Malacasta and Gardante seem to have always been lying in wait for her. To put it another way, Chastity needs them in order to be what it is, and they need Chastity. As the Britoness continues to wander she will negotiate the ongoing perils and rewards of heroic and erotic life, but this negotiation will not depend primarily on deliberate choices that might *shape* the narrative.

As the foregoing comments already imply, the priority of narrative over choice emerges in part from the medium in which Spenser writes: allegory rapaciously turns plot into meaning, subordinating consciousness to essence, persons to personifications. Allegorical narrative gradually creates the impression that events follow one another due to a conceptual necessity hovering just above the literal action. The allegory implicitly demands that its conceptual dimension "make sense," and so we come to feel that events of the narrative are in the service of this sense, that they point to something other than themselves.[13] This otherness need not result in the annulment of the literal story, and we do not generally read allegories in the hope of forgetting about the action and characters before us. Paul Suttie, in a recent and very lucid discussion of allegorical otherness that extends the work of Charles Singleton, points out that allegory can function according to the disparate logic of "this *for* that" and "this *and* that."[14] In the former, the literal image or action is taken *only figuratively* to signify some nonfictional meaning outside the world of the story. Christ makes clear to his disciples that his parables are to be applied allegorically to the "real" world; the figurative vineyard laborers exist in a world that is distinct from, and comments upon, the world of the disciples. By contrast, "this *and* that" allegory allows figurative events to participate in the world whose reality they signify. Moses' parting of the Red Sea allegorically signifies Christ's baptism, but both events occurred in the same world. Protestant exegetes sometimes preferred to call this kind of allegory "typology" when they applied it to the history in the Hebrew Testament. Yet Suttie extends this idea to overtly fictional allegories. Redcross Knight's journey along the "broad high way" leading to the House of Pride (*FQ* I.iv.2) allegorically signifies the idea that the way to sin is easy and frequently chosen. Suttie observes that Spenser in fact allows this abstract idea to participate in the fictional world of the path, when Dame Caelia teaches the knight the significance of "the broad high way" (I.x.10.5), encouraging him to develop an allegorical understanding of his own adventures.[15]

Suttie's fine insights reveal that an allegory's conceptual otherness interacts with its literal dimension in more than one way, and they suggest that I should be cautious in claiming that allegorical meaning simply imposes a necessity on the fiction from the outside. Yet, although readily granting the variety that Suttie discerns in allegory, I want to reemphasize the fact of *secondariness* that must always inhere in the mode. However present the literal elements remain in the fiction, they exist *for the sake of* an alternative order of nonfictional ideas. They announce, with greater and lesser degrees of explicitness, their secondariness to this order. This explicitness does vary: Tasso is concerned that the allegory of his poem will be hard to spot—that it won't *seem* allegorical enough—and so he offers a figure-by-figure translation, whereas Spenser expresses concern that his readers may find the allegory of his poem too heavily or tediously imposed.[16] Yet both writers assume that in allegory the actions and images of a story are to be seen as instrumental, not as ends in themselves. The "broad high way," whatever its persistence as a real element in a fictional world, exists for the sake of the idea of the human alacrity to sin, not vice versa. Spenser does not use the idea of sin-inclined humanity as a juicy occasion to represent a broad path any more than Christian exegetes thought that readers should study the baptism of Christ to learn more about Moses. It's not "this and that" so much as "this and, even more importantly, that." Of course, no allegory will ever perfectly translate its narrative action into ideas; there will be semantic drift and decay. But the allegorical action must at least seem secondary. A narrative that offers *no* sense, however diffuse, of the priority of idea over image is not an allegory. It is with this notion of secondariness that I claim that allegory promotes the impression that its characters' choices are themselves consequences of prior causes, that the narrative grips them with a certain necessity. *The Faerie Queene* is special, as we will see, in that it imagines the secondariness of the characters as potentially allowing them to cooperate with narrative necessity, to will it, if not exactly choose it.

PERSONIFICATIONS AND DAEMONS

Critics routinely and sometimes sternly warn us not to assume that personification has anything to do with allegory.[17] The former is an oratorical device, whereas the latter is a narrative mode. The confusion between the two has resulted, we are told, from an anachronistic imposition of post-Renaissance literary taste onto the Renaissance. This warning is worth heeding, since practically no commentator before the seventeenth century makes any formal connection between allegory and personification. Yet the warning also risks ignoring what everyone recognizes: personification—especially the personification of abstract concepts—seems to work like allegory, offering an image that signifies an idea. Jon Whitman has discussed the manner in which both personification and allegory rely on a double structure of interior reality and external façade, *prosopon* and *allos*.[18] Similarly, Isabel G. MacCaffrey has usefully described allegory's tendency to turn adjectival characters (the shamefast man) into noun-characters (Shamefastness).[19] My own emphasis on allegorical secondariness likewise tends to link personification to allegory. We might say that personification is the logical (if not always fully realized) fate for any character we think of as allegorical, that is, who exists mostly for the sake of something else. Personification expresses the sense that the necessity imposed by the order of nonfictional ideas has gotten inside the character, shifting adjective to noun, imbuing her with an essence that compels behavior from within as well as without. Personification, then, promotes the subordination of choice that I have been discussing in the poem.

Of course, neither personification nor allegory is unique in this respect, since plenty of other literary factors can create a priority of necessity over choice. Plot itself, as an artifice of human imagination, structurally depends on the idea that the conclusion of a narrative is foregone even if not foreknown at the present moment of reading.[20] Genre is another kind of example. Epic tends to overdetermine choice by exerting teleological necessity on its characters, whereas romance often underdetermines choice by obliging characters to wander from episode to episode, the links between which frequently remain mysterious. Yet both plot design and genre expectations can still allow for and even promote the impression free, deliberate choice.[21] Personification allegory almost never promotes such an impression because it functions by making a character's actions fulfill the needs of an alternative order of ideas. This alternative order possesses personifications, as it were, with a magical presence, or programs them with complex computer software, so that their decisions appear to resonate with, and emerge from, a preexisting conceptual necessity. A literary character can sometimes own its choices to the degree these choices appear to come from the inside and not only the outside; yet a personification's inside already seems as if it came from the outside. A personification has an agency that does not quite appear to belong to it.

Consider, for example, a Spenserian reference which would seem to demand the ascription of original agency: the character of Lucifera, whom we find in the underworldly House of Pride (I.iv–v). Spenser here glances at the tradition in which the prideful Lucifer's choice to rebel in heaven leads eventually to the Fall from Eden, "and all our woe," as Milton will put it.[22] And, indeed, Spenser has Lucifera initiate an allegorical procession of traditional deadly sins: Idleness, Gluttony, Lechery, Avarice, Envy, and Wrath (I.iv.18–35). Yet even as we prepare to identify Luciferian pride as the volitional originator of a chain of postlapsarian consequences, the allegory suddenly traps us in a feedback loop, when Spenser tells us: "And after all, upon the wagon beame/Rode Sathan, with a smarting whip in hand,/With which he forward lasht the laesie teme" (I.iv.36.1–3). It is curious that Satan follows *after* the procession of sins—as if he were an eighth deadly sin—even though he was the agent who, as the archangel Lucifer, long ago *begot* these sins. Yet when we look back to the beginning of the parade of sins to recapture this historical agency, we find that the allegory has already coopted it, rewriting Lucifer-the-agent as Lucifera-the-personification, turning cause into effect. The procession of personified evils thus absorbs the original evil-doer into the very chain of consequences he supposedly set in motion long ago.

This demonic feedback model of agency is not the only version of personification allegory that Spenser employs. However, it *is* the version that we find in modern theories of personification, which usually treat personification as a figure of volitional limitation or stasis. Angus Fletcher has influentially discussed allegorical characters as "obsessed" personae, and Steven Knapp has pointed out their fanatically self-absorbed nature. In Paul de Man and J. Hillis Miller, personification imposes a death-dealing petrifaction, recapitulating the rift between life and signification.[23] These accounts tend to rely, directly or indirectly, on Walter Benjamin's now famous description of modern (post-Renaissance) allegory as an expression of the gap between the order of nature and the order of meaning, wherein the attempt to impose significance on the world drains life from the world: "The greater the significance, the greater the subjection to death, because death digs most deeply the jagged line of demarcation between physical nature and significance."[24] For Benjamin, the two personae who best figure the allegorist are the melancholic, who drains energy, and the sadist, who humiliates the object of his attention.[25]

Likewise, much Spenser criticism, and some of the best, has followed this theoretical model in its treatment of the agency of allegorical characters. In this view, allegory and personification exert a tyrannically constraining or deadening pressure on the poem's characters. Gordon Teskey has recently discussed the necrotic dimension of personification: "the very liveliness of the allegorical figures, their frenetic, jerky, galvanic life, makes us think of dead bodies through which an electric current is passed," and he intriguingly observes the danger that allegory's "shadow of absolute, determinate meaning" poses to "whatever it is in the poem that keeps the poem alive."[26] In a similar vein, Jeff Dolven, elegantly extending Teskey's earlier work on allegorical capture, considers allegory as a form of poetic justice, one which emblematically includes the consequences of crime with the crime itself. He concludes his wide-ranging discussion by noting "how close to the conceptual root of personification allegory the idea of punishment lies."[27] Kenneth Gross has likewise given us a rich discussion of allegory as a fantasy of conceptual desire, wherein personifications "work to lend a human substance, a human face or gesture, to ideas, energies, structures, and influences, which otherwise seen to live a different life, a less or more than human life." The cost of this lending, for Gross, is an enervating fixity of thought, resulting in "the sense of something dead or inert in allegorical writing. Its rigidly diagrammed actions seem a mode of exhausting imaginative energy."[28]

These ideas of death, punishment, and fixation in Spenserian allegory are anticipated to some degree by Susanne Wofford's 1992 book, *The Choice of Achilles*, which sees Spenser's poem governed by "an apparently inevitable link between prosopopoiia and imprisonment, bondage, enclosure, or death."[29] To make her interpretation, Wofford draws on Angus Fletcher's description of personification as "daemonic possession," yet she associates Fletcher's mythic daemons with infernal demons, arguing that in the poem "sin itself comes to be defined as the moment when a human being allows a daemon to overtake him or her, becoming as it were completely 'obsessed' by the one devouring trait."[30] By contrast, Wofford reads Britomart's realization of her character at the end of Book III as a function of her successful escape from the daemonic compulsion that the allegorist Busirane tries to impose on women. Britomart emerges from the book as a "fictional heroine," not an allegorical personification. This interpretation strongly implies that we might generally distinguish the titular heroes of *The Faerie Queene* from the narrow personifications that surround them in terms of the heroes' greater freedom from allegorical compulsion.

As we can see from the Lucifera/Satan episode, such accounts of Spenserian allegory have great merit—personifications do sometimes operate as reduced or immobilizing agents. Yet it is important to remember that no commentator before the eighteenth century speaks of *prosopopoeia* in this manner.[31] The emphasis on volitional stasis or compulsion thus appears to derive in part from a modern bias toward psychologically mimetic, "well-rounded" characters, in comparison to which personifications appear narrow, inauthentic, or flat. Renaissance readers surely did see a difference between a character such as Britomart and characters such as Gardante or Fancy, but there is no evidence they measured this difference in terms of greater or lesser freedom, or that they thought Britomart was a fictional *as opposed to* allegorical character. Indeed, Renaissance readers had no formal category, as we do, of "non-allegorical fiction"; all fiction, unlike history, could take on a secondariness and signify an alternative order of ideas.[32] They clearly did not think it worthwhile to pursue an allegorical meaning in every fiction, but every fiction was susceptible to allegory. In this respect, I seek to supplement interpretations about the compulsive nature of personification by observing that the other side of allegorical compulsion is not necessarily life, freedom, or fiction, but sometimes something else—more allegory.

When Renaissance commentators discuss *prosopopoeia*, they do not talk about static or flat characters; instead, they follow the ancient rhetoricians in emphasizing the act of animation, the vitalization of nonliving or nonreasoning things with living attributes and personhood. George Puttenham writes that poets use *prosopopoeia* when they "attribute any human quality, as reason or speech, to dumb creatures or insensible things, and do study (as one may say) to give them a human person."[33] Henry Peacham likewise describes the trope as "when to a thing senseless and dumb we fain a fit person," attributing to it "speech, reason, and affection." By means of *prosopopoeia*, Peacham explains, the poet temporarily reverses the effects of mortality: "sometime[s] he raiseth again as it were the dead to life, and bringeth them forth complaining or witnessing what they knew."[34] Indeed, he insists that *prosopopoeia* is the last, best defense of a besieged orator, "not unlike to a champion, having broken his weapons in the force of his conflict, calleth for new of his friends . . . or to an army having their number diminished, or their strength enfeebled, do crave and call for new supply."[35] Personification, for these commentators, is energy.

If the rhetoricians found a kind of oratorical agency in *prosopopoeia*, Renaissance neoplatonists found a cosmological agency in a related figure from Greek literature and philosophy. In Plato, Euripides, and Aristophanes, characters with names like Necessity or Ambition are sometimes referred to as *daemons*, and they appear to hover between personified abstraction and actual deity.[36] The Italian classicist Marsilio Ficino devoted a considerable part of his commentary on the *Symposium* to Plato's claim that Love was the daemon offspring of Poverty and Resource, part mortal and part immortal.[37] Ficino, and the writers influenced by him, developed an elaborate theory of daemons, the messengers of God who, like angels, deliver divine gifts to humans on earth. Theresa Krier has, in two groundbreaking articles, recently applied the mediatory function of daemons to literary personification, arguing that personifications potentially represent productive linking between concepts, producing unconstrained thinking.[38] In a related approach, I wish to note the *volitional* potential of neoplatonic daemons. For Ficino, the universe is a mixture of necessity and freedom, since God's productive love naturally produces an ordered universe, but God loves that universe willingly.[39] Daemons are an expression of God's will—we might even say they personify that will. They are the agents who actively connect the various levels of the universe, bringing the passions of the cosmos into the hearts of men and women. Such daemonic possession can become tyrannical, and Ficino acknowledges that love often entails the loss of self-possession.[40] Yet he usually emphasizes the willing quality of daemonic love, describing at one point "that one great love [that Plato] called 'the great daemon,' which, dwelling in everything throughout the whole universe, allows no heart to sleep, but everywhere arouses it to loving."[41] This daemon of love does not so much constrain as it inspires and enables.

The oratorical and neoplatonic traditions thus allow us to think of the daemon as a figure of *either* obsession *or* inspiration, giving us a more varied sense, I think, of the possessed will in Spenser's poem. Obsession does indeed sometimes trump agency in *The Faerie Queene*, and personification turns out to be compulsion. Malbecco's transformation into Gelosy, for instance, forces upon him a new face, or *prosopon*, that eats him from the outside in: "all his substance was consum'd to nought,/And nothing left, but like an aery Spright" (III.x.57.3–4). The Snowy Florimell provides another example: the Witch carefully constructs her body, piece by piece, but the wicked Spright that possesses this *prosopon* does not achieve animation so much as animatronics: "and in the stead/Of life, she put a Spright to rule the carcase dead" (III.viii.7.8–9). The Witch does not quite manage to raise the dead to life, as Peacham describes, but only effects a kind of undead simulation. In both cases a daemon sadistically forces these characters to advertise the extent to which they signify something other than themselves, and they become examples of Teskey's necrotic mannequins or Dolven's self-accusing emblems of just punishment.[42]

But not all of Spenser's daemons impose such grotesque zombification. Think of the angel who protects Guyon after his faint, a figure who certainly arrives as an *angelos*, or messenger of God, but whom the narrator also compares to "Cupido on Idaean hill" (II.viii.6.1), clearly glancing at the neoplatonic association between angels and daemons. This messenger does not only protect the knight of temperance, but he promises that renewed life will be instilled in the lifeless body. The angel assures the anxious Palmer, "But dread of death and dolor doe away;/For life ere long shall to her home retire,/And he that breathlesse seems, shal corage bold respire" (II.viii.7.7–9). "Corage" means life, of course, but combined with "bold" it also promises life energy, force, will. We ought to have this Cupid-like angel in mind near the beginning of Book III, when the narrator, addressing love as that "most sacred fire," observes that

Well did Antiquitie a God thee deeme,
That over mortall minds hast so great might,

To order them, as best to thee doth seeme,
And all their actions to direct aright;
The fatall purpose of divine foresight,
Thou doest effect in destined descents,
Through deepe impression of thy secret might,
And stirredst up th'Heroes high intents,
Which the late world admyres for wondrous moniments.

(III.iii.2)

Here the god of love, aligned with providential power, does influence the will—he can "direct aright" the actions of men. Yet this direction does not simply compel or constrain, but rather motivates: "stirredst up th'Heroes high intents." Daemonic love does not set the heroes free exactly, but it does inspire their intentions, encouraging them to will.

In this respect it is worth remembering that Spenser has little admiration for *liberty* where erotic experience is concerned. When Mirabella was "Ladie of her libertie" she "Did boast her beautie had such soveraine might,/That with the onely twinckle of her eye,/She could or save, or spill, whom she would hight" (VI.vii.31.5–8). Likewise, Prince Arthur confesses that his time of "libertie" (I.ix.10.7 and 12.4) was characterized by the "looser life" (12.6) of adolescent sadism, when he "joyed to stirre up strife,/In midst of their mournfull Tragedy,/Ay wont to laugh, when them I heard to cry,/And blow the fire, which them to ashes brent" (10.3–6). Along these lines, readers have sometimes been slightly misled by Britomart's Chaucerian dictum that "Ne may love be compeld by maistery;/For soone as maistery comes, sweet love anone/Taketh his nimble winges, and soone away is gone" (III.i.25.7–9), which out of context suggests that lovers must be free to *choose* to fall in love or not. But Britomart's exception to mastery responds to the Redcross Knight's report that Malacasta's knights want him "To change my liefe, and love another Dame,/That death me liefer were" (III.i.24.3). No question of freedom here: love comes upon you, sometimes with a speed of an arrow, and one's moral responsibility at that point is to maintain a fidelity to that unchosen object of desire.

In Spenser, then, virtuous desire and action reside not so much in "freeing" oneself from the mastery of love as willing it toward virtuous ends with the available resources of moral character. After all, Britomart is on a mission to impose the same mastery on Arthegall, to fetch him back to Britain "firmly bound with faithful band"

(III.iii.27.6). Spenser knows that the ethic of the "band" risks association with the sadistic versions of erotic bondage abounding in his poem, but such is the way of daemonic will. Once Love captures Arthur and Britomart it does *force* them to signify, bringing the praise-seeking Arthur closer to Praysdesire and the chaste British princess to the ideas of Chastity and Dynasty. It makes them, in a sense, more secondary than they were before. (Indeed, this contrast seems to be the point of providing them each with pre-capture biographies.) Daemonic possession does not simply foreclose their agency, however, but rather enables agency to extend in a certain direction. Extrapolating to the poem more broadly: to the degree that the titular characters of *The Faerie Queene* succeed in their quests, they do so not by outgrowing their allegorical natures, but by affirming their daemonic essence.

BRITOMART'S VOLITIONAL MASTERY

Britomart's behavior in the House of Busirane illustrates just such an affirmation. She offers a good test case for the foregoing argument, since to a greater degree than any other character in the poem readers have seen in her the presence of psychological complexity or character development. I do not deny these effects, but it is a mistake to see them as the cause of Britomart's success, as if outgrowing the allegory puts her in touch with free will, authentic humanity, or life itself. This is not how Spenser thinks of either character or will. We ought to remember that Canto xi begins with the narrator's hope to transition from "Fowle Gealosy" (III.xi.1)—which Malbecco's demonic transformation has just described for us—to "Sweete Love" (III.xi.2), which allows "faire Ladies" to "governe wisely well" the hearts of men. Both Jealousy and Love daemonically possess the human soul, but the first merely obsesses while the second inspires. In exploring this contrast, the episode asks: how might someone gain a voluntary purchase on the largely involuntary experience of desire? How might someone be an agent, and not only a victim, of love?

The famous victim of the episode is Amoret, the captive of Cupid's allegorical masque: "She dolefull Lady, like a dreary Spright, / Cald by strong charmes out of eternal night, / Had Deathes owne ymage figurd in her face" (III.xi.19). Much as jealousy consumes Malbecco until he is "like an *aery* Spright," so does Busirane's demonic compulsion make Amoret "like a *dreary* Spright." Personification is imposed on her, a *prosopon* of terrifying stasis: "Deathes owne ymage figurd in her *face*." Whatever their ethical differences, both Malbecco and Amoret experience daemonic possession as a violent self-dispossession. Indeed, part of Amoret's problem is that she has been transformed into one of the consequences of a psychological process that she could have chosen to initiate. Traditionally, as Thomas Roche noted some time ago,[43] it is the courtly lady who inspires in the male admirer the experiences personified by Cupid's allegorical masque: Fancy, Desire, Doubt, Danger, Fear, Hope, etc. (III.xii.7–18). Amoret is in fact held by two personifications, Despite and Cruelty, who would otherwise represent the agency of a woman to refuse love. This may be an intentional irony in the episode: you play the Petrarchan game, you reap the consequences. Yet, if so, Spenser opts to represent these consequences as daemonic compulsion, pushing the adjectival idea of a spiteful and cruel woman into the nouns of Despite and Cruelty. Like Satan in the House of Pride, whose historical agency is rewritten as an allegorical consequence in Lucifera, Amoret is reduced from agent to consequence.

Britomart for the most part escapes Amoret's fate, establishing herself as an agent, rather than mere casualty, of desire. Although her final encounter with Busyrane is important, the experience that determines her agency occurs at the statue of Cupid and the subsequent masque, and it is on these sections that I will focus. Spenser signals Britomart's agency, in part, by repeatedly designating her as "bold." This distinguishes her will from the too bold will of Scudamour (the over-eager lover), which degenerates into mere willfulness, and the insufficiently bold will of Amoret, which remains too vulnerable to the other daemonic agents that afflict her. As Dorothy Stephens has discussed, the "be bold" and "be not too bold" messages that Britomart sees implicitly pull her into an erotic relationship with Busirane. These messages come from the folk tale about Bluebeard, the homicidal husband who warns his new bride not to look in the closet containing the corpses of his past wives, admonishing her, "Be bold, be bold, be not too bold, lest that thy heart's blood should run cold."[44] I suspect that Spenser found this folk tale an apt analogue to Britomart's situation because of the threat of daemonic stasis: Busirane's sadistic love turns the blood cold, freezes the will, imposes an immobilizing *prosopopoeia*.

Nonetheless, Britomart does not refuse the bait of daemonic allegory. She risks looking at the procession holding the bloody Amoret, Busirane's wished-for bride, and at the triumphant Cupid who follows; "she saw both first and last" (III.xii.27), the narrator tells us. How does she maintain her agency in the face of this compulsive

spectacle? According to Isabel MacCaffrey, "For Britomart, the drama-
tization is an exorcism."[45] This remark aptly points to the daemonic
context of the episode, but it assumes that agency rests only in escap-
ing or refusing the determinism of allegory. The association between
the neoplatonic daemon and Renaissance psychology may offer a
more nuanced account of how Britomart keeps her distance from
the spectacle without simply renouncing it. Genevieve Guenther
has recently demonstrated how Renaissance psychologists revised the
Platonic notion of the ideal image—which works on the imagination
to inspire virtue—by coupling it with evaluative resources of reason.
Spenser's knights "apply their desire instrumentally by setting the
image of the object cathected in the imagination within the 'stay'
fashioned by the discourse of the understanding."[46] For Guenther,
the mechanism that keeps one close but not too close to the daemonic
image is *wonder*, which obliges one to acknowledge the image but
assumes an imperfect understanding of it.

Although she is more interested in the Protestant anxiety about
infernal demons existing in the real world and less interested in the
protocols of allegorical fiction, Guenther's account of wonder, poised
between cathexis and mediatory process, nicely captures the manner
in which Spenser dramatizes the workings of daemonic agency. It
goes far in explaining how Britomart allows the daemon of love to
possess her without obsessing her. Shortly before watching Cupid's
masque she sees his statue holding bow and arrow in his cruel hand
and standing over the wounded dragon:

> That wondrous sight faire Britomart amazd,
> Ne seeing could her wonder satisfie,
> But evermore and more upon it gazd,
> The whiles the passing brightnes her fraile sences dazd.
>
> (III.xi.49.6–9)

Spenser presents Cupid as a stone statue at this point to signal the
threat of daemonic compulsion: desire can turn you into stone, much
as Bluebeard can freeze your blood, and much as Amoret now wears
her prosopopoetic death mask. Britomart does not bow down to the
statue in idolatry, as do the other inhabitants of the castle, but she
does gaze at it in "wonder" (49.7), almost overcome. Critics usually
read this moment as an illustration of the danger of erotic desire
and/or Britomart's susceptibility to that desire. Yet I would argue
that Britomart is not so much making an error here as she is taking

a risk. It is a necessary risk, since in the neoplatonic scheme Cupid's statue is, for all its tyranny, a version of the noble image of Cupid the ancient god in Canto iii. Britomart's encounter with the statue does not stymie her will, since in the following stanza the narrator begins referring to her as "bold": "She was no whit thereby discouraged,/From prosecuting of her first intent,/But forward with bold steps into the next roome went" (xi.50). By allowing herself to undergo the wonder of daemonic possession, Britomart can engage Busirane's sadistic eroticism without accepting its consequences as inevitable. There are alternative stories to tell, alternative endings toward which to will. Her volitional mastery lies in making the daemon of love inspire her, rather than obsess her.

Spenser returns to the delicate balance between inspiration and obsession at the end of the 1590 version of the episode, where he makes clear that Amoret's deliverance does not simply amount to a freedom from allegorical possession. Her body, "late the prison of sad paine," has now become "the sweet lodge of love and deare delight" (III.xii.45.3,4). Here we have the fulfillment of the poet's hope, expressed at the beginning of the episode (III.xi.1–2), to shift from jealousy to love. Yet this shift is not one from compulsion to liberty, but rather a move to a new kind of daemonic possession, when Amoret and Scudamour embrace:

> But she faire Lady overcommen quight
> Of huge affection, did in pleasure melt,
> And in sweete ravishment pourd out her spright:
> No word they spake, nor earthly thing they felt,
> But like two senceles stocks in long embracement dwelt.
>
> (III.xii.45.5–9)

It is tempting to read this passage as an ironic commentary on Britomart's rescue of Amoret. "Senceles stocks" reminds us of the constraining versions of personification elsewhere in the poem, and the "ravishment" of Amoret's "pourd out . . . spright" here uncomfortably recalls what Busyrane tried to do when he presented Amoret "bleeding forth her fainting spright" (xii.20.7). Yet, again, the risk of such associations is the way of daemonic love. Once we give up the erroneous expectation that Spenser will associate love with freedom or choice, we can understand the alienation of "sweete ravishment" and "long embracement" as love's potential for virtue. Spenser elsewhere conceives of virtuous love in this manner: at the betrothal ceremony of Redcross and Una, the angel's voice—like a neoplatonic daemon—leaves the listener "ravished with rare impression in his sprite" (I.xii.39.9).

No doubt, daemonic ravishment *does* pose a risk, and Britomart must be cautious in the way she identifies with the reunited couple, who in their embrace resemble "that faire Hermaphrodite" (III.xii.46.2). Ovidian perils aside for the moment, Lauren Silberman has noted what is most distinctive about this classical reference: Spenser cites not Hermaphroditus but rather an (absent) *statue* of Hermaphroditus, "of white marble wrought" (46.3).[47] With this fact in mind, we can appreciate the care with which Spenser here replays Britomart's earlier encounter with Cupid's tyrannical statue. She again confronts and responds to a potentially petrifying version of love, and again she maintains a distance ("*halfe*-envying their blesse" [46.6]) without rejecting the vision, "much empassiond in her gentle sprite" (46.7). To the degree that this vision inspires her to continue the search for her own love, it also reveals the degree to which Britomart, through an exertion of virtuous will, has reclaimed love from Busirane's sadistic and moribund representations. The reunited lovers, likened to a statue, still bear the trace of the tyrannous Cupid but do not simply recapitulate its tyranny. This is as much as Britomart can do for them, and Spenser suggests that, whatever her will's limitation, it amounts to a great deal.

This reading of the House of Busirane has tried to demonstrate the manner in which Spenser's characters express their wills in the narrative, deliberately and voluntarily, without exactly choosing. One character's compulsion can be another character's inspiration. Spenser's sense of the possessed will ranges from the sublime to the quotidian: the prophet is possessed by the gods but still speaks as the prophet, much as we sometimes casually say that "something got into me" but still own that something as something we *willed*. Possession by this something or by the gods necessarily compromises our volition's independence, making it contingent on an external presence, an effect that Spenser gestures at stylistically with the secondariness of allegorical fiction. Yet this contingent secondariness does not only compel or deaden; instead, it can serve as the basis of immensely powerful exertions of the will. In Britomart's case, this amounts to saying that she is not simply free from the allegory of love, but that she has the potential to will it to ends other than the destructive ones preferred by Busirane. Britomart succeeds not because she manages to overcome her allegorical nature and move toward authentic personhood, but, on the contrary, because she is able to intensify her daemonic nature and become what she is: *chastity*, which for Spenser is always a bold engagement with desire.

Ohio University

NOTES

1. Alpers, *Poetry of* The Faerie Queene (1967; rpt. Columbia: University of Missouri Press, 1982), 332.

2. *Julius Caesar*, ed. William Montgomery (New York: Penguin, 2000).

3. *Paradise Lost*, ed. Gordon Teskey (New York: Norton, 2004).

4. As Jacque Bos demonstrates, before the late-seventeenth century the term "character" signified a *type* of person, not an individual. See "Individuality and Inwardness in Literary Character Sketches of the Seventeenth Century," *Journal of the Warburg and Courtauld Institutes* 61 (1998): 142–57. Elizabeth Fowler, in her acute study of literary character, likewise discusses character in terms of the "social person" whose recognition depends on convention: "Social persons are models of the person, familiar concepts of social being that attain currency though common use . . . . As conventional kinds of person, social persons are very much like literary genres, because they depend upon the recognition of convention" (Fowler, *Literary Character: The Human Figure in Early English Writing* [Ithaca: Cornell University Press, 2003], 2).

5. See Lee D. Ross, "The Intuitive Psychologist and His Shortcomings: Distortions in the Attribution Process," in *Advances in Experimental Social Psychology*, ed. Leonard Berkowitz, vol. 10 (New York: Academic Press, 1977), 174–77; and Lee D. Ross, Mark Lepper, and Michael Hubbard, "Perseverance in Self-Perception and Social Perception: Biased Attributional Processes in the Debriefing Paradigm," *Journal of Personality and Social Psychology* 32 (1975): 880–92. For an intriguing if slightly schematic application of the Fundamental Attribution Error to literary character, see Richard J. Gerrig and David W. Allbritton, "The Construction of Literary Character: A View from Cognitive Psychology," *Style* 24:3 (1990): 32–43.

6. Aristotle, *Nicomachean Ethics*, bk. 6, chap. 2 (1139a 30–35); in *The Basic Works of Aristotle*, ed. and trans. Richard McKeon (New York: Random House, 1941), 1024.

7. Woods, "Making Free with Poetry: Spenser and the Rhetoric of Choice," *Spenser Studies* 15 (2001): 1–16, 3.

8. Spenser, *The Faerie Queene*, ed. A. C. Hamilton (New York: Longman, 2001).

9. Oram, "Characterization and Spenser's Allegory," in *Proceedings of the Nineteenth International Congress on Medieval Studies*, ed. Francis G. Greco (Clarion: Clarion University Press, 1984), 91–122, 98, 96. Oram goes on perspicaciously to observe that "[t]his blank past does not, however, leave Spenser's characters free. They are, in fact, peculiarly limited by the explicitness of their own futures" (97).

10. Aristotle, *Nicomachean Ethics*, bk. 6, chap. 3 (1139b 5–10), 1024.

11. Thomas P. Roche, Jr., *The Kindly Flame* (Princeton: Princeton University Press, 1964), 70–71.

12.   This account owes much to Gordon Teskey's description of the distinction between Milton and Spenser: "From Allegory to Dialectic: Imagining Error in Spenser and Milton," *PMLA* 101 (1986): 9–23.

13.   "In complex allegories . . . we seem to be directed, through the process of interpretation, toward a point where all mystery is dispelled in the presence of truth . . . . The existence of an ineffable center of meaning where all interpretations seem to converge is something that the reader is encouraged to accept in order to enjoy the process of trying to get there" (Gordon Teskey, "Allegory," *The Spenser Encyclopedia* [Toronto: University of Toronto Press, 1990], 16).

14.   Suttie, *Self-Interpretation in "The Faerie Queene"* (Cambridge: Boydell & Brewer, 2006), 15–38.

15.   Ibid., 26.

16.   Tasso: "if the allegory of anything be not well expressed, with these beginnings [Tasso's notes] every man by himself may easily find it out" ("Allegory of the Poem," *The Recovery of Jerusalem*, trans. Edward Fairfax [London, 1600], sig. A3r.). Spenser: readers might "rather have good discipline plainly in the way of precepts, or sermoned at large, as they use, then thus clowdily enwrapped in Allegorical devises" ("Letter of the Authors," *Faerie Queene*, ed. Hamilton, 716). Of course, the letter to Ralegh, absent from the 1596 edition, is an imperfect guide to Spenser's intentions. Yet whether or not he *really* expected readers to find his allegory distractingly heavy, he seems to have felt that his readers would find such an expectation comprehensible.

17.   One of the classic and most persuasive warnings comes from Michael Murrin, *The Veil of Allegory: Some Notes Toward a Theory of Allegorical Rhetoric in the English Renaissance* (Chicago: University of Chicago Press, 1969).

18.   Whitman, *Allegory: The Dynamics of an Ancient and Medieval Technique* (Cambridge: Harvard University Press, 1987), 269.

19.   "By introducing 'adjectival' characters, the Temperate Man or the Just Man, into a sequence of adventures, Spenser causes them gradually to become transparent to the reader's vision, so that behind each of them we come to see the outlines of a noun: Temperance, Justice. This noun becomes a character itself in Shamefastness . . . " (MacCaffrey, *Spenser's Allegory: The Anatomy of the Imagination* [Princeton: Princeton University Press, 1976], 84).

20.   Peter Brooks puts it this way: "If the past is to be read as present, it is a curious kind of present that we know to be past in relation to a future we know to be already in place, already in wait for us to reach it. Perhaps we would do best to speak of the *anticipation of retrospection* as our chief tool in making sense of narrative, the master trope of its strange logic." See Brooks, *Reading for the Plot: Design and Intention in Narrative* (New York: Knopf, 1984; rpt. Cambridge: Harvard University Press, 1992), 23.

21.   For example, few readers (and probably few of the fictional characters) would claim that they understand all the conceptual links between the disjointed episodes of Chrétien de Troyes's romance *The Knight of the Cart*, but a number of these episodes do dramatize characters making deliberate decisions that appear to shape (temporarily) the direction of the plot. Lancelot, when told that to find Guinevere he must ride in the shameful cart, hesitates and appears briefly to deliberate about

the conflicting claims of reason (which counsels him to avoid reproach) and love (which counsels him to find his mistress at any cost). His choice to ride in the cart ends up producing important consequences for his future, and the narrative refers back to this decision repeatedly. See *Arthurian Romances*, trans. William W. Kibler (New York: Penguin, 1991), lines 355–75, pages 211–12.

22. Thomas Roche compares this episode to Milton's Satan in "Spenser, Milton, and the Representation of Evil," in *Heirs of Fame: Milton and Writers of the English Renaissance*, ed. Margo Swiss and David A. Kent (Lewisburg: Bucknell University Press, 1995), 18–20.

23. Fletcher, *Allegory: The Theory of a Symbolic Mode* (Ithaca: Cornell University Press, 1964), chap. 1; Knapp, *Personification and the Sublime: Milton to Coleridge* (Cambridge: Harvard University Press, 1985), 4; De Man, "Anthropomorphism and Trope in the Lyric," in *The Rhetoric of Romanticism* (New York: Columbia University Press, 1984); Miller, *Versions of Pygmalion* (Cambridge: Harvard University Press, 1990).

24. Benjamin, *The Origin of German Tragic Drama* (1928), trans. Jonn Osborne (London: Verso, 1994), 166.

25. Melancholy: "If the object becomes allegorical under the gaze of melancholy, if melancholy causes life to flow out of it and it remains behind dead, but eternally secure, then it is exposed to the allegorist, it is unconditionally in his power. . . . For the only pleasure the melancholic permits himself, and it is a powerful one, is allegory" (ibid, 183, 185). Sadism: "It is indeed characteristic of the sadist that he humiliates his object and then—or thereby—satisfies it. And that is what the allegorist does in this age drunk with acts of cruelty both lived and imagined" (ibid., 184).

26. Teskey, "Death in an Allegory," in *Imagining Death in Spenser and Milton*, ed. Elizabeth Jane Bellamy, Patrick Cheney, Michael Schoenfeldt (Basingstoke: Palgrave, 2003), 66, 82–83.

27. Dolven, "Spenser's Sense of Poetic Justice," *Raritan* 21:1 (2001): 127–40, quotation at 139–40. Dolven's analysis is very subtle, and he carefully avoids an argument "that might simply equate allegory and punishment. One could say, after all, that allegory is about *thinking*—and that it is no more violent or punitive than extended analogy" (134).

28. Gross, "The Postures of Allegory," in *Edmund Spenser: Essays on Culture and Allegory*, eds. Jennifer Klain Morrison and Matthew Greenfield (Burlington: Ashgate, 2000), 170–71, 175.

29. Wofford, *The Choice of Achilles* (Stanford: Stanford University Press, 1992), 303.

30. Ibid.

31. See the survey of the literature in James J. Paxson, *The Poetics of Personification* (Cambridge: Cambridge University Press, 1994), 8–29.

32. Some readers will be quick to point out that Renaissance commentators did sometimes treat history allegorically, as Providence or typology. But when commentators did this they thought of history as God's story, something he had "written" and infused with signs of his dispensation. No one thought that Livy or Foxe or Holinshed *intended* their histories as allegories, even if God's Providence could be glimpsed in them.

33. Puttenham, *The Arte of English Poesie* (London, 1589), 246.

34. Both passages from Peacham, *The Garden of Eloquence*, 2nd ed. (London, 1593), 136.

35. Ibid., 137.

36. For an overview of such appearances in Greek texts, see Emma Stafford, *Worshipping Virtues: Personification and the Divine in Ancient Greece* (London: Duckworth, 2000), 1–44.

37. Ficino, *Commentary on Plato's Symposium* (1475), trans. Sears Reynolds Jayne (Columbia: University of Missouri Press, 1944), 190–200.

38. Krier, "Psychic Deadness in Allegory: Spenser's House of Mammon and Attacks on Linking," in *Imagining Death in Spenser and Milton*, ed. Elizabeth Bellamy, Patrick Cheney, and Michael Schoenfeldt (Basingstoke, England: Palgrave Macmillan, 2003); and "Daemonic Allegory: The Elements in Late Spenser, Late Shakespeare, and Irigaray," *Spenser Studies* 18 (2003): 315–42, esp. 330–32.

39. Ficino, 179.

40. Ibid., 202.

41. Ibid., 192.

42. These images also resonate with the pervasive trope of paralysis in the poem, surveyed by William Oram, "Spenserian Paralysis," *Studies in English Literature, 1500–1800* 41:1 (2001): 49–70.

43. Roche, *Kindly Flame*, 72–88.

44. Stephens, *The Limits of Eroticism in Post-Petrarchan Narrative* (Cambridge: Cambridge University Press, 1998), 31–32.

45. MacCaffrey, *Spenser's Allegory*, 112.

46. Guenther, "Spenser's Magic, or Instrumental Aesthetics in the 1590 *Faerie Queene*," *English Literary Renaissance* 36:1 (2006): 194–226, 209.

47. Silberman, *Transforming Desire: Erotic Knowledge in Books III and IV of "The Faerie Queene"* (Berkeley: University of California Press, 1995), 68.

ELIZABETH JANE BELLAMY

Spenser's "Open"

Continental postmodernism's influential "return to ethics" has recently revisited such figures as Bataille, Girard, Kristeva, Lacan, and others in order to pursue the question of the animal as the repressed other of Western culture. At the same time, a recent trend in early modern cultural studies has begun investigating sixteenth—and seventeenth-century perspectives on human-animal difference. This essay does not attempt an impossible—and, perhaps, even undesirable—bridging of early modern and early modernist inquiries into animal being. But, in its broadest scope, it is concerned with how *The Faerie Queene* opens up beyond its own historicity to take its place in a genealogy of Western culture's ongoing discourse, from Aristotle to Descartes to Heidegger, on the question of the animal as bearer of absolute alterity. This essay offers no polemic on whether Spenser's poetry anticipates a liberal humanist preoccupation with animal rights. Rather, it eventually focuses on a particularly moment early in *The Faerie Queene* that reveals Spenser's anxiety that our access to animality—more particularly, to insect-being—is less mediated than we might think.

*I*N THE APOCALYPTIC CONCLUSION of *The Faerie Queene*, Book 1, Contemplation shows Redcrosse a vision of "The blessed Angels to and fro descend[ing]/From highest heuen, in gladsome companee" (x.56).[1] But the prophet says nothing about whether the relations between animal and human will assume a new form; nothing about whether an eschatological vision will reveal a deeper understanding of the complex economy of relations between the animal and the human; no indication that, following Redcrosse's defeat of

Spenser Studies: A Renaissance Poetry Annual, Volume XXII, Copyright © 2007 by AMS Press, Inc. All rights reserved.

Errour and the dragon, we can anticipate a return of animality to the human. All of which prompts a revisiting of those brief, scattered moments throughout *The Faerie Queene* that constitute Spenser's tentative meditations on the animal as both radically distant, yet intimately proximate to the human.

Continental postmodernism's influential "return to ethics" has recently revisited such figures as Bataille, Girard, Kristeva, Deleuze and Guattari, Lacan, and others in order to pursue the question of the animal as the repressed other of Western culture.[2] At the same time, a recent trend in early modern cultural studies has begun investigating sixteenth- and seventeenth-century perspectives on human-animal difference.[3] This essay does not attempt an impossible—and, perhaps, even undesirable—bridging of early modernist and modernist inquiries into animal being. But, in its broadest scope, it is concerned with how *The Faerie Queene* opens up beyond its own historicity to take its place in a genealogy of Western culture's ongoing discourse, from Aristotle to Descartes to Heidegger, on the question of the animal as bearer of absolute alterity. In particular, a persistent undercurrent of this essay reads Spenser against the grain of Heidegger, whose "theoretical" biology many have judged as twentieth-century philosophy's most notorious effort to separate the animal from the human. The complete lack of relationship—the utter non-reciprocity—between Spenser and Heidegger must be acknowledged and respected. But to place them in otherwise strange proximity with one another—to read Heideggerian biology "with" Spenserian poetics—is to offer a further perspective on ongoing investigations, both early modern and postmodern, into how the animal remains the traumatic limit of Western thought.

Despite Aristotle's remarks, in *Historia Animalium*, on the kinship of the human and the bestial, Greek antiquity quarantined the category of *bios* from the sphere of politics proper. In early modernity, Descartes perceived the animal as a programmed machine, a creature with neither language nor consciousness.[4] Many of the revered predecessors of continental philosophy's recent, influential "turn to ethics"—Kant, Nietzsche, Heidegger, Levinas, Lacan—all stumbled on the animal as the traumatic Thing that, ever since Aristotle, has served as the limit of human knowledge. In such a discursive context, when Derrida, musing on what separates the animal from the human, confesses that "the discourse of animality remains for me a very old anxiety, a still lively suspicion," one can welcome his wise reluctance to foreclose on the complexities of animal-human difference.[5]

This essay offers no polemic on Spenser's ethical attitude toward animals, no speculation on whether Spenser's poetry anticipates a liberal humanist preoccupation with animal rights—on whether, for example, Spenser, as the creator of the sixth book's adopted bear-baby, would have abhorred the monkey and bear-baiting of London's Bear Garden in the mid-1560s. Rather, this essay eventually focuses on a particular moment early in *The Faerie Queene* that reveals, echoing Derrida, Spenser's own "very old anxiety" that our access to animality—more particularly, to insect-being—is less mediated than we might think.

In Western thought, the categories of consciousness and conscience have persistently marked the animal's difference from the rational human. In his 1596 *A Discourse of Conscience*, William Perkins, in a Piconian moment, expounds on the difference between the human and the animal: "The proper subjects of co[n]science are reasonable creatures, that is men and Angels. Hereby conscience is excluded . . . from bruit beasts: for though they haue life & sense, and in many things some shadowes of reason, yet because they want true reason, they want conscience also."[6] More than three hundred years later, this early modern philosophical-theological reflection on the non conscience of "bruit beasts" survives virtually intact in Heidegger's sophisticated, though chilling, 1929–30 Freiburg lectures on biology—perhaps, as mentioned earlier, twentieth-century philosophy's most notorious effort to separate the animal from the human. Attempting to think the difference between the simply living being and Dasein, Heidegger asserts that the behavior of the animal is never an apprehending of something *as* something; that the animal has no access to being *as such*; and that animals have no relationship to consciousness or selfhood. In the realm of authentic thought, only humans can apprehend the "unconcealedness" of being.[7] In his "Letter on Humanism" Heidegger goes so far as to perceive not just a species-difference between the human and the animal but an absolute break, an abyss (*Abgrund*), a caesura of essential separation between the human and the animal.[8]

In his biology lectures, Heidegger rarely speaks of mammals, referring mostly to snails, bees, moths, and praying mantises. These lectures, centering on a persistent critique of insect-*praxis* as opaque and unrelatable, can thus provide a useful backdrop for probing the mysteries of Spenser's insect worlds. One could argue that Spenserian poetics and Heideggerian philosophy both converge and diverge in the insect as a trauma for Western thought.

A passage from *The Faerie Queene* that readily comes to mind is the pastoral gnat-simile of the Errour episode, where the monster's repulsive brood, swarming "all about" Redcrosse's legs, are compared to annoying gnats (I.i.23). But before we can do justice to the complexities of this simile, many layers of insect observation—both entomological and literary—will have to be peeled back.

Necessary first is a revisiting of Spenser's earliest experiment in a poetics of the gnat, an insignificant creature with a nonetheless venerable literary history. The pseudo-Virgilian *Culex*, whose Latin original was presumed to be one of Virgil's juvenilia, was one of many poems that prompted Vida, in his 1527 *De arte poetica*, to advise younger poets to make their debuts not by writing "long *Iliads*" but rather by versifying small, trivial topics, such as "the fearsome fates of a gnat."[9] Thus, in his 1579–80 poem *Virgils Gnat*, Spenser narrates a sad shepherd erecting a memorial tomb for "a litle noursling of the humid ayre" (282).[10] The shepherd had fatally swatted the gnat, only to be told by the gnat's returning ghost that the insect had heroically stung the dozing shepherd—"His little needle there infixing deep" (286)—to save him from a predatory snake. In Spenser's epyllion *Muiopotmos*—whose subtitle, *The Fate of the Butterflie*, explicitly echoes Vida's injunction to write of the "fearsome fates" of insects—insect triviality is allegorized not as heroism but as vanity: Spenser's proud butterfly-protagonist Clarion, "hated foe" (256) of the spider Aragnoll, preens himself as the possessor of "the Empire of the Aire"—until fatally ensnared in Aragnoll's web.

Both Spenser's vigilant gnat, concerned for the shepherd's safety, and his vain butterfly traffic not in real entomological worlds but rather in mimetic worlds of human heroism or of the "airy empires" of human vanity. (Here, one is well reminded that the lavishly embellished *Muipotmos*, in particular, transpires not in rural woods, but in highly stylized "gay gardins."[11]) For Vida, the pursuit of poetic ambition begins with adroit exercises in anthropomorphisms. Thus, Spenser's gnat and butterfly are not insects but rather signifiers of how deftly a young poet on the threshold of a career can distill the truths of human experience from triviality—that is, to echo Vida, "the fearsome fates of a gnat."[12]

One associates Heidegger with the category of humor at one's peril. Nevertheless, his speculative biology does cast further light on the distinctive comic appeal of the beast-fable genre. For Heidegger, insects, like all animals, are dazed, stupefied, "benumbed" (*Benommen*)—capable of "perishing," but never of attaining a state of "being-toward-death." From a Heideggerian perspective, the anthropomorphic humor of Spenser's *Virgils Gnat* is generated by the return of the gnat's angry ghost, evidence that the fatally swatted gnat has not simply "perished." The absurd prospect of a vigilant, "unbenumbed" gnat earlier apprehending an endangered shepherd *as* endangered,

and later reproaching him for his ingratitude and thereby inducing
guilt in a human being, is risible because real gnats are presumed to
suffer what Heidegger, in his biology lectures, termed an animal's
"poverty-in-the-world" (*Weltarmut*). Moreover, the comic appeal of
yet another Spenserian beast-fable, *Mother Hubberds Tale*, whose political satire dictates a decidedly "unbenumbed" fox and ape speaking
as humans, reminds us that the beast-fable's endowing animals with
the gift of speech foregrounds language as the principle mode of
apprehension that animals lack. The beast-fable is the comic point at
which animals mime the rational, human soul, the living being who
possesses speech.

Heidegger would not have assented, but Spenser's beast-fable implies that animal muteness may be more a problem for *us* than the
animal. The beast-fable's desire for speaking animals exposes a lack
inherent in its readers—a lack that must posit animal muteness as
problematic, as distinctly "other" to the speaking human. Put another
way, animals lack the lack by virtue of which the human becomes a
subject of the signifier. But Derrida asserts that the attempt to think
the complex economy of relations between the animal and the human
"*would not be a matter of 'giving speech back' to animals*, but perhaps of
acceding to a thinking . . . that thinks the absence of the name and
of the word otherwise, as something other than privation."[13] The
beast-fable's articulate animal is, among other things, an aesthetic
escape from the vexed *dis*-articulation between the category of language and the category of species. One could argue, therefore, that
the most "beastly" of human acts would be a misreading of the beast-
fable—that is, a failure to perceive the human in a talking animal. At
the same time, however, the humor of the beast-fable also begs the
question: what if animals have no particular need of speech?

The "unspoken" given of the anthropomorphic beast-fable is not
just the real animal's muteness but also, as Heidegger terms it, its
status as "just-plain-life" (*Nur-noch-leben*).[14] The martyrdom of Spenser's fictive gnat distills humor from the presumption that a real gnat
is utterly inaccessible to mourning or an *experiencing* of death. But
Spenser's later epic poetry does—however tentatively—acknowledge
real insects as potentially dwelling in more than "just-plain-life,"
perhaps even achieving Heidegger's ultimate marker of humanness,
that is, a "being-toward-death" that is neither a lowly "perishing"
nor a glorified anthropomorphic, mock-heroic martyr-death.

The unpacking of this argument calls for a (temporary) abandonment of Heidegger in favor of a more historicized turn back to early
modern naturalist inquiry into animal being which, unlike the period's beast-fable, studied real entomological worlds. But their investigations tended to be less inductive than discursive—even, for that

matter, closer to fiction than empirical observation. Pertinent here is Thomas Mouffet, a Frenchman and court physician in the reign of Elizabeth, who wrote a treatise entitled *The Theater of Insects* (the third volume of Edward Topsell's *The History of Four-Footed Beasts and Serpents and Insects*) that was published posthumously in 1634 by Theodore Mayerne, also a court physician.

In his chapter 13, "Of Gnats," readers encounter not so much the gnat as Mouffet's entanglement in a semantic web spun from classical poetry, drama, anthropology, and geohistory—a "gnat-ological" jumble of examples from Homer, Aristotle, Strabo, Herodotus, Aristophanes, Hippocrates, Theophrastus, Tertullian, Pliny, Plautus, and others. On the Empides, a species of river-gnat, Mouffet observes, "It maketh a shril-like noise as the other kindes of Gnats do, whence *Chaerephon* in *Aristophanus* his *Nubibus* demands of *Socrates, whether he thought that the Empides did make that sound with their mouth or their tail?*"[15] Mouffet's contemplation of the river-gnats' "shril-like" sounds impels him not forward to his own naturalist observations but rather back to classical antiquity's curiosity about the gnat—a curiosity Mouffet leaves unresolved.

At one point, Mouffet launches his own inquiry into the physiognomy of the gnat when he writes:

> For in these so small Insects and as good as none almost, what reason is there? What force? What inextricable perfection? Where hath nature placed so many senses in the Gnat? Where his sight, where his taste, where his smelling? Where is begotten that terrible and great sound which that little body makes? With what curiosity are the wings fastened, and the shanks and legs to the body? An empty hollow place for a belly which causeth such a thirst after bloud, of mens especially?
>
> (952)

"[W]hat reason? . . . What force? What inextricable perfection?" Mouffet demands to know. But his questions can strike us as less a prelude to scientific speculation than a Keatsian affinity ("What mad pursuit? What struggle to escape?") for the lyrical power of rhetorical questions.

Early modern naturalism arguably took a step forward into more empirical insect-worlds when the aforementioned Theodore Mayerne, in his dedicatory epistle to William Paddy, physician to Charles I, looks forward to the future of an emergent science of entomology when powerful microscopes will reveal with greater precision the mechanics of insect predation: "How wilt thou be pleased to see the small proboscis of butterflies wreathed alwaies into a spiral line, after they have drawn forth nutriment from flowers . . . ."[16] Mayerne's anticipation of one day viewing the "wreathed, spiraled" proboscis of a butterfly entertains the possibility that insects really are, *pace* Heidegger (or, for that matter, Mouffet), "world-forming" (*weltbildend*). Mayerne calls for, at the very least, a sharper focus on how the insect is related to the circle within which it nourishes itself and pursues its prey.

At this juncture, it is appropriate to move (back) to the future to Giorgio Agamben's *The Open*, an ambitious study of how to define animality in a postmodern era. Agamben devotes a chapter to the baron Jacob von Uexkull, one of the twentieth century's greatest zoologists and proto-ecologists, whose research Heidegger had read. The resulting difference between Uexkull's and Heidegger's insects speaks volumes about the difference between biological observation and a philosophical "thinking" of insect-being.

Uexkull forayed into what he termed "excursions in unknowable worlds," particularly intent on uncovering the mysteries of such minute beings as sea urchins, jellyfish, sea anemones—even the lowly tick.[17] He perceived no unified world that includes both the animal and the human. In Agamben's paraphrase,

> Too often . . . we imagine that the relations a certain animal subject has to the things in its environment take place in the same space and in the same time as those which bind us to the objects in our human world. This illusion rests on the belief in a single world in which all living beings are situated. Uexkull shows that such a unitary world does not exist . . . . The fly, the dragonfly, and the bee that we observe flying next to us on a sunny day do not move in the same world as the one in which we observe them, nor do they share with us—or with each other—the same time and the same space.[18]

Although Uexkull contended that insect-being transpires in a parallel universe to human experience, he was less interested in "othering" the fly or dragonfly or bee than in teasing out the uniqueness of insect predation. The "carriers of significance" (*Bedeutungstrager*) that attract these insects, such as the nectar of a flower or the blood of human veins, are not objects as such, but rather constitute a close functional—or, as Uexkull prefers to say, musical—unity with the animal's receptive organs that are assigned to perceive the mark (*Merkorgan*) and to react to it. Everything happens as if the external carrier of significance and its receiver in the animal's body constituted two elements in a single musical score, almost like two notes of the "keyboard on which nature performs the supratemporal and extraspatial symphony of signification" . . . .

(41)

When, in early modernity, Mouffet described the gnat's "empty hollow place for a belly which causeth such a thirst after bloud," he understood insect predation to be a linear relationship of cause and effect: the emptiness of the gnat's belly causes a thirst for blood as an "object" as such. When Uexkull's insects, however, approach their "carriers of significance," the process reveals not a cause-and-effect sequence but rather a harmony between object and receiver, composed within a symphonic "musical score" of interrelated movement. All of which complicates Heidegger's positing of an abyss between the animal and the human, and calls for much-needed alternatives to the philosopher's attribution of "mere-aliveness" to the insect.

As Agamben observes, Heidegger programmatically overlooked the care with which Uexkull avoided denying the "world-forming" capabilities of animals in favor of *reconstructing* the perceptual world of tiny organisms. As if rejecting the vitalism of Uexkull's harmonious metaphors (i.e., the insect-world's "musical unity" and nature's "keyboard" and "symphony of signification"), Heidegger downgraded the insect's intense fixation on its "carriers of significance" as a state of mere captivation (*Benommenheit*). Uexkull's acute sensitivity to the perceptual world of insects metamorphosed into Heidegger's theorizing of the insect's "poverty-in-the-world," its incapacity to reveal itself as a being. Heidegger, utterly tone deaf to the harmonious resonances of Uexkull's research on insect-*praxis*, was never one to take to the fields; and thus, in his "thinking" of insect-being, he transformed Uexkull's biological observation that a unitary world between insect and human does not exist (i.e., that the fly, dragonfly, and bee "we observe flying next to us on a sunny day do not move in the same world as the one in which we observe them") into the following philosophical axiom: the opaque insect, lacking an openness-to-the-world (*Weltoffenheit*), is not just different from the human, but also separated from the human by an abyss.

The Faerie Queene's most prominent gnat-simile, mentioned at the essay's beginning, is evidence that Spenser, unlike Heidegger, probably at least on occasion took to the fields, opening an abyss between Heidegger's bio-philosophy and Spenser's poetics.

But we should approach this simile with caution, first revisiting the many other "litle stinges" of *The Faerie Queene*'s swarming insects, largely borrowed from epic literary history. From Homer to Milton, a recurring epic simile compares the enemies of epic destiny to swarming insects. Ariosto's dynastic epic *Orlando furioso* compares the Saracens attacking Charlemagne's army as "A swarm of importuning flies assail[ing],/Making with strident wings a buzzing haze" (14.109). Variants of this simile appear five times in *The Faerie Queene* where, as A. C. Hamilton points out, gnats and flies become a "common emblem in the poem of what is merely troublesome."[19] Maleger's troops attack Arthur and Guyon like "a swarme of Gnats at euentide," such that "Ne man nor beast may rest, or take repast,/For their sharpe wounds, and noyous injuries" (II.ix.16).[20] Arthegall aids Burbon in slaying his enemies, "Who flocking round about them, as a swarme/Of flyes upon a birchen bough doth cluster,/[and] Did them assault with terrible allarme" (V.xi.58). Calidore rescues Pastorella from the brigands, depicted as

> Many flyes in whottest sommers days
> Seiz[ing] vpon some beast, whose flesh is bare,
> That all the place with swarmes do ouerlay,
> And with their litle stinges right felly fare.
>
> (VI.xi.48)

If, in the beast fable, insects such as Spenser's Clarion mock-heroically accede to human ambition, epic's gnat and fly similes work in reverse to diminish the ambition of the human opponents of epic destiny by comparing them to "noyous" insects. In such a scheme, the epic simile effectively attempts to restore insect triviality to its "proper place" in the Great Chain of Being as, echoing Hamilton, "a common emblem for what is merely troublesome." But the "noyous" gnats and flies of Spenser's similes also provide *The Faerie Queene*'s readers with tantalizing naturalist glimpses into the realities of insect experience, an interest for its own sake *in what insects do*.

To place Spenser's epic forays into insect "world-making" in sharper perspective, we can briefly return to *Virgils Gnat*, where the gnat-protagonist awakens the sleeping shepherd by "His little needle there infixing deep." As we have seen, the gnat's "infix[ed] little needle" is less a product of Spenser's naturalist observation than his nod toward the beast-fable's highly mannered, mock-heroic decorums. But the mock-heroic gnat's "infix[ed] little needle" cedes place to the increasingly real and eminently predatory "stinges" of *The Faerie Queene*'s epic gnats, flies, and bees. As "swarm[ing] Gnats at euentide," Maleger's troops, to be sure, conventionally recall the many other swarming enemy troops of epic literary history. But Spenser's simile also specifies dusk as the gnats' preferred feeding time, a temporal detail briefly lifting his readers out of epic—or, perhaps, even pastoral—aesthetics into a real world of insect cravings and predation. Similarly, Burbon's enemies, likes flies swarming around a "birchen bough," evoke the flies' particular attraction to the sweet sap of birch trees. And the brigands-as-flies of Book VI are portrayed as specifically seeking out mammalian flesh as the target of their highly motivated "litle stinges." In sum, Uexkull's "world-forming" insects, reacting to their "carriers of significance," are anticipated in any number of places in *The Faerie Queene*.

At one point in his aforementioned chapter "Of Gnats," Mouffet, Spenser's contemporary, leaves behind the gnats of ancient Greece, Egypt, and Mesopotamia long enough to satisfy his readers' curiosity about their native gnats. Typically, Mouffet does not offer his own eyewitness observation, but rather turns to another source—in this case, the antiquarian John Stow's account of a battle between two giant armies of gnats:

> Upon a certain time there was seen in the air between the Monasteries of *Sion* and *Shene* in England, such a pitch'd battel of Gnats, that you could not see the Sun at mid-day. The sight was maintained for four hours, as long as the Armies could stand; at length a mighty slaughter being made on both sides, so many dead carcasses of Gnats were found in the hedges and highwaies, that they were feign to sweep the corn fields and medows with beesoms. There followed upon this the banishment of the Monks in both the Monasteries.
>
> (956)

Interestingly, Mouffet's summary of Stow's account turns the gnat-similes of epic literary history on their head: if epic compares real enemy armies to fictive gnats, Stow compares real gnats to fictive armies. But even here, the entomological realities of gnat-being cede place to antiquarianism's affinity for local legend: the point of the story seems to be that the gnats' "pitch'd battel," rendering the monasteries' grounds polluted, unsacred sites of insect carnage, directly led to the banishment of the monks. When Mouffet adds, "Whether this be true or not, I leave to those that can resolve such truth," he slides out of insect worlds into the realm of human experience: he seems less interested in what entomological conclusions can be drawn from the observable group behavior of gnats than in demonstrating skepticism concerning the monks' legendary banishment.

Spenser brings his readers closer than Mouffet to the gnats of the British Isles. Though indebted, as we have seen, to the larger scope of continental epic literary history, *The Faerie Queene*'s gnat-similes invite us to imagine these insects as neither epic poetic nor antiquarian embellishments but as products of Spenser's own local, naturalist observations in England and in Ireland's fens of Allan.[21] And we can imagine the gnats that annoyed Spenser in England and Ireland as lending a local habitation and a name to the gnats of the Errour episode. Early in Book I, Redcrosse is "encombred sore" by Errour's deformed, "swarming" spawn as they crawl about his legs. To reinforce his depiction of this "swarming" spawn, Spenser turns to a pastoral simile that offers a very different kind of encounter between shepherd and gnat than the mock-heroism narrated in *Virgils Gnat*:

As gentle Shepheard in sweete euentide,
  When ruddy *Phoebus* gins to welke in west,
  High on an hill, his flocke to vewen wide,
  Markes which doe byte their hasty supper best,
  A cloud of cumbrous gnattes doe him molest,
  All striuing to infixe their feeble stinges,
  That from their noyance he no where can rest,
  But with his clownish hands their tender wings,
He brusheth oft, and oft doth mar their murmurings.

(i.23)

Spenser's interest in the relationship between the animal and its environment-world is perhaps never so minutely explored as in this, *The Faerie Queene*'s first gnat-simile—as if Spenser is activating something that had lain dormant in his poetry since *Virgils Gnat*. The gnats of epic literary history may indeed be nothing more than common emblems of annoying insignificance; but here Spenser is compelled (paradoxically) to devote an entire stanza to gnat-being.

Jeffrey Knapp has offered the most recent sustained commentary on this stanza, arguing that it constitutes an "overt pastoral uncannily reenter[ing]" the narrative and reintroducing a pastoral theme even as the narrative recounts Redcrosse's "battle to end pastoral error"—that is, the error that has entangled Redcrosse and Una in the Wandering Wood.[22] As Knapp suggests, the overall effect of the stanza is an odd deferral of the end of pastoral error by inserting yet more pastoral into the epic narrative.

Knapp's argument opens up other possibilities, beyond comparative genre, for noting how the stanza, as Spenser's "thinking" of agrarian time, delays, or even stops time altogether. The leisurely passage of time is foregrounded in Spenser's allusion to "ruddy *Phoebus* gin[ning] to welke in west"—one of *The Faerie Queene*'s many allusions to Phoebus, Aurora, Tithonus, Cynthia, and Night that, as Theresa Krier has marvelously observed, "establish, border, and shape various temporal intervals within the narrative and so help to establish the very sense of given world and time" in Spenser's epic.[23] Here, we are well reminded that posited worlds and times—in particular, parallel worlds and times—are the precise origins of Uexkull's investigation of the difference between the insect and the human.

As "ruddy *Phoebus*" sets, time slows down dramatically to reveal the insect-world of Spenser's "cumbrous gnattes" as they search for patches of bare skin in which "to infixe their feeble stinges." In this simile, the shepherd and the gnat emphatically do not, echoing Uexkull, inhabit the same time and place, as they do in *Virgils Gnat*. The shepherd's world is one of seeing to it that his sheep complete the day's last grazing, while the gnats' world is one of awaiting the right moment to *begin* their feeding—to, biologically speaking, pierce the sebaceous follicles of the shepherd's perspiring skin. What, for the shepherd, is a momentarily restful "sweet euentide" at sunset becomes, for the gnats, a fading light that activates their receptive organs to search for nourishment. Absent is the mock-heroic tone of *Virgils Gnat*. But neither are we left simply with the Heideggerian insect as experiencing a benumbed "poverty-in-the-world." And thus, as this essay nears conclusion, I offer some (very) tentative thoughts on what replaces the mock-heroism of Spenser's earlier poetics of the gnat, admittedly struggling to find a way to talk about these gnats that is neither anthropomorphic nor a disappearance into a Heideggerian "poverty-in-the-world."

From a Heideggerian perspective, the simile's gnats appear to be in a benumbed state of "mere-aliveness," dependent on a stimulus, unable to apprehend their world as such. Yet, so attuned are the gnats to the falling evening temperature, so reactive are they to the

odor from the shepherd's sweat glands and blood vessels that, if nothing else, we should pause to consider the gnats' intense relationship
to their world—an intensity that should make us wonder if humans
have a similarly intense relationship with their (presumably richer)
world. Accordingly, readers might pause to ask themselves exactly
what is taking place in the concluding alexandrine—so often a crucial
moment in Spenser's poetics. Every foot of the alexandrine, particularly the repetition of "oft"—"He brusheth oft, and oft doth mar
their murmurings"—labors to depict the tedious repetitiveness with
which the shepherd's "clownish," rustic hands brush away the persistent gnats. But within the surging and ebbing rhythms of attack and
repulse lies a moment of . . . what? Perhaps a moment of neither
attack nor repulse, but a moment that arrests the gnats on a threshold,
their "marred murmurings" suspending them beyond their predatory
impulses, beyond Heidegger's insistence on their opaque, unrelatable
captivation to mere drives.

The stanza lifts its readers out of any exegetical space, pushing
toward no definite conclusion or direction, awarding neither the
shepherd nor the gnats "victory" in their battle. In the absence of
any manifest point to the stanza, questions continue to arise. Have
the gnats, to echo Agamben's resonant term, "opened" themselves
out to something? Do the gnats' "marred murmurings" suggest a
state "beyond captivation"? During their "marred murmurings," do
they signal an awareness of themselves *as* gnats? Do their "marred
murmurings" exhibit intimations of mortality? Do they anticipate
an experience of death by "clownish" human hands?

One conclusion is certain. In this odd stanza, Spenser's gnats become something more than simply icons or emblems of annoying
insignificance. All similes, by their very nature, are tropes of experi-
mentation: seeking to compare two things which otherwise might
not invite linkage, similes cross a threshold. Spenser's gnat-simile
begins by comparing Errour's brood to gnats. But by its conclusion,
the gnats have moved away from Spenser's allegory, seemingly dis-
persed into Agamben's "open."

In his reading of Heidegger's biology lectures, David Farrell Krell,
countering the philosopher's othering of animal-being, poses an intriguing question: "Is it the living creature in the seas and the mountains
that is 'unfamiliar,' 'not dwelling'? Or is it not *man* who is the least
familiar, most uncanny, most monstrous, most violent, most nomadic,
and least homey of creatures?"[24] As Spenser's sheep graze peacefully
and as the gnats prepare for their own evening feeding, the shepherd
gradually emerges as a nomad, a "not-dwelling" intruder in this sunset world. Perhaps the gnats perceive the shepherd's swatting hands

as "clownish." What if, during their "marred murmurings," it is a case of Spenser's gnats having gained insight into the "clownish" shepherd as the most uncanny and "least homey" of creatures? Perhaps the "marred murmurings" are the point at which insect compulsion cedes place to an apprehension of the shepherd *as* a shepherd in ways that the anthropomorphic gnat of *Virgils Gnat* could never have discerned.

University of New Hampshire

NOTES

1.　All references to *The Faerie Queene* are taken from *Edmund Spenser: "The Faerie Queene,"* 2nd ed., ed. A. C. Hamilton, text edited by Hiroshi Yamashita and Toshiyuki Suzuki (London: Longman, 2001).

2.　For an overview of the postmodernist "return to ethics" and its problematic encounters with the animal, see Cary Wolfe, "In the Shadow of Wittgenstein's Lion: Language, Ethics, and the Question of the Animal," in *Zoontologies: The Question of the Animal*, ed. Wolfe (Minneapolis: University of Minnesota Press, 2003), 1–57.

3.　For recent studies of early modern perceptions of human-animal difference, see Erica Fudge, *Perceiving Animals: Human and Beasts in Early Modern English Culture* (Urbana: University of Illinois Press, 2000); Bruce Boehrer, *Shakespeare Among the Animals* (London: Palgrave, 2002); Gail Kern Paster, *Humoring the Body: Emotions and the Shakespearean Stage* (Chicago: University of Chicago Press, 2004); and Laurie Shannon, "Actaeon's Coat: Renaissance Zoographies of the Body's Edge," paper delivered at the Early Modern Seminar, Leslie Humanities Center, Dartmouth College, April 2005.

4.　Rene Descartes, *The Philosophical Writings of Descartes*, Vol. I, trans. John Cottingham, Robert Stoothoff, and Dugald Murdoch (Cambridge: Cambridge University Press), 139–40.

5.　Jacques Derrida, *Of Spirit: Heidegger and the Question*, trans. Geoffrey Bennington and Rachel Bowlby (Chicago: University of Chicago Press, 1989), 11.

6.　In *The Workes of That Famous and Worthy Minister of Christ in the Vniuersitie of Cambridge, Mr William Perkins*. Quoted in Fudge, *Perceiving Animals*, 34.

7.　Martin Heidegger, *The Fundamental Concepts of Metaphysics: World, Finitude, Solitude*, Part 2, Chaps. 2 and 3, trans. William McNeill and Nicholas Walker (Bloomington: Indiana University Press, 1995).

8.　"Letter on Humanism," trans. Frank A. Capuzzi and J. Glenn Gray, in *Martin Heidegger: Basic Writings*, ed. and trans. David Farrell Krell (New York: Harper and Row, 1977).

9.　Quoted by Renwick, *Var.* 7:240.

10.　All references to Spenser's short poems are from R. E. Neil Dodge, ed., *Spenser: The Cambridge Edition of the Poets* (Cambridge: Riverside, 1936).

11. On *Muiopotmos* as a precursor of *The Faerie Queene*'s Bower of Bliss, where nature also vies with art, see Don Cameron Allen, "On Spenser's *Muiopotmos*," *Studies in Philology* 53 (1956): 141–58.

12. On *Virgils Gnat* as a window into Spenser's Virgilian ambitions, see David Lee Miller, *The Poem's Two Bodies: The Poetics of the 1590 "Faerie Queene"* (Princeton: Princeton University Press, 1988), 62.

13. Jacques Derrida, "The Animal That Therefore I Am," trans. David Wills, *Critical Inquiry* 28:2 (2002), 416; italics mine. The essay was first published in French in *L'Animal autobiographique: Autour de Jacques Derrida*, ed. Marie-Louise Mallet (Paris: Galilee, 1999).

14. *Being and Time*, trans. John Macquarrie and Edward Robinson (New York: Harper and Row, 1962), 75.

15. Thomas Mouffet, *The Theater of Insects*, vol. 3 of Edward Topsell, *The History of Four-Footed Beasts and Serpents and Insects* (rpt. of the 1658 London edition, copy in the Rare Book Collection of the Library of the American Museum of Natural History), intro. Willy Ley (New York: Da Capo Press, 1967), 953.

16. Qtd. in Emma Phipson, *The Animal-Lore of Shakespeare's Time: Including Quadrupeds, Birds, Reptiles, Fish and Insects* (London: Kegan Paul, 1883), 390.

17. Qtd. in Giorgio Agamben, *The Open: Man and Animal*, trans. Kevin Attell (Stanford: Stanford University Press, 2004), 40.

18. Qtd. in Agamben, 40.

19. Hamilton, 37, note to X.i.23.

20. Two cantos later, Arthur pierces Maleger's body with his sword, but "Ne drop of blood appeared to bee, / All were the wound so wide and wonderous" (II.xi.38). Spenser compares Maleger and his "raskall routs" to swarming gnats; but, ironically, Maleger lacks the human blood that gnats crave.

21. Maleger's "raskall routs" that attack Arthur and Guyon outside Alma's Castle are specifically compared to the swarming gnats that "Out of the fennes of Allan do arise" (II.ix.16).

22. Jeffrey Knapp, *An Empire Nowhere: England, America, and Literature from "Utopia" to "The Tempest"* (Berkeley: University of California Press, 1992), 113.

23. The Kathleen Williams Lecture, May 2006. I am grateful to Professor Krier for sharing her lecture manuscript with me.

24. David Farrell Krell, *Daimon Life: Heidegger and Life-Philosophy* (Bloomington: Indiana University Press, 1992), 191; italics in original.

JOSEPH LOEWENSTEIN

Gryll's Hoggish Mind

This essay begins from the observation that Spenser has virtually no affective engagement with fauna, an observation supported with details from *The Shepheardes Calender.* Yet Spenser asserts the kinship of certain humans and certain animals, in moments throughout *The Faerie Queene,* especially its first two books. This kinship Spenser thinks out through the traditions of philosophical skepticism and its particular totem animal, the pig (as in Plutarch's *Gryllus* or Gelli's *Circe*), traditions that demote the human and human reason, and/or insist on the animal nature of the human. The essay considers not only Spenser's Grylle in *FQ* II.xii, but also the lion of *FQ* I.iii, who focuses the centrality of a virtue difficult for Redcrosse, that of fellow-feeling, or what we now call the problem of other minds.

> Piggie is the super-best dancer. So light on his feet.
> —Lorelei Lee (Marilyn Monroe), *Gentlemen Prefer Blondes*
> (1953)[1]

*A*SKED TO WRITE ABOUT SPENSER'S animals, I responded with bafflement and slight alarm. Of course there *are* animals in Spenser—one can recall an ape, a kid, and a couple of foxes, all voluble; a lion, more eloquent (though mute) than those Aesopian others, and a bear, also silent—in fact, silenced to death. There are many sheep and a few contrastive goats; there is the allegorical crab and various accessory horses, including a quite necessary one, to be stolen and missed and fought over. Early on in *The Faerie Queene,* there is an ass to signify and disappear and *not* to be missed. In the end, there are the zodiacal creatures. In the course of the epic, dozens of ornamental or totemic beasts, many of them mythological, are

---

Spenser Studies: A Renaissance Poetry Annual, Volume XXII, Copyright © 2007 by AMS Press, Inc. All rights reserved.

enlisted to assist with similes; and many beasts are broken up for
signifying *parts*, the hindquarters proving especially useful. Thus my
bafflement and alarm didn't echo from a vacant memory. What worried me was that to write of animals in Spenser would almost inevitability eventuate in my betraying what I take to be one of the most
unattractive defects, however arguably minor, with which a person
may be hobbled—that I have no imaginative sympathy with animals,
that I feel no spontaneous affection for them. While this *self*-betrayal
cannot matter to Spenserians, it may in fact matter to allege that
Spenser, too, seems to have virtually no affective engagement with
fauna, to surmise that they're no more than an imaginative convenience for him, like trees or pagans.

It would take some doing, or some emotional and intellectual not-
doing, for an Early Modern poet to be unengaged with animals—to
care little about the hunt; or about the dignity of horses, the aimless
exaltation of birds, or the sheepish vulnerability of lambs. I am, that
is, alleging something quite different from what Boehrer calls "absolute anthropocentrism," the confidence of human radical difference
from, superiority to, and proper dominion over the animals.[2] In most
of his compelling study, Boehrer is addressing matters of philosophical
principle, whereas I am, for the next few pages, concerned with
affect. Even a clumsy artist like the person who carved the woodcuts
for *The Shepheardes Calender* seems to register that sheep—even the
doggy sheep of "October"—have something like an ethos, some
gestural distinctiveness and some force. (Despite its hilarious failures
of draughtsmanship, even the "September" woodcut insists that
flocks, of sheep and birds, *dwell* in the world, staking claims to grass
and air.) Spenser betrays his limits when lovesick Colin, taking in
the ill-kempt, weak-kneed state of his sheep, addresses his flock:
"mayst witness well by thy ill-government/Thy masters mind" ("Januarye," 43).[3] "Mayst . . . thy . . . ": grammatical number is telling:
Colin recognizes only a flock of sheep and not the several sheep.
Indeed, the flock takes its place in a series of inanimate addressees:
"Thou barren ground, . . . You naked trees, . . . Thou feeble flocke
. . . Wherefore my pipe" ("Januarye," 19, 31, 43, 67).

Nor does Spenser often transcends these limits; Spenserian pastoral
is more detached from nature than usual. In "Maye," Piers commends
the goat to Palinode and to us, albeit not *as* goat, "But for she had a
motherly care/Of her young sonne." When "Shee set her youngling
before her knee" she is imaged as a human mother and not a goatly
one ("Maye," 180–82). Yet something more sweetly inhuman quick-
ens as Piers turns his attention to the youngling—

That was both fresh and lovely to see,
And full of favour, as kidde mought be:
His Vellet head began to shoote out
And his wreathed hornes gan newly sprout.

Spenser's Piers doesn't preserve the kid in this lovely inhumanity,
although the partial swerve back towards the human leaves us in a
powerfully uncanny middle creaturely ground—"The blossomes of
lust to bud did beginne,/And spring forth ranckly under his
chinne" (183–88).

The lambs of "August" quicken similarly. The work "enchased"
on Perigot's mazer is alive to vocationally pastoral (as opposed to
generically pastoral) concern, to the pastoral concern of others—or
perhaps to the decorative resources of others' tenderness toward animals—

Thereby is a Lambe in he Wolfes jawes:
But see, how fast renneth the shephearde swayne,
To save the innocent from the beastes pawes.

And Perigot's answering pledge is even a bit more tender—

Thereto I will pawn yonder spotted Lambe,
Of all my flocke there nis sike another:
For I brought him up without the Dambe.

("August," 31–33, 37–39)

This latter suggests that what secures Spenser's pastoral engagement
is precisely what would hold his imagination throughout his writing
career—the spotted lamb as motherless child and as subject of taming
and training. Spenser would not be alone among his contemporaries
in engaging animals *for* their educability. But there is an odd blood-
lessness to Spenserian training. If the adoption of the bear-baby of
Book VI attests to a sustained interest in domestication, taming, and
training, the animal-child is rendered lapidary, not creaturely, by
education: Matilde and Sir Bruin are left to "enchace/Whatever
formes" they wish to incise within this child (*enchace*, even though
the child be "soft and fit them to embrace").[4] And as for the pubes-
cent goat of "Maye," what attracts Spenser is transforming growth
itself, again an abiding engagement:

> So he him dubbed, and his Squire did call.
> Full glad and ioyous then young *Tristram* grew,
> Like as a flowre, whose silken leaues small,
> Long shut vp in the bud from heauens vew,
> At length breakes forth, and brode displayes his smyling hew.
>
> (*FQ* VI.ii.35.5–9)

Returning to the kid's new beard, we notice how it is registered: "The blossomes of lust to bud did beginne." As when he renders the stripling Tristram, Spenser seems to be able to capture the ravishments of maturation in floral terms—a Garden of Adonis and not a Park or Jungle.

That Spenser *does* seem genuinely charmed by Virgil's gnat and the butterfly of *Muiopotmos* does not amount to evidence of a faunal imagination, since the attraction in these instances almost certainly has to do with scale—with Spenser's especially warm participation in a fashionable taste for the intricately lapidary and minute.[5] This interest in insects is far easier to explain than Spenser's general unresponsiveness to other animals—this in a period of burgeoning empirical correction and augmentation of the natural historical record—which would seem to require explanation, like the dog that didn't bark in the night. The explanation might have something to do with a repression of the brutal conversion of pastoral to arable agriculture in Ireland, but satisfactory explanation lies beyond the aims of this essay.

*

Spenser is not much interested in animals as such, but he is more than a little interested in animals *not*-as-such. Lévi-Strauss can help us focus on the highly theoretical character of Spenser's interest in fauna. I'm thinking here of Lévi-Strauss's slogan—Sapir called it a shibboleth—that animals are taken up as totems not so much because they are good to eat, *bon à manger*, but because they are *bon à penser*, good to think.[6] There's an unfortunately long tradition of quoting this formulation with little respect for the original context, but it *does* pertain here, since the totemic assertion, of the curious kinship, and not just the revealing resemblance, of (particular) humans and (particular) animals, is very close to what's at stake at the close of Book II, as well as in such not so distantly related encounters as that between Una and her lion or the interactions with wild men. But there's a fortuitous pertinence to Lévi-Strauss's phrase, for when he observes that animals are *bon à penser*, he is speaking of their special utility in the classificatory work of culture—good to think with—whereas there is also a powerful tradition, in which *The Faerie Queene* affiliates itself, in which animals have a different epistemological utility.[7] Dogs and cats have a place in this tradition, but its totem is the pig.[8]

The cultural history of the pig is too large to broach at this juncture. Many years ago, Peter Stallybrass and Allon White took a run at the task, but it can't be claimed that they finished the job.[9] Like the lamb, the pig is a Christian beast, though its Christianity is diacritical; Christianity as non-Jewishness. I take it that the use of the pig as a totem in *The Lord of the Flies* captures the fact that the pig signifies by negation and that such signification is intrinsically volatile: the Christian pig is always available as a diabolical sign. The semiotic volatility of the pig may be observed in the festivity that attends on its butchering, and especially that which attends on the rituals of Fat Tuesday. Yet within the contested history of cleanliness and odor, in which the pig has a privileged place, it signifies with a distinctive lack of volatility, for whereas the fæces of cow and horse are easily convertible, by means of a kind of affective composting, as manure, and hence as "sweet," pig shit is always pig shit, and always offensive. The Bavarian smiles over the *Misthauffen*, in all its earthy, mounded plenitude, the sign of *Heimat*; the sink of the pig wallow, on the other hand, would be the essence of dirt, if dirt partook of essence and though it has everything to do with fixity, it has nothing to do with domesticity. The pigs that glare at Dürer's Prodigal Son—the fierce hostility of their stare weakly serving to depict that sharp but invisible stench that eludes depiction—mark the Son's unhoused exile, from dignity, from family, from civil conversation.

But they're quite intelligent really, as people with farming in their family will insist. To offer such a reminder is, admittedly, not so much as to say that the pig is a philosophical totem, *bon à penser*, for *that* assertion one has to turn to Plutarch's *Moralia*, and specifically to his unfinished *Beasts are Rational* (*Bruta Animalia Ratione Uti*). Otherwise known as the *Gryllus*, this dialogue comes late in the *Moralia*, and although it is framed as a disputation between Ulysses and Gryllus, with Circe standing by and smirking, the pig does most of the talking, and disputation effectively dissolves into mock encomium, for which the pig might be said to be become a kind of generic marker. But to say *only* that would be to trivialize Gryllus's function, as Ulysses also seeks to do as he comments on the dialectical abilities of the pig, though he means for us to understand thereby that he regards the pig as a sophist. But that is not *Plutarch's* intention, as I understand it. Plutarch is simply interested in what may be gained by treating the pig as an interlocutor.

The *Gryllus* takes its place as one of a small suite of works that situate Plutarch in the history of philosophical skepticism.[10] The most decisive of these is lost, unfortunately, a treatise *On the Ten Modes of Pyrrho*, which has left its traces only as entry 158 in Lamprias's ancient catalogue of Plutarch's works. What does survive is another of the *Moralia*, the *Reply to Colotes*, which is a defense of academic skepticism against epicurean assaults.[11] On the basis of a remark in the *Suda*, many members of the Early Modern intelligentsia—like a few modern classicists—believed Plutarch to be the uncle of Sextus Empiricus, the most influential exponent of Pyrrhonian skepticism.[12] Although Erasmus recalls the *Gryllus* as a mock encomium in *The Praise of Folly*, it is not so easily trivialized and dismissed once we place it in its skeptical context, since it performs two critical functions, each different, but both similar, and both characteristically skeptical—that is, first, the demotion of the human and, especially, the denigration of human reason, and second, the insistence on the animal nature—and hence the non-privilege—of the human.

Whereas Gail Paster has carefully mapped the relatively unfamiliar Early Modern physiological psychology of the human-animal border, the cruder epistemological border disputes provoked by Renaissance skepticism have not received as much attention recently. Those disputes were once notorious.[13] Gassendi makes a detailed argument that animals think; in the *Meditations*, Descartes strenuously attempts to demonstrate the automatism of animal intelligence.[14] Descartes's demonstration draws a line not only between the human and the animal but also between his skepticism and the similarly constructive, but still more daring form developed by Gassendi. But Montaigne's engagement with the problem of animal intelligence is perhaps still familiar; certainly it goes deeper than his delightful speculation about whether he plays with his cat or his cat plays with him.[15] The passage comes from *The Apology for Raymond Sebond*, Montaigne's most sustained intervention on behalf of skepticism, and it proceeds to twenty pages on the dignity of animals.[16] There is a scholarly consensus that these arguments, and the *Apology* as a whole, leap from Montaigne's deep engagement with the Latin edition, in 1562, of the *Pyrrhonian Hypotyposes* of Sextus Empiricus, and with the *Life of Pyrrho* by Diogenes Laertius, which Henri Estienne appended to the *Hypotyposes*.[17] But Montaigne is also deeply influenced here by the Plutarch, whose Gryllus speaks of the spontaneous animal production of craft, and contrasts it with painstaking human specialization and deliberation.

In arguments deeply indebted to those in Plutarch, Montaigne asserts that the non-propositional problem-solving of animals is an intelligence, and entertains, as Gryllus insists that Ulysses entertain, the possibility that this intelligence is superior to human intelligence. Gryllus effects a sharp denigration of human *techne* and its dependence on education: "nor do we receive our arts as alien products or pay to be taught them. Our intelligence produces them on the spot unaided, as its own congenital and legitimate skills."[18] He urges the preeminence of animals as "self-taught and self-sufficient." All of this is reproduced and extended in Montaigne's *Apology*.

But somewhat more important for my purposes is the passage from the fourteenth essay of Book One, "That the taste of good and evil depends on our opinions," in which Montaigne adduces an anecdote on the effects of fear from Diogenes Laertius: "the philosopher Pyrrho happened to be aboard ship during a mighty storm; to those about him whom he saw most terrified he pointed out an exemplary pig, quite unconcerned with the storm; he encouraged them to imitate it" (57). The anecdote is famous and repeated far more often than Diogenes's observation that Pyrrho so little assented to the superior dignity of humans that he was in the habit of washing his pig. An ideal from which the Odyssean Guyon might have learned, the serenity of the pig in the storm models *ataraxia*, the tranquility of skeptical indifference. For the Pyrrhonians, as for the Montaigne of the *Apology*, this tranquility is the product of that philosophical discipline which leads to *epoche*, or suspension of judgment.

This discipline was as methodical as perhaps any intellectual activity in antiquity. The fullest surviving account of skeptical method is Sextus's *Pyrrhonian Hypotyposes*, though there are supplementary accounts in both Diogenes Laertius and Philo Judaeus—and Plutarch's lost *On the Ten Modes of Pyrrho* would have gone over a good deal of the same territory. "Modes" in this case translates *tropos*, although the skeptics also used the term, *tupos*, and modern philosophers render both terms variously as "modes," "argument," or "schemata."[19] These are intellectual routines designed to disable dogmatic assertion and so to lead to *epoche*. They come down to us, via Sextus, as several canons—the ten modes, the five modes, the two modes.[20] For my purposes here—since this will go a long way towards explaining the centrality of the problem of animal intelligence in Gassendi, Descartes, and Montaigne—it's enough to know that the first of the Ten Modes disables faith in human assertion by adducing the variability of apprehension across various animal kinds:

> First . . . is the argument according to which animals, depending on the differences among them, do not receive the

same appearances from the same things. This we deduce both from the differences in the ways in which they are produced

—and it may be observed that this is a decidedly weak feature of the First Mode—

and from the variation in the composition of their bodies.[21]

(*PH* I, 40)

Different bodies, different perceptions; different perceptions, different intelligences; hoggish body, hoggish mind.[22] The principle has a stubborn materialism entirely pertinent to "The Legend of Temperance."

Also relevant to Book II, to *The Faerie Queene* at large, and to Spenser's involvement with skeptical concerns is Gianbattista Gelli's wonderful *Circe*, which expands the *Gryllus* into several dialogues between Ulysses and various victims of Circe's enchantments—a snake, a goat, a hare, deer, lion, calf, horse, dog, a mole, an elephant, and an oyster.[23] Despite its very unSpenserian vivacity, Gelli's dialogues are, I think (and I take my cue from James Nohrnberg in this) as much on Spenser's mind as is Plutarch's *Gryllus*, for, like Guyon, Gelli's Ulysses is frustrated and baffled by what he takes to be the unregeneracy of the animals.[24] Within the traditions of natural philosophy, animals generally illustrate life in a streaming of passion, unchecked by reason.[25] As such, they may be pressed into contrastive service, available for differential definition of the human. But the tendency of skepticism is to renounce such contrast, however nervously.

In a painstaking technical analysis of the Pyrrhonian Modes, Julia Annas and Jonathan Barnes note that none of the Pyrrhonists offers examples of the First Mode; that none of them actually attempts to describe the difference between what a dog sees and what a cow sees. Whether or not the difference is describable, it remains undescribed. But Annas and Barnes fail to remark on a more haunting lacuna in the Pyrrhonian corpus, that the First Mode, based on differences between animal kinds, is always mobilized (on behalf of suspense of judgment) as a contrast between the perceptions of some particular animal kind and humans.[26] That is, the skeptic identifies the human as a kind of animal, a different kind of animal, but no more different from cats than cows would be. Of course, this is at odds with the argument of Plutarch's Gryllus, and it's at odds with the arguments

of Gelli's animals, from oyster to elephant. Characteristically, and
with characteristically cheerful abandon, Montaigne entertains both
the idea of radical human–animal differentiation and of radical continuity.

When Spenser takes up the story of Gryll, he seems to join Plutarch
and Gelli in asserting human–animal differentiation:

> Said Guyon, See the mind of beastly man,
>   That hath so soone forgot the excellence
> Of his creation, when he life began,
>   That now he chooseth, with vile difference,
>   To be a beast, and lacke intelligence.

But Plutarch's Gryllus is voluble, as are Gelli's animals; they insist
that they would regard the return to human form as a transformation,
and an unpleasantly transgressive one. Spenser's chief innovation—beyond the fact that he transforms Gryll, as his source texts do
not—is to silence those bestial men whom Guyon "liberates":

> And streight of beasts they comely men became;
>   Yet being men they did unmanly looke,
>   And stared ghastly, some for inward shame,
>   And some for wrath, to see their captive Dame:
> But one above the rest in speciall,
>   That had an hog beene late, hight Grille by name,
>   Repined greatly, and did him miscall,
> That had from hoggish forme him brought to naturall.

Here Spenser turns the narrative, with whatever misgivings, towards
a contemplation of human–animal continuity. This is not the full,
skeptical trope, but insofar as the emphasis falls on degeneracy, regen-
eration, and unregeneracy, Spenser moves here under the influence
of the first skeptical Mode, and hoggish Gryll distantly resembles
Pyrrho's pig.

Red Crosse's horse and Una's ass may be the poem's first beasts,
but the first beast to present itself with anything that partakes of will,
or consciousness, or anything that interrupts a pure objectivity, is the
"ramping Lyon" of Canto iii, and he makes his appearance under
the aegis of fellow-feeling. The canto begins with the poet's declaration of his own "deare compassion of mind" for Una, and the same

affect wells up in Una when the amazed lyon begins to lick her hands: "Her hart gan melt in great compassion." The great labor of Cantos ii and iii is to disrupt the tyrannous subjectivity of Red Crosse, "he my Lyon, and my noble Lord," as Una now describes him. The Fradubio episode, with which Canto ii had concluded exposes Red Crosse as incapable of imagining Others as comparable Selves: as far as Red Crosse can see, Fradubio is an alien species—"once a man Fradubio, now a tree"—irreducibly an object and inconceivable as what he is and what we come to understand him to be, as Red Crosse's second, perhaps his first, Self. What philosophy will shortly propose as the problem of other minds, Book I demonstrates as a psychological and spiritual exercise, one too difficult for its hero.

Canto iii continues this unfinished business. For the imagination of Una—as comparable subject and not as objective principle—has been even more difficult than the imagination of Fradubio. Spenserians will not need reminding that for Red Crosse, Una's very speech calls forth dragons and demons, that the possible independence of her will, the possibility that she might have claims *on* him, splits her and dissolves him; and that the possibility of her subjectivity reconstitutes her as a beauteous form with a witch within. Indeed, when we ourselves are invited to see Una, alone and relieved of the burden of signifying-for-Red Crosse, the narrative is hardly unperturbed: her manifest grief, the sign of her inwardness, calls forth a fury—a noble, leonine fury—soon tamed. Compassion, though not impossible, is a dangerous potency. Note that the force of the episode depends on the skeptical principle of species continuity, of a *fellow*-feeling almost inconceivable, given the apparent alterity of animals.

In *Shakespeare Among the Animals*, Bruce Boehrer distinguishes what he refers to as "relative anthropocentrism" from the "absolute anthropocentrism" discussed above.

> The difference between absolute and relative anthropocentrism is that the former distinguishes between humanity and the animal world without qualification, whereas the latter associates large and variable subsets of the human community to a greater or lesser extent with the realm of nature, while reserving full human status only for specific, arbitrarily defined social groups.
>
> (17)

As Boehrer frames it, relative anthropocentrism serves primarily as an ideological instrument for the maintenance of invidious social distinctions, relying on a lamentable principle of species-continuity to shift individuals (Acrasia's Gryll, say) or even whole classes of people—"that raskall many" of V.x.65.2, for example, "Who flocking round them, as a swarme / Of flyes vpon a Birchen bough" (V.xi.58.1–2) —into a subhuman or animal status. The skeptical deployment of species-continuity, of which Montaigne's practice is exemplary, is not unrelated, though its function is hardly invidious. Its kindly task is to humiliate human reason; in doing so, skepticism compromises, sometimes radically, the force and function of anthropocentrism.

The pertinence of all this to the conclusion of book II might now almost go without saying—or, at least, its pertinence will be obvious to those familiar with Theresa M. Krier's great discussion of Guyon's adventure on the sacred soil of Acrasia's bower.[27] To her treatment of objectification and of the failure of fellow-feeling with which Guyon should be taxed as he makes his way through the gateways of Acrasia's dainty paradise, the foregoing intellectual history may serve as supplement. The presence of the skeptical totem, Gryllus, at the end of the book may now be understood as a rebuke to that dogmatism with which Guyon had addressed the entire population of Book II. But by this point of the poem, the illusion of intellectual sovereignty may be the least of Guyon's worries. As Krier suggests, the conclusion of Book II once again rehearses Red Crosse's difficulty, the problem of the reality of others, although in this case the problem is less a matter of crediting others than of coping with their creaturely warmth. Guyon is far more capable of compassion than Red Crosse; indeed, in the final cantos of Book II he shudders between awkwardly flexed self-restraint and an unbalanced looseness of affective assent. Yearning towards a principled incorporeality, he traverses seascapes and landscapes of eruption and intromission, the world itself in the throes of bodiliness.

Hence the relevance of skeptical animals. If animals serve the skeptical tradition as guarantors of the irreducible variability of mental experience, they also serve to subdue the philosopher to humble, because embodied and creaturely, fellowship. Thus the skeptical lion of Book I is heroic, a model of comparable subjectivity. Like Durer's pigs, the frowning Gryll, on the other hand, is a parodic temptation. For when Guyon announces that Gryll "chooseth, *with vile difference* / To be a beast,*" we could answer, slanging, "you *wish.*" Guyon here somewhat desperately bespeaks Boehrer's relative anthropocentrism, stiff in his defensive superiority. From the very first canto, Guyon has been confounded by the inevitability of the body, which he experiences as an ineradicable stain, and his quest, across the Legend of Temperance, is to construct a vile difference, a difference from the creaturely that eludes him to the parodic end. The palmer's "let Gryll be Gryll" is desperately optative, though it be uttered with dogmatic confidence. Gelli, Montaigne, and perhaps Una know better; even Pyrrho's pig would grunt with philosophical dismay.

Washington University in Saint Louis

NOTES

1. Directed by Howard Hawks, screenplay by Charles Lederer.

2. *Shakespeare Among the Animals: Nature and Society in the Drama of Early Modern England* (New York: Palgrave, 2002), 6–7. In fact, Spenser's philosophical position entails both absolute and, at least in Book II, what Boehrer refers to as "relative anthropocentrism" (17–18).

3. *The Yale Edition of the Shorter Poems of Edmund Spenser*, ed. William A. Oram et al. (New Haven: Yale University Press, 1989).

4. *The Faerie Queene*, ed. A. C. Hamilton et al., 2nd ed. (London: Longman, 2001), VI.iv.35.

5. More might be said of the bug poems that's of relevance to what follows here, however. As with Gryll, the bugs are an object of identification, though not of philosophical identification. In the case of the gnat and butterfly, it's the sense of human or rather the poet's marginality (and, in the case of the butterfly, the specific problem of ornamental marginality).

6. The phrase is turned in *Totemism*, trans. Rodney Needham (Boston: Beacon Press, 1962), his book-length review of the work of Radcliffe-Brown (1963), 89. Lévi-Strauss is summarizing the conceptual achievement of Radcliffe-Brown's Huxley Memorial Lecture for 1951, entitled "The Comparative Method in Social Anthropology," a substantial reworking of Radcliffe-Brown's thinking after a long career of work on the ethnography of totemism.

7. For a useful survey of anthropological approaches to cultural relations between humans and animals, see the collection of essays edited by Tim Ingold, *What Is an Animal?* (2nd ed., London: Routledge, 1994). R. L. Tapper's essay "Animality, Humanity, Morality, Society," 47–62, takes time to survey the tradition that responds to Lévi-Strauss, and his summary of Sapir's attempt to complicate and refine Lévi-Strauss's account of totemic thought is especially efficient: "Through *non-human metaphor* they [i.e., animals] allow teachers and learners to avoid articulating difficult or embarrassing truths about humanity [as when, e.g., we invoke the birds and the bees or we speak of a dog-eat-dog world]; at another level they *create a distinction* between humans and other animals; and they *reinforce human morality* by giving it a 'natural' basis" (51).

8. The pig is not the only skeptical totem of animal intelligence. The other key exemplar of animal reason is Chrysippus's dog, for which, see Sextus Empiricus, *Outlines of Pyrrhonism*, I.69–70, where Sextus records Chrysippus's assertion that his dog employs the fifth complex indemonstrable syllogism in deciding which of three roads to choose in pursuit.

9.   *The Politics and Poetics of Transgression* (Ithaca: Cornell University Press, 1986), 44–66.

10.   The chief work on this topic, albeit inevitably outdated, is Johannes Schroeter, *Plutarchs Stellung zur Skepsis* (Greifswald, 1911).

11.   The defense is marshaled specifically on behalf of the work of Arcesilaus.

12.   On the genealogical question, see Luciano Floridi, *Sextus Empiricus: The Transmission and Recovery of Pyrrhonism* (Oxford: Oxford University Press 2002), 6–7.

13.   In *Humoring the Body: Emotions and the Shakespearean Stage* (Chicago, 2004).

14.   Pierre Gassendi, *Syntagmatis Philosophici Pars Secunda seu Physica*, III.8.4–5 and III.9. Descartes raises the question of animal thought in his grapplings with the Second through Sixth Objectors, *Meditations on First Philosophy*, John Cottingham et al. trans., *Philosophical Writings of Descartes* (Cambridge: Cambridge University Press, 1984), II:88, 96, 128, 144, 161–62, 183–89, and 279–89.

15.   Montaigne, *The Complete Essays*, trans. M. A. Screech (New York: Penguin, 1991), I:12, 505.

16.   See Hugo Friedrich, *Montaigne*, ed. Philippe Desan, trans. Dawn Eng (Berkeley: University of California Press, 1991), 121–22. Of course, traditions distinct from philosophical skepticism preserve this respect for animals. Notable, and arguably relevant to the reception of skeptical urgings of animal intelligence, is Xenophon's *Art of Horsemanship*, a treatise much read and much mined in the Early Modern period, which insists on equine intelligence.

17.   Diogenes Laertius's *Life of Pyrrho* had its *ed. princ.* in Greek in 1533.

18.   Plutarch here surveys precisely the territory A. L. Kroeber traversed in "The Superorganic," in *The Nature of Culture* (Chicago: University of Chicago Press, 1952), 31—his rebuttal to the pathbreaking work of Lewis Henry Morgan on animal intelligence, *The American Beaver and His Works* (1868).

19.   Julia Annas and Jonathan Barnes provide a useful introduction in *The Modes of Scepticism: Ancient Texts and Modern Interpretations* (Cambridge: Cambridge University Press, 1985).

20.   Sextus describes the Ten Modes as the legacy of the "older skeptics," and chiefly of Aenesidemus, who wrote in the first century BC.

21.   Annas and Barnes, trans., *Sextus Empiricus: Outlines of Scepticism* (Cambridge: Cambridge University Press, 1994).

22.   In *The Modes of Skepticism*, Annas and Barnes review the discussion of the first mode not only in Sextus but also in Diogenes Laertius (*Lives of the Philosophers*, IX, 79–80) and Philo (*On Drunkenness*, part of his commentary on Genesis, IX). In all three cases "the Pyrrhonists pointed to observable differences among animal species, and they inferred that it is 'likely' (to use Sextus's term) that things appear differently to different animal species" (40). They point out that the Pyrrhonists never treat this inference as problematic. (Neither does Plato, incidentally: when Socrates asks, "Would you insist that every color appears to a dog—or to any other animal—in just the same way as it does to you," Theaetetus replies, "Of course not." *Theaetetus*, 154A.)

23.   The seriousness of Gelli's enterprise never functions as a bulwark against the silliness of the invention. Gelli lets Ulysses betray himself as a snob, so that his argument for the superiority of men to beasts gives way to exasperation that he

should be trying to reason with animals who had once been men of inferior status, the Oyster originally a fisherman, the Mole a plowman. The Oyster and the Mole call him on his elitism, effectively exposing the disputation on matters of natural philosophy to the imaginative suspicion that it is similarly prejudiced, the idealized human merely a facile ideological transformation of the aristocrat or magistrate. The critical effect here is quite unstable: one can hardly determine whether the suggestion that Ulysses' position is what we could now call speciesism is meant to lampoon all forms of anti-elitism or whether it indeed serves as quite a traditional skeptical elaboration of a skeptical formula—"if we can suspect the evaluative arguments of a privileged social group, can we not suspect the evaluative arguments of a privileged species, indeed can we not suspect all evaluative arguments as interested arguments for privilege?" My own sense is that the balance tips a bit in the latter direction; that is, I think Gelli is attempting something a bit more radical than the genially submissive skepticism of an Erasmus, something more like what's to be found in Agrippa.

24. James Nohrnberg, *The Analogy of* The Faerie Queene (Princeton: Princeton University Press, 1976), 501–02. That Spenser continues to take refuge from the faunal into the vegetable is evidenced by a final representation of Gryll's unregeneracy as "repining" (II.xii.86.8).

25. My formulation here is indebted to Paster's elegantly nuanced account of the operations of the passions in animals in chapter 3 of *Humoring the Body*; the specific figure of the stream of passions derives from Thomas Wright, *The Passions of the Minde in Generall*, ed. Thomas O. Sloan (Urbana: University of Illinois Press, 1971), 74.

26. The argument runs thus:

"x appears F to animals of kind K"
"x appears F★ to animals of kind K★"
"we cannot prefer K to K★"
"we must therefore suspend judgment as to whether x is really F or F★"

Jonathan Barnes provides a fuller, more intricate analysis of the first mode in "Diogenes Laertius, IX, 61–116: The Philosophy of Pyrrhonism," *Aufstieg und Niedergang der römischen Welt*, eds. W. Haase and H. Temporini, II, 36.4 (de Gruyter: Berlin, 1992), 4273–79.

27. *Gazing on Secret Sights: Spenser, Classical Imitation, and the Decorums of Vision* (Ithaca: Cornell University Press, 1990), 99–112.

ELIZABETH D. HARVEY

Nomadic Souls:
Pythagoras, Spenser, Donne

This essay examines Spenser's intertextual relationship to John
Donne's fragmentary poem, *Metempsychosis*, or *The Progress of
the Soul* (1601), a satiric narrative that charts the progress of a
migratory soul through a series of vegetable, animal, and human
incarnations. Donne's use of a modified Spenserian stanza for
his poem forges a link with Spenser, but we do not know
what part of Spenser Donne meant to evoke. I propose two
possibilities: The *Complaints* (*Mother Hubberds Tale* and *Visions
of the Worlds Vanitie*) and Book II of *The Faerie Queene* (The
Castle of Alma and Grill in the Bower of Bliss). The portrayal
of unrestrained sexual and predatory appetite in *Metempsychosis*
retrospectively illuminates important aspects of Spenser's medical depiction of the body, the senses, the mental faculties, and
their interactions in the castle of the soul. I argue that reading
Spenser through Donne allows us to understand both the philosophical foundations of Spenser's representation of body-soul
relations (Pythagoras, Plato, Aristotle, Ralegh, La Primaudaye)
and the ethical dimensions of his depictions of animals (in relation to Plutarch and Montaigne) and the animal or sensible soul.

"THE SOUL IS EVER THE SAME," says Pythagoras in Book XV
of Ovid's *Metamorphoses*, "though it passes into ever-changing bodies."[1] Pythagorean metempsychosis, here distilled into a passionate
oration on mutability that is mediated through Ovid, offered a
powerful theory of human and natural transformation. Pythagoras
functions as an ironic philosophical muse for Ovid's poetic method;

Spenser Studies: A Renaissance Poetry Annual, Volume XXII, Copyright © 2007 by
AMS Press, Inc. All rights reserved.

although he implicitly sanctions and even inspires Ovid's great theme
of metamorphosed bodies, which are often violently transmuted from
human to plant and animal form, Pythagoras prohibits the consumption of meat, cautioning that it contain the reincarnated souls of
parents or brothers.[2] Yet Ovid's ventriloquistic incorporation of Pythagorean philosophy within his poem is an ingestion that enacts a
metaphorical poetic transmigration, implicitly shaping Ovid's treatment of his other epic precursors and licensing his often irreverent
assimilations of their work. Indeed, the idea that the souls of great
poets could be reborn in the bodies of their literary successors furnished classical and Early Modern writers with a fantasy of poetic
genealogy that rendered the boundaries of the individual dangerously
and intoxicatingly porous, making him both vulnerable and accessible
to the inhabitations of poetic precursors. The Roman poet Ennius
relates at the beginning of the *Annals*, for example, how in a dream
Homer's soul was transposed into him; since sleep was thought to
free the soul, allowing it to wander, it was an ideal state for psychic
exchange.[3] Francis Meres, in a much-cited formulation in *Palladis
Tamia*, says that "As the soule of *Euphorbus* was thought to live in
Pythagoras : so the sweet wittie soul of *Ovid* lives in mellifluous &
hony-tongued *Shakespeare*,"[4] a description that joins metempsychosis
with mellification, Seneca's metaphor for literary imitation.[5] Just as
the bee gathers nectars from a variety of flowers, distilling them into
honey, and the writer collects commonplaces, digesting them in order
to produce his own work, so is the vagrant poetic soul translated
into different bodies. Reincarnation and imitation share an emphasis
on difference, registered through bodily transformation, and sameness, evoked through the mnemonic echo of an earlier state or form.
Dryden famously summarized Spenser's own figuration of this rein-
carnative relationship when he said that "Spenser more than once
insinuates that the Soul of Chaucer was transfused into his body,"[6]
as if the soul were an enduring liquid that could be poured from one
bodily container into another.[7] That the conditions of Early Modern
education and poetic composition made the writer permeable to past
incarnations of ideas and forms is a concept that is at once familiar and
foundational to our imagining of poetic relationships in the period.

   I will concentrate here on an aspect of this genealogical transposition that has received comparatively little critical attention: the idea
that the soul, both as poetic figure and philosophical concept, could
itself be an instrument of transfer. Spenser's intertextual relationship
to John Donne's fragmentary poem *Metempsychosis*, or *The Progress of
the Soul* is central to my discussion not only because Donne's poem
narrativizes reincarnation, charting the progress of a migratory soul

through a series of vegetable, animal, and human incarnations, but also, as I will argue, because it incorporates Spenser's own speculations about the natural historical, philosophical, and medical dimensions of souls. Donne's poem becomes in this way a space of poetic cohabitation. The presence of Spenser's poetic soul is registered through a series of allusions to his *Complaints* and through Donne's echo of the Spenserian stanza, moments of intertextual transfer that Donne reflexively extends to embrace Spenser's representation of the psyche in the Garden of Adonis and the Castle of Alma. My interest in this Pythagorean philosophical legacy is concentrated on the Platonic and Neoplatonic traditions of psychology and its transformation by the Judeo-Christian tradition and Renaissance Platonism. I am equally concerned to explore the pervasive doctrine of the Aristotelian tripartite soul (composed of vegetable, sensible or animal, and intellective aspects) that is formulated in *Parva naturalia* and *De anima* and assimilated by scholasticism, natural philosophy, and medical writings (Galen and Avicenna, among others). These syncretic ideas are further complicated by the doctrine of bodily spirits, what the Stoics called *pneuma*, the "subtile" bodies that meditated between the body and the soul, and which accounted for the operations of body and mind.[8] Spenser may have known some of these writings directly, but many of these ideas were for him also filtered through such popular treatises as Pierre de la Primaudaye's *The French Academie* and Stephan Batman's translation of Bartholomeaus Anglicus's *De Proprietatibus Rerum, Batman uppon Bartholome*. According to many Renaissance thinkers, the rational soul subsumes the organic souls into itself, harnessing powers of growth and reproduction from the vegetative soul, and movement, emotion, and sensation from the sensitive soul.[9] While the lower souls are thus often thought to be assimilated, governed, and even forgotten by the inorganic rational human soul, I claim that these lower souls are sometimes much less neatly segregated into hierarchical components than humanist discourses and natural philosophy suppose or desire. Pythagorean metempsychosis disturbs the already delicate intersection between established psychic theories inherited from classical philosophy, medicine, and Christian doctrine because it questions foundational ideas: the nature of the body-soul connection and the relationship between the material and immaterial realms.

The doctrine of reincarnation interrogates the nature of the tripartite soul in fundamental ways: if the rational soul is unique to human beings, can it be translated into a vegetable or animal body? Conversely, can a soul that formerly occupied an animal body be reborn in a human host, and if so, will it then acquire an intellective dimension? Are the aspects of the tripartite soul immanent and enabled only if the body that shelters the soul possesses the necessary faculties? If a rational soul migrates into an animal body, does it retain memory and consciousness of its earlier life but without the power to articulate it? These questions were urgently debated by philosophers and theologians, and Donne's skeptical portrait of the soul and the interrelationship among its components is in part a response to these controversies.[10] His depiction anatomizes the human subject's linkages both with the ambient vegetable and animal worlds and with his or her own mental, sensory, and passional nature. Donne's poem reveals a dark, satirical image of the human soul's relationship to its vegetal and sensitive counterparts, a very different version of the intellective psyche that was celebrated by humanist treatises as safely cordoned off from its lower souls and the natural world over which it purportedly presided. The savage portrayal of unrestrained sexual and predatory appetite in *Metempsychosis* retrospectively illuminates aspects of Spenser's medical depiction of the body, the senses, the mental faculties and their interactions in the castle of the soul, allowing us to glimpse the philosophical dimensions of these psychic conjunctions.

1.

The ligature between Spenser and Donne's poem is the stanza, the poetic unit that Giorgio Agamben, following Dante in his *De Vulgari Eloquentia*, describes as a capacious room, a receptacle of technique.[11] Dante activates the etymological sense of stanza, derived from the Latin *stare*, to stand, which designates a room or standing place. If the *canzone* is the "womb" or "whole essential thought" of the poem, according to Dante, the stanza embodies the "elements" that constitute it. [12] Dante offers an analogy to explain why it is essential to anatomize the stanza: just as attaining a true knowledge of rational man entails a comprehension of his constituent elements, namely the body and the sensible soul, he tells us, so too must one seek to know the component parts of the stanza in order to apprehend the poem's thought, the *canzone*.[13] Spenser's famously enigmatic geometrical and arithmological stanza (II.ix.22) in the Castle of Alma furnishes a crucial key for understanding *The Faerie Queene*'s thought, and in keeping with Dante's analogical parallel, it describes a cognate linkage of body and soul. As Kenelm Digby's intricate gloss of 1644 makes clear, Pythagorean theories of the soul and mathematics are intimately coupled.[14] Yet none of these analyses, even Alastair Fowler's extended numerological commentary, explain the arithmological riddle as a description of the stanzaic form itself.[15] Kenneth Gross has suggestively claimed in an argument that mirrors my own that the stanza describing the creative order in the Garden of Adonis (III.vi.42) becomes a commentary on its own poetic form: the garden offers "a mythic emblem of the stanza's life," and "[f]or a moment, the stanza *is* the Garden."[16] Without discounting the clearly accurate references to Pythagorean, Aristotelian, and Platonic numeric systems that critics of the arithmological stanza make, I contend that its numerological enigmas refer both to the philosophical traditions of psychic and corporeal union and also to the poetic numbers of the stanza itself. If "Nine" is "the circle set in heauens place," that number simultaneously designates the Spenserian stanza's nine lines. The "quadrate" that stands "twixt" the circle and triangle alludes not just to the four humors that join the body to the mind, but also to the quatrains themselves. Lines four and five, the first and last lines respectively of the stanza's quatrains, marry through their (feminine) rhyme the mortal and the immortal proportions, the body and the soul: "The one imperfect, mortall, fœminine;/Th'other immortal, perfect, masculine" (II.ix.22).[17] This stanza thus provides a microcosmic metacommentary on the poetic form Spenser invented for *The Faerie Queene*. It also suggests a rationale for Donne's choice of stanza for his poem about the migration of the soul between bodies, a form that he at once mimicked and transformed.

Scholars have long speculated about Donne's echo of the Spenserian stanza, for *Metempsychosis* is composed of fifty-two modified Spenserian stanzas, ten-line sequences made up of nine pentameter lines and an alexandrine, what Kenneth Gross terms a kind of "impertinent" overwriting that ruins the "subtle mathematics of Spenser's form."[18] While there is also a potent thematic connection between Donne's poem and Spenser's *Complaints*, Donne's choice of verse form leads us inevitably back to the Castle of Alma in *The Faerie Queene*, Spenser's meditation on the interlacing of somatic and psychic elements. Spenser's sources for this figuration are multiple, and they include both Platonic and Aristotelian influence. Plato claimed in the *Timaeus* that the soul was immortal but that it contained mortal souls that were aligned with specific bodily zones or stations: the head lodged the immortal soul and was separated from the body by the isthmus of the neck. The two inferior souls were relegated to the upper and lower parts of the thorax respectively. The soul that was housed in the heart embodied bravery and emotion, and the nutritive soul, voracious for meat and drink, was separated from the other mortal soul by the diaphragm and confined to a region that was "a sort of manger for the food of the body."[19] This appetitive soul was, Plato tells us, "bound . . . down like a wild animal which was chained up with man" (70e), as far as possible from the brain or "council chamber" (71a), relegated to the "house of the lower nature" (71b), the liver. Aristotle, who was more concerned with the soul's en-meshment in matter, posited three psychic entities to explain the animating principle that humans shared with plants and animals, and this tripartite soul so familiar to the early moderns also shapes Spen-ser's figuration of Alma's house in ways that extend the physiological allegory.[20] The stanzas in Spenser's body allegory correspond to the body's rooms, which accommodate these three souls: the kitchen houses the vegetative soul, the parlor is the seat of the animal soul, and the ventricles of the brain harbor the faculties of the intellective soul. In an analogous way, the stanzas of *Metempsychosis* correspond roughly to the different vegetable, animal, and human hosts the soul occupies in its transmigratory journey, as if the stanzas are themselves bodies, standing places or rooms, animated by the nomadic soul. Donne's supernumerary line becomes not just a ruin, but a vitalizing anomaly, an active principle that refuses the stately confines of the Spenserian architecture. Spenser explores the nature of these souls in detail in the Castle of Alma, but I want to turn first to his *Complaints*, because they provided particularly rich evocations for Donne of Spenser's animal or sensitive souls.

2.

The *Complaints*, that anthology of "fugitive pieces,"[21] was published in 1591, just ten years before Donne's poem was written. Brian Blackley has argued that *Prosopopoia. Or Mother Hubberds Tale* is the most obvious source for *Metempsychosis* because it features a fox and an ape as its central protagonists and because its satire of the estates of Early Modern society corresponds closely to Donne's veiled satiric treatment of the court.[22] However, while acknowledging the impor-tance of this resonance, I will also explore an additional source text: *Visions of the Worlds Vanitie*, one of the three *Visions* that conclude the *Complaints*. This poem features twelve Spenserian sonnets, ten of which offer miniature emblematic visions. The poet is a dreamer, and his spirit, "shaking off her earthly prison," enters into a deep meditation of things that exceeds the "reach of common reason" (V: 1–4). The dream, frequently represented as a state in which the soul can range unfettered, freed temporarily from its corporeal container, here becomes a medium for exploring different registers of being. The ten subsequent visions, each circumscribed by the "room" of the sonnet, depict relationships between creatures from the vegetable, animal, and insect worlds: a bull and a brize or gadfly, a crocodile and a tedula (a small Egyptian bird), an eagle and a scarab beetle, a dragon and a spider, a cedar and a worme. Each encounter illustrates the inevitable tragic fall that is associated with the *de casibus* tradition; the concluding couplet of every sonnet pits greatness against insignificance, and in each case, the subordinate creature is the precipitating factor in the destruction and downfall of its more powerful host. Each sonnet describes a corporeal penetration of one creature by another, an insidious, intimate occupation that breaches the boundaries of the larger body. The narrator is himself also infiltrated by what he sees, his "spright" "is greatly moved," and new passions are born in his "engrieved brest," as if the animal contests he witnesses have stirred the working of his own sensible soul, which is temporarily liberated from the confines of human reason during his visions.

Two pairs of antagonists are particularly relevant for their relationship with Donne's poem: the first is the whale whose throat is speared by the swordfish, causing him to "spewe" the contents of his stomach. Like Spenser's *Visions of the Worlds Vanitie*, *Metempsychosis* also features an extended episode of a whale gored by a swordfish, a battle that would have been familiar to both Spenser and Donne from the account of Stephan Batman's 1582 translation of Bartholomaeus's *De Proprietatibus rerum*, *Batman uppon Bartholome*.[23] The political and psychic implications of the encounter are amplified for Donne; the whale's "vast womb" becomes a rapacious net, allowing him to suck everything into his "gulf-like throat." The whale "drinks . . . up seas," "eats up flocks," "jostles islands," and "shakes firm rocks" (317–32),[24] and in this "roomful house" the soul floats, sending "like a Prince . . . her faculties/To all her limbs, distant as provinces" (334–35). The incorporated soul animates the body or kingdom, a familiar image that sutures theories of government, the body politic, to philosophical and medical understandings of the somatic-psychic nexus, the body natural. Sensory spies are dispatched by the prince to gather intelligence from the outer reaches of the kingdom, and the ability to process this information determines the prince's success in governing. Isaac Oliver immortalized the iconography of political and sensory espionage in his representation of Elizabeth I, "The

Rainbow Portrait," depicting the queen's cloak strewn with disembodied eyes and ears, emblems of her visual and acoustic vigilance. Just as the senses mediate between the inner body and the exterior world, the swordfish's sojourn within the whale makes manifest the soul's investiture within the body. The incorporation literalizes the idea that the lower souls, which in Donne's poem manifest themselves as actual vegetable and animal components, inhabit the human body as vital presences. The whale and the swordfish epitomize the sensible soul, which includes the nutritive and reproductive aspects of the vegetative soul now augmented by the powers of movement, the capacity to experience emotion, and the ability to gather knowledge though the faculties of sensation.

That the depiction of animals in *Visions of the worlds vanitie* troubles the border between human and animal is made even more apparent in the main title Spenser chooses for: *Prosopopoia*. George Puttenham named this rhetorical figure "counterfeit impersonation," the attribution of "any humane quality, as reason or speech to dombe creatures or other insensible things."[25] Spenser's use of this figure as a structural principle in *Mother Hubberds Tale* involves a transfer of human characteristics to beasts, but it also implicitly creates a juxtaposition between the animal and the human, a complex mirroring that calls into question for the skeptical reader the philosophical nature of the distinction between species. Prosopopeia's etymological meaning, from the Greek, *prosopon*, person or face + *poiia*, to make, is significant here because, as Helkiah Crooke reminds us in *Mikrokosmographia* (1615), human beings are distinguished from other animals by their upright stance, a position that situates the face looking forward, giving it a primacy that renders the visage a signifier of the human. The face, Crooke asserts, registers the "comely conformation and Beauty whereof the elegancy of humane nature doth most appear."[26] Because the organs of sense are situated in the front of the head, he tells us, the face is "truly called the Image of the mind" (532). *Prosopopoia* describes the impersonation by the fox and ape of the figures that represent the three estates of man (beggar/shepherd; priest; courtier/king). The animals transform themselves through clothing, a sartorial display usually designed to cloak a uniquely human nakedness, and through language, a linguistic expression that was considered the special preserve of rational humanity. The strangeness of the animals' assumption of clothing in *Prosopopoia* is registered in the nomination of their attire and behavior as foreign: "His breeches were made after a new cut,/ *Al Portuguese*" (P: 211–12), "the fond Ape himselfe uprearing hy/Upon his tiptoes, stalketh stately by,/As if he were some great *Magnifico*" (P: 663–65), "But his behavior altogether was/

Alla Turchese" (P: 676–77). The animals' speech is almost always designated by a parenthetical aside ("sayde the Ape" [P: 973]), and even though this mode of introducing dialogue also characterizes the inception of Mother Hubberd's narrative, the frequency with which it prefaces beastly language accentuates the counterfeit or "Puppit" (P: 931) nature of these utterances. We might conceive of prosopopeia as a kind of rhetorical metempsychosis, then, for it installs a speaking soul, an anima, in a body that was formerly "inanimate" in the sense that it lacks an intellective soul and the articulate speech that expresses human thought.

Paul de Man's influential theorizing of prosopopoeia as "de-facement" identified the trope's anthropomorphizing tendency, its impulse to impose its own animate characteristics on the inanimate other.[27] Derrida augmented this point in his tribute to de Man, *Memoires for Paul De Man,* and further extended it to animal-human relations in his essay, "The Animal That Therefore I Am (More to Follow)."[28] Derrida's analysis is historically grounded in his meditation on Montaigne's *Apologie of Raymond Sebond,* a chapter that Derrida termed "the greatest pre- or anti-Cartesian text on the animal."[29] The pivotal Montaignean moment for my purposes is the encounter that Derrida and others focus on, Montaigne's description of playing with his cat, a reciprocal gaze that elicits Montaigne's radical critique of human rational sovereignty. Montaigne asks, "When I am playing with my cat, who knowes whether she have more sport in dallying with me than I have in gaming with her? We entertain one another with mutuall apish tricks."[30] The chiasmic structure of this ludic interaction, culminating in Montaigne's designation of the reciprocal play as "apish," couples the animal and human through a signifier of mimicry, the ape, the animal simulacrum of the human. The encounter with his cat evokes Montaigne's speculation about communication, language, and gesture, and these questions introduce and subtend his broader interrogation of the social and philosophical subordination of animals. This subjection relies upon the privileging of reason, a faculty assumed to be uniquely human. Montaigne questions the presumed exclusivity of rationality, encapsulated in Helkiah Crooke's assertion about bipedality, the distinctness of the human face, and its transparent ability to express the mind. Montaigne judges the "prerogative" that is signaled by human upright stature to be "meerely poeticall," "for there are so many little beasts that have their sight directly fixed towards heaven."[31] As Montaigne observes, many creatures have their face pointed forwards, including the "vilest and filthiest of all the rout," the ape, who, he reminds us, is the beast that most resembles man. And the animal whose "inward and vitall parts" bear the closest resemblance to the human, he asserts, is the hog.[32] Montaigne insists on the physical and philosophical kinship with the beastly that a Platonically inspired humanism sought to disavow. He seeks to extend this alliance of resemblance between species by understanding animals on their own terms, intuiting what kinds of languages and mental powers they might possess, and even attempting to glimpse humans from the perspective of the beast. Montaigne's idea of language expands here to encompass what we might call non-linguistic forms of communication: emotional valence in expression, the tone of a bark, an alphabet of gesture, a bodily inflexion.[33] Spenser's *Mothers Hubberds Tale* uses the beast fable as a kind of narrative prosopopoeia, animating the fox and ape by, in Puttenham's phrase, attributing language to "dombe creatures," an adjective that engages both ideas of speechlessness and the linked denotation of stupidity. As Puttenham's definition reveals, and de Man and Derrida corroborate in theoretical terms, the trope functions anthropomorphically, performing the same rhetorical subordination that social structures do in their relegation of animals to a philosophical category that does not permit a genuine looking or talking back.

Montaigne's *Apologie of Raymond Sebond* and Donne's *Metempsychosis* upset the humanist hierarchy, both because they insist on a real, "face-to-face" encounter between the animal and the human, and because they indict reason as the highest good. Where Pico della Mirandola's "Oration on the Dignity of Man" provided an authoritative articulation of the widespread belief that reason radically distinguished men from animals,[34] Donne used the ideas of the tripartite soul and Pythagorean transmigration of souls to examine humanism's underbelly: if the vegetable and animal souls are not finally subsumed into the rational soul, but rather coexist with it, then the dominion over all living things that God supposedly conferred upon human beings is called into question. If human beings are not distinguished as fundamentally different from the plants and animals with which they share the world, if men make no effort to understand the "inward and secret motions of beasts," then their natural sovereignty is no longer an innate privilege, but rather what Montaigne calls an "over-weening," "vanitie," or "presumption."[35] Indeed, the erosion of the distinction between animal, vegetable, and human urges a redefinition of the nature of humanity and the prerogatives that reason should bestow. The narrator's soul in Spenser's *Visions* poetically and imaginatively infiltrates itself into the animals he depicts, a psychic analogy to the smaller creature's insinuation of itself into a larger body. Although Spenser's poem converts its beastly exemplars into a lesson for human readers, Donne's *Metempsychosis* echoes the eighth sonnet in *Visions of the Worlds Vanitie,* powerfully expanding the Spenserian implications of this corporeal ingression in directions that are cognate with Montaigne's critique.

The sonnet paints a picture of an elephant "gorgeouslie" adorned with "bells and bosses," bearing on his back a "gilden towre" (100–103). He is "puffed up with passing surquedrie" (105) until an ant creeps into his "nosthrils," puncturing the foolish vanity of the ornamented beast by causing him to cast down his "towres," thus deforming both his "borrowed pride" and his "native beautie" (109–10). In the corresponding episode in Donne's *Metempsychosis,* a mouse crawls up the proboscis of a sleeping elephant, the great hall of the brain, and there chews the "life cords," and "like a whole town/Clean undermined, the slain beast tumbled down" (394–95). The episodes share the image of a small, insignificant creature infiltrating the elephant's head, thus bringing about its destruction. Donne's version, however, integrates a telling intertext. When the mouse enters the elephantine skull, it inspects the surrounding architecture:

> In which as in a gallery this mouse
> Walked, and surveyed the rooms of this vast house,
> And to the brain, the soul's bedchamber, went,
> And gnawed the life cords there.
>
> (391–94)

Donne's joke, of course, is that the description of the elephant's cranial cavity from the rodent's perspective exactly replicates the language of anatomy treatises and the poetry, most notably the Castle of Alma in Spenser's *Faerie Queene* and Sir John Davies's *Nosce Teipsum,* that draws on them. Pierre de la Primaudaye, the sixteenth-century Protestant encyclopedist, begins the second part of *The French Academie,* for instance, with the same familiar anatomical trope. In his address to the reader, la Primaudaye says that he will reveal not only the "outward members of man's body," but also the "most hidden & inward parts thereof": "Heere may you see the exquisite frame & composition of the head, as it were the upper lodging of this house, the severall ventricles of the braine, as so many sundry chambers for the intertainement of the *Animal Spirits.*"[36] The elephant holds a privileged place in natural histories, for it is often, as la Primaudaye himself acknowledges in the third volume of *The French Academie,* the animal nearest to the "sense of man" in its "so excellent

witte, discretion, and memorie."[37]   Giovanni Battista Gelli's 1549
dialogue, *Circe*, makes the elephant the only animal willing to be
changed back into a human being, and it is the elephant who celebrates with Ulysses the glories of human reason.[38] The mouse's inhabitation of the elephant brain in Donne's poem anticipates both the
last transmigration in *Metempsychosis* when the soul is incorporated
in a human form and assumes a rational soul, with all the attendant
speculative faculties that this would enable, and also the way that the
intellective soul is always subtended (and often thwarted completely)
by the impulses of its lower souls. In this case, the appetitive nature
of the organic souls causes the mouse to consider the "sinewy strings"
"which do our bodies tie" to the "tender well-armed feeling brain"
(502–03) not as the essential tether to life itself but as a snack.[39] The
mouse's infiltration of the elephant's skull, what Helkiah Crooke calls
the soul's "throne of state,"[40] presents the obverse of the prosopopoeic
encounter. Rather than anthropomorphizing its other, this incorporation is a theriomorphizing moment, for the mouse converts the
brain, the signifier of the rational (and thus the human), into an
animal other, its prey and physical nourishment.

3.

If *Visions* provide some of the matter for *Metempsychosis*, Donne's real
Spenserian source, as its stanzaic form intimates, is *The Faerie Queene*.
The most obvious enactment of metempsychosis in the poem is the
cycle of souls in the Garden of Adonis, but that metaphysical vision
of ceaseless psychic generation is supplemented by the physiological
and anatomical representation of the tripartite soul in the Castle of
Alma. The knights' entry into the castle is a penetration of a larger
allegorical body that aligns them simultaneously with the insinuating
creatures of Spenser's *Visions* and with the speculative gaze of the
anatomist. The poem places the knights in the position of Donne's
mouse, for they too "survey" the "rooms of this vast house" that
constitute the body's architecture, and they too make their way to
the brain, "the soul's bedchamber."[41] The allegory would seem to
represent a straightforward body/soul dichotomy, since Alma, the
embodiment of the Christian and rational soul, presides over the
castle of the body in an ostensible relationship of sovereignty. In fact,
once the knights enter the castle, the psychic/somatic dialectic is
complicated by the "self-predicating" nature of allegory[42] itself and

by the epistemological conundrum of surveying the faculties that make consciousness possible in the first place. This intensified self-reflexivity manifests itself as a series of enigmatic scenes that are invested with significance but whose meaning is always slightly elusive. The riddling nature of the body's interiority is compounded by the fact that the knights' guide, Alma, never speaks. Rather, she gestures, "leading" the knights into the body through the mouth (an image of ingestion) and to the various tableaux in the hall of the belly, the parlor of heart, and the turret of the brain. Although Alma is given a figure and a face through the trope of personification—fair skin, golden hair, a "lilly white robe" with a train of gold and pearl, and a crown of "sweet Rosiere" (II.ix.18–19)—she is never animated, as prosopopeia conventionally is, by language. Her muteness, in fact, expresses her psychic nature, for as John Donne put it of the dialogue between the lovers' rational souls in "The Ecstasy," there is no need for audible language because "both meant, both spake the same."[43] The language of the inorganic soul, in other words, is silent because it is coterminous with thought. Alma's muteness thus figures a soul standing outside of the intellective faculties that lend it speech. Her silence has the paradoxical effect of foregrounding the nature of language, both the rational soul's relationship to linguistic expression and the poetic and allegorical devices through which Spenser represents the operations of the mind and the soul.

The relationship between the intellective soul, housed in the brain's ventricles, and its lower counterparts, represented in Spenser's allegory by the kitchen and the parlor, was vigorously debated by early modern thinkers, and the controversies frequently focused on the doctrine of metempsychosis and whether it was possible for a human soul to occupy a plant or animal body. The distinctness of the rational soul was closely tied to the idea of a perfect consonance between body and soul. In the opening line of his *Treatise of the Soul*, for instance, Sir Walter Ralegh insists on the absolute distinction rationality confers: "There are two kinds of souls, one void of reason, another endued with reason." Later in the *Treatise,* he makes it clear that the faculty is unique to human beings: "The other power of the soul, which is proper to man and denied to beasts, is understanding; this, together with the will, are the proper and only faculties of the reasonable soul." He argues that these faculties both confer language and also allow man to "dispute, and foresee, and mount to heaven."[44] Spenser would seem to concur. In the Garden of Adonis, the garden beds are planted with "[i]nfinite shapes of creatures" and "vncouth formes" that are "ranckt in comely rew." Each of these shapes is destined for a particular soul: "some fit for reasonable soules t'indew,

/ Some made for beasts, some made for birds to weare" (III.vi.35). Creation thus provides a range of bodily hosts that are arranged in neat categories conceived to suit specific souls, animal, plant, or human. The great psychic "wheele" of generation is guided in this vision by an infallible principle of order, a kind of cosmic matchmaking.

Pierre de la Primaudaye's influential defense of the uniqueness of the human rational soul is augmented by his attack on the potential chaos that a random transmigration of souls might engender. In the second part of *The French Academie*, his "naturall historie of the body and soule of man," four allegorical interlocutors discuss the nature of the soul in general and the status of metempsychosis in particular. La Primaudaye's insistence on the distinctiveness of human reason is matched by the scathing treatment he gives to those—Pythagoras and Plato, among others—who believed in the "passage of the soule from one body to another."[45] As he asserted in his discussion of instrumentality, the human soul must "of necessitie have another body, with other instrumentes and of another nature, then the soule of beastes may have: and the soule of beastes another then the soule of plants, according as every one of them differeth from other both in nature and offices" (435). Plato and Pythagoras did not believe in literal transmigration, he asserts; their meaning was rather to "withdraw men from beastly affections" (509). Men have the capacity to transform themselves at any time into sheep, wolves, hogs, dogs, bears, or lions, just as they can also transfigure themselves as angels, for as Plato tells us, the "nature of man" is "monstrous" in its ability to house multiple natures.[46] Reincarnation, in other words, served a monitory function, a figuration of what the predominance of the sensible over the rational soul would look like, an imaginative portrait of a depraved inner soul displayed in the outward form of a beastly body. La Primaudaye here reiterates humanist beliefs in the human and rational capacity to triumph over the mortal, inferior souls that all humans harbor within them, to submerge the sensual in the speculative. Just as Adam was given dominion over the animals, a superiority marked by language and reason, so, too, could all human beings vanquish the animal and vegetable affinities bequeathed to them by their mortal souls.

The confident pronouncements of la Primaudaye about the absolute distinction between souls and the impossibility of random reincarnation wavers at several points. While these moments do not approach the radical skepticism of Montaigne's interrogation of human and animal intelligence in the *Apologie of Raymond Sebond* or Plutarch's *Moralia* to which Montaigne recurrently refers, they do anticipate Donne's subversion of the humanist principles that la Primaudaye so vehemently articulated. La Primaudaye's contention that the rational soul was unique to human beings is itself undermined by the etymology that he furnishes and then almost immediately disavows. "[T]his worde *Animal* [is] derived from *Anima*," he writes, which means that a human being "is altogether animal, that is, naturall and sensuall both in body and soule without Christ Jesus."[47] Religion allows humans to slough off the animal soul within them, to extinguish or sublate its "naturall" and "animall" aspects. La Primaudaye's account of the gestation of the infant, which accords with the psychology of Aristotle and Aquinas, also acknowledges the rational soul's root in the natural souls that form its foundation: "we see how the child, so long as it is in the Mothers wombe, differeth almost nothing at all from plantes; and after it is borne, how it differeth but a little from brute beastes."[48] La Primaudaye clings to an idea of natural hierarchy that depends on the orderly cleaving of specific souls to matching bodies. An arbitrary transmigration that is motivated by destiny or appetite would produce the chaotic universe that sometimes appears at the edges of his encyclopedic work, but that is always quickly relegated to the strictly systematized world governed by an intrinsic correspondence between soma and psyche.

The Castle of Alma, although constantly under siege from without, offers a refuge of relative psychic order within its walls. Arthur and Guyon ascend the ivory staircase of the spine to the head and to the three ventricles of the brain, which is, as Helkiah Crooke reminds us, "the seate of the Sensative Soule" and the "seate of all the Animall faculties, Imagination, Reason or discourse & Memory."[49] The ventricles are animated by spirits, the intermediaries between somatic materiality and the ethereal, transcendent soul. Generated by heat and composed of invisible hot vapours, spirits were conventionally divided into three types: natural, vital, and animal. The vital spirits, bred in the heart and associated with the passions, are carried by secret sinews and channels throughout the body. We see the movements of these spirits in the parlor of the heart where the repeated blushings of Arthur, Guyon, and Shamefastnesse display the heart's secrets in a suffusion of blood in the skin, a vaporous exhalation "as cloud from sea arise" (II.ix.42). The spirits are then transported to the brain and filtered through the *rete mirabile*, where they breed animal spirits, which flow through the three ventricles of imagination, reason, and memory, the animal faculties.[50] The term "animal spirits" ultimately derives from the territorialization of the souls, since the sensitive or animal soul defines what is common among humans and animals, namely, motion and feeling or sensation. But the term also forges a kinship among species, a commonality that is disavowed but that nevertheless manifests itself as a residue in language, especially in metaphor. The ventricle of imagination in the Castle of Alma is, not surprisingly, full of animals, human and beastly ("Apes, Lions, Ægles, Owles" [II.ix.50]), the flies and bees associated with fantasy, and the hybrids generated by the imagination, centaurs and "*Hippodames.*" Spenser's erroneous name for the seahorse converts it into an animal-human composite, which he substitutes for "hippocampus," the correct word, and the term that, ironically, eighteenth-century neuro-anatomy would use to designate that portion of the frontal lobe that governs the retrieval of names and words. Creatures also seem to invade the description of Phantastes: he is of "crabbed hew," expressing in his outward nature the refractory character of the crustacean, and he possesses "hollow beetle brows." Helkiah Crooke relates that some philosophers believed the eyebrow to be the seat of the soul because of its capacity to express thought or emotion, and here that privileged location is metaphorically occupied by a beetle.[51]

Spenser's representation of the soul in the Castle of Alma, while strongly inflected by Platonic psychology (particularly as articulated in the *Timaeus*) in its insistence on the geometrical expression of the soul's immortal dimension and on the moral governance of the appetitive souls, is nevertheless Aristotelian in some aspects. Aristotle's formulation of the tripartite soul in *De anima* and *Parva naturalia* is anchored in natural philosophy, and his observations are often comparative, taking into account as he does the communalities among, and the distinctions between, vegetative and animal life. Aristotle was not only the chief source for Elizabethan faculty psychology; he was also a major progenitor of the discourses on the senses.[52] His account of the soul seeks to explain its relationship with matter, and he thus devotes a great deal of attention to explaining the physiology of the senses, those faculties that Helkiah Crooke termed "the intelligencers between the body and the soule."[53] Bartholomaeus offers a succint description of the action of the senses: by means of the sinews, the animal spirits pass out of the innermost chambers of the brain, some being sent to each sense organ to quicken and heighten the senses. His account of the sense of smell contains a long passage on the olfactory power of four-footed beasts, from apes and hounds to fowles and gryphons, whose ability to smell carrion is renowned.[54] Where these creatures stand as exemplars of the acuity of smell for Bartholomaeus, for Spenser they also form the "monstrous rabblement" that besiege Alma's castle. They are the raw sensory data that assail the body, a kind of anti-masque or procession of animals and hybrid creatures that evoke a cognate array of animals and composite creatures in Phantastes's chamber, the ventricle of imagination. Aristotle believed that sensory faculties were the gateway to the soul, and information entered by means of the senses. While sensation had to be physically present in order to be received, according to Aristotle, fantasy or imagination reconstructed images from this sensory data in new ways, a kind of phantasmatic afterimage, manifested most commonly by dreams.[55]

When Guyon and the Palmer leave the castle, Maleger and his troops renew their attack, focusing their ferocious assaults on the five bulwarks of the senses. The third troupe "cruelly assay[s]" the third fort, the bulwarke of smell, and the hideous shapes include apes, hounds, and puttocks, carrion birds, the same animals that for Bartholomaeus epitomize olfactory acuity. The faculty of smell is itself assailed not just by aggressively unfiltered sensory data, but by the very creatures that emblematize the faculty they attack. Among the fourth battalion, whose "cruell battery [is] bent" against the bulwark of taste, are animals renowned for omnivorous and undiscriminating appetite, such as the ostrich, as well as creatures "fashioned in the wast/Like swine" (II.xi.12). Not only does the "troupe" include animals in which a particular sense is especially highly developed, but also those creatures whose indulgence in the pleasures of a particular sense manifestly distorts their bodies. The designation of the distended middle of the swine-like creatures as "wast" itself suggests a surfeit of meaning in its doubleness, as if the rhyme between "tast" and "wast" had engendered lexical offspring. One meaning points to indulgent eating, a prodigal consumption that exceeds necessity and produces "waste," and the other gestures proleptically toward the bodily consequences of this greed, the engorged "waist." Instead of depicting the senses as receptors allured by the pleasures of vision, smell, touch, taste, and hearing, the castle is bombarded by crowds of hostile creatures, a cacophonous rout of "fowle misshapen wights"(II.xi.8), whose manifestation is a distorted vision of medieval iconographic depictions of the sensorium. The vividness of these figurations exemplifies both the way the senses are besieged by unprocessed sensory information, and the way the poetic imagination can create the illusion of sensory data through the vestigial but phantasmatic residue of these impressions.

The contiguity between animal and rational souls reveals itself most forcefully, however, in the ventricle of memory. The "wormeeaten" parchment scrolls in this cranial room figure time's destruction as well as the consumption of one animal by another, a kind of digestive translation. The vermiculated animals skins recount the origins of Briton, an archive whose physical record is deteriorating in ways that mirror the uncertainty of the land's beginnings: "But when they sprong, or how they were begot,/Vneath is to assure; unneath to wene" (II.x.8). The land was originally occupied by "hideous Giants" and "halfe beastly men," who "like wilde beasts lurking in loathsome den" (II.x.7), behaved like animals until Brutus subdued them and brought civilization. Civilized culture emerged from beastly origins, and it is the eponymous hero of Briton, "Brute," who subdues the aboriginal inhabitants. Although Brutus brings a new, "royall stocke" to Albion, his progeny is superimposed upon the land occupied by the descendants of the putative coupling between Diocletian's daughters and the native "feends and Filthy Sprights" (II.x.8). Their pollution of the land caused even their mothers to loath the giants' "beastlinesse" (II.x.9). Spenser takes the name of Brutus, of course, from his sources, Geoffrey of Monmouth and the Tudor chronicles, but because he and his contemporaries used the word "brute" to modify or designate "beast," it is difficult not to catch the irony produced by the activation of the name's etymological meaning (L. *brutus*, heavy, dull, irrational). Martha Craig reminded us long ago of the tradition exemplified by Homer, theorized in Plato's *Cratylus*, and systemized by the Ramists: etymology often reveals the essential nature of the thing it names.[56] Like Adamic language, which posited an originary world in which a perfect correspondence existed between word and thing, between a name and the essence of an animal, etymology furnishes a linguistic root, a residue of that ideal consonance. The operations of civilization depend not only on conquering the "saluage" nation of giants, but also upon subduing the human propensity towards beastliness, and the residue of that subjection endures as a homonymic vestige in Brutus's name. Brutus is at once the instrument of what Norbert Elias called the civilizing process and the subjected residue of that conquest, an embodiment of an animal soul without its rational superstructure.

If vanquishing these beast-men lies at the root of English history as an almost obliterated memory, the struggle to contain the animal impulses that is exemplified in the Platonic and moral version of the organic soul must nevertheless be fought continually. Guyon's confrontation with Grill after the destruction of the Bower of Bliss is the most dramatic encounter of the animal-human interface. Not only is Grill a figure of human-animal transformation, having been changed into a hog by Acrasia, and then restored to human form by Palmer's rod, but he is also an intertext, a poetic transmigration, from Plutarch's *Moralia*. In Plutarch's theriophily, "Beasts are Rational,"

Gryllus is given a voice, and he debates with Odysseus and Circe about the superiority of animals to humans. If human beings with rational souls are superior to beasts, argues Gryllus, why do the poets invent epithets to describe their bravery that exemplifies animal qualities, such as "lion-hearted" or "like a boar in valour"?[57] Indeed, Gryllus asserts that the courage of men is compromised by their propensity to think and to calculate, a feature of the rational soul that tempers and dulls the "cutting edge of courage."[58] Most pertinent for Spenser's Grill is the discussion of temperance in Plutarch's dialogue. Gryllus argues that beasts are naturally more able to curtail and govern their desires than men are, for they never wish for the superfluous, for anything beyond what is essential. Human desire, on the other hand, is a deluge, an "overwhelming" "alien rabble" of wishes, longings for luxurious living, for gorgeous attire, gold ornaments, spices, perfumes, exotic food. Gryllus's description of luxury's allure necessarily recalls the assaults on the bulwarks of the five senses in the Castle of Alma. Animals are immune to these sensory sieges, claims Gryllus, since taste in animals is not distorted by superfluous desire.

Gryllus's indictment includes even the human appetite for animal flesh, for like man's desire for the exotic, hunger for meat goes beyond what is essential for survival and nourishment. The organ of taste in animal is itself a faculty of sober government, he argues, that is used to admit what is proper and reject what is alien.[59] Animals are similarly regulated when it comes to sexual pleasure, which they celebrate according to the natural laws of the seasons. Human beings, on the other hand, are driven by lusts that violate natural order and distinction, leading them to consort even with animals. The progeny that these unions produce are the hybrids that populate Phantastes's chamber: minotaurs, sphinxes, centaurs. Plutarch's theriophilic arguments, which are echoed in Gelli's dialogue and Montaigne's *Apologie of Raymond Sebond,* thus impugn the unquestioned sovereignty of human rationality. That Spenser's Grill "repines" at the end of Book II, resisting his transformation to human form and preferring his "hoggish mind," is a less simple choice than the Palmer suggests. If the status of the intellective soul is associated with unrestrained desire and sensory indulgence, then the animal soul is a much more natural ally of the virtue of temperance. Spenser's hierarchy of souls in the Castle of Alma and the Palmer's interpretation of Grill's resistance would seem to support the primacy of the rational soul. The Palmer's portrait of Grill as a figure of moral choice recalls La Primaudaye's allegorical conversions, where the beast stands for "filth and foule incontinence," the possibility that a human will choose to "be a beast, and lacke intelligence" (II.xii.87). But Grill and his Plutarchan intertext, as well as the Pythagorean tradition that subtends it and with which it shares fundamental principles, disturbs this simple relegation of the animal to its Platonic place, below the isthmus of the neck. Grill's repining offered a different, more troubling and complex way for Spenser's later readers, including Donne, to read "the mind of beastly man" (II.xii.87).

University of Toronto

NOTES

I am grateful to the superb work of two research assistants, Mingjun Lu and Adele Wilson, and to those who listened to an early version of this essay at the International Spenser Society Conference in Toronto.

1. Ovid, *Metamorphoses*, trans. Frank Justus Miller (Loeb Classical Library, 1916; repr., 1976), xv: 171–72.

2. Ovid, xv: 459–60.

3. *The Annals of Quintus Ennius,* ed. Ethel Mary Steuart (London: Cambridge University Press, 1925).

4. Francis Meres, *Witts Academy. A Treasurie of Goulden Sentences Similes and Examples* (London, 1636), 281ᵛ. I have silently modernized i, j, u, v, and long s, and expanded contractions in all references to Early Modern prose.

5. Seneca's 84th letter in *Epistulae morales.*

6. John Dryden, Preface to *Fables Ancient and Modern, Translated into Verse from Homer, Ovid, Boccaccio, and Chaucer, with Original Poems,* in *Literary Criticism of John Dryden,* ed. Arthur C. Kirsch (Lincoln: University of Nebraska Press, 1966), 148.

7. Peter Stallybrass, "Shakespeare's Writing Table," paper delivered at the Shakespeare Association of America annual meeting, Philadelphia, April 15, 2006. Stallybrass described Early Modern writing practices as frequently including the material presence of other authors, either through the physical presence of these works on the desk or as a mnemonic record on one side of a double-columned page, which typically functioned as a kind of commonplace book, filled with excerpts from the writings of favorite authors. See also Peter Stallybrass, Roger Chartier, J. Franklin Mowery, Heather Wolfe, "Hamlet's Tables and the Technologies of Writing in Renaissance England," *Shakespeare Quarterly* 55:4 (2004): 379–419 for a discussion of erasure and memory in the material practices of writing. These discussions of memory describe some of the material ways in which poetic inspiration could be translated from one poet to another.

8. For a fuller discussions of these ideas, see Katharine Park and Eckhard Kessler, "The Concept of Psychology" in *The Cambridge History of Renaissance Philosophy,* general ed. Charles B. Schmitt, ed. Quentin Skinner and Eckhard Kessler (Cambridge: Cambridge University Press, 1988), 455–63. See also E. Ruth Harvey, "Psychology," and Robert L. Reid, "Psychology, Platonic" in *The Spenser Encyclopedia,*

ed. A. C. Hamilton et al. (Toronto: University of Toronto Press, London: Routledge, 1990), 565–68; 568–70.

9.   Katharine Park, "The Organic Soul" in *The Cambridge History of Renaissance Philosophy*, 465–84. See also Emily Michael, "Renaissance Theories of Soul" in *Psyche and Soma: Physicians and Metaphysicians on the Mind-Body Problem from Antiquity to Enlightenment,* ed. John P. Wright and Paul Potter (Oxford: Clarendon; New York: Oxford University Press, 2000), 147–72.

10.   These arguments are given in fuller form in my essay "The Souls of Animals: John Donne's *Metempsychosis* and Early Modern Natural History" in *Environment and Embodiment in Early Modern England*, ed. Garrett Sullivan and Mary Floyd-Wilson (Houndsmills, Hampshire, New York: Palgrave Macmillan, forthcoming, 2007).

11.   Giorgio Agamben, *Stanzas: Word and Phantasm in Western Culture*, trans. Ronald L. Martinez, Theory and History of Literature, 69 (Minneapolis: University of Minnesota Press, 1993), xiv–xix.

12.   Marianne Shapiro, *De Vulgari Eloquentia: Dante's Book of Exile* (Lincoln: University of Nebraska Press, 1990), 82.

13.   Shapiro, *De Vulgari Eloquentia*, 82.

14.   For a useful analysis of Pythagorean thought, see Christoph Riedweg, *Pythagoras: His Life, Teaching, and, Influence*, trans. Steven Rendall (Ithaca: Cornell University Press, 2005).

15.   Kenelm Digby, *Observations on the 22. Stanza in the 9th Canto of the 2d. Book of Spencers Fairy Queen* (London, 1644). See also Alistair Fowler, *Spenser and the Numbers of Time* (London: Routledge and Kegan Paul, 1964), especially Appendix I, "The Arithmological Stanza," 260–88.

16.   Kenneth Gross, "Shapes of Time: On the Spenserian Stanza," *Spenser Studies* XIX (2004): 27–35, 31 (italics mine).

17.   Edmund Spenser, *The Faerie Queene*, ed. Thomas P. Roche, Jr. (New Haven: Yale University Press, 1981). Subsequent references are to this edition.

18.   Gross, 33.

19.   Plato, *Timaeus*, trans. Benjamin Jowett in *Collected Dialogues of Plato*, ed. Edith Hamilton and Huntington Cairns (Princeton: Princeton University Press, 1961): 1151–1211, 1193–94: 70e. Subsequent references are to this edition. See the commentary on the souls in *Plato's Cosmology: The* Timaeus *of Plato*, trans. Francis MacDonald Cornford (Indianapolis: Bobbs-Merrill, 1957), 281–87.

20.   Aristotle, "On the Soul" in *Aristotle: On the Soul, Parva Naturalia, On Breath*, trans. W. S. Hett, Loeb Classical Library, ed. G. P. Goold, Aristotle VIII: 288 [1936, repr., 1995], 415b.

21.   William Oram, introduction to *The Yale Edition of the Shorter Poems of Edmund Spenser*, ed. William Oram (New Haven: Yale University Press, 1989): 217. Subsequent line references are to this edition: *Prosopopoia. Or Mother Hubberds Tale* is indicated as (P) and *Visions of the Worlds Vanitie* as (V).

22.   Brian Blackley, "The Generic Play and Spenserian Parody of John Donne's *Metempsychosis*," (PhD diss., University of Kentucky, 1994).

23.   *Batman uppon Bartholome: His Booke De Proprietatibus Rerum* (London, 1582), viii: 200.

24.   *John Donne: The Major Works*, ed. John Carey (Oxford: Oxford University Press, 1990). Subsequent references in the text are to this edition.

25.   George Puttenham, *The Arte of English Poesie* (Menston, England: Scolar Press, 1968; facsimile of the 1589 edition), 200.

26.   Helkiah Crooke, *Mikrokosmographia. A Description of the Body of Man. Together with the Controversies thereto Belonging. Collected and Translated out of all the Best Authors of Anatomy, Especially out of Gasper Bauhinus and Andreas Laurentius* (London: William Jaggard, 1615), 533.

27.   Paul de Man, "Autobiography as De-facement," *MLN* 94 (1979): 919–30, and 926–29 for de Man's discussion of prosopopeia. See also Rei Terada's discussion in *Feeling in Theory: Emotion after the "Death of the Subject"* (Cambridge: Harvard University Press, 2001), particularly her discussion of de Man's prosopopoeia and Derrida's Psyche (134–40).

28.   Jacques Derrida, *Memoires for Paul de Man*, trans. Cecile Lindsay, Jonathan Culler, and Eduardo Cadava (New York: Columbia University Press, 1986). Jacques Derrida, "The Animal That Therefore I Am (More to Follow)," trans. David Wills, *Critical Inquiry* 28:2 (2002): 369–418.

29.   Derrida, "The Animal That Therefore I Am (More to Follow)," 375.

30.   *The Essayes of Michael Lord of Montaigne*, trans. John Florio (London: George Routledge, 1893), 226.

31.   Montaigne, *The Essayes*, 244.

32.   Montaigne, *The Essayes*, 244.

33.   Montaigne, *The Essayes*, 227.

34.   Giovanni Pico della Mirandola, "Oration on the Dignity of Man," trans. Elizabeth Livermore Forbes, in *The Renaissance Philosophy of Man*, ed. Ernst Cassirer, Paul Oskar Kristeller, John Herman Randall, Jr. (Chicago: University of Chicago Press, 1948): 215–54.

35.   Montaigne, *The Essayes*, 224–26.

36.   Pierre de la Primaudaye, *The Second Part of the French Academie* (London, 1605), A2. The earliest date of publication in England for *The Second Part* is 1594. I cite from the 1605 edition.

37.   Pierre de la Primaudaye, *The Third Volume of the French Academie, Contayning a notable description of the whole world, and of all the principall parts and contents thereof.* (London, 1601), 378.

38.   *Circes of John Baptista Gelli, Florentine*, trans. Henry Eden (London, 1557).

39.   Donne, *Metempsychosis*, lines 502–03.

40.   Helkiah Crooke, *Mikrokosmographia*, 431.

41.   Donne, *Metempsychosis*, lines 392–93.

42.   Gordon Teskey, "Allegory, Materialism, Violence," *The Production of English Renaissance Culture*, ed. David Lee Miller, Sharon O'Dair, and Harold Weber (Ithaca: Cornell University Press, 1994), 293–318, especially 296–300.

43.   "The Ecstasy" in *John Donne: The Major Works*, ed. Carey, line 26.

44.   Sir Walter Ralegh, *Treatise of the Soul. The Works of Sir Walter Ralegh, Kt. Now first collected*, vol. III, *Miscellaneous Works* (Oxford: The University Press, 1829), 571–91, 571, 587. See Pierre Lefranc, *Sir Walter Ralegh, écrivain, l'œuvre et les idées* (Paris: Librairie Armand Colin, 1968), 57–58 for a discussion of the attribution of this work to Ralegh. The text exists in a single manuscript copy, transcribed by Elias Ashmole (8161 in Ashmole's Museum), and there are no external confirmations

of the author's identity. It was first published in 1829, and the attribution of authorship rests on the comparison between the *Treatise* and Ralegh's comments on the soul in *The History of the World*, which are in general more Platonic than the Aristotelianism of the *Treatise*. Nevertheless, the *Treatise* summarizes well the prevailing Aristotelian assumptions about the tripartite soul and the status of the rational soul.

45.   Pierre de la Primaudaye, *The Second Part of the French Academie*, 508. First published in French in 1577, *The French Academie* began to be translated into English in 1586. Its currency is indicated by the numerous editions in the 1590s and first two decades of the seventeenth century. Madalene Shindler ("The Vogue and Impact of Pierre de la Primaudaye's 'The French Academie' on Elizabethan and Jacobean Literature," PhD diss., University of Texas, 1960) asserts that in 1658 it was the second most popular book in England (vi).

46.   Pierre de la Primaudaye, *The Second Part of the French Academie*, 510.

47.   Pierre de la Primaudaye, *The Second Part of the French Academie*, 446.

48.   Pierre de la Primaudaye, *The Second Part of the French Academie*, 447.

49.   Crooke, *Mikrokosmographia*, 453.

50.   See D. P. Walker, "The Astral Body in Renaissance Medicine," *Journal of the Warburg and Courtauld Institutes*, 21:1/2 (1958): 119–33; James J. Bono, "Medieval Spirits and the Medieval Language of Life," *Traditio* 40 (1984): 91–130.

51.   Crooke, *Mikrokosmographia*, 541.

52.   See Ronald A. Horton, "Aristotle and his Commentators" in *The Spenser Encyclopedia*, 57–60.

53.   Crooke, *Mikrokosmographia*, 6.

54.   *Batman uppon Bartholome,* 18–20.

55.   Aristotle, "On the Soul," 427b–429a.

56.   Martha Craig, "The Secret Wit of Spenser's Language," in *Elizabethan Poetry: Modern Essays in Criticism*, ed. Paul J. Alpers (New York: Oxford University Press, 1967): 447–72, especially 451–54.

57.   Plutarch, "Beasts Are Rational" in *Moralia*, trans. Harold Cherniss and William C. Helmbold, Loeb Classical Library, ed. Jeffrey Henderson, Plutarch XII: 406 [1957, rept., 2001], 988D. Both of these examples are taken from the *Iliad*.

58.   Plutarch, "Beasts Are Rational," 988.

59.   Plutarch, "Beasts Are Rational," 989–90.

GARRETT A. SULLIVAN, JR.

Afterword

This afterword considers the different ways Shakespeare and
Spenser take up the problem of the human. Whereas Shakespeare grounds his examination in *subjectivity*, Spenser focuses
on *vitality*, a difference that contributes to the perception, often
encountered in the classroom, of Shakespeare as familiar and
Spenser as alien. This essay concludes by championing Spenser's
seeming alterity—by, that is, noting the continued significance
of Spenser's conception of human vitality as both untethered
to subjectivity and continuous with animal and vegetable life.

A problem routinely faced (and, it must be said, strategically exploited)
by teachers of early modern literature is the outsized role played by
Shakespeare in our students' thinking about the Renaissance. This
problem was again brought home to me through two recent incidents
from different classes. One took place in a course entitled "Pairing
Shakespeare," in which I taught *The Merchant of Venice* next to *The
Jew of Malta, The Spanish Tragedy* next to *Hamlet*, and so on. As part
of an attempt to draw conclusions from the semester's reading, I
asked students to articulate the similarities and differences between
Shakespeare and those contemporaries of his we had studied. It was,
more than anything, Shakespeare's psychological realism that capti-
vated those students who addressed my question—a realism, they
suggested, that captured something of what it is to be human.
Whereas Barabas is a caricature, Shylock's actions and deliberations
bear some relationship to the actions and deliberations we perform
today. Although none of the students claimed that Shakespeare invented the human, they did imply that he is our contemporary. (So
much for a semester's worth of scrupulous historicizing.)

Spenser Studies: A Renaissance Poetry Annual, Volume XXII, Copyright © 2007 by
AMS Press, Inc. All rights reserved.

The second incident takes us from Shakespeare to Spenser. In a course focused on epic and romance, I taught Book 2 of *The Faerie Queene*, and we found that it abides very different questions from those that a Shakespeare play does. One student asked, of the two "naked Damzelles" in the Bower of Bliss that C. S. Lewis dismissively dubbed "Cissie" and "Flossie," "What are their motives in trying to seduce Guyon?"[1] This question, it became clear, doesn't work directly, as put. But it opened up a large space in which we could ponder the nature of character and person in Spenser's poem, for it is a Shakespearean question, asking something psychological in a modernist sense about a character's depth or interiority. This question registers what for the students was the sheer alterity of the Spenserian text. To them, and many like them first encountering *The Faerie Queene*, Spenser is emphatically *not* their contemporary. Indeed, this student's question about motive resonates with the claims made in my other class about Shakespeare.

I offer these anecdotes to underscore a meaningful difference between Spenser and Shakespeare—a difference powerfully informed but not determined by the divergent genres in which they worked. Unlike Spenser in *The Faerie Queene*, Shakespeare in his most famous works is a poet of subjectivity.[2] Moreover, it is Shakespeare's depiction of subjectivity that has conventionally grounded assertions about his insights into what it is to be human.[3] What, then, of the "non-subjective" poet? What kind of claims can he or his characters make about (or to) humanity? It is to this last question that recent Spenser criticism, as admirably represented by essays in this volume, so powerfully responds. Two topics frequently represented in this collection are memory (Helfer, Owens) and the relationship between human and animal (Bellamy, Harvey, Loewenstein, and, indirectly in his discussion of *prosopopeia*, Escobedo)—topics that *could* be developed in relation to subjectivity (and, in Shakespeare criticism, frequently are). And yet, subjectivity plays little role here. We are invited by Gordon Teskey to consider what is distinctive about Spenser's thinking, but the thinking of his characters is another matter altogether.

This "neglect" of subjectivity, if that is the right way to conceive it, gets at something important about Spenser. Whereas for Shakespeare memory and the human are routinely tethered to the subject—consider Hamlet's opposition between the avenger who remembers his filial obligations and the "beast that sleeps and feeds," an opposition developed in a famous soliloquy that stands as a benchmark for the representation of subjectivity—Spenser's approach to these topics is importantly different. Questions of memory and humanness matter deeply to him, but not primarily as understood in relation to the subject.[4] If Shakespeare is a poet of subjectivity, Spenser tends to approach the question of what it is to be human from the perspective of the vitality of *all* forms of life. Indeed, he presses us to consider what it is that constitutes (human) life in the first place. (The slipperiness of distinctions between animal and human life is central to a number of essays in this volume.) Spenser wants us to ask not, "What are the motives of 'Cissie' and 'Flossie'?"—my student's "Shakespearean" question—but, "What are 'Cissie' and 'Flossie'?" Are they *human*? Are they *alive*, and, if so, in precisely what senses of those two words?[5] How do we differentiate them from other temptations of the Bower to which they bear an obvious functional resemblance, like the "ioyous birds" and golden ivy? What is their place in the broader landscape of the Bower, a landscape that famously accommodates nature and artifice so completely as both to confound the distinction between them and to demand that we try to forge it anew?

The question of the relationship between vitality and humanity is one that Spenser pursues repeatedly in *The Faerie Queene,* especially in Book II. We can see this through two examples centered upon sleep, a basic somatic activity performed by animals and humans and understood in the Renaissance as antithetical to memory.[6] Because it is common to man and beast, sleep, which is located by Aristotle in the sensitive or "animal" soul, troubles the stability of definitions of the human. Such instability informs one of the most famous moments in *The Faerie Queene*, in which Guyon swoons and is then attended to by a "blessed Ange[l]." It is here that Spenser poses his famous question, "And is there care in heauen?" (II.viii.1)—the answer to which is never in doubt. What is important about this question is, first, that it is provoked by Guyon's swoon. That is, it is Spenser's response to the image conjured at the end of the previous book of a sleep resembling death: "The life did flit away out of her nest,/And all his senses were with deadly fit opprest" (II.vii.66).[7] Also important is the reason given for Spenser's affirmative answer: without care in heaven, "much more wretched were the cace/Of men, then beasts" (II.viii.1). "Care in heauen" does the rhetorical work of differentiating men from beasts—of distinguishing between forms of life. This process of differentiation is undertaken here because Guyon's sleep blurs the line not only between life and death, but also between man and beast. The work of the angel is to redraw that line; "care in heauen" serves as the basis for a putatively stable definition of the human.[8]

The second example returns us to the Bower of Bliss and concerns my favorite sleeper in all of Spenser, Verdant.[9] Verdant is the perfect

figure for undifferentiated (or undifferentiatable) vitality. Until rescued by Guyon, he is without a name, all traces of his heroic identity
having been erased along with the markings on his shield. That is,
he has forgotten his identity and, like the sleeping Guyon, his very
humanness is also in jeopardy. The stakes are raised in this episode,
however, because Acrasia's post-coital and quasi-vampiric "suck[ing
of] his spright" intimates his fate: to become one of the men-turned-
animals that populate her Circean pleasure garden. At the same time,
while Verdant's very name associates him with life, it is specifically
vegetable life that is evoked (compare, e.g., "verdant gras," I.ix.13,
III.i.5). In short, Spenser's Verdant exists at the intersection of the
animal, vegetable and human.[10] Guyon's great achievement is to turn
sleeping life, in all its indeterminate vitality, into human life by restor-
ing the sleeper to his identity, his name. The irony, though, is that
that identity both marks him as human—as a man and a martial
hero—and suggests his ineradicable affinity with other forms of vitality, with vegetable life. In this regard, Verdant resembles one of
his co-inhabitants of the Bower of Bliss, the reluctantly transformed
"beastly man," Grill. As Joseph Loewenstein suggests, Grill, like Verdant, is a figure for that which both constitutes the human and is
repudiated by it.[11]

Loewenstein also points out that Spenser's Grill does not speak.
Nor do we know much about his thinking, beyond his unarticulated
reluctance to remain human, his desire to evade cognition. When
Guyon asks us to "see" Grill, what we witness bears a confused and
confusing relationship to thought, subjectivity, and humanness:

> See the mind of beastly man,
> That hath so soone forgot the excellence
> Of his creation, when he life began,
> That now he chooseth, with vile difference,
> To be a beast, and lacke intelligence.
>
> (II.xii.87)

How does one "see" the mind of a man—especially of a "beastly
man," an oxymoronic figure that lacks higher-order cognition or
subjectivity? Does Grill forget the excellence of his creation, of the
beginning of his (human) life? Or does he forget that excellence when
he *begins* his (animal) life? As with Verdant's life as a sleeper, Grill's
as a beast is constituted out of an act of self-forgetting, understood
here as the forgetting of "the excellence" of one's creation in God's

image, one's divinely underwritten humanness. It is also the forgetting of that model of humanness installed by "care in heaven."
Whereas self-forgetting in Shakespeare is a figure for subjectivity, in
Spenser it is a figure for life that troubles and transgresses the boundaries of the human.[12] In that the beastly man has a mind—in that
he forgets and chooses—he is a man. In that the beastly man lacks
intelligence—in that he is as forgetful as animals proverbially are and
that he has made the bad choice that he has—he is a beast. So, what
finally *is* he, man or beast? How can we begin to account for his
"hoggish mind" (II.xii.87)? This is the insoluble problem, persisting
beyond Guyon's (in)temperate destruction of the Bower, that Spenser
leaves us with at the end of Book II—a problem the Palmer and
Guyon leave *behind* when they depart, "Let[ting] Grill be Grill"
(II.xii. 87). While angelic care distinguishes man from beast, Verdant
and Grill—vegetable and animal life—blur that distinction.

Spenser, then, is responsible not for inventing the human but for
troubling it so entirely and so imaginatively as to flummox my students. And it is with the pedagogy of flummoxing that I would
like to conclude. Teaching Shakespeare and teaching Spenser each
requires different responsibilities and provides different challenges. In
the case of Shakespeare, part of the challenge is to defamiliarize the
text for the students—to try to disrupt the operations of the "timeless
verities" machine into which they so readily plug Shakespeare's
works. (My opening anecdote tells you just how successful I've been
at doing this lately.) Spenser, on the other hand, necessitates that we
work to make the text more accessible, more (but not entirely) familiar, as he powerfully resists being plugged into that same machine.
Put differently, most of us try to cultivate in our students a sense of
Shakespeare's alterity, whereas Spenser's alterity is already fully on
display for them. What our students need to and can be convinced
of is both the range of strange pleasures Spenser's alterity provides
and, paradoxically, the profound relevance of that which at first
glance might seem entirely alien. After all, there are few more pressing political, environmental or epistemological questions than what
it is that constitutes the human, how some are ascribed human status
while others are not, and how the "human" relates to the physical
world that all life inhabits.[13] Even the application of a "Shakespearean" question to the "Spenserian" text—what does the Other (Cissie,
Flossie, Grill) think?—has led us, albeit indirectly, to a very non-
Shakespearean place, in which subjectivity recedes before vitality
and the "timeless verities" find little secure purchase. In this regard,
Spenserian alterity stands as a powerful example of what Nietzsche

dubs the "untimely," that which runs counter to the *present's* "time-less verities" in the service of other possibilities and thus of a future radically different from the present.[14] What I find bracing and signifi-cant about the essays in this volume is, finally, their own untimeli-ness—the ways they put to exciting use the critical potential latent in Spenser's alterity. In this regard, they admirably fulfill the pedagogical mission alluded to above: making Spenser more (but not entirely) familiar while also harnessing his alterity to defamiliarize that which we think we know—such as, what it is to be human.[15]

NOTES

1.   Edmund Spenser, *The Faerie Queene*, ed. Thomas P. Roche, Jr. (New York: Penguin Books, 1978), II.xii.63. Henceforth cited in the text.

2.   Of course, *The Amoretti* are a different matter. Moreover, in referring to Shake-speare as a "poet of subjectivity," I mean to describe not an authorial predisposition but a characteristic of a number of his texts.

3.   On the very first page of *Shakespeare: The Invention of the Human* (New York: Riverhead Books, 1998), Harold Bloom answers the question, "Why Shakespeare?" by asserting, among other things, "Inner selves do not exactly abound in the works of the creators of Tamburlaine and of Sir Epicure Mammon. . . . No one, before or since Shakespeare, made so many separate selves" (1).

4.   As Owens's essay suggests, memory is linked in Spenser less to interiority than to heroic agency.

5.   As formulated, these questions might seem to ignore the gender dynamics of a scene in which the "naked Damzelles" kindle lust in the male knight of Temperance (II.xii.68). I would suggest instead that the question of what constitutes the human has a particular urgency in the case of women, whose putatively passionate natures render them closer by temperament to beasts. Also relevant in Canto xii are the hints of pedophilia; "faire Ladies" are joined by "lasciuious Boyes" in preserving through "song" and "light licentious toyes" Verdant's post-coital sleep (II.xii.72).

6.   John Willis writes in *Mnemonica; or, The Art of Memory* (London: Leonard Sowersby, 1661) that "*Sleep* offendeth *Memory*" (140). It is "overmuch" sleep that is the real culprit here (140). On sleep's links to forgetting, see Garrett A. Sullivan, Jr., *Memory and Forgetting in English Renaissance Drama: Shakespeare, Marlowe, Webster* (Cambridge: Cambridge University Press, 2005).

7.   Sleep is conventionally associated with death in this period. Moreover, it is routinely defined in terms of the binding of the senses. Thus, while a swoon might be understood as distinctive from sleep, Spenser is undoubtedly asking to think in terms of the latter here.

8.   Important to this is the establishment of an affinity between man and a higher form of "life," the angel, rather than with a lower, the beast.

9.   For more on Verdant and sleep, see Alan Stewart and Garrett A. Sullivan, Jr., " 'Worme-eaten, and full of canker holes': Materializing Memory in *The Faerie*

Queene and *Lingua*," *Spenser Studies* 17 (2003): 215–38; and Mary Floyd-Wilson and Garrett A. Sullivan, Jr., "Introduction: Inhabiting the Body, Inhabiting the World," *Environment and Embodiment in Early Modern England*, ed. Floyd-Wilson and Sullivan (Basingstoke: Palgrave, 2007), 1–13.

10.   Obviously relevant here is the distinction between animal, vegetable, and rational souls. For more on this, see especially Harvey in this volume.

11.   "The division of life into vegetal and relational, organic and animal, animal and human, . . . passes first of all as a mobile border within living man, and without this intimate caesura the very decision of what is human and what is not would probably not be possible" (Giorgio Agamben, *The Open: Man and Animal* [Stanford: Stanford University Press, 2004], 15). For more on Agamben and Spenser, see the essay by Bellamy in this volume.

12.   See Sullivan, *Memory and Forgetting*.

13.   On the former, see Loewenstein's discussion of "relative anthrocentrism," a concept he derives from the work of Bruce Boehrer.

14.   Friedrich Nietzsche, "On the Uses and Disadvantages of History for Life," in *Untimely Meditations*, ed. Daniel Breazeale, trans. R. J. Hollingdale (Cambridge: Cambridge University Press, 1997): 59–123.

15.   Thanks to Theresa Krier for her helpful suggestions with this essay.

Index